The Communist States in Disarray 1965-1971

THE COMMUNIST STATES IN DISARRAY 1965–1971

Edited by
Adam Bromke
and
Teresa Rakowska-Harmstone

University of Minnesota Press, Minneapolis

Printed in the United States of America
at Lund Press, Minneapolis.
Published in the United Kingdom and India by the Oxford University
Press, London and Delhi, and in Canada
by the Copp Clark Publishing Co. Limited, Toronto

Library of Congress Catalog Card Number: 78-187166

ISBN 0-8166-0638-2

Preface

This volume is the fifth in a series sponsored by the Soviet and East European Studies Program, Carleton University, Ottawa. Like most of its predecessors it stems from public lectures on communist affairs which are given biannually at Carleton. Seven of the chapters originated as lectures delivered in January through March 1970; the others were written especially for the book to round out the coverage of the subject.

The present work is largely intended as a sequel to *The Communist States at the Crossroads* which, we thought, had an encouraging reception among readers. More than half of the authors contributing to this volume are the same as those whose essays appeared in the earlier publication. Also the format of the book, although we have tried to introduce a few improvements, remains basically unchanged.

The Communist States at the Crossroads treated developments from the time the Sino-Soviet dispute came into the open in the spring of 1960 until the end of the Khrushchev era in the fall of 1964. It analyzed the nature of the schism between Moscow and Peking and the resulting rise of "polycentrism" in international communism.

The Communist States in Disarray considers the events from the time of the Brezhnev-Kosygin take-over in 1964 through the remainder of the 1960s. It continues the discussion of the twin themes: the aggregation of the Sino-Soviet conflict and the spread of nationalism in the communist world, especially in Eastern Europe. Attempts to project the current trends into the remaining 1970s are made.

As in the past, we have been encouraged in our work by many people at Carleton University. We are particularly grateful to Dean G. C. Merrill, Professors B. R. Bociurkiw and J. W. Strong, and Mrs. D. W. Jones. The interest and support of the Department of External Affairs also have been greatly appreciated. Mrs. A. Burns, of the office of political science, efficiently and cheerfully assisted in preparing the manuscript for publication.

A. B.
T. R. H.

NOTE: Because of the different languages involved in this book, all diacritical and accent marks have been deleted from foreign words, with the exception of those words that have been adopted into the English language.

The Carleton Series in Soviet and East European Studies

The Communist States at the Crossroads: Between Moscow and Peking. Ed. Adam Bromke. Intro. Philip E. Mosely. New York: Frederick A. Praeger, Publishers, 1965; London: Pall Mall Press, 1965. (Japanese translation, Jiji Press, Tokyo, 1967; Marathi translation, Janapad Prakashan, Bombay, 1969.)

East-West Trade. Ed. Philip E. Uren. Intro. Hon. Mitchell W. Sharp. Toronto: The Canadian Institute of International Affairs, 1966.

The Communist States and the West. Ed. Adam Bromke and Philip E. Uren. New York: Frederick A. Praeger, Publishers, 1967; London: Pall Mall Press, 1967.

The Soviet Union under Brezhnev and Kosygin: The Transition Years, 1965–1968. Ed. John W. Strong. New York: Van Nostrand Reinhold, 1971.

The Communist States in Disarray, 1965–1971. Ed. Adam Bromke and Teresa Rakowska-Harmstone. Minneapolis: University of Minnesota Press, 1972.

Contents

The Communist States in Disarray 1965-1971

1

Polycentrism in Eastern Europe

BY ADAM BROMKE

In the last decade a profound change has taken place in Eastern Europe.[1] The communist monolith established by Stalin in the late 1940s and consolidated by Khrushchev in the late 1950s largely disintegrated in the following decade. In its place separate national entities have reemerged, creating in Eastern Europe a situation which is truly polycentric. At least four distinct brands of communism exist in the area. At one extreme Albania adheres to the militant Chinese type of communism. At the other extreme Yugoslavia has developed its own version of communism, the most moderate of all and the one most resembling Western social democracy. Rumania has also evolved a separate national brand of communism which ideologically stands in the middle, thus allowing Rumania to remain on good terms with both China and Yugoslavia. The remaining five Eastern European communist states, Poland, Czechoslovakia, Hungary, Bulgaria, and East Germany, have basically followed the Soviet model. Nevertheless, the differences among them have grown, as each nation has developed some unique features of its own. The Poles, for example, have refrained from collectivizing agriculture and have accorded a special place to the Catholic Church; the Hungarians have advanced with the most comprehensive economic reforms; and the Czechs and the Slovaks in 1967–68 moved a long way toward democratizing their entire political system.

Yet, despite increasing diversity along national lines, there paradoxical-

1. For a review of the developments in Eastern Europe in the first half of the 1960s see Adam Bromke, "Eastern Europe in a Depolarized World," *Behind the Headlines* (Canadian Institute of International Affairs) May 1965.

ly exists a good deal of uniformity in political trends in Eastern Europe as a whole. This has been manifested in four different ways. First, there has been a marked decline in the role of communist ideology. Doctrinal pluralism in turn has led to the growth of pragmatism. The continued adherence of the ruling communist elites to Marxism-Leninism has increasingly assumed the form of mere rationalization of a desire to remain in power. Secondly, there has been a noticeable growth of nationalism. National traditions have been revived and the communist governments have shown greater concern for national interests. Thirdly, there has been a steady widening of personal freedoms, although this has not been a simple process. There have been advances and retreats, or to paraphrase Lenin's dictum, two steps forward and one step back. However, looking at the situation from a dynamic point of view, the communist regimes have responded at least partly to popular pressures. Finally, there has been a gradual restoration of Eastern Europe's relations with the West, and especially its traditional bonds with Western Europe. Virtually all the countries in the area have expanded their economic, cultural, and even political contacts with the Western world.

Close interdependence also has developed among all the political trends in Eastern Europe, each one reinforcing the others along both horizontal and vertical lines. Horizontal interdependence among changes in the different Eastern European countries has been demonstrated on several occasions. The 1956 revolution in Hungary was encouraged by Poland's successful defiance of the Soviet Union; in fact it started with a meeting in Budapest to express Hungarian solidarity with the Poles. The students' rebellion in Poland in 1968, in its turn, was inspired by the progress of reform in Czechoslovakia; the students' slogan called for the replacement of Gomulka by "a Polish Dubcek." Yugoslavia's, and more recently Rumania's, independent courses from Moscow have been widely admired and envied in other East European countries.

Vertical interdependence in political changes within a single country also has been quite conspicuous. Acceptance of nationalism, as developments in Ceausescu's Rumania have shown, leads to a growing reconciliation between the communist regime and the populace. In turn, the ruling communist elite, feeling more secure in its position, is somewhat more tolerant toward personal freedom. Again, as was the case under Dubcek in Czechoslovakia, increased popular influence over a communist government pushes it in the direction of expanding relations with the West. Yet, the closer the country moves to the nondoctrinaire West, the less chance there is to preserve communist orthodoxy.

Horizontal and vertical lines of interdependence in the developments in Eastern Europe frequently overlap. There have been numerous examples of group interactions cutting across national boundaries such as those of economic reformers or rebellious intellectuals. Needless to say, because of the influence that these groups exert on their own societies, the interdependence of their actions has often been crucial in the process of leveling off reforms in the area as a whole. Working class pressure for an improved standard of living in one country, such as the impact of the workers' rebellion in Poland demonstrated, could have far-reaching effects in some other states. Political dynamics, then, push Eastern Europe in the direction of continuing change.

The tendencies toward reemergence of separate national entities have been opposed by the forces striving to preserve communist unity. Continued close ties between some Eastern European states and the USSR are due to three main factors. First, in the case of some countries their national interests converge with those of the Soviet Union. Czechoslovakia and especially Poland are still apprehensive about Germany and look to Russia for protection from their Western neighbor. Secondly, the ruling communist elites have vested interests in maintaining close bonds with Moscow. Even if they increasingly regard communist ideology as a mere rationalization of a desire to continue in power, proletarian internationalism is sufficiently an integral part of Marxism-Leninism that it cannot be removed without threatening the very basis of their political legitimacy. This is even true of the highly nationalistic Rumanian regime. Moreover, at least some communist governments still find Soviet support, and, indeed, the presence of Russian troops in their territory, a useful counterbalance against popular pressure. This is the case not only of the repressive East German regime, but also of the relatively moderate Hungarian government. Last but not least, there is the reality of the preponderant Soviet power in the area. The events in Hungary in 1956 and those in Czechoslovakia in 1968 clearly demonstrated that Moscow is ready to use its superior military force whenever it feels its vital interests are at stake. Indeed, since the invasion of Czechoslovakia the direct Soviet threat has been considerably intensified. It is now enshrined in the Brezhnev doctrine which openly justifies Moscow's interference in the domestic affairs of other communist states.

Yet, there is little reason to suppose that Brezhnev's recent efforts to restore the cohesion of the Eastern European states will be any more successful than those of Stalin and Khrushchev in the past. The fact that, as a last resort, communist unity has been maintained by the paramount Soviet power has aroused a good deal of resentment, if not hatred, of the Russians on the part of the Eastern Europeans. These sentiments are widespread among the masses and are also present among the ruling elites. Moscow's repeated use of force in some ways has strengthened the tendencies of the different Eastern European nations to try to escape from Russian suzerainty. The record of Soviet influence in the area is a sorry one. In the last two decades, of the eight communist states in Eastern Europe, three have successfully defied the USSR: Yugoslavia in the late forties, Albania in the early sixties, and Rumania in the mid-sixties. Of the remaining five, four tried to do so and failed: East Germany in 1953, Poland and Hungary in 1956, and Czechoslovakia in 1968; moreover, in 1970 a new serious political crisis ensued in Poland. The only country where as yet there has been no open revolt against Russian influence is Bulgaria. However, had the attempted coup in Sofia in April 1965 been successful, political developments in that country probably also would have taken a different turn. It is clear that after over two decades of Soviet hegemony in the area the will of the Eastern Europeans for independent national existence has by no means been extinguished.

I

The Soviet invasion of Czechoslovakia in August 1968 and the enunciation of the Brezhnev doctrine has slowed down, but has not reversed the disintegration of the communist monolith in Eastern Europe. Czechoslovakia was forcibly returned to the communist bloc, yet movements toward polycentrism throughout the area have not been stamped out. Indeed, in some respects at least, the new demonstration of naked Soviet power has strengthened the resolve of Eastern Europeans to resist it.

In the southern tier of communist states in the Balkans, polycentrism has remained dominant. Bulgaria is the only country in that region which has steadfastly remained on the Soviet side. Albania has reasserted its independent position; in fact it used the invasion of Czechoslovakia as a formal excuse to withdraw from the Warsaw Pact. Tirana has continued to denounce the Soviet brand of communism as a betrayal of true Marxism-Leninism and has maintained its close ties with Peking. And, it is of great significance that, at the same time, it has mitigated its attacks against Belgrade; indeed, Albania has stressed that in the event of a Russian attack on Yugoslavia, it would side with the Yugoslavs — all their ideological differences notwithstanding. Finally Albania's relations with neighboring Greece, as well as several Western European countries, have taken a turn for the better.

Yugoslavia has also reaffirmed its independence, emphasizing strongly that it would resist Soviet invasion with arms. Belgrade's ideological rift with Moscow has widened with the Yugoslavs openly repudiating the Brezhnev doctrine. At the same time Yugoslavia's relations with Rumania have remained quite close, and its relations with China have undergone a marked improvement. Yugoslavia, however, is faced with mounting domestic problems – its economy is passing through a difficult period of adjustment and the country is increasingly ridden with nationalistic rivalries. Moreover, President Tito is aging, and soon the political situation may be further complicated by the struggle among various factions to succeed him. There is a danger that the Soviets may try to exploit this situation by meddling in Yugoslav domestic affairs.

Rumania, despite its exposed position next to the USSR and its continued membership in the Warsaw Pact, has maintained an independent course. The Rumanians did not participate in the invasion of Czechoslovakia; they were openly critical of the action taken by the Warsaw powers as well as of its justification by the Brezhnev doctrine. Like the Yugoslavs they stressed that, if invaded, they would defend themselves. At the same time the Rumanians tried to improve their country's position vis-à-vis Russia through broad, and brilliantly executed, diplomatic moves. They have developed good relations with many countries in different parts of the world belonging to different alliances, and each one of these contacts enhances Rumania's prestige in the international sphere. Bucharest has maintained friendly relations with Albania and China, as witnessed in President Ceausescu's visit to Peking in June 1971. At the same time Rumania and Yugoslavia have remained very close, with Ceausescu and Tito holding frequent meetings. By bridging the gap between the two diametrically opposed brands of communism, the Rumanians have hinted at a possibility of Sino-Balkan cooperation in opposing any further Soviet hegemonical claims. Rumania has also enjoyed good relations with several Western powers, notably France and Italy. It was the first East European country to establish diplomatic relations with West Germany, and the only communist state which has maintained diplomatic relations with Israel after 1967. Since 1964 Rumania has also had friendly relations with the United States. A visit by President Nixon to Bucharest in August 1969 – the first call by an American president on a communist capital – and a visit by President Ceausescu to the United States in October 1970 dramatized to the entire world Rumania's independent stance in foreign policy.

There seems to be little doubt that Bucharest's independent course represents a continued irritant to Moscow, and that the Russians would gladly dispose of it, if they could. Yet, for the time being the only way that the Soviet Union could suppress a defiant Rumania would be by resorting to outright invasion. The Ceausescu regime, precisely because of its nationalistic attitude, has enjoyed broad popular support in the country and has successfully managed to preserve unity in the ranks of the Rumanian Communist party. In addition, the Rumanians, while following their own course, have avoided being unnecessarily polemical so as not to provide the Russians with a pretext for attacking them. The price that Moscow would have to pay for forcibly returning Bucharest to communist orthodoxy would be high. The invasion of Rumania could well lead to a small war in the Balkans, which would tarnish Soviet prestige in the international sphere even more than did the occupation of Czechoslovakia. Still this does not guarantee, especially should internal opposition develop against the Ceausescu government, that Moscow will necessarily continue to abstain from meddling in Rumanian domestic affairs. Soviet-Rumanian relations are likely to continue to be potentially explosive for some time to come.

In the northern tier of communist states in Central Eastern Europe, which has always been strategically more important to Russia than the Balkans, Soviet influence has been enforced more effectively. But latent polycentric tendencies continue to be present in virtually all the countries in this region. The damage that the invasion of 1968 did to Soviet-Czechoslovak relations can hardly be exaggerated. The Czechs and Slovaks, who traditionally had been more friendly toward the Russians as their big Slavic brothers and protectors from the Germans, have now become some of the most ardently anti-Soviet peoples in Eastern Europe. The capital of popular goodwill has been squandered by Moscow, and it is doubtful that it can ever be regained; hatred and contempt of the USSR are today almost universal in Czechoslovakia.[2] The Czechs and the Slovaks bitterly resist restoration of the Soviet-type communism in their country, and should the opportunity arise they would turn in vengeance against the Russians.

On the surface the political situation in Czechoslovakia has been normalized. Beneath the surface, however, the struggle between the "centrist" forces led by the present communist party secretary, Husak, and his conservative opponents of the former President Novotny vintage still goes on. Husak has removed the Dubcek liberals from positions of influence in the

2. The Czechs' contempt for the Russians was well illustrated by a poster that this writer saw displayed in Prague even in the fall of 1969. Under a photograph of Dubcek and Svoboda was a quotation from Karl Marx: "Only those nations are free, who do not deprive other nations of their freedom."

party and the government, and has gone a long way in meeting Soviet demands for the revival of communist orthodoxy. Yet he has stopped short of reintroducing mass terror and generally has refrained from taking punitive measures against his liberal opponents. His objective appears to be to establish a political system basically similar to that in Kadar's Hungary — with the communist party firmly in control, but tolerant of a fairly broad range of personal freedom. Husak's conservative opponents insist on more drastic measures. They would like to revive the oppressive Novotny system and bring the liberals to trial; and, in a few cases, as for example that of General Prchlik, they have succeeded. Naturally both Husak and the conservatives have been vying for the support of Moscow. In order to win Soviet favors Husak went a long way to justify the Soviet invasion of his country. The Czechoslovak-Soviet friendship treaty of May 1970 explicitly endorsed the Brezhnev doctrine, and at the Party Congress in Prague in May 1971 Husak personally thanked Brezhnev for saving socialism in Czechoslovakia. There is little doubt, however, that such declarations do not reflect changed popular attitudes. If anything, by adding insult to injury, they only strengthen the anti-Soviet sentiments of the Czechs and the Slovaks.

In the late sixties a serious political crisis developed also in Poland. The popular dissatisfaction with the conservative policy of the Gomulka regime was steadily mounting and eventually culminated in its open defiance. The first explosion coincided with the Prague spring. In February 1968 the Warsaw writers protested against the banning of the play by the great nineteenth-century Polish poet Adam Mickiewicz because of its anti-Russian overtones. In March the students in Warsaw and several other cities joined the protest and took to the streets. The students' rebellion was forcibly suppressed, but the tension in the country persisted. At the Party Congress in November 1968, with Brezhnev's personal blessing, Gomulka was again reelected first secretary, but his political influence was clearly waning. As a result of the deteriorating economic conditions there was growing restlessness among the workers. The announcement of increased food prices on the eve of Christmas in 1970 led to violent workers' outbursts in several coastal cities. Gomulka, who himself had been brought to power by workers' riots in 1956, was now replaced as first secretary by Gierek.

Gierek succeeded in appeasing the workers by withdrawing unpopular economic measures, but his position remains difficult. He has no choice, but in order to improve its performance he has to undertake the drastic overhaul of the economic system in the direction of greater market influence on production. This, at least in the short run, may adversely affect workers' wages. Moreover, the political situation in the country continues to be tense. The workers could not fail to observe that by taking to the streets, for the second time they succeeded in removing from power unpopular communist leaders. Should conditions become unbearable, they may try to do it again. This, in turn, may bring about Soviet intervention.

The workers' outburst in Poland was remarkably free from anti-Russian overtones. The Poles, remembering well the recent fate of Czechoslovakia, carefully abstained from anything which could have justified Soviet intervention. Their self-restraint, however, is not unlimited. Should Moscow try to frustrate domestic reforms, Polish nationalism may acquire a sharply anti-Russian edge. Such a development might prove tragic. Soviet efforts to suppress changes in Poland could lead to another Czechoslovakia, or even a Hungary, for in line with their tradition the Poles would be prone to resist Russian military intervention with arms. As such the situation in Poland is probably more explosive than that in any other country in Eastern Europe.[3]

In Hungary it seems that not only the people but the Kadar regime as well were unhappy about the invasion of Czechoslovakia. Apart from sympathy for the plight of the Czechs and the Slovaks so similar to their own in 1956, the Hungarians were concerned that the reversal of democratization in Czechoslovakia could adversely affect the changes in their own country. Yet nothing of the sort has happened. In the domestic sphere the Kadar regime has maintained its relatively liberal course. It has quietly but steadfastly pressed on with economic reform. In foreign policy, while carefully siding with the Soviet Union on all major issues, Hungary has maintained correct relations with various Western countries, notably the United States. In 1969 it clearly welcomed the signs of a new East-West détente and the prospect of establishing diplomatic ties with West Germany.

East Germany survived the Czechoslovak crisis with apparent calm. The presence of a large Soviet garrison, Ulbricht's totalitarian control, and relative economic prosperity prevented the manifestation of any serious dissatisfaction in the country. Yet, beneath the surface there have also been signs of discontent in the German Democratic Republic. Youths' scattered protests against the invasion of Czechoslovakia and brawls with the police during the celebrations of the twentieth anniversary of the GDR

3. The political developments in Poland are discussed in some detail in Adam Bromke, "Poland's Political Crisis," *World Today*, 25, no. 3 (1969), 117–26, and in "Beyond the Gomulka Era," *Foreign Affairs*, 49, no. 3 (1971), 480–92.

in East Berlin, in the context of Ulbricht's oppressive political system, might well have signaled growing restiveness on the part of the younger generation. The reaction of the East German regime to the workers' riots in Poland revealed some concern over the position of East German workers, especially in view of the worsening economic conditions in the country. In addition, Ulbricht's stepping down from the leadership in April 1971 may aggravate the situation. To a very large extent the GDR has been a personal creation of Ulbricht, and despite the orderly initial transfer of power to Honecker, it may find the transition difficult to cope with. Last but not least there is the question of how Pankow will adjust to Bonn's new posture toward it. The initial response of the GDR to Brandt's *Ostpolitik* indicated at least some signs of nervousness. Pankow seems to be apprehensive either of finding itself increasingly isolated or of having to intensify its contacts with the Federal Republic beyond its capacity to control them; each of these alternatives would result in the reopening of the perennial issue of German unity.

It is clear, then, that the latest demonstration of Soviet force in Czechoslovakia failed to accomplish its objective. It did not stabilize Moscow's rule in Eastern Europe. At best it postponed, but certainly did not resolve, the problems with which the Russians are faced in the area. The process of change there will continue in the years to come. Whatever opportunities may arise for emancipation from the Soviet hegemony will be exploited by the Eastern European peoples. Eastern Europe will remain basically unstable, and in some respects a dangerous area, throughout the 1970s.

II

Another major development which took place in the communist orbit in the 1960s was the transformation of Sino-Soviet relations from an alliance into a bitter conflict. It was in the spring of 1960 that an ideological dispute between Moscow and Peking first came into the open. Nearly a decade later, in the spring of 1969, the two former allies fought bloody battles along their boundary and there was talk of an impending nuclear war between them. The dramatic change in Asia, in turn, affected Eastern Europe.

China's own brand of communism had no great appeal in Eastern Europe. The Chinese abandonment of the short-lived "hundred flowers" course in 1957 and their renewed tight restrictions on personal freedom were in direct opposition to the aspirations of the Eastern Europeans. The excesses of the Cultural Revolution ten years later only widened the gap between them. And China's militant stance toward the West, and especially the United States, evoked little sympathy in Eastern Europe. Thus, among the communist states in the area only Albania sided with China. In all other countries, pro-Chinese sentiments were of no political significance; they were basically confined to small groups of unrepentant Stalinists.

The indirect influence of the Sino-Soviet rift in Eastern Europe, however, was considerable; indeed, through the 1960s it represented a major catalyst of change in the area. The schism between the two centers of communism – each proclaiming itself to be the only true exponent of Marxism-Leninism – compromised the universalist pretensions of communist ideology. As has already been mentioned, the emergence of doctrinal pluralism led to the growth of pragmatism in the Eastern European communist parties. Moreover, Sino-Soviet rivalry made the Chinese encourage the revival of nationalism in other communist states. Peking openly denounced Moscow's suppression of the Eastern European peoples and posed as a champion of their rights to independence.

The Sino-Soviet contest also provided the Eastern Europeans with an opportunity of political maneuver vis-à-vis Moscow. As long as the two communist giants had remained united, the smaller communist states had little choice but to follow their lead; in fact, the reconsolidation of Soviet influence in Eastern Europe (except Yugoslavia) in the late 1950s was effectively assisted by China. Once Moscow and Peking fell apart, the position of smaller communist countries improved considerably; they were now regarded by each side as prospective partners in opposing the other. In this way the Eastern European states obtained at least some leeway from the USSR.

The changed atmosphere in the communist world strengthened the independent position of Yugoslavia. While its rivalry with Peking persisted, Moscow, in order not to be caught in a struggle on two fronts, has avoided aggravating its ideological rift with Belgrade. The new situation also greatly helped Rumania. By taking a neutral stand in the Sino-Soviet dispute Bucharest managed to play off Peking against Moscow, and in doing so, it has emancipated itself from the influence of both of them. Hungary's more pragmatic course and Poland's independent agricultural policy probably also have been the manifestations of a greater latitude which the Eastern European countries have won from Moscow in the aftermath of the Sino-Soviet quarrel.

The Soviet invasion of Czechoslovakia has only increased China's role in Eastern Europe. Despite its pronounced dislike of the reformist Dubcek regime, Peking came out strongly against Soviet interference in Czechoslovak internal affairs and denounced the Brezhnev doctrine as "imperialist." At the same time the Chinese policies in Eastern Europe, after a period of withdrawal during the Cultural Revolution, have been revived. The pro-Chinese communists from the parties loyal to Moscow now in exile in Tirana, notably the Poles, have intensified their activities. Chinese-Albanian relations have continued to be very close, and Chinese-Rumanian relations have remained friendly. Even more significantly, there have been signs of improvement in relations, culminating in the exchange of ambassadors, between China and Yugoslavia. Apparently, their common opposition to the USSR has brought the two diametrically opposed brands of communism closer together, pointing to the possibility of, should the Russians persist with their hegemonical claims, a Sino-Balkan alliance. China's determined anti-Soviet stand has gained it sympathy among the other Eastern European peoples too. This was well illustrated in the spring of 1969 by the students in Prague who, in their anger and helplessness, shouted at the Russian soldiers: "The Chinese will teach you a lesson!"

China's emergence from its self-imposed isolation during the Cultural Revolution and its more active participation in international politics should expand its diplomatic opportunities in Eastern Europe. The improved relations between China and various Western countries, including the United States, should enhance the appeal of Peking in that part of the world. They would make easier the position of those countries, such as Rumania, which strive to counterbalance Soviet pressure by preserving good relations with both Peking and Washington. In the 1970s, then, China is likely to retain substantial political influence in Eastern Europe. Should the Eastern Europeans be denied other opportunities of emancipation from Moscow's authority, they will increasingly look to Peking for support.

It is more likely, however, that as in the past so in the years to come, China will play an indirect rather than a direct role in Eastern Europe. The protracted conflict with China (and there are few signs that it will abate soon)[4] might push the USSR in the direction of reducing tensions with the West. This would be in line with the traditional pattern of Russian diplomacy which has always tried to avoid simultaneous entanglements on

4. This evaluation of the future Sino-Soviet relations was confirmed to this writer, late in 1969, by a high-ranking official from one of the pro-Moscow Eastern European countries, who, after praising the virtues of peaceful coexistence, added pointedly: ". . . and all this applies to our relations with some socialist countries too." Clearly the best he hoped for in Sino-Soviet relations was the avoidance of cold war.

its two flanks: in the Far East and Central Asia, and in Europe. Moscow, moreover, seems to be well aware of the precariousness of its present strategic position. On March 11, 1969, the East German paper *Neues Deutschland* accused the Chinese of a betrayal by deliberately provoking the clashes on the Ussuri River at the very moment when the communist countries had been engaged in a confrontation with the West over Berlin. It is quite probable, therefore, that to avoid similar situations in the future, at one time or another in the 1970s, the Soviet Union will seek a détente in Europe. The relaxation of East-West tensions would have far-reaching repercussions in Eastern Europe. A climate of détente, as has been evident ever since the "Geneva spirit" in the mid-fifties, would be conducive to the expansion of contracts between the two parts of Europe. In turn, erosion of communist ideology and revival of aspirations to independence among the nations in the Eastern part of the continent would set up a chain reaction.

III

The West played a relatively small role in Eastern Europe in the 1960s. Since the end of the Second World War, and especially since the Hungarian Revolution in 1956, the Western powers have recognized that they cannot challenge Soviet supremacy in that area without risk of a military confrontation. Even the attempt to keep the Eastern European issue on a diplomatic agenda posed some difficulties – it stood in the way of improving the climate of East-West relations. The Western countries have believed that their restrained policy (even though they may have occasionally used this as an excuse for ignoring Eastern Europe altogether) is also the best possible alternative for the Eastern Europeans. To try to liberate Eastern Europe by nuclear war would not make sense, while a climate of détente, as the experience of the 1950s demonstrated, could be conducive to gradual changes in that region.

The acceptance of severe limitations on their policy in Eastern Europe did not mean, however, that the Western powers were prepared to sanction Soviet rule by force in that region. There were several reasons for this reluctance. To ignore the legitimate aspirations to independence of the Eastern Europeans would mean repudiating the very principles on which the policy of the West rests, and the Western powers could not do this without appearing hypocritical. In addition, an acceptance of the division of Europe along the present lines would perpetuate a confrontation there between the two superpowers with the danger of a conflict between them (which could be provoked by some upheaval in Eastern Europe spilling over into the Western part of the continent), and a resulting mutual distrust which could hinder progress in some other spheres of East-West relations. Last but not least a formal recognition of the present status quo in Europe, especially by the United States, could well be counterproductive. For the paradox of the European division is that it is tolerable only as long as it remains provisional; were it to be declared permanent it would become unstable. If hope of overcoming the present barriers in Europe were to be crushed, forces would be released in both parts of the continent which, in succumbing to a council of despair, would threaten its very stability. The Eastern Europeans, denied their hopes for freedom, could become even more restive; and the Germans, frustrated in achieving national unity, could resort to an unpredictable, nationalistic policy.

The West, thus, welcomed the trend toward polycentrism in Eastern Europe. The developments in that region were in line with its two objectives: on the one hand, they widened the scope of independence from the USSR of at least some of the Eastern European nations; on the other hand, they did not preclude chances for an East-West détente. Indeed it was hoped that with their gradual emancipation from Soviet hegemony, the countries in the region might play a constructive role in bridging the ideological gap dividing the two blocs. In the mid-sixties, then, at least two Western powers, the United States and France, cautiously attempted to encourage changes in Eastern Europe. Neither one was successful.

The United States adopted the so-called "building bridges" policy toward Eastern Europe. In his speeches of May 1964 and October 1966 President Johnson proclaimed the American intention to expand economic, cultural, and diplomatic contacts with the various Eastern European countries. In Washington it was expected that, in line with the dynamics of change in the region, increased cooperation with the United States would assist the Eastern Europeans in gradually enlarging their independence from Moscow. The policy of "building bridges," however, never really got off the ground. The Johnson administration, preoccupied with the war in Vietnam, paid little attention to Europe in general, or to Eastern Europe in particular. As a result, except for some improvement in relations with Rumania in 1964, nothing much was done. The proposals to adopt a more constructive course of action regarding Eastern Europe were ignored.[5]

5. Notably those advanced by Zbigniew Brzezinski in his book, *Alternative to Partition: For a Broader Conception of America's Role in Europe* (New York, 1965). For an early critique of the American policy of "building bridges" see also Adam

Since 1964 de Gaulle's France also followed a sort of "building bridges" policy of its own. France's relations with various Eastern European countries, notably Poland and Rumania, improved markedly. Economic, cultural, and even political contacts were considerably expanded. De Gaulle's diplomatic gambit was to use the Paris dispute with Washington as a lever to win concessions from Moscow in Europe. He hoped that in exchange for restricting the American role in Western Europe, he could obtain a proportionate reduction of Soviet influence in the Eastern part of that continent. De Gaulle, however, grossly overestimated Paris' bargaining position vis-à-vis Moscow. The USSR was glad to use France to erode the American position in Europe, but offered no quid pro quo in its own sphere of influence. Opposed by both the Americans and the Russians, the French Eastern European policy soon ran into difficulties.[6] De Gaulle's offer of political cooperation to the Poles, made during his visit to Warsaw in September 1967, was coldly rejected by Gomulka, and his visit to Bucharest in May 1968 was cut short by the students' rebellion in Paris, which dramatically revealed France's internal weakness.

When the Czechoslovak crisis came to a head in mid-1968 there was really no Western policy toward Eastern Europe, unless the absence of a policy can be regarded as one. Washington adopted a studied indifference toward Prague, and Paris remained silent. Indeed, after the Soviet intervention the French Foreign Minister M. Couve de Murville promptly declared that this action should not stand in the way of a continued East-West détente, and President Johnson was soon ready to go to a summit meeting with Premier Kosygin.[7] The Western goal of improving relations with the USSR clearly overshadowed that of assisting the Eastern Europeans in their efforts to free themselves from Soviet control.

Since the change of administration in Washington, the balance in American policies has been at least partly restored. President Nixon has shown less eagerness than his predecessor to rush to summit talks with the Russians, but he has paid more attention to Europe, including the

Bromke, "The United States and Eastern Europe," *International Journal*, 21, no. 2 (1966), 211–18.

6. For an evaluation of the impact of de Gaulle's policy in Eastern Europe see Adam Bromke, "Poland and France: The Sentimental Friendship," *East Europe*, 15, no. 2 (1966), 9–15.

7. For an evaluation of American policy at the time of the Czechoslovak crisis see Adam Bromke, "Czechoslovakia and the World," *Canadian Slavonic Papers*, 10, no. 4 (1968), 581–91; John C. Campbell, "Czechoslovakia: American Choices, Past and Future," and Bromke, "The Aftermath of Czechoslovakia," in *Canadian Slavonic Papers*, 11, no. 1 (1969), 23–30.

Eastern part of the continent. His visit to Rumania in August 1969, though carefully avoiding any overt anti-Soviet overtones, served to emphasize a continued American interest in the fate of Eastern Europe. Yet, few concrete steps to expand American-Rumanian relations, even in the economic sphere, have followed. Also, so far, no new American program for Europe has been clearly formulated; the attention of the United States continues to be diverted from that continent by persistent conflicts in Southeast Asia and in the Middle East.

In 1969 a more dynamic policy toward Eastern Europe was adopted by West Germany. The new *Ostpolitik* actually had been launched by the Kiessinger-Brandt coalition government in 1966, but not until the spring of 1969 did it elicit any positive response from the Soviet side, and it was put into practice only after Brandt took over as chancellor in the fall of that year. Since then Bonn has engaged in extensive, three-pronged negotiations with Moscow, Warsaw, and Pankow; these soon were supplemented by negotiations among the Four Great Powers on the status of Berlin. In August 1970 the treaty on the renunciation of force was signed by West Germany and the Soviet Union; in the following December a similar pact, stressing somewhat more the inviolability of the existing boundaries, was concluded between the Federal Republic and Poland.[8] Bonn, however, made the ratification of the two treaties contingent on the prior settlement of the Berlin problem.

The new West German policy has striven to overcome the dilemma facing the West in Eastern Europe. It has recognized that the reunification of Germany cannot be achieved by a confrontation. Instead, it has proceeded from the belief that reunification can be advanced only as a part of a broad East-West détente in Europe, a process in which Germany would have to play a major part. By concluding treaties renouncing the use of force and respecting the integrity of existing boundaries with Moscow and Warsaw, Bonn has hoped to allay the Russians' and Poles' fear of West Germany and, in a new international climate, to obtain their consent to improve the position of West Berlin and to bring the two Germanies closer together. A formal reunification has been relegated to the distant future — it has now become accepted as the final, rather than the first, step in the tedious process of overcoming the division of Europe. In the meantime, Bonn has declared its readiness to expand its official contacts with

8. For an analysis of the impact of the *Ostpolitik* on Poland see Adam Bromke and Harald von Riekhoff, "Poland and West Germany: A Belated Détente," *Canadian Slavonic Papers*, 12, no. 2 (1970), 195–210; and "The Polish-West German Treaty," *East Europe*, 20 (1971), 2–8.

Pankow, but has stopped short of granting the GDR formal recognition, a step which it has regarded as detrimental to the long-range prospect of national unity.

Brandt's foreign policy has been fraught with serious risks. It has been regarded with apprehension by a considerable segment of the German electorate as well as by some of Germany's Western allies. The opponents of the *Ostpolitik* fear that the Soviet Union would use a rapprochement with West Germany solely to consolidate the status quo in Europe, and especially the position of the GDR. They claim that in the Moscow and Warsaw treaties most of the concessions were made by West Germany, while in negotiations on the status of Berlin as well as on closer bonds between the two Germanies, there has been little progress. Indeed, as was the case with France in the sixties, the chances of West Germany alone extracting a satisfactory quid pro quo from the Soviet Union appear to be remote. Brandt, therefore, has deliberately tied his *Ostpolitik* to the broad pattern of East-West negotiations. His best hope seems to be that the West German policy of movement could spread into other areas of East-West relations, preparing the way toward the gradual emergence of a genuine détente in Europe.

Late in 1969 and early in 1970 the Western powers, in addition to undertaking negotiations with the Russians on Berlin, cautiously but persistently explored other avenues of improving the European political climate. The communist proposal of March 1969, to hold a conference on European security, was noted but not accepted by the NATO ministerial meeting in December. The agenda put forward by the communists calling for a renunciation of the use of force and the expansion of economic and scientific contacts among the European states was criticized by the West as too nebulous. A meeting with such vague terms of reference could only achieve an illusion of a détente without resolving any issues of substance in East-West relations. Indeed, U.S. Secretary of State William Rogers, in a speech delivered during his stay in Brussels, went further and explicitly posed the question of whether the real objective of the proposed European conference was to "draw a veil over [the] subjugation of Czechoslovakia." [9]

At the same time, however, the NATO ministers declared that they are receptive to the idea of reducing tensions with the communist countries, and they made various concrete suggestions on how this could be achieved. They proposed that, in addition to economic and scientific con-

9. *New York Times,* December 7, 1969.

tacts, cultural exchanges promoting the free movement of people and ideas should be expanded; they revived the plan, originally advanced at the NATO meeting in June 1968, to undertake a mutual and balanced force reduction in Europe. At the NATO conference in Rome in May 1970 it was agreed that a formal proposal for troop reduction, significantly including nuclear force, should be presented to the communist countries. In a speech in Tiflis in May 1971, Brezhnev responded favorably to the Western initiative and proposed that a conference to discuss force reductions in Europe should be convened. At the same time the Americans and the Russians, who since 1969 had been engaged in bilateral negotiations to limit strategic arms, agreed to turn over negotiations on the reduction of nuclear weapons in Central Europe to NATO and WTO.

Thus, the two opposing blocs gradually have expanded the scope of their negotiations. Taken together the various East-West talks presently under way clearly amount to the most serious effort to reduce the confrontation in Europe since the end of World War II. "The purpose of all these initiatives," declared a communiqué issued by the NATO ministerial meeting in Lisbon in May 1971, "is to seek just solutions to the fundamental problems of European security and thus to achieve a genuine improvement of East-West relations." [10] Should satisfactory agreements be reached on Berlin and some progress made in negotiations on eventual troop reductions the road would be free for a European conference.[11]

Should a European meeting take place, it would be unrealistic to expect too much from it. Even if there were mutual goodwill, progress would be slow. A true European settlement is too complex to be achieved all at once; it will require certainly more than one attempt to devise a viable security system in Europe. Before that end is achieved a series of conferences, spread throughout the seventies and perhaps even beyond, will be needed. Moreover, it is doubtful if there is sufficient goodwill on both sides. For, in the early seventies, it can be seen that the Western and Soviet goals are still far apart. The Western goal is progressively to reduce and ultimately to overcome the division of Europe, while the USSR objective is to preserve, and, indeed, to consolidate the status quo. The chance of an early change in the Soviet position, as its continued emphasis on the Brezhnev doctrine testifies, does not appear likely.

10. *New York Times,* June 5, 1971.

11. For a more detailed discussion of the Western response to the communist proposal for a European security conference see Adam Bromke, "Eastern Europe on the Threshold of the 1970's," *Slavic and East European Studies,* 14 (1969), 31–48, on which this chapter is largely based.

Yet if the West maintains its course, the Russians, in the long run, may become more amenable to a genuine resolution of the European problem. It should not be forgotten that there are important forces in the communist orbit which eventually may bring the Soviet Union to the conference table on Western terms. The Russians may one day realize that perpetuating their rule by force does not strengthen their position in Eastern Europe, but in fact weakens it. A continued confrontation with China might also make them perceive the need for a true détente in Europe. Despite Soviet efforts, the Eastern European question played an important role in East-West relations in the 1960s. It will certainly remain on their diplomatic agenda throughout the 1970s.

2

The Sino-Soviet Dispute

BY JOHN W. STRONG

Since 1965 Sino-Soviet relations have progressively deteriorated to the point where during 1969 there was much talk and discussion regarding the possibility of a full-scale war between the Soviet Union and the People's Republic of China.[1] How this split evolved and deepened, and how the diplomatic and ideological relationship between the USSR and the PRC has degenerated from the stage of general dispute to a level of increasing struggle are the major questions to be dealt with in this chapter. The conflict between the Soviet Union and China is an important development not only because of its impact on the two nations themselves, but also because it has destroyed whatever unity there was in the communist world, and it has greatly affected the attitudes and policies of other nations toward the socialist states. One could even say that the conflict has been a major cause of the East-West détente and of the end to the cold war rigidity so characteristic of the 1950s.

Before Nikita Khrushchev's unceremonious retirement in October 1964, the view that perhaps the Sino-Soviet dispute was a matter of personal antagonism between Chairman Mao and the Soviet premier could be justified. When relations became further strained during 1965, however, it became obvious that the struggle had transcended specific issues. The antagonism had developed an all-inclusive nature in which its components (ideological differences, national interests, personalities, race, etc.) were inseparably interwoven. It might even be argued that the dispute had developed into a type of Hegelian phenomenon where the whole was greater than the sum of its parts.

1. See for example, Harrison E. Salisbury, "Will There Be War between Russia and China?" *New York Times Magazine*, July 27, 1969.

Speculation along these lines has been reinforced, if not confirmed, by the diplomatic talks on border problems conducted by the two powers in Peking since October 1969. Even if these negotiations should produce some mutually acceptable solution to the boundary disputes, it seems unlikely that they will do very much to improve the overall relations between the Soviet Union and China. This becomes more apparent when one considers the following statements issued by the government of China in October 1969 — statements which give a clear indication of Peking's attitude toward its northern neighbor.

> The Chinese Government has never covered up the fact that there exist irreconcilable differences of principle between China and the Soviet Union and that the struggle of principle between them will continue for a long period of time.[2]
>
> The Soviet revisionist renegade clique has consistently been hostile toward the Chinese people. Filled with hatred and fear, it has redoubled its efforts to carry out anti-Chinese activities especially since China launched the Great Proletarian Cultural Revolution and won great and decisive victories.[3]

It seems quite obvious that even a miraculous solution of these "irreconcilable differences of principle" would offer little prospect for a settlement of these two powers' conflicting national interests.[4]

I

After the open split between Moscow and Peking burst on the international scene in the early 1960s, Western observers began searching intensively for the origins of this dispute. A favorite possibility was Khrushchev's "de-Stalinization" oration at the Twentieth Congress of the Communist party of the Soviet Union (CPSU) in 1956, and the resulting turmoil within the socialist bloc.[5] Khrushchev's blunt attack on personality cults could not help but have exacerbated Chairman Mao's distrust and dislike of the post-Stalin Soviet leadership.

In a recent interview, Premier Chou En-lai frankly asserted that "the split between Moscow and Peking developed because Nikita S. Khrush-

2. *Statement of the Government of the People's Republic of China*, October 7, 1969 (Peking, 1969), p. 5.

3. *Down with the New Tsars!* (Peking, 1969), p. 4.

4. It is assumed that when the Chinese refer to "differences of principle," they mean the ideological differences between themselves and the Soviets.

5. John W. Strong, "Sino-Soviet Relations in Historical Perspective," in Adam Bromke (ed.), *The Communist States at the Crossroads: Between Moscow and Peking* (New York, 1965), p. 40.

chev took the road of revisionism and peaceful coexistence rather than continuing vigorous revolution after he came to power in the nineteen fifties." [6] However, with a perspective of sixteen years, one can see that perhaps the Twentieth Congress of the CPSU has been overemphasized as a source of Sino-Soviet difficulties. It undoubtedly contributed to the dispute, but was it a basic source of the troubles?

In September 1962 Chairman Mao himself commented on the origins of the dispute: "The roots for [the conflict] were laid earlier. They did not allow China to make revolution. This was in 1945, when Stalin tried to prevent the Chinese revolution by saying that there should not be any civil war and that we must collaborate with Chiang Kai-shek. At that time we did not carry this into effect, and the revolution was victorious. After the victory they again suspected that China would be like Yugoslavia and that I would become a Tito." [7] Mao's statement does not mention the disputes and disagreements between Stalin and him in the twenties and thirties, but it does emphasize the existence of serious Sino-Soviet difficulties before 1956. It shows that the current struggle is not a superficial contemporary problem, but one which has rather deep historical roots. Whenever a conflicting international relationship has a long historical background and becomes imbedded in the national psyche, it is not inclined to lend itself to easy, piecemeal, or even rational solution. European history for the past five hundred years is testament enough to this unfortunate fact.

In the current phase of the Sino-Soviet struggle, both sides have what they consider to be legitimate fears and concerns. It is evident that these concerns are not propagandistic devices used for domestic purposes but are an authentic expression of the climate of thought in the USSR and China.

For a person in the West, it has been easier to understand and to share some of the Soviet fears of China than to identify with Chinese apprehensions regarding the USSR. The Soviet fears, based on real dangers, seem more rational. Such an assumption, however, may be more of a comment on the closer identity of Western and Soviet thought processes than a realistic analysis of the problem. China's reiterated accusations concerning Soviet-American collusion against the PRC [8] are difficult for a Westerner to appreciate, and may thus seem ludicrous. On the other hand, the Soviet

6. *New York Times*, May 21, 1971.

7. Mao Tse-tung, "Speech to the 10th Plenary Session of the Eighth Central Committee, September 24, 1962," *New York Times*, March 1, 1970.

8. See for example, "Intensified U.S.-Soviet Collaboration Against China," *Peking Review*, no. 46 (November 14, 1969), 28.

fear of China's verbal militancy, backed as it is by an atomic arsenal, is easily understood and shared by the western world.[9]

Soviet fears regarding China, which have in their own way contributed to the tension between the two countries, are numerous and only a few examples need be given. First and foremost are China's proximity and its ever-growing demographic size. Although the Soviet concern that millions of Chinese are waiting breathlessly for an opportunity to settle in the harsh lands of Eastern Siberia is no doubt exaggerated, it does express the underpopulated USSR's worry about an "expanding China." Repeated Chinese allegations that Siberian and Central Asian territory was wrongfully taken from them by Russian imperialism [10] do little to calm Soviet nerves. China's military capacity for causing grave mischief along its 4000-mile boundary with the USSR has contributed greatly to war jitters felt throughout the Soviet nation. Military bases and kinship relations among minority ethnic peoples on both sides of the long boundary of course aggravate the border problem. Statements by Soviet authorities which maintain that the Chinese know full well that the Soviet Union's military power is huge, and thus that China would never cause real trouble, are designed more to bolster self-confidence than to convince. These assertions are also predicated on the dubious reasoning that the Chinese will reason and develop plans just as the Soviets believe they should.

Another major Soviet concern is the development of Maoism as a socialist ideology, its implementation in China, and its potential to expand beyond Chinese borders. The Soviets' condemnation of the ideological component of such developments in China as the Great Leap Forward, the commune system, and the role of the military in Chinese political life has not helped to lessen the friction between the two countries. The Soviets have gone so far as to accuse the Chinese on many occasions of that ultimate communist sin: Trotskiism. "It is now quite obvious that the Maoists are determined to smash the Party and the organs of people's power with the object of consolidating the cult of Mao Tse-tung and establishing a military-bureaucratic regime. The Mao Tse-tung personality cult has reached monstrous proportions: in fact, it has come to the stage where

9. Harrison E. Salisbury (ed.), *The Soviet Union: The Fifty Years* (New York, 1968), pp. 511–12.

10. "The treaties relating to the present Sino-Soviet boundary are all unequal treaties imposed on China by tsarist Russian imperialism in the latter half of the 19th century and the beginning of the 20th century when power was in the hands of neither the Chinese people nor the Russian people." *Statement of the Government of the People's Republic of China*, October 1, 1969, p. 32.

Mao Tse-tung is being deified." [11] Without reserve, the Soviets have bitterly and sarcastically attacked Mao and his development of communism in China.

> The proclamation of the Chinese People's Republic and the transition to the building of a new society required that Mao Tse-tung, too, should make his contribution to the solution of the manifold problems that faced China in connection with the new tasks arising from the development of the revolution. As history has shown, he was unable to solve these problems.
>
> His subjective idealism in analysing social development, his petty-bourgeois limitations resulting from the semi-natural, semi-feudal economy of the Chinese village, the dogmatism of the Chinese patriarchy, his twenty-year old habit of settling all important questions as the leader of an army and with the help of the army made it impossible for Mao to understand and master the Marxist-Leninist principles of socialism and communism.
>
> Mao's socialism and communism are a version of utopia, an "ideal world," based on the semi-natural economy of the backward Chinese village.[12]

The Soviets have openly said that the only hope for China will be to overthrow Mao and his philosophy: "The victory of those forces which are resisting the policies of Mao Tse-tung and his supporters would be the beginning of a return for China toward a normal economic life, . . . and even the beginning of the solution of all those economic problems which have accumulated in China during the past decade." [13]

China's fears regarding Soviet Russia are also numerous and an obstacle to any rapprochement. The Maoists are absolutely certain that they are ideologically correct and pure. Thus they have become almost religious fanatics in their convictions, and with this fanaticism have emerged a growing intolerance, contempt, and fear of the Soviet model of a socialist society, which they condemn as "revisionism" of the Marxist-Leninist-Stalinist-Maoist truth.[14] The Maoists' struggle against what they felt were the cancerous effects of Soviet revisionism was surely one of the motivating forces of the Great Proletarian Cultural Revolution.[15]

11. Zanegin, Moronov, and Mikhailov, *Developments in China* (Moscow, 1968), p. 38. For a bibliography of recent Soviet literature on China see Klaus Mehnert, "Mao and Maoism: Some Soviet Views," *Current Scene*, 8, no. 15 (September 1970).

12. V. Gelbras, *Mao's Pseudo-Socialism* (Moscow, 1968), pp. 154–55.

13. *Bol'shoi Skachok i Narodnye Kommuny v Kitae* (Moscow, 1968), p. 142.

14. See for example, "Soviet Revisionist Renegades Step Up Capitalist Reorganization of Economy," and "Soviet Revisionists: Sordid Salesmen of Reactionary Western Culture," *Peking Review*, no. 44 (November 1, 1968), 23–28.

15. Lin Piao, *Report to the Ninth National Congress of the Communist Party of China* (Peking, 1969), pp. 84–86.

From the Chinese point of view a major cause for concern is the possibility of a meaningful Soviet-American détente. Convinced that collusion between the two superpowers already exists, the Chinese grow increasingly apprehensive when such conferences as the SALT talks convene. They tend to see these developments not as steps toward a more peaceful world, but as diabolical plots against themselves. The Chinese Communist party has even embodied in its new constitution a determination to fight the united forces of "U.S. imperialism" and "Soviet revisionism." "The Communist Party of China upholds proletarian internationalism; it firmly unites with the genuine Marxist-Leninist Parties and groups the world over, unites with the proletariat, the oppressed people and nations of the whole world and fights together with them to overthrow imperialism headed by the United States, modern revisionism with the Soviet revisionist renegade clique as its centre and the reactionaries of all countries, and to abolish the system of exploitation of man by man over the globe, so that all mankind will be emancipated." [16] Although its nature is still vague, the Brezhnev proposal of a system of collective security in Asia is viewed in Peking as a design to "contain" the Chinese and as added verification of their fears and suspicions. A Chinese representative in the West stated in early 1970 that the Chinese nation was on a war footing and that the government was absolutely convinced that joint Soviet-American action would eventually be taken against them.[17]

II

Sino-Soviet relations must also be seen and analyzed against the background of what history may yet prove to have been the major event of the sixties – the Great Proletarian Cultural Revolution. The development of the Cultural Revolution was influenced by Sino-Soviet relations, and in turn it had a worsening effect on them. However, caution should be exercised not to exaggerate this interaction. There is little evidence to suggest that the Cultural Revolution either caused the recent Sino-Soviet quarrel, or was caused by it.

Much has already been written about the Cultural Revolution and it will undoubtedly continue to be a favorite topic for the historians of twentieth-century China. We are now still close enough to the event to be confused about many aspects of this momentous internal upheaval in China.

16. *The Constitution of the Communist Party of China* (adopted, April 14, 1969) (Peking, 1969), pp. 10–12.

17. Statements to this effect frequently come from Peking. The source of this particular remark, however, must remain anonymous.

There are many guesses but there are still few clear-cut answers to the basic question, What was this event all about? Interpretations have varied from the very narrow (it was a power struggle among the top leaders of the CCP) to the very broad (it was an attempt to rebuild Chinese society and to create a new way of life — the Maoist man living in an ideal Maoist world).

In looking for the origins of the Cultural Revolution one is faced with the same type of problem as in looking for the origins of the Sino-Soviet dispute. If the Cultural Revolution is seen as a narrow, political movement, its genesis could be found in Mao Tse-tung's launching of the Socialist Education Movement in 1963 and its concomitant purge of intellectuals. If, however, it is viewed in its broad, philosophical and cultural context, its beginnings could be traced back to Mao's writings and thoughts from the twenties onward.[18]

Following the economic dislocation caused by the Great Leap Forward, Mao's political position within the communist hierarchy suffered a serious decline and he was retired as president of the People's Republic. Always the leader of the "ideologist" faction of the party, Mao was eclipsed during the early sixties by the "experts" or "technocrat" faction led by his replacement as president, Liu Shao-ch'i. It was Liu and his supporters who supervised China's recovery from the Great Leap. It was they who apparently attempted to free China from the rigid ideological bonds imposed by the Maoists, and in so doing release China's potential for more realistic economic development. Thus Chairman Mao was faced with a double challenge — to his personal prestige and political position, and, more importantly, to his basic beliefs regarding how a truly revolutionary and self-reliant China should develop. In Mao's opinion, his former comrades like Liu had betrayed not only him personally, but the Chinese revolution by favoring a revisionist, or Khrushchevian-"goulash approach" to communism. From this belief developed the anti-Soviet component of the Cultural Revolution.

Where the Maoist opposition misjudged the situation was in underestimating the aura, or personality cult, which the party itself had created around Mao as *the* leader of Chinese communism. Utilizing this asset, Mao began to mobilize his forces about 1963 for a counterattack on his enemies and their ideas. The weapon to be used in this struggle was the Great Proletarian Cultural Revolution.

What is ironic concerning China's relations with the Soviet Union is

18. See, K. H. Fan (ed.), *The Chinese Cultural Revolution: Selected Documents* (New York, 1968), pp. 3–32.

that the open break between them in 1962–63 came when Mao's position was apparently at a low ebb, and when the supposedly more pro-Soviet elements were theoretically on the ascendancy. This apparent contradiction can only be understood if one begins to view the Sino-Soviet dispute not in terms of personality conflict only, but in its broader context of national, political, and ideological differences. When seen in this light, it becomes clear that alterations in the leadership of either country have had little effect on the course of the dispute.

In an interview with Premier Chou reported on May 21, 1971, Chou stated that ". . . when Leonid I. Brezhnev came to power in Moscow, China had hoped for a change in the revisionist policy. . . . [China] discovered that the change in leadership in Moscow was not a result of a change in party policy . . . but was motivated by a struggle for power in the leadership which was very disappointing to the Chinese." [19]

What could be called the background phase of the Cultural Revolution (1964–66) was obviously unsatisfactory to Chairman Mao. It convinced him that he could not achieve his objectives by using the conventional establishment institutions of party and government. Although Mao might well have been able to regain his personal political position by struggle within these institutions, he no longer felt that they could be utilized to achieve his broader objectives: a revolutionized China; an end to Soviet "neo-capitalist" tendencies; and the development of an orthodox (Maoist) system of communism. For these objectives Mao was forced to go outside the party and the government and appeal directly to the masses, the army, and especially the youth of China. It was as if Mao had decided that heaven's mandate to rule China had been withdrawn from the party and government, and that the people should now exercise their right to rebel against the corruption of those institutions. This prompted many Maoist sympathizers to erroneously view the Cultural Revolution as a vast exercise in popular democracy.

The purge of Peking's mayor, P'eng Chen, in May 1966, and the unleashing of the Red Guard Movement in August marked the beginnings of a new, more radical, and more violent phase of the Cultural Revolution. The precedent of a communist leader appealing to forces in society to strive against the ruling party bureaucracy was naturally viewed with horror by the Soviet leaders and prompted many comments such as the following:

> The present developments in China are a tragedy for the Chinese people.

19. *New York Times*, May 21, 1971.

> . . . These developments acquire a sinister meaning also because the "cultural revolution" threatens the socialist gains of the Chinese people and makes remote the prospects of China's socialist development.
>
> The home and foreign policy which the Maoists are pursuing in defiance of the will of the Communist Party and people of China has bared its adventurist substance and completely discredited itself. The "new order" which the Maoists plan for China can only conserve her economic and cultural backwardness, revive the material hardships of the "big leap" years and throw China many decades back.[20]

Mao's emphasis on the idea of continuous stages of revolution also must have disgusted the Soviets, especially because of its vague similarity to Trotskii's concept of "permanent revolution."

The ideological fuel of the Cultural Revolution was the Thought of Mao Tse-tung. As Marshal Lin Piao wrote in December 1966, "Comrade Mao Tse-tung is the greatest Marxist-Leninist of our era. He has inherited, defended and developed Marxism-Leninism with genius, creatively and comprehensively and has brought it to a higher and completely new stage."[21] Although ridiculed in the West and in the USSR, Mao's thoughts and the Maoist cult provided the youth of China with new standards of behavior and ethics with which to transform Chinese society. This was the glue which held the Cultural Revolution together, and which in the end held China together when confronted by the traditional centrifugal forces generated by the revolution itself.

During the developing stages of the Cultural Revolution from 1966 through 1968, the Maoists seem to have made two serious errors – one of judgment, the other of tactics. They misjudged the strength of the conservative opposition and its determination to resist. This firm resistance undoubtedly accounted for much of the widespread physical violence and economic disruption in the country. They made the tactical error of not appreciating the inclination toward anarchy which can be generated by movements like that of the Red Guards. As in practically all revolutions, the forces born of the Cultural Revolution ran beyond the control of the leaders. This is clearly indicated by the many reports of violence between rival Red Guard units whose only quarrel was apparently that each claimed to be more loyal to Mao than the other.

These two errors could have been the undoing of Mao, the Cultural Revolution, and perhaps of China itself. They were compensated for, however, by other factors. Foremost was the ability of the Maoists, led by

20. Zanegin et al., *Developments in China*, p. 83.

21. *Quotations from Chairman Mao Tse-tung*, 2nd ed. (Peking, 1967), p. 1.

Lin Piao, to retain (for the most part) the loyalty and support of the People's Liberation Army.[22] There were also the adroit compromising activities of China's grey eminence, Chou En-lai – activities which managed to pacify and control a potentially vast opposition among bureaucrats, technocrats, and intellectuals. Another neutralizing element was the repeated calls throughout the Cultural Revolution for national unity in the face of supposedly grave external threats from "Soviet revisionism" and "American imperialism." Finally there was again this almost mystical unity provided by Chairman Mao himself as the semideified symbol of China's revolution and of the Chinese nation, and by Mao's thoughts as the binding ideology of the new China.

With the benefits of hindsight one can see that by the spring of 1967, the Maoists had, for all practical purposes, won the political phase of the Cultural Revolution. The CCP establishment was in total disarray and its effective leadership of the country was broken. This is an indication that the potentially large opposition to Mao had been, in fact, very poorly organized and led. It is an odd characteristic of the Cultural Revolution that the opposition was there, but was nebulous, difficult to identify, and seemingly always floundering in a leaderless vacuum. Men like Liu Shao-ch'i were more a symbol of opposition than actual leaders of resistance.

The Maoist victory in Shanghai and the ousting of Mayor Tsao Ti-chiu were followed by similar victories across China, all of which were the result of bitter emotional and physical struggle, since those people loyal, or sympathetic, to Liu Shao-ch'i resisted the Cultural Revolution. Those who condemned the revolution often called on the peasantry of China for support in hopes that the peasant's traditional conservatism would be repelled by the radicalism of the Red Guards, as manifested in campaigns such as the destruction of the "four olds" (old thought, old culture, old customs, and old habits). The Maoist's victory shows that the opposition was generally unsuccessful in its efforts to divide and confuse the peasant's loyalty to the new China which they believed Mao had created for them.

The attacks on and by the opposition forces naturally led to excesses perpetrated by both sides. Maoist leadership made attempts to control the Red Guard excesses,[23] but on the whole seemed to condone the more ex-

22. See "Carry the Mass Movement for the Creative Study and Application of Chairman Mao's Work to a New State," Comrade Lin Piao's call to the Chinese People's Liberation Army, *Peking Review*, no. 42 (October 14, 1966), 5–8. See also Fan, *Chinese Cultural Revolution*, pp. 203–4.

23. For example see "Cadres Must be Treated Correctly," *Peking Review*, no. 10 (March 3, 1967), 5–9.

treme measures as long as they furthered the development of the revolution. Mao's comment on August 23, 1966, remained the guiding principle: "The principal question is what policies we should adopt regarding the problem of disturbances in various areas. My views are as follows. I firmly believe that a few months of disturbances will be mostly for the good and that little bad will result from these disturbances." [24]

As party authority broke down at the local levels under the attacks of Maoist Red Guards, it was gradually replaced with new organs of authority known as the Revolutionary Committees, which were composed of representatives from the army, Red Guards, and progressive workers. In most cases the Revolutionary Committees' basic functions were to exercise local leadership, promote military training, clean up local administrations, and instill confidence in the confused local population. In retrospect one can see that the Revolutionary Committees were also the vehicle through which the military was able to control and subdue the anarchistic tendencies of the youthful Red Guards. Excerpts from comments on a draft resolution presented by the Shanghai Municipal Revolutionary Committee on February 24, 1967, give a good indication of committee objectives:

> The armed core of the militia, the People's Liberation Army and other people's forces are the strong pillars of the provisional organ of power at each level.
>
> The Draft Resolution also calls on the revolutionary masses in the rural people's communes, factories and enterprises, and the departments of culture, education and health to pay attention to certain questions in production and to strive to win victories on every front.
>
> The draft Resolution pointed out that every mass organization and individual should strictly observe the state plan and the state regulations. No one is allowed to make free use of state property.[25]

It is the dominant role of the PLA in the Cultural Revolution which has convinced the Soviets that China under Mao has become a "military-bureaucratic dictatorship," and is no longer a socialist state.

Marking the exact end of a revolution is about as difficult as identifying its point of origin. More or less as a convenience, people now say that the "recent phase" of the Cultural Revolution ended with the convening of the Ninth Congress of the CCP in April 1969. The Maoist political victory was

24. Mao Tse-tung, "Talk before the Central Committee Work Conference, August 23, 1966," *New York Times*, March 1, 1970.

25. "Shanghai Municipal Revolutionary Committee Holds Grand Meeting," *Peking Review*, no. 10 (March 3, 1967), 11.

complete, and efforts were concentrated on rebuilding the reorganized party's control over China. The emphasis of the Congress was on unity. "The unification of our country, the unity of our people and the unity of our various nationalities – these are the basic guarantees of the sure triumph of our cause." [26] To promote national unity the Maoists again could use the old formula of arousing fear in the people of an external danger. The clash of Soviet and Chinese border forces on Damanskii-Chenpao Island in March 1969 was extremely convenient for this purpose. There has been inconclusive speculation that Peking may have perpetrated the border crisis as a means to that very end.

What were the accomplishments of the Cultural Revolution in China other than the obvious political victory of the Maoists and the consolidation of power in their hands? To mention a few: A new approach to education was initiated, which radically reevaluated the significance of education for the individual and for its role in Chinese society. Chinese cultural life as a whole was given new direction based on the principles of "serve the people" and "self-reliance." Although the prestige of the Chinese intellectuals declined, that of the technocrats actually did not suffer. Their role is still considered vital to China's development. The influence of the military increased substantially during the Cultural Revolution and will undoubtedly remain a determining force in the affairs of the country for some time to come.[27] This is a major deviation from the Soviet system in which the military remains subordinate to the party and under its civilian control.

The Cultural Revolution established the Thought of Mao Tse-tung as the guiding philosophy for China's future, and Maoism has almost completely submerged the ideology of Marxism-Leninism.[28] China's prestige abroad suffered as the outwardly irrational developments of the Cultural Revolution became known. However, this was at worst a temporary setback, and one which apparently was of little concern to the leaders in Peking. The doctrine of "continued revolution" has been established.[29] More cultural revolutions are to occur so that China's revolutionary-socialist society may be continually rejuvenated and kept immune from bourgeois-revisionist tendencies.

26. Lin Piao, *Report to the Ninth National Congress*, p. 103.

27. It is estimated that around 60 per cent of the new Central Committee ot the CCP is composed of military personnel.

28. *Constitution of the CCP*, pp. 4–5.

29. *Ibid.*, p. 8.

Where the Great Proletarian Cultural Revolution obviously failed was in its inability to create the new China of Mao's dreams. The three-thousand-year weight of China's history, heritage, and tradition could not be overturned in an instant even by an upheaval of this magnitude. Needless to say, only the historians of the future will be able to assess the lasting impact of the Cultural Revolution. It may well be judged as merely a superficial aberration from the historical development of China.[30]

That the Cultural Revolution had a worsening effect on Sino-Soviet relations need hardly be said. The Soviets were appalled at what happened in China, considered it to be the ultimate in national madness, and were completely frustrated by their inability to influence the course of events. Whatever they did or said only further strained relations with Peking. It is not difficult to imagine how the Soviets feel when they hear the USSR continually vilified as neo-capitalist, when they are called by China its "No. 1 Enemy," when they are forced to tolerate their embassy in Peking being put under practically a state of siege, and when they learn that Soviet citizens in China are spat on and roughed up, etc. The Revolution taught the Soviets another painful lesson on the limitations of a great power's ability to influence and control events beyond its border. It is not surprising that there were discussions concerning a possible Soviet preemptive nuclear strike against China. Such irrational thoughts have unfortunately become an indication of the frustrations of the great powers in the twentieth century.

One must remember that the Great Proletarian Cultural Revolution did not alter the basic objectives of China's foreign policy in any substantive way. It disrupted China's relations with other nations, but this was only temporary and did not affect long-range goals. The Cultural Revolution did worsen Sino-Soviet relations, yet this was a result not of the upheavals of the Revolution, but primarily of the violent Soviet reaction to them.

III

While the Cultural Revolution ran its course, other events transpired around the world which contributed to the deterioration of Sino-Soviet relations. Three of these will serve to illustrate the trend – the situation in Vietnam, the Arab-Israeli War of 1967, and the Soviet invasion of Czechoslovakia in 1968.

Seen logically, one might have surmised that the escalated war in Viet-

30. For a brief, but solid analysis of the Cultural Revolution see A. R. H. Thomas, *China: The Awakening Giant* (Toronto, 1971), chap. 13.

nam would have helped to better Sino-Soviet relations. A fraternal socialist government was in a de facto state of war with the "American imperialist" enemy. It should have been in the interests of both the Soviet Union and China to forget their differences and cooperate in giving assistance to Hanoi. As things worked out, the assistance was given, but in the process, Sino-Soviet differences were aggravated rather than reconciled.

The Chinese accused the Soviets of failing to give Hanoi and the Vietcong sufficient aid. To the Chinese this meant that the Soviets were in effect cooperating with the United States to prevent a communist victory in Vietnam. The reason for this, according to Peking, was that new communist regimes in Southeast Asia would naturally gravitate into the Chinese orbit. To the Soviets, an American presence in Southeast Asia was preferable to Chinese influences in the region. The Brezhnev doctrine seems to indicate that there is probably more than a small grain of truth in this Chinese argument.

The USSR countered the Chinese accusations with repeated charges that Peking was doing little except paying lip service to the North Vietnamese cause. Worse than that, the Chinese were continually interfering with Soviet aid to Vietnam and actually stealing some Soviet military hardware being sent by rail across China to Hanoi. That the bulk of Soviet aid to Vietnam had to be sent by ship from Vladivostok to Haiphong indicated that the Soviet's accusations were serious and had some substance. The Chinese also may have hoped that with Soviet ships going in and out of Haiphong harbor, and with American bombers in the vicinity, an accidental but serious Soviet-American confrontation might occur.

All in all, the war in Vietnam was not seen in either Moscow or Peking as dangerous enough to warrant a cooperative effort on their part. One cannot help but feel that as long as the Vietnam War remained limited (and U.S. policy always seemed determined to keep it so), it was rather pleasing to both China and the Soviet Union. It provided the Chinese leaders with visible proof (on the doorstep of China) of "American aggressiveness," and of China's need to remain united and vigilant against further U.S. moves. The war in Vietnam also provided them with an excellent propaganda weapon to use against the USSR. It did not really matter whether the Soviets did nothing, too little, or too much; they were bound to be exposed to Chinese criticisms which were embarrassing and difficult to answer.

To the Soviet Union, the limited war in Vietnam offered multiple advantages: (1) It kept the United States heavily committed in East Asia and thus incapable of concerted action elsewhere in the world. (2) It maintained a U.S. presence in Southeast Asia, which served as a deterrent to Chinese expansion into that region, and which concomitantly relieved the Soviets of any need for action in this regard. (3) World opinion was definitely turned against American policy in Southeast Asia. (4) The war created a serious domestic crisis within the United States. (5) It gave the Soviets an opportunity to test some of their modern military equipment, such as ground-to-air missiles, under combat conditions. (6) It provided the USSR with rather effective propaganda for use against the Chinese. The Chinese could be accused of failing to aid North Vietnam because of the internal weakness of China caused by Mao's Cultural Revolution. In this way the Cultural Revolution was working to sabotage the world communist cause.

For the USSR, the Arab-Israeli War of 1967 was both a benefit and an embarrassment. The Arab's debacle left them badly weakened and heavily dependent on the Soviets for help. For the first time in history an age-old Russian dream had been realized as the Soviets were able to capitalize on the situation and gain a firm position of influence in the Middle East-Mediterranean region. The Six Day War was an embarrassment, however: it indicated that Soviet military equipment was worthless in the hands of incompetents, and that in spite of their aid the Soviets were unable to control or restrain their Arab friends; it was a staggering financial loss; and it left the Soviets exposed to Chinese accusations that the USSR was responsible for the war, but afraid to intervene in order to secure victory. In China's view, the Arab cause had been sacrificed on the altar of American-Soviet collusion. Peking feels that the Soviets actually have little interest in the Arab nations' struggle, but are simply using it to increase their own imperialistic ambitions in the Arab world.

It is easy to see why, for the Chinese, the 1967 conflict in the Middle East was ideal. On the one hand, China could effectively criticize every action, or lack of action, in the Middle East taken by its Western and Soviet enemies. The Big Four committee seeking a solution to the Middle East crisis is to Peking simply another example of Soviet-Western cooperation to suppress revolutionary forces in order to maintain their own imperialist controls.

> Social-imperialism has always worked hand in glove with U.S. imperialism against the Palestinian people. It has viciously slandered and abused the Palestinian people's armed struggle as "terrorist operations," thus revealing its fear and hatred of the Palestinian people's armed struggle. In so doing it has only greatly discredited itself. Recently social-imperialism changed its tactics and hypocritically pretended to "support" the Palestinian people's armed strug-

gle. It is clear to everyone that the purpose of this is to get control of the Palestinian armed forces and use them as chips in its dirty deals with U.S. imperialism in the Middle East, so as to realize its criminal plot of stamping out the Palestinian armed struggle and divide up the Middle East with U.S. imperialism.[31]

Since the events in Czechoslovakia will be dealt with at length later in this volume, here it need only be pointed out that again the Chinese were able to utilize a world crisis as an effective propaganda weapon. At first the situation in Czechoslovakia was a disconcerting dilemma for the Chinese. They were dismayed by the liberal social and economic reforms of the Dubcek government, but at the same time, they took pleasure from the difficulties which these reforms were causing the Soviet Union.[32]

When the Soviet invasion came in August 1968, the reaction from Peking was slow for the obvious reason that the Chinese approved in principle of Moscow's action in crushing "counterrevolution," but to say so publicly would endorse the Soviet move. By the summer of 1968, the Chinese were not about to sanction anything the Soviet Union did. Approving the Soviet invasion of a socialist country, could also imply endorsing a rather dangerous precedent in relations between communist states. The Chinese were caught: they could condone neither the Czechoslovak spring nor the Soviet's invasion to crush it. However, it did not take Peking long to realize that the Soviet move into Czechoslovakia was a blessing in disguise. By halting the dangerous Czechoslovak experiments, the Soviet Union's prestige and image throughout the world had suffered a severe blow.

The Chinese interpretation of the events in Czechoslovakia became one of rather smug satisfaction. The Dubcek government had been misled by following the Soviet revisionist line. The situation in Prague then had gone out of control, counterrevolution had materialized, and it had become necessary for the Soviets to crush it before it spread throughout the satellite empire of Eastern Europe and even into the USSR itself. To the Chinese, these events substantiated their belief that the "revisionist, neo-Khrushchevian" policies of the Brezhnev-Kosygin government were not only wrong, but extremely dangerous for any socialist nation to follow. The Chinese

31. "Palestinian People's Armed Struggle Forges Ahead Victoriously," *Peking Review*, no. 3 (January 16, 1970), 27.

32. For Chinese-Albanian feelings on the situation in Czechoslovakia just before the Soviet invasion see "Soviet Revisionism and Czechoslovakia," *Peking Review*, no. 33 (August 16, 1968), 16–19. This article states: "We are not at all surprised that the Soviet and Czechoslovak revisionists would arrive at such an impasse, for we know and we have said that bandits settle accounts among themselves by using the ways of bandits."

quickly began to denounce the Soviet invasion of Czechoslovakia as a revival of old Russian imperialism. "They have ruthlessly plundered and brutally oppressed the people of some East European countries at will, and even sent several hundred thousand troops to occupy Czechoslovakia and turned a vast expanse of land in East Europe into their sphere of influence in an attempt to set up a tsarist-type colonial empire." [33]

In Czechoslovakia, Peking again saw evidence of Soviet-American collusion.[34] The idea of Soviet-American collusion has clearly become an obsession with the Chinese. Since August 1968, the Chinese have used conditions in Czechoslovakia many times in their continuing propaganda tirade against the USSR. This propaganda centers on the theme that the Soviets are using imperialist-fascist means to control their satellite empire in Eastern Europe, and that they are doing so with the support and blessing of the United States. The following excerpts from comments on the October 1968 Soviet-Czechoslovak treaty exemplify the Chinese propaganda line: "The treaty also stipulates that no Czechoslovakian is allowed to resist the Soviet revisionist troops' fascist occupation. The treaty unscrupulously tramples on Czechoslovak sovereignty and reduces the country to a virtual vassalage of Soviet revisionist social-imperialism. All facts indicate that this treaty . . . is meant to meet the needs of U.S.-Soviet collusion in redividing the world and intensifying their global counter-revolutionary collaboration." [35]

It is clear that events such as those in Vietnam, the Middle East, and Eastern Europe were not a direct cause of the troubles between Peking and Moscow, although they were utilized as convenient weapons in the struggle. This seems confirmed by the fact that in the opinion of both the Soviets and Chinese, their opponent can do no right. Any Soviet or Chinese statement or action in international affairs has been — and probably will continue to be — promptly and thoroughly condemned by the other.

IV

Tension between the USSR and the PRC had become so strained by the late sixties that the outbreak of armed clashes along their border came as no surprise. The conflict of March 2, 1969, on Damanskii-Chenpao Island

33. *Down with the New Tsars!* p. 5.

34. "Washington and Moscow Collaborate as Well as Contend over Czechoslovakia," *Peking Review*, no. 35 (August 30, 1968), 19–20.

35. "Diabolical Social-Imperialist Face of Soviet Revisionist Renegade Clique," *Peking Review*, no. 43 (October 25, 1968), 8–10.

in the Ussuri River made big headlines, but was probably only one in a series of such incidents. In this case the incident was too great to conceal, and obviously neither Peking nor Moscow had any desire to do so, since it offered both sides an ample opportunity to make propaganda mileage out of the supposed hostility and aggression of their opponent.

From the official statements issued by both governments it is nearly impossible to judge who was to blame for starting outbursts like that on Damanskii-Chenpao. Attempts to assess complete blame become little more than exercises in academic speculation. One can construct a good case to show that China was responsible for these clashes because the Maoists needed evidence of an external threat from their major enemy in order to promote and harness Chinese unity and national sentiment. An equally suitable case can be made to show Soviet responsibility for the USSR wanted demonstrable evidence to prove its contention that Mao's China is aggressive, militaristic, expansionist, and power hungry. It really does not make much difference who was to blame, for these border clashes in themselves are not so much the cause of Sino-Soviet animosity as they are an outward manifestation of it.[36]

It is interesting to note that regardless of who is responsible, both sides have been careful to keep the border clashes limited. The Damanskii-Chenpao incident itself was an example of self-restraint. Choosing as a cause célèbre a worthless island about to be inundated by the spring runoff from the Ussuri was a fairly safe guarantee that the incident would not escalate out of control, but nevertheless would be sufficient to prove the antagonists' point.

Although it is speculation, it may be argued that what may well have happened with the Damanskii-Chenpao clash was that the incident itself was kept safely limited, but the propaganda tirades which ensued went beyond the original plans. Looking at two publications from Peking, both entitled *Down with the New Tsars!* one finds that the language of the second, issued in the fall of 1969, is much harsher and more provocative than that of the first, which appeared in the summer.[37] The escalated propaganda battle was supplemented by demonstrations in both Peking and Moscow. These demonstrations were, as usual, well organized and carefully controlled, but were also intensely emotional. On television and movie

36. An excellent account of the Damanskii-Chenpao incident may be found in Harold C. Hinton, "Conflict on the Ussuri: A Clash of Nationalisms," *Problems of Communism*, 20 (January–April 1971), 45–59.

37. *Doloi Novykh Tsarei!* (Peking, Summer 1969); and *Down with the New Tsars!* (Peking, Fall 1969).

screens in both countries the citizens were provided with gory accounts of their enemy's barbaric behavior. In such an atmosphere of suspicion and hatred, accidents could have occurred to make the fears of war a reality. The USSR and the PRC had maneuvered themselves to the brink. Vehicles of communication, such as the meeting at Khabarovsk of the Joint Commission for Boundary River Navigation, were incapable of breaking the deadlock.

On September 11, 1969, Premier Kosygin and Premier Chou En-lai held a hastily arranged meeting at the airport in Peking. That this meeting even took place indicates that both the Soviet Union and China were deeply concerned that their relations had dangerously disintegrated. The two sides quickly agreed that *the dispute on principle* should not hamper the normalization of state relations. The Kosygin-Chou meeting led to the opening of the talks in Peking on October 20, 1969, which are being conducted at the Deputy Foreign Minister level. As of this writing, the talks have remained deadlocked. Rumored reports are that the Chinese insist on three points before they will discuss an overall border agreement or other problems: (1) agreement to cease all clashes on the border; (2) withdrawal of troop concentrations to sixty to one hundred miles from the frontier on both sides; (3) agreement to renounce the use of force in settling disputes.[38] The Soviet position is that a frontier demarcation agreement must be the first order of business. Success for these Peking talks appears doubtful, although they have succeeded in easing the extreme tension which existed in the summer and fall of 1969. In late 1970 the Sixteenth Conference of the Joint Commission on Navigation of Border Rivers reached an agreement. A protocol was signed regulating Chinese and Soviet shipping on the Amur, Argun, Sunghua, and Ussuri rivers as well as on Lake Khanka.[39] If the border talks should break down completely, an ominous situation would arise once again. It appears that perhaps the best one can hope for is that the talks will continue to follow their inconclusive course while the border itself remains relatively quiet.

The pessimism expressed here regarding a future Sino-Soviet border settlement is based on the existence of China's newly born and intense feelings of national pride and dignity and on the Soviet Union's apparent inability or reluctance to recognize these feelings and to consider them in negotiations. A mutually acceptable border solution could be reached if the USSR could overcome its own national pride, admit that its present

38. *New York Times*, March 1, 1970.

39. *Toronto Globe & Mail*, December 22, 1970.

boundaries in Asia are the result of unequal treaties forced on China by Tsarist imperialism, and then negotiate a new boundary treaty with the PRC on the basis of national equality. The contrast between the Sino-Indian and Sino-Burmese boundary settlements should provide the Soviets with ample evidence of China's attitude in these matters.[40] For over twenty years one of the overriding objectives of China's foreign policy has been to establish the national sovereignty of the People's Republic, protect that sovereignty, and to insist that other nations respect it with dignity and equality. The Soviet Union to date has shown little inclination to accept China and its policies on this basis.

V

During the sixties the Sino-Soviet dispute was the catalyst creating the disarray in the communist world.[41] Relations between the communist giants in the seventies will continue to play a major role in determining the future of world communism. Political, economic, and ideological relationships between other socialist states and the Soviet Union will be directly affected by the Sino-Soviet dispute as will the relations between the Soviet satellite states themselves. As the individual socialist states strain toward more independence and self-sufficiency, the cohesion (or lack of cohesion) within the communist world will continue to depend on the state of relations between Peking and Moscow. There are three alternate roads along which Sino-Soviet relations may proceed in the seventies. Two of the alternatives, however, appear rather unlikely.

The first unlikely alternative is that Sino-Soviet relations will completely collapse into a state of full-scale (nuclear?) war. There is no evidence whatsoever that either the USSR or the PRC desires such a war. Both regimes have a sober, realistic understanding that war would solve nothing and would more likely be their ruination. A "balance of horrors" should preserve the peace.

For the foreseeable future China's armed forces and economic structure will be no match for the Soviets. A Chinese aggression against the USSR would therefore become an exercise in national suicide which could only be provoked by unpredictable and extreme domestic or foreign tensions. For the Soviet Union to attack China would probably bring military vic-

40. For a detailed coverage of China's attitude toward its national boundaries see Ishwer C. Ojha, *Chinese Foreign Policy in an Age of Transition* 2nd ed. (Boston, 1971), chap. 6.

41. Adam Bromke, "Eastern Europe on the Threshold of the 1970's," *Slavic and East European Studies*, 14 (1969), 39.

tory, but the price would be so horrendous that even the most rabid Soviet hawk would have cause to hesitate. A war initiated by the USSR would be an anathema to the average Soviet citizen and could produce an internal explosion which could tear the country apart. The prospect of even one Chinese bomb delivered on one Siberian city would be a terrible disaster to the Soviet Union. An occupation of China could well bleed the USSR into social and economic bankruptcy and would result in social chaos.[42] Unlike the expansion of communism following World Wars I and II, a Chinese-Soviet war would surely mark the end of communism as an acceptable system for any society.

The realization that these would be the consequences of war makes the prospect of war improbable. If it should come, it would be accidental, unwanted, and an unprecedented disaster for all mankind. Both the USSR and the PRC would deny that it was a conflict between socialist states. Both would undoubtedly claim that war between them had developed because the other had renounced socialism in favor of "fascistic-imperialism" or some other such doctrine.

China's "opening to the United States" in early 1971 by way of what has come to be called "ping-pong diplomacy" was a positive response to the hints from Washington of a desire to normalize Sino-American relations, and may also have been motivated by China's continued differences with the Soviet Union. Presidential adviser Kissinger's surprise trip to Peking and President Nixon's announcement that he would visit China in early 1972 are major steps toward an improved balance in international relations for the seventies. However, the long-term results of these steps are difficult to foresee or predict. Improved relations with the United States would undoubtedly create for the Chinese a better overall position in international affairs than that which existed for them throughout the sixties. This dramatic shift in Sino-American relations can be viewed as a sign of China's renewed confidence in itself following the disruptions of the Cultural Revolution. As indicated by its exchange of diplomatic relations with Canada and Italy, China is gradually returning to normal diplomatic contacts with other nations and is expanding its role in world affairs. It is obvious that the Chinese wish to play a larger role in the international arena of the seventies, that this role will be in line with their own conception of China as a major power, and that they will insist other nations accept China on the basis of national equality.

For the Chinese, this new attitude and projection of China as a third

42. Andrei Amalrik, *Will the Soviet Union Survive Until 1984?* (New York and Evanston, 1970).

major force in world politics are particularly important whenever signs of a new United States-Soviet Union détente appear. They are also related to the important and persistent Chinese objective of establishing Peking as the center (or alternate center) for the international communist movement. The government of China feels that this goal is a vital necessity for the future of communism because of its belief that the Soviets have fallen into hopeless reaction and corruption. The Chinese now seem to be aware that in order to realize their objective of becoming a new center for world communism, they cannot resort to force or to excessively radical experimentation. The damage done to China's world image by the Cultural Revolution has been a useful lesson. Winning friends and supporters from both within and without the communist bloc can best be achieved by the examples of efficiency at home and normal contacts abroad.

The second unlikely alternative for Sino-Soviet relations in the seventies is that the two sides will arrive at a rapprochement leading to close and friendly ties. Such a rapprochement is possible, but only in the sense that anything is possible in the long run of history. If it should come, it could only be predicated on such improbable developments as: (1) an abject, total surrender by either Peking or Moscow to the other's position and beliefs; (2) a new leadership in both nations which had formulated an entirely new outlook on international and ideological relationships; (3) an external threat to both the USSR and the PRC so acute that they would be forced to end their differences for the sake of survival.

The third and most probable alternative for the seventies is that Sino-Soviet relations will continue, much the same as they are at present, in a state of hostile coexistence, characterized by bitter propaganda polemics, limited border disputes, and mutual national suspicions, fears, and hatreds. Party contacts, border commissions, "Peking talks," and even official diplomatic relations can come and go without substantially affecting that underlying base of antagonistic coexistence. As Professor Richard Lowenthal recently wrote, "The continuation of limited and controlled conflict between Russia and China thus remains a far more plausible prospect than its end by either reunion or catastrophe." [43] It is one of the great ironies of history that the relations between the two major communist powers have come to be best described by a phrase coined long ago by Lev Trotskii, communism's most notable unperson: "No Peace – No War."

43. Richard Lowenthal, "Russia and China: Controlled Conflict," *Foreign Affairs*, 49, no. 3 (April, 1971), 518.

3

Czechoslovakia

BY H. GORDON SKILLING

The fall of Novotny in January 1968 came as a surprise, as did its exciting aftermath, the Prague spring, and to a lesser degree, its tragic denouement, the August invasion. For many years Czechoslovakia had been a stable and loyal satellite of the Soviet Union, an apparently passive object of Soviet policy, and an almost stagnant backwater of continuing Stalinism. Suddenly this small country became a source of independent initiative, acting on its own to reform the old order of things and to create a new model of socialism, and exercising a decisive impact on the Soviet Union and the communist bloc. The main impulse for change came not from Moscow or from the Kremlin leaders, but from Prague and Bratislava, and not only from the Castle, or the Central Committee headquarters on the Vltava, but from "below," from political activists, and even from the masses of the Czech and Slovak people. These forces of popular spontaneity and national independence, unleashed after January, were set back by the August invasion, but continued to make their influence strongly felt for another eight months, at least until Husak's succession to power in April 1969. Czechoslovakia thus became, for the first time in two decades, a serious problem for Moscow and world communism, comparable to Yugoslavia or other dissident communist states in the past, and no less serious than China or Rumania. It continues to be a source of grave concern for the future. Armed coercion and political repression could curb the forces released in 1968 but could not fully eliminate them as a factor in the future development of Czechoslovakia and world communism.

Czechoslovakia

I

For more than a decade after the Twentieth Congress of the CPSU in 1956 Antonin Novotny had shown an extraordinary capacity to survive. Paying lip service to the Khrushchevian doctrine of de-Stalinization, Novotny had been able to maintain more or less intact the political and economic system which he had inherited from Gottwald in 1953, and to weather the storms of 1956. Having successfully checked reform tendencies at home, the Czechoslovak regime emerged as a pillar of strength for the Soviet Union and for communism in Eastern Europe in its hour of trial.[1] Again in 1961, when Khrushchev renewed his attack on Stalinism, Novotny was able to deflect all blame from himself, by sacrificing some of his closest and most reliable colleagues, such as V. Siroky and K. Bacilek.[2] The economic collapse of 1962–63 was partly surmounted by the introduction of cautious reforms and by the recovery of the economy from its lowest point. The rising tide of dissent among writers, journalists, and scholars, which reached a high point in 1963, was dammed back by various forms of repression. Novotny seemed to have successfully squared the circle, throwing his full support to Moscow in all controversies within the bloc and on all world issues, and yet at the same time avoiding any serious reforms, such as those espoused by Khrushchev.[3] The latter's ouster in 1964 no doubt awakened concern in Prague and was reportedly even the occasion of a bitter telephone conversation between Novotny and Brezhnev. Novotny nevertheless remained in power.

Yet, in retrospect, the sixties may be seen as a period of Stalinism in decline, as Novotny's power and legitimacy were progressively undermined. The seeds of change had been planted by Stalin's death and by Khrushchev's erratic course of denigrating Stalinism. Beneath the surface of a stagnant and inefficient dictatorship forces were stirring that were to bring about the fall of the discredited Czech leader. Long before the dramatic removal of Novotny in January 1968, he had personally become an object of scorn and hatred in Prague and Bratislava. His power was buttressed by

1. See Edward Taborsky, "Czechoslovakia in the Khrushchev-Bulganin Era," *American Slavic and East European Review*, 16, no. 1 (1957), 50–65, and "Political Developments in Czechoslovakia since 1953," *Journal of Politics*, 20, no. 1 (1958), 89–113.

2. Ivo Duchacek, "Czechoslovakia: The Past Reburied," *Problems of Communism*, 11, no. 3 (May–June 1962), 22–26.

3. See H. Gordon Skilling, "Czechoslovakia," in Adam Bromke (ed.), *The Communist States at the Crossroads: Between Moscow and Peking* (New York, 1965); Edward Taborsky, "Changes in Czechoslovakia," *Current History*, 48, no. 283 (March 1965), 168–74.

coercive measures against dissenters, mixed with occasional halfhearted concessions, but opposition was possible, and the risks of dissent were tolerable. Especially among the intellectuals – research scholars, professors, students, writers, journalists, playwrights, film makers, folk singers, and cabaret satirists – the ferment of creative ideas became more and more uninhibited. Prague and Bratislava became the freest cities in the communist world. Bursts of creative energy manifested themselves in novels, plays, films, scholarly works, or newspaper commentaries and became elements in an intellectual unrest which ultimately affected wide sectors of the population and proved fatal to the regime.[4]

The general malaise reflected the deep antagonisms and fundamental problems that had developed in the sixties and the failure of the regime to deal with them adequately.[5] The crisis in the economy continued, as the reform left the system of overcentralized planning and management largely intact. The long simmering conflict between the regime and its literary and intellectual critics flared up in the summer of 1967 at the Writers' Congress, where discussions went far beyond literary matters and included biting criticisms of domestic and foreign policy. Among students the party had lost almost all support and was further discredited in November 1967 by a brutal police assault on students protesting dormitory living conditions. Even more serious was the smoldering discontent among Slovaks, who yearned for equality and a greater autonomy within a reformed dualist or federalist system. The Slovak party, headed by Alexander Dubcek, was unable to defend Slovak interests effectively because of the complete centralization of power in Prague. Gustav Husak, after a decade of imprisonment in the fifties, was kept on the sidelines unable to resume a political role. A vivid memory of the terror of the fifties and the resentment of the regime's failure fully to rehabilitate its victims added to Czech and Slovak discontent. All these factors threw into sharp relief the inherent defects of the political system, characterized by the concentration of personal power in the hands of Novotny, the domination of all aspects of society and all institutions by the party and its apparatus, and the absence of any real political life in the bureaucratic order that Novotny had inherited and perfected.

4. Bromke, *Communist States at the Crossroads*, and Skilling, *Communism, National and International* (Toronto, 1964), chap. 7.

5. For the following, see Pavel Tigrid, *Le Printemps de Prague* (Paris, 1968), and Z. A. B. Zeman, *Prague Spring: A Report on Czechoslovakia 1968* (Harmondsworth, 1969). See further Karel Bartosek, "Revoluce proti byrokratismu?" *Rude pravo*, July 18, 24, 26, 30, 1968, March 11, 1968.

Still, the regime had the support of powerful forces: the institutions of the police, the army, the party *apparat*, and the state bureaucracy, as well as the vested interests attached to the regime; the deep-rooted habits of thought and action; and the silent consent of those who benefited from an obsolete economy and a backward social system. While it was possible to discern the forces encouraging change, it was unclear whether, and how, they could make themselves successfully felt against the powerful entrenched elements of the status quo, headed and personified by Antonin Novotny.

The actual fall of Novotny came unexpectedly as the culmination of the growing dissatisfaction with his leadership among his closest colleagues in the topmost party organs.[6] From October 1967 to January 1968, largely unknown to the general public, or even to the rank and file of the party, a bitter discussion ranged within the Central Committee and the Presidium on the methods of party work and, at first implicitly, and then openly, on the concentration of power in Novotny's hands. The issue of the debate was euphemistically termed "the accumulation of functions" by party leaders; in fact it was centered on the holding of the two posts of first secretary and president by Novotny. The Central Committee was sharply divided, and there was a deadlock in the Presidium with five supporting and five opposing Novotny's continuance as first secretary. The offensive against Novotny was launched by Alexander Dubcek, and continued by Ota Sik and Josef Smrkovsky. Novotny, with substantial support, waged an intense struggle in defense of the traditional conception of the leading role of the party. A personal appeal to Leonid Brezhnev was not successful. During a one-day visit in Prague in December, Brezhnev apparently left the matter to be decided by the Czechs, thus in effect consigning Novotny to his fate. When the latter was eventually ousted, there was no evidence of displeasure in Moscow, and indeed there were public indications of support for the January changeover.

Another feature of the crisis which remains shrouded in mystery was an apparent attempt by certain high-ranking military officers either to exert pressure on the Central Committee or to prevent Novotny's ouster by

6. For the fall of Novotny, see Pavel Tigrid, "Czechoslovakia: A Post-Mortem," *Survey*, no. 73 (Autumn 1969), 133–64; Skilling, "The Fall of Novotny in Czechoslovokia," *Canadian Slavonic Papers*, 12, no. 3 (1970), 225–42. For fuller detail, see V. Mencl and F. Ourednik, "Jak to bylo v lednu," *Zivot strany*, no. 14–19 (July, August, September 1968); and "Ceskoslovenske jaro 1968," *Svedectvi*, 9, no. 34–36 (1969), 147–82. A partial translation of the Mencl and Ourednik articles is given in R. A. Remington (ed.), *Winter in Prague: Documents on Czechoslovak Communism in Crisis* (Cambridge, Mass., and London, 1969), pp. 18–39.

force. General J. Sejna, party leader in the Ministry of National Defense, worked hard and long to secure army backing for Novotny. The deputy minister of defense, General V. Janko, who later, during the spring of 1968, committed suicide, sympathized with Sejna's efforts and reportedly placed certain military units in a state of readiness. The minister, General B. Lomsky, however, and General V. Prchlik, the head of the Ministry's Main Political Administration, rejected Sejna's overtures. Sejna's last minute success in securing a resolution of the party committee in the Ministry in favor of Novotny's continuance came too late. In the meantime the Presidium had agreed to remove Novotny as first secretary and to replace him with a compromise candidate, Dubcek, and the Central Committee had unanimously approved this solution.

The replacement of Novotny by Dubcek, like the change of first secretaries in any communist country, was bound to have momentous effects. At first, however, it did not seem to involve much more than a change of guard, with the possibility of some reforms in party procedures. Novotny remained as president of the Republic, and, more important, as a member of the party's Presidium. No other major changes were made in the top leadership. The composition of the Central Committee remained unaffected. Dubcek, little known prior to the fall of 1967, had not revealed himself to be a proponent of reform. Indeed, as Slovak first secretary, he had had to implement Novotny's policies in that region. He was a longtime *apparatchik*, who not only had spent his childhood in the Soviet Union, but had studied at the Higher Party School in Moscow. True, this had been at the highpoint of Khrushchev's first de-Stalinization campaign, and this experience may well have had an impact on his later actions. Dubcek's early pronouncements as party leader did not suggest the beginning of a period of revolutionary change, or even radical reform.

Nonetheless Dubcek represented a new generation of leaders, not directly responsible for the crimes and errors of the fifties, and, as soon became evident, he favored a new style of leadership and substantial reforms. Although he lacked the qualities for decisive leadership or a clear conception of the future, he was ready to consult specialists and to take account of conflicting interests and viewpoints in the formation of public policy. In his first major speech, to the Slovak Central Committee in late January, unpublished at the time, Dubcek declared:

> We are not changing the general line, either in domestic or foreign policy . . . We are not changing the mission of the Party; we must, however, adapt its activity and methods to the new quality of the development of society . . .

Real democracy assumes discipline, too, and conscious discipline is proportional to the democratic character of decisions and decision-making. In this sense there will never be enough democracy. Democracy is not only the right and the possibility to express one's opinion; democracy is also the circumstances and the method of dealing with the opinions of the people; it is also whether functionaries, and the working people generally, have a real feeling of co-responsibility, of co-decision-making. . . .[7]

The ensuing "process of revival," as it came to be called, and its sudden termination by Soviet military intervention were not preordained results of the change of leadership. They can best be regarded as the products of the collisions and interactions of two sets of conflicting forces during the seven and a half months following the January event.[8] On the one hand, there was the interplay between the cautious and uncertain leadership of Dubcek and the popular pressures from below generated by the removal of Novotny, which included demands by reformers as well as counterpressure from more conservative elements, so that Dubcek was pushed and pulled in opposite directions. On the other hand, there was the interaction of these indigenous forces and the outside pressures exercised in Moscow and the rest of the bloc. As the pace of reform was stepped up in Czechoslovakia, the pressure from outside intensified. This in turn affected the participants in the domestic conflict, pushing some to a more cautious, and others to a more radical, position.

Dubcek was well aware of the extent to which the party and its methods had been discredited and of the necessity of substantial changes in the system of governance. He had, however, no clear conception of what needed to be done and for several months he confined himself to general statements of major objectives. It was only in early April that the Action Program, drafted hurriedly by a team of intellectuals from inside and outside the party apparatus, delineated the broad outline of the changes to be

7. See a collection of Dubcek's speeches published in October 1968, *K otazkam obrodzovacieho procesu v KSC* (Bratislava, 1968), pp. 61–62.

8. The fullest analysis of the politics of the post-January development is given by Remi Gueyt, *La mutation tchecoslovaque* (Paris, 1969). See also Zeman, *Prague Spring*; Pavel Tigrid, *Le printemps de Prague*; Edward Taborsky, "The New Era in Czechoslovakia," *East Europe*, 17, no. 11 (1968), 19–29; A. H. Brown, "Political Change in Czechoslovakia," *Government and Opposition*, 4, no. 2 (1969), 169–94; and Skilling, "Czechoslovakia's Interrupted Revolution," *Canadian Slavonic Papers*, 10, no. 4 (1968), 409–29, and "Crisis and Change in Czechoslovakia," *International Journal*, 23, no. 3 (1968), 456–65. For the main documents, see Remington, *Winter in Prague*, and Paul Ello (ed.), *Czechoslovakia's Blueprint for "Freedom"* (Washington, D.C., 1968). For all official party documents issued in 1968, see *Rok sedesaty osmy* (Prague, 1969).

made in all aspects of public life.[9] The general aim was, in the words of the Program, "to embark on the building of a new model of socialist society, one which is profoundly democratic and conforms to Czechoslovak conditions."

Although in some respects this was a radical document envisaging substantial alterations in many spheres, it was in other respects relatively moderate and was designed to buttress the position of the party by the removal of the worst evils of the past. The Program provided for legal guarantees of freedom of expression and of freedom of association, including the formation of genuine interest groups. Other reforms were to be substantial, almost revolutionary in the context of communism, such as a judicial guarantee of the rights of the individual; the full rehabilitation of all victims of terror; a full implementation and extension of the economic reform, including the formation of workers' councils in the factories; a federalization of the constitutional system, guaranteeing equality to the Slovaks; broad rights to the national minorities; and religious freedom.

The proposed reforms created, however, an insoluble dilemma for the future. A new relationship of party and public was to ensure an independent role for the National Assembly and the government, for the revived mass associations, and for the regenerated Czechoslovak People's and Socialist parties. Yet there was to be no place for an opposition party or parties, or for an electoral struggle which might endanger the ruling position of the communist party. No political activity was to be permitted outside the National Front, which would form a partnership of all political parties and interest groups based on a common platform of action. In other words, the democratization of the political system was somehow to be reconciled with the maintenance of the leadership of the communist party, which, it was assumed, would be legitimized by popular endorsement in the aftermath of the reforms. In the minds of some, however, freedom of expression and association would inevitably jeopardize the position of the party and of the entire system of "socialism" established in 1948. Others, on the other hand, feared that the continued predominance of a single party would be incompatible with democratization and would prevent the establishment of full democracy.

These reforms were considered to reflect the special conditions of the country, and in that sense to embody a "Czechoslovak way." This was regarded as perfectly compatible with close association with the USSR and the other socialist countries. No basic change in the international orienta-

9. *Rude pravo,* April 10, 12, 1968. Translations of the text are given in Remington, *Winter in Prague,* pp. 88–137; Ello, *Czechoslovakia's Blueprint,* pp. 89–178.

tion of Czechoslovakia was proposed. Membership in the Warsaw Pact and in Comecon would be preserved. Support for the Soviet position within the world communist movement would be continued. Prague would pursue a foreign policy fundamentally in consonance with Moscow's, for instance, in relation to European security and the German question, the Middle East, and Vietnam. No rapprochement with China was heralded, or any new alignment with Yugoslavia. The maintenance of these traditional features of Czechoslovak foreign policy did not exclude, thought the Prague leaders, some initiatives by Czechoslovakia, especially in Europe, that would reflect its specific national interests, including the development of greater trade with West Germany and substantial loans from Western sources. As envisaged in the spring and early summer of 1968, none of these initiatives would lead Czechoslovakia along a course as independent as Rumania, let alone Yugoslavia. Changes within Comecon and the Warsaw Pact were hinted at, but none as far-reaching as those sought by Rumania, and none designed to lead to withdrawal.

Dubcek's tactics gradually crystallized during the early months of his regime. It represented a middle-of-the-road approach, designed to consolidate the political situation and to advance step-by-step toward the goals of the Action Program. The formation of a government under Cernik and the election of Smrkovsky as chairman of the National Assembly were to pave the way for legislative implementation of the major reforms. Alterations in the Central Committee would be kept to a minimum and deferred to a party congress, to be held, at the earliest, in the first part of 1969. "The ultimate goal was a more perfect type of socialist democracy corresponding to Czechoslovak conditions," Dubcek declared at the Central Committee plenum at the end of March. This would involve the eventual establishment, under the party's continued primacy, of what he called a "well-thought-out and well-functioning system of institutions, organs and organizations." [10] He tried to assure the more fearful conservatives that the democratization process would not threaten the bases of socialism or communist party rule, and to persuade the more impatient reformers that the process would not stop halfway but would go steadily forward to completion. The March plenum did in fact stabilize the situation; Novotny was replaced as president by General Ludvik Svoboda; the Action Program was adopted; and Novotny and some of his closest associates were dropped from the Presidium and the Secretariat. The Central Committee (its composition still unchanged) approved all these decisions. By the

10. Dubcek's report to the March plenum, *Rude pravo,* April 2, 1968. See also text in Ello, *Czechoslovakia's Blueprint,* pp. 29–81.

time of the party congress in 1969, the major reforms presumably would have been implemented, and the party's prestige, severely damaged by the decades of Gottwald and Novotny rule, would have been restored. Under new leadership, the party would then proceed to the next phase, elaborating a long-term program and advancing with confidence toward general elections.

The tactic, however, was difficult to maintain in the face of the pressures on Dubcek from many sides. The more vigorous reformers or "progressives," within and outside the party, who dominated the public stage through their access to the mass media, were dissatisfied with the slow tempo of reform and with the continuation in office of many conservatives. They feared that the full application of the Action Program would be hindered and that the post-January course might even be reversed. Their most urgent tactical demand was the convocation of an extraordinary party congress, in 1968 if possible, to elect a more progressive leadership to the Central Committee and to accelerate the pace of reform. The removal of Novotny from the presidency in March, and his ouster from the Central Committee in May were in part the result of these pressures.

A further factor complicating Dubcek's strategy was the emergence of public opinion as a force which was moving, on many substantive issues, ahead of the leadership or even of its more vigorous reform spokesmen, such as Smrkovsky, Kriegel, and Spacek. The unrestrained debate in the mass media acquainted the public with radical viewpoints of communists and noncommunists and presented the leadership with awkward challenges. Although all were ready to endorse "socialism," the demands for reform often went far beyond the provisions of the Action Program which had in a sense been outdated by events. The model of Soviet socialism, as it had been applied in Czechoslovakia, was subjected to devastating criticism. A wide-ranging comment on the future political system touched on a multi-party system, a parliamentary opposition, completely free elections, the abolition of censorship, and the like. The ferment penetrated the lower party ranks, and large-scale changes of local leadership occurred at the district and regional conferences. The forming of political clubs, such as KAN (the Club of the Non-Party Committed), the attempted revival of social democracy, and the revivification of the existing noncommunist parties and mass interest groups opened up the possibility of a vigorous competition, in which the communist party would have to fight hard for its supremacy.

On the other side, Dubcek met the strong resistance of more conservative elements, fearful of the loss of their own status, and anxious to slow down the pace of change, or even to reverse it. Less willing to voice their opinions in the mass media, and often resorting to closed meetings and illegal leaflets, the conservatives still enjoyed positions of power and influence which made them a force impossible to ignore. Some would have liked to restore the old system, with or without Novotny. Others were willing to support Dubcek in a moderate and controlled program of change, but were fearful that he would yield too much to popular pressures. For all of them, progressive demands represented "antisocialist forces," which threatened the very existence of the socialist system and the position of the communist party, and hence created a danger of "counterrevolution."

The bitter political struggle between opposing forces was clearly reflected at the Central Committee plenum at the end of May and early June.[11] The decision to hold an extraordinary congress in September 1968 was a decisive victory for the progressives, as was the removal of Novotny and several close colleagues from the Central Committee. On the other hand, the membership of the Central Committee and of its organs, the Presidium and Secretariat, was largely unchanged, and no significant shift in policy occurred. To appease the conservatives the plenum warned of the danger of antisocialist forces and appealed to the mass media to moderate their radical tone. Dubcek's middle-of-the-road policy was bound to satisfy neither of the opposed forces, as was soon clear. The plenum, however, represented a new stabilization, at a point of balance which, while somewhat further to the conservative side, was likely to shift in the other direction in September.

The ultimate outcome of this conflict, had there been no Soviet intervention, was uncertain. Certain concrete reform measures were introduced in June and July, including a law on rehabilitation and a reform of the press law, abolishing censorship. The law on association, however, had not been passed, or a revised electoral statute, so that it was not clear whether the party could be effectively challenged by other political movements. Nor was it evident how far the party would be internally democratized, although the draft statute, published in the middle of August,[12] constituted a far-reaching revision, including the legitimization of minority dissent. Meanwhile the elections of delegates to the forthcoming congress, which were held during July and August, pointed to the probability of a decisive shift in the balance of power in the direction of vigorous reform.

11. For the May plenum documents, see Ello, *Czechoslovakia's Blueprint*, pp. 185–274.

12. *Rude pravo*, August 10, 1968, supplement; Remington, *Winter in Prague*, pp. 265–87.

Nonetheless both extremes expressed their dissatisfaction. The *Two Thousand Words* manifesto in late June expressed the progressives' concern that reform was slowing down and their determination to press hard for its continuance.[13] The conservative People's Militia, in a letter published in Moscow's *Pravda*, expressed some uneasiness over developments and declared their loyalty to the Soviet Union and the socialist bloc.[14] Although he had accepted the necessity of an extraordinary congress, Dubcek had not given up his faith in the step-by-step tactic. He believed that the measured implemention of the Action Program would consolidate the party's position by restoring confidence in the leadership and by undercutting both the more conservative opponents, and the impatient protagonists, of reform. The congress, he hoped, would contribute to the stabilization by eliminating the most conservative elements and by uniting the party on the basis of his centrist policy.

II

The developing political situation reflected not only the changing counterpoint of the Prague leadership and domestic factors, but also the dialectical relationship of indigenous forces and external pressures.[15] The Soviet leaders did not actively oppose the January changeover, and they accepted the necessity of at least moderate reforms. The Action Program was on the whole approved, although certain of its features were criticized. From March on, however, Moscow became more and more disturbed by the course of events in Czechoslovakia. In particular the elements of spontaneity that increasingly began to appear were utterly contradictory to the entire Soviet concept of politics. There was mounting concern that Dubcek would lose control of the situation. The decisions to remove Novotny and to hold the congress in 1968 were regarded as warnings. The freedom of expression in the media of communications was particularly frightening, as it made possible the unbridled discussion of sensitive issues, including severe criticism of Soviet practices, and the presentation of widely opposed

13. Text of the *Two Thousand Words* was published in *Literarni listy*, June 27, 1968. See Remington, *Winter in Prague*, pp. 196–202.

14. *Pravda* (Moscow), June 21, 1968; quoted in *Rude pravo*, July 19, 1968.

15. For the international aspects of the Czechoslovak crisis, see Philip Windsor and Adam Roberts, *Czechoslovakia, 1968: Reform, Repression and Resistance* (London, 1969), and Robert Rhodes James (ed.), *The Czechoslovak Crisis, 1968* (London, 1969). Postoccupation descriptions of Czechoslovak-Soviet relations after January 1968 were given by V. Bilak, *Rude pravo*, September 3, 1969, and by G. Husak, *ibid.*, August 20, 1969, September 29, 1969. See also Gueyt, *La mutation tchecoslovaque*, pt. III.

views in a manner alien to Soviet practice. The emergence of such political organizations as KAN and of a revived social democracy, and the discussion of a revised electoral system, including even the possibility of an opposition, threatened the supremacy of the communist party. The Russians interpreted these trends as the seeds of counterrevolution, perhaps less bloody than that in Hungary in 1956, but nonetheless fatal to the continuance of communism in Czechoslovakia.[16] Even if this danger was not an immediate one, it was regarded as a future probability, arising out of the potentialities of the situation.

Actually the Soviet fears ran even deeper. Although they were perhaps sincere in their concern for counterrevolution as the *ultimate* danger, they were equally worried by the prospect of a substantial reform of the communist system in Czechoslovakia or of a more independent course by Prague in foreign relations. Such changes were unacceptable to Moscow, especially in a country so strategically located as Czechoslovakia, and within the context of similar developments elsewhere in Eastern Europe. The impact of a "humanized socialism" would weaken the existing Soviet model of socialism elsewhere, especially in Poland and in the German Democratic Republic, and in the Soviet Union itself, and therefore undermine the position of the current ruling elites. The emergence of a more independent communist regime would impair the entire Warsaw security system as conceived and controlled by Moscow. For a regime as conservative as Brezhnev's, even the most modest changes in either respect were intolerable. Unless checked in time, it was feared such changes might lead to drastic reforms, and these in turn to counterrevolution. There was no sympathy for the idea that communism in Czechoslovakia and elsewhere might emerge stronger and more stable as a result of such changes, as was believed by many communists throughout the world, including the powerful Italian, and the ruling Rumanian and Yugoslav, parties.

Thus, the conflict of the Soviet Union and Czechoslovakia arose from the Soviet perception of the "actualities" of the situation and from Moscow's judgment of its implications for the future. The Action Program certainly did not envisage the dismantling of socialism or communist rule in domestic affairs, but the changes it contemplated would have resulted in a system more pluralist and democratized than that in any other communist state, including Yugoslavia. This alone was unacceptable to the Soviet Union which was willing to tolerate only a moderate degree of controlled

16. The term *counterrevolution* was used in Soviet comment on the *Two Thousand Words*. See I. Alexandrov, *Pravda* (Moscow), July 11, 1968. For texts of this and other Soviet comments, see Remington, *Winter in Prague*, pts. II and III.

differentiation in countries under its influence. In regard to foreign policy, the Dubcek regime did not profess a desire for national independence but was determined to assert a greater degree of autonomy than in the past, a stand quite unacceptable to Moscow. Worse still, the continuance of their course might eventually lead to a more independent stance, going beyond that of Rumania and approaching that of Yugoslavia.

Beginning with the bloc conference at Dresden in March, the Soviet Union and its allies began to express their fears, at first privately to the Prague leaders, and then openly in press comment and in official statements. The pressure gradually intensified and took many forms – meetings with Czechoslovak leaders; newspaper attacks on individuals and certain aspects of the democratization process; regular diplomatic action in Prague by Soviet representatives; military maneuvers on the borders of Czechoslovakia, and then, in the latter half of June, on Czechoslovak territory; and the long delay in the withdrawal of Warsaw Pact troops after the completion of the June exercises. These measures culminated in formal and public condemnation of the Prague course in the Warsaw letter in mid-July [17] and in secret diplomatic negotiations in Cierna and Bratislava several weeks before the invasion.[18] The Warsaw letter set forth publicly what was no doubt the tenor of earlier confidential statements and closed discussions. Arguing that a situation had arisen in Czechoslovakia which threatened the foundations of socialism and that this was the common concern of all the socialist countries, the letter urged the Czechoslovak party to conduct an offensive against the antisocialist forces, to forbid the activities of antisocialist political organizations, to control the mass media, and to enforce democratic centralism in the party.

In retrospect the purpose was clear – to persuade the Czech leaders themselves to moderate the policy of reform and to curtail the so-called antisocialist forces. The Soviet moves were also presumably designed to strengthen the hands of the more conservative associates of Dubcek and to weaken the position of the progressive elements, thus influencing the domestic political struggle. Although their distrust of Dubcek was by this time substantial, the Soviet leaders did not seek to replace him with a more malleable leader. It was presumably their hope that, by such political and diplomatic pressures, they could succeed in decelerating the pace of reform and thus ward off the potential dangers of the future.

17. For the text of the Warsaw letter, see Remington, *Winter in Prague*, pp. 225–31; for the Czechoslovak reply, *ibid.*, pp. 234–43.

18. The communiqués are given in *ibid.*, pp. 255–61.

To some extent Soviet strategy was successful. Dubcek, and even strong reformers such as Smrkovsky, were anxious not to alienate the Soviet Union and were themselves worried by developments in Czechoslovakia that might weaken the socialist system and threaten the party's hegemony. The Czechoslovak leaders could therefore use the pressures from outside as arguments for caution. At the May plenum, they warned of the danger "on the right" and thereafter sought to restrain the more radical trends of public opinion. But criticism by the allies only spurred large segments of the population to greater determination to push on with reform and to urge Dubcek not to yield to outside pressure. The *Two Thousand Words* manifesto was a striking example of this boomerang effect. Moreover, the external pressures stirred up the patriotic feelings of many Czechs and Slovaks and added an important national element to the situation by merging the notion of humanizing communism with the idea of national independence. As a result, especially after the Warsaw letter, Dubcek began to articulate the determination of the majority of the two nations to resist Soviet importuning and to continue along the chosen path of reform. This in turn led the Soviet Union, which interpreted the Czechoslovak national mood as an anti-Soviet one, to draw the conclusion that increased pressure was necessary.

Little is known of the proceedings of the Cierna conference at the end of July. Four days of talks culminated in an apparent Soviet-Czechoslovak agreement which was implicitly endorsed by the other bloc leaders at Bratislava on August 3. The Cierna communiqué was brief and revealed nothing of the nature of any specific agreements reached. The Bratislava declaration was couched in generalities and proclaimed certain common theoretical principles, such as the leading role of the party, but included also an endorsement of the sovereignty and independence of bloc members. At the time Dubcek claimed that these meetings had resolved the controversy symbolized by the Warsaw letter and left the way clear for the implementation of the Action Program.[19] Although it was denied that any other agreements were reached, there was admittedly an understanding that mutual polemics in the mass media would be terminated, thus implying that Czechoslovak authorities would place some limits on freedom of expression.[20] Instructions were apparently issued by the Prague regime

19. See his television address, *Rude pravo*, August 5, 1968.

20. Dubcek later stated that there were no "secret agreements" at Cierna but that the Czechs had informed the Russians of measures they planned to take against certain political organizations. See his speech at the Central Committee plenum in September 1969, as given in *Svedectvi*, 10, no. 38 (1970), 275–76.

to the mass media requesting "positive treatment" of the conference and of relations with the socialist countries.[21] In retrospect the two meetings might be interpreted as an exercise in deceit by governments which had already resolved on military action. More likely, they represented a final effort by the Soviet government and its allies to settle the dispute with Prague through political methods and in agreement with the existing Dubcek leadership. Their success seemed to be demonstrated by the completion of the withdrawal of Warsaw Pact troops from Czechoslovak territory during the Cierna talks.

A little more than two weeks after this apparent compromise, however, Moscow and its allies invaded Czechoslovakia. If Cierna was indeed a sincere effort at agreement, the reasons for the shift in tactics remain clouded in mystery. Perhaps it was the growing conviction in Moscow that the Cierna "agreements" were not being carried out by Prague. The successive visits by Tito and Ceausescu to Prague, even though prearranged, must have intensified the fears of an independent Czechoslovak course. The brief visit by Ulbricht, who was coldly received, might have added to this assessment, as did a secret meeting of Kadar and Dubcek on August 17. Certainly the publication of the draft party statute, within a few days of Bratislava, testified to the determination of Prague to carry through a radical modification of "democratic centralism."

Perhaps a decisive factor in convincing the Soviet Union of the inherent dangers of the situation was the gloomy picture of "antisocialist activity" and the impending changes of cadres at the forthcoming extraordinary congress, which was painted in a report prepared by the CPCZ apparatus in early August. This was submitted to the Presidium by Indra and Kolder, with recommendations for appropriate action, on August 13 and then again on August 20.[22] Although the date of the extraordinary congress

21. For text of these instructions, see the interview with O. Svestka, the editor-in-chief, in *Rude pravo*, August 21, 1969.

22. The report was later published for inner-party circulation under the title *Studijni texty, Zprava o soucasne politicke situaci Ceskoslovenske socialisticke republiky a podminkach cinnosti Komunisticke strany Ceskoslovenska (srpen 1968).* Dated July 23, and 116-pages long, it was transmitted to the Presidium on August 12. The report, without its appendices, was published in *Rude pravo*, July 2, 1969, and *Tribuna*, February 2, 1969, and July 2, 1969. The text of the proposals prepared by Indra and Kolder was given in *Rude pravo*, August 23, 1969. See also the interview with Svestka, cited above. Another description of the August 20 Presidium by an eye witness was published in *Rude pravo*, August 23, 1968, and is given in *Sedm prazskych dnu, 21.–27. srpen 1968* (Prague, 1968), pp. 8–13. An English text is given in Robert Littell (ed.), *The Czech Black Book* (New York, 1969), pp. 12–18. For Dubcek's version of these events, see his speech, September 1969, *Svedectvi, ibid.*, pp. 276–278.

had been known for some months, the report dramatically reminded the Soviet leaders of the crucial political shift that would occur at the congress. If this critical turning point were to be avoided, action had to be taken before September 10, and indeed preferably before August 26, the date to which the Slovak party congress had been advanced. It may have been hoped that acceptance of the Indra-Kolder proposals by the Presidium would have forced a change of course by Dubcek. The Presidium's eventual rejection would presumably be regarded as the ultimate test of Dubcek's willingness and capacity to carry out the understandings of Cierna. On August 20, however, when the Presidium rejected the proposal, the invading forces were already moving toward the frontier.

III

Whatever the exact reasons for and the timing of the decision to invade, this action signified a fundamental change of Soviet tactics. Their previous efforts to achieve their goals by political means, through cooperation with, and pressure on, Dubcek, had failed. Having come to the conclusion that the dangers were more acute than previously estimated and that Dubcek was no longer to be relied upon for a satisfactory solution, the Soviet Union decided to resort to military intervention, coupled with an attempt to find an alternative political solution. Ordering the arrest of Dubcek, Cernik, Smrkovsky, and Kriegel, the Soviet regime presumably hoped that General Svoboda could be persuaded to cooperate in forming a new, more compliant regime. Whether Moscow had assurance of support from alternative leaders or whether they were simply assuming that such support would emerge cannot be determined for want of evidence. The group of party and state leaders, who, in the initial postinvasion statement in *Pravda,* was said to have requested Soviet aid, was never identified.[23] Certainly the more conservative elements in the Presidium were known to include Kolder, Indra, Svestka, and others. On August 20 these persons had emerged as the supporters of the Indra-Kolder proposals, and after the news of the invasion they opposed the majority declaration which condemned the invasion as contrary to international law. Several of these persons, with others representing perhaps one-third of the Central Committee membership, participated in an improvised meeting on the day after the invasion in the Hotel Praha. This meeting, it is reported, endorsed the Presidium's condemnation of the invasion, but called for respect for the "hard

23. *Pravda* (Moscow), August 22, 1968.

reality" and urged "normalization" through negotiations with the local Soviet military leaders.[24] It is also reported that a new regime, a Workers-Peasant government, headed by Indra, was proposed to President Svoboda that same day.[25]

Although the invasion was a military success, it was not a political triumph. In fact the alternative political framework on which the Soviet Union had counted collapsed in the first hours of the occupation. There was, it would appear, a group of top communists who were prepared to provide an alternative leadership under Soviet sponsorship. They were unable to do so, however, because President Svoboda refused to sanction such a government and insisted on direct negotiations with Moscow. An act of personal courage, it was influenced and made possible by the massive, nonviolent resistance of the overwhelming majority of both Czechs and Slovaks in the seven days following August 21.[26] The invasion was condemned by all the official leaders of party and state and of all public associations and institutions; the people as a whole refused to cooperate with the invaders. The extraordinary Fourteenth Party Congress, which was held secretly in a large factory in Prague, unified the mass of the party against the occupation and led to the selection of a new progressive Presidium, of a largely new Central Committee, and of an acting first secretary, Silhan, in the absence of Dubcek. These events isolated potential collaborators, and made it impossible for them to seize the reins of power.

Less than a week after the invasion, a new and surprising political alternative came into being. Dubcek and his closest colleagues were restored to power; the price was their acceptance, in substantial part, of Soviet demands for a basic change in Czechoslovak policy. On the Soviet side this arrangement reflected the failure to find a more amenable regime and the absence of any alternative other than direct Soviet military rule. This was combined with the expectation that a chastened Dubcek would halt the reform program and stamp out "counterrevolutionary forces." The chief architect of democratization was to demolish his own work. No doubt, on the Czechoslovak side, the policy of "collaboration" served to avert worse

24. See *Sedm prazskych dnu*, pp. 74–75. For the text of the Hotel Praha resolution, see an interview with J. Piller, *Rude pravo*, September 17, 1969. The meeting was said to have appointed a three-man group to attend the proposed "conference of delegates," which was eventually held as the Fourteenth Party Congress.

25. Gueyt, *La mutation tchecoslovaque*, pp. 309–10.

26. For these events, see *Sedm prazskych dnu*. For the documents of the Fourteenth Party Congress, see J. Pelikan (ed.), *Le Congres clandestin* (Paris, 1970).

alternatives, such as, for instance, military rule, or the breakup of the country and its incorporation in the Soviet Union. It was, moreover, accompanied by the hope of continuing in a limited degree the post-January policy and of resisting the most extreme Soviet demands. Smrkovsky, in his television address after his return from Moscow, spoke of the alternative of armed resistance. The Moscow delegates, he said, had chosen the path of "compromise," a decision which might be regarded by history and by the people as "a wise solution or as treason." [27]

The first steps toward "collaboration" already had been taken by the original decision not to resist the invasion by force, and by President Svoboda's expressed readiness to negotiate with the Soviet leaders. His insistence on the participation of Dubcek and others who had been imprisoned set the stage for the Moscow conference, in which the entire Soviet leadership met with almost all the Czechoslovak leaders.[28] The meeting, which resulted in a joint communiqué and an agreement on a secret fifteen-point protocol,[29] created a new political context.

The communiqué noted that an understanding had been reached on measures aimed at "the swiftest possible normalization of the situation" in Czechoslovakia, but did not indicate the nature of the measures to be taken to that end, except vaguely referring to the need to implement the "joint decisions" of Cierna and the "propositions and principles" of Bratislava. Contradictorily, the Soviet side affirmed its support for the Czechoslovak leaders' intention to proceed "on the basis of the January and May plenary sessions" of the CPCZ Central Committee. The communiqué did not explicitly condone the military occupation, referred to as the "temporary entry" of troops, and provided for their eventual withdrawal when the situation had been "normalized." In the meantime, the troops would not "interfere in the internal affairs" of Czechoslovakia.

27. Text in *Sedm prazskych dnu*, pp. 400–6; Remington, *Winter in Prague*, pp. 384–86.

28. With a few exceptions all members of the CPCZ Presidium and all secretaries were included in the delegation. Among the notable absentees were Kolder and Kriegel. Gustav Husak, not then a Presidium member, was present, as was Z. Mlynar, secretariat member.

29. The communiqué was published in *Pravda*, August 28, 1968. See Remington, *Winter in Prague*, pp. 376–78, for English text. What is said to be the text of the protocol was published in the Paris journal, *Svedectvi*, 9, no. 34–36 (Winter 1969), 228–31. See also Remington, *Winter in Prague*, pp. 379–82. This text corresponds closely to what was termed, in a document published for inner-party use, the "true content" of the confidential protocol. See *O zasedani Ustredniho Vyboru KSC dne 31. srpna 1968* (Prague, 1968), pp. 34–37.

The secret protocol gave a clearer picture of the concrete meaning of "normalization." This included the invalidation of "the so-called Fourteenth Congress"; the calling of an early Central Committee plenum to discuss policy and to discharge "certain individuals" from their posts; the immediate imposition of control on the mass media and the proscription of "antisocialist" political organizations; early economic negotiations between the USSR and the CSSR; consolidation of the Warsaw defense system; "coordinated action in international relations"; a demand for the withdrawal of the Czechoslovak question from the U.N. agenda; and further negotiations between the two regimes "within a short period."

As though by a miracle, the preinvasion Big Four, Svoboda, Dubcek, Smrkovsky, and Cernik (three of whom had been imprisoned by the invaders), was again in power, and the organs of party and government were once again functioning. The major leaders all rejected the view of some that any other course, such as resistance, was feasible.[30] In Dubcek's words there was "no other way out but to fulfill the Moscow protocol." [31] "We regard the Moscow protocol," he said, "as a reality which opens wide the possibility of developing still further the work of our Party and our country and gives us a certain leeway to find a way out of the present situation." Dubcek apparently believed that the Moscow agreements would permit the continued implementation of the post-January policy, although it should be noted that neither the Action Program nor the March plenum had been mentioned in them. "Normalization" was to come first, however, including administrative measures to correct the "negative" features of the post-January developments. The fulfillment of the Moscow protocols, Dubcek believed, would result in the complete withdrawal of troops, to be attained by successive stages and by agreement of the governments concerned. Significantly, he reiterated his unwillingness to accept the Soviet evaluation of developments in Czechoslovakia prior to the invasion or the justification of the military intervention. It was a "decisive political fact," he said, that "the people do not regard this intervention into the life of their country as a protection against counterrevolution, but as an intervention into their civil rights, freedoms, and state and national sovereignty."[32]

30. For the speeches of the top leaders, see *Sedm prazskych dnu*; Remington, *Winter in Prague*; and *O zasedani U.V.*

31. Speech of September 14, in *Rude pravo*, September 15, 1968; Remington, *Winter in Prague*, p. 389.

32. Speech of August 31, 1968, at Central Committee in plenum, *O zasedani U.V.*, pp. 5–17.

IV

For eight months after the occupation a paradoxical political situation, full of strange contradictions, prevailed.[33] Although the context of politics had been fundamentally changed by the occupation, the two sets of opposing forces which had been present from January to August continued to operate – the persisting counterpoise of Moscow and Prague, and the action and interaction of the Prague regime and domestic forces. The Dubcek leadership again found itself between two mutually opposed pressures, internal and external.[34] On the one hand, Moscow, in spite of the enormous shift of the balance of power in its favor, was unable to impose its will fully on occupied Prague. On the other hand, the Prague regime was unable to win complete support for its policy of compromise from the Czech and Slovak people. Progressive forces were still active, both outside and within the regime, seeking to defend something of the post-January line and urging greater resistance to outside pressures. Conservative forces were equally active, also within and outside the regime, urging speedier adaptation to the "reality" of the occupation and a more decisive correction of the "negative aspects" of the post-January policy.

The domestic balance of forces had not shifted as much as might have been expected. The Big Four remained in their key positions. The plenum in late August invalidated the extraordinary Fourteenth Party Congress (a step demanded by the Slovak party Congress, at Husak's insistence),[35] but the leading party organs were in fact more progressive in composition than before the invasion. The Central Committee was broadened by the coopting of eighty delegates to the Fourteenth Party Congress who had been nominated before the occupation. The enlarged Presidium embraced most of the preinvasion leaders, including Bilak, but with two key conservatives, Svestka and Kolder, and the progressive Kriegel dropped, and Husak added. The removal from their posts of key reform spokesmen, such as the economic reformer Sik, the Foreign Minister Hajek, and the Minister of the Interior Pavel, represented a shift away from reform. Nonetheless, even at the crucial November plenum, when the party organs were reorganized and their membership reshuffled, both the enlarged Presidium and the new eight-man Executive Committee maintained a rela-

33. See Jan Provaznik, "The Politics of Retrenchment," *Problems of Communism*, 18, no. 4–5 (July–October 1969), 2–16. See also Gueyt, *La mutation tchecoslovaque*, pt. IV.

34. Michal Lakatos, *Zitrek*, January 8, 1969.

35. See Husak's speech at the Slovak party Congress, *Pravda* (Bratislava), August 29, 1968.

tively centrist character.[36] Two men emerged into positions of prominence. Strougal, a minister under Novotny (including five years as minister of the interior) and deputy prime minister under Dubcek, became a key figure, as a member of both the Presidium and the Executive Committee and as the head of the newly created Bureau for the Czech party. Husak, with a firm base in Slovakia as first secretary, also won membership in the two top organs of the party.

The Moscow agreements marked the beginning of a series of retreats by Dubcek on fundamental aspects of the post-January program. Censorship was reestablished and the powers of the security forces were increased; a ban was imposed on social democracy and such organizations as KAN; the Fourteenth Party Congress was invalidated, and in November, both the regular Fourteenth Congress and the Czech party congress, which had been designed to bring into existence a Czech party parallel to the existing Slovak party, were postponed indefinitely. At first, these measures were justified as necessary to create the conditions for the ultimate withdrawal of Soviet troops. By October, however, it was clear that such a withdrawal had been indefinitely postponed. The conclusion, in that month, of the special treaty on the presence of military forces in Czechoslovakia adumbrated the details of the "temporary" occupation, without indicating the number of forces to remain, or referring to any future date of withdrawal. Although the treaty did not endorse the invasion itself, it legitimized the indefinite presence of occupation forces. This agreement, concluded in secret and then ratified by the National Assembly, represented a major step backward from the original hopes entertained by leaders and people alike.[37]

Yet, the retreat was not complete. In his report to the November plenum, Dubcek defended the necessity of "normalization" and criticized the "negative features" of the post-January policy and the "antisocialist forces" currently active. Nonetheless, he made a spirited defense of the main tendencies of the preinvasion course and did not accept the thesis of "counterrevolution" or the legitimacy of the occupation. He emphatically declared his determination to continue to implement the positive features of the post-January program.[38]

36. For the November plenum, see *Rude pravo,* November 15–19, 1968. For the Central Committee resolution, see Remington, *Winter in Prague,* pp. 430–41.

37. Text of the treaty on stationing of troops, in Remington, *Winter in Prague,* pp. 420–24. Four deputies voted against the treaty, ten abstained.

38. For Dubcek's report, see *Rude pravo,* November 15, 1968. A much fuller version

In some respects his hopes to salvage some elements of reform were justified. The establishment of a federal system was achieved, as planned, on October 28, the fiftieth anniversary of the Republic. On January 1, 1969, the federal state of two equal republics, Czech and Slovak, came into existence. The legislative process, both in the new bicameral Czechoslovak Assembly, and in the two republican National Councils, retained many democratic features. Rehabilitation continued, and many victims of injustice were judicially exonerated and financially compensated. The organization of interest groups, such as new youth associations, continued apace. The idea of economic reform was still the subject of vigorous public discussion. The legalization of workers' councils, already established in many enterprises, was still planned. Moreover, although censorship had been reintroduced, the press and the other media retained a great deal of freedom of expression, and there were almost no restrictions on scholarly work or the creative arts.

Strong pressures from below continued to make themselves felt. Reform elements were active, seeking to discourage the Dubcek regime from excessive retreats and urging it to preserve as much of the Action Program as possible. A wide range of critical views on public policy were published in the press, especially in the newspaper of the Writers' Union, reborn under the name *Listy*, in the Union of Journalists' magazine, *Reporter*, and in two new weeklies, *Zitrek*, linked with the Socialist party, and *Politika*, weekly of the party's Central Comimttee. There was also much room for action by the mass organizations, including the reinvigorated trade unions, the creative unions (writers, etc.), the Academy of Sciences (especially its institutes in the social sciences), and party organizations and institutions.[39] Students at the universities took a leading role, with a successful three-day general strike in late November in support of the post-January program.[40] The conclusion of formal alliances between students and trade unions, the establishment of a coordinating committee of creative unions, and other forms of cooperation among progressive groups, provided an organizational framework for the defense of reform. Mass demonstrations

is given in *Zasedani Ustredniho Vyboru KSC ve dnech 14.–17. listopadu 1968* (Prague, 1968), pp. 3–34.

39. For instance, the Institute of History published, for private circulation, a 500-page volume on the occupation and its aftermath, entitled *Sedm praskych dnu (21.–27. srpen 1968)* (Prague, 1968).

40. The Ten Points of the student strike included statements in favor of the Action Program, the temporary nature of censorship, freedom of assembly and association, freedom of research and of literary and cultural expression, and personal and legal security of the citizen. See *Lidova demokracie*, November 21, 1968.

in the streets, on the anniversaries of October 28 and November 7, contributed to the spirit of resistance.

Dubcek's conditional retreat and his permissive attitude toward oppositional forces could only awaken profound dissatisfaction among conservative forces at home and in the invading countries. The Prague leaders were under direct and constant pressure from the Soviet Union, through high-level talks during visits to Moscow in October and to Kiev in December; through frequent exchanges of visits by top party and government leaders; and through the influence of Deputy Foreign Minister Kuznetsov during his residence in Prague and of the Soviet ambassador. The Czechoslovak situation was sharply criticized in the Soviet and bloc mass media, as well as by the Czech-language newspaper *Zpravy*, distributed by the occupation forces, and the Czech-language radio station Vltava, operating until February from East German soil. This unrelieved outside intervention was intertwined with internal pressures from more conservative Czechs and Slovaks. The most extreme critics voiced their discontent with Dubcek and his moderate policy in closed meetings and in the organ of the Czech party bureau *Tribuna*, edited by Svestka. Similar, although less extreme, views were expressed in the Central Committee and in the press by conservative leaders, such as Strougal, Bilak, and Husak. Indeed the latter adopted an increasingly conservative position, emphasizing the need for normalization of relations with the Soviet Union and its allies, and criticizing ever more sharply the negative features of the reform period.[41]

This climate of clashing views and crisscrossing pressures made September 1968 to April 1969 a period of intense political conflict, characterized by a succession of serious crises. The student strike in November was followed by efforts of reform-oriented groups in December 1968 and January 1969 to prevent the ouster of Smrkovsky from the chairmanship of the National Assembly in the federal reorganization. Husak strongly articulated the Slovak insistence that this post be occupied by a Slovak (the president and the prime minister being Czechs). The resulting crisis was settled by a compromise, when Professor Colotka, a progressive Slovak, was appointed to the position in question, and Smrkovsky, retaining his top party posts, became deputy chairman of the Assembly and chairman of one of its two houses, the People's Chamber. This episode brought into relief the instability of the political balance. Almost immediately thereafter the suicide by fire of the student Jan Palach re-created for a

41. See his speech, *Rude pravo*, November 14, 1968, in which he spoke of two stages of "deformation" of Marxism-Leninism, the first under Novotny, and the second after January 1968.

few days the atmosphere of August and added anew to the political tension.

In retrospect the eight months after the invasion were a transition period which was bound sooner or later to come to an end because of its inherent contradictions. Dubcek tried to steer a middle course between total surrender and outright resistance to Soviet demands, but his popular support declined somewhat and his reputation was increasingly tarnished by his concessions to Moscow and his retreats from the January program. Among his critics there were some who bitterly condemned the entire policy of "surrender"; there were others who had serious reservations about the official policy, but who sought to strengthen Dubcek's hand in withstanding pressures from Moscow. On the other side were those who advocated a more realistic policy of even closer collaboration and a harder line against opponents at home. The Soviet Union no doubt estimated Dubcek as a person who could be cajoled and coerced into carrying out the emergency measures of normalization, but who could eventually be dropped in favor of a more subservient successor.

V

The opportunity for a change in leadership came with a new political crisis at the end of March after the Czechoslovak ice hockey victories over the Russians in Stockholm. This led to massive popular demonstrations in many cities and to violent actions, in several places, against Soviet installations, including the Aeroflot offices in the center of Prague. Deputy Soviet Foreign Minister Semenov and Marshal Grechko suddenly arrived in Prague, reportedly to present a Soviet ultimatum demanding drastic political changes. There were rumors of an effort at a take-over by high-ranking Czechoslovak army officers. The party Presidium, describing the situation as being "on the edge of catastrophe," immediately took special measures, particularly against certain newspapers.[42] Under heavy pressures at home and from abroad, Dubcek yielded. At a Central Committee plenum in mid-April, he resigned as first secretary, proposing Husak as his successor. This appointment was overwhelmingly approved, and a smaller Presidium, including Dubcek, but excluding Smrkovsky, was formed. Within the Central Committee opposition to the change was minimal. Popular resistance did not materialize since the opposition forces were tired and dispirited and Dubcek himself had proposed the change-

42. For the Presidium statement, see *Rude pravo,* April 3, 1969.

over. The press was already muzzled. A student strike fizzled out. Anticipated action by the trade unions did not take place.

Husak had already emerged as a possible alternative leader in the preceding months. Increasingly vigorous in his criticism of so-called "pressure groups" which were creating constant tension, he had offered, as a model for the entire country, the "middle-of-the-road current" in Slovakia, where the relative weakness of extreme conservative or progressive tendencies and his own strict control had in fact produced a quieter political scene than that in the Czech lands.[43] As Husak had become deputy prime minister only in April 1968 and had held no high party position until after the invasion, his responsibility for post-January "excesses" could be minimized.

In April 1969, he assumed the full burden of finding "a way out of the difficult crisis situation." There was to be no change in the political line, he declared, but a change in the attitude toward its implementation. Once the situation had been consolidated, all problems with the Soviet Union — "without exception" — could be solved.[44] There were hopes that Husak, a victim of persecution under Novotny and a supporter of the January reform movement, would avert a return to the "fifties" and total subjugation to Soviet demands, and by "normalizing the situation," through draconic measures, might even create the conditions for the withdrawal of Soviet troops and for a resumption of at least part of the reform movement. There were, at the same time, many fears that his past record of ruthless and autocratic leadership and his current hard line, coupled with continuing Soviet pressures and the influence of extremists at home, would lead to a complete reversal of the post-January gains and pave the way for a return to the "fifties," either under his aegis or under even tougher successors. In the words of a slogan which had been used by students during the November strike and which had played on the meaning of the name Husak (a male goose), "socialism with a human face" seemed to have been replaced by "socialism with goose-flesh."

The ensuing months witnessed the gradual unfolding of Husak's neo-conservative policy of "consolidation."[45] Attention was first given to the

43. *Ibid.*, November 20, 1968. See also his speeches in *ibid.*, January 11, March 13, and April 12, 1969.

44. See Husak's speeches at the close of the plenum, *ibid.*, April 18, 1969.

45. See Husak's speech at the May plenum, *ibid.*, June 2, 1969. For a review of events, see Wolf Oschliess, "Die Tschechoslowakei nach Dubcek," *Osteuropa*, 19, no. 8 (August 1969), 575–88, and Wolf Oschliess, "Prags schwarzes Jubilaum:

systematic replacement of party functionaries, especially at the regional and district levels, and of leading figures in the mass associations, radio and television, party and government institutions, and newspapers and journals. The appointments of Bruzek as minister of culture and of Professor Hrbek as minister of education initiated a policy of drastic repression of so-called "revisionist" ideas and persons. Freedom of expression was limited by the banning of reformist journals, such as *Politika*, *Listy*, and *Reporter*, the removal of editors from other key newspapers, and tighter control and censorship of the mass media in general. This was accompanied by a mounting campaign against "rightists" and a reevaluation of the post-January period, replete with sharp criticism of leading persons, including Dubcek himself. Significantly, the Soviet paper *Zpravy* ceased publication, since its purposes were being fulfilled by other means. There was continued moral and intellectual resistance to the new course, especially by the creative unions, by the rank and file of the party and the trade unions, and by intellectuals in research and educational institutions, but tightening repression made overt opposition increasingly difficult.[46]

Street demonstrations during the week of the anniversary of the invasion were crushed by strict police action and served as the grounds for issuing emergency measures for preserving public order. The campaign against Dubcek intensified.[47] At the September 1969 plenum he was removed from the Presidium; at the same time seven persons, including Smrkovsky, were expelled from the Central Committee, and nineteen others resigned; major Central Committee resolutions from July and August 1968, including those condemning the invasion, were rescinded. This was followed in October by the removal of Smrkovsky, Dubcek, and others from their posts in the National Assembly Presidium, the resignation or removal of a number of deputies, and the annulment of many 1968 Assembly resolutions. Several months later Smrkovsky and others were forced to resign their parliamentary seats. A new stage of the drive against the "guilty"

Nach dem 21. August 1969," *ibid.*, 20, no. 1 (January 1970), 1–25. See also Gueyt, *La mutation tchecoslovaque*, pp. 401–20.

46. The Ten Points Manifesto, signed by a dozen leading intellectuals, was circulated illegally in Czechoslovakia and published abroad. The manifesto, addressed to the governmental organs and the CPCZ Central Committee, condemned the Moscow protocol and described the presence of Soviet troops as the "cause of unrest." The document expressed disagreement with "the policy of constant concessions" and with the abolition "point by point" of the Action Program, and criticized the introduction of censorship, the abandonment of economic reform, the postponement of elections, and other actions of the regime.

47. This was initiated by Husak's speech, *Rude pravo*, August 20, 1969.

rightists came in January 1970 with the resignation of Dubcek from the Central Committee (following his appointment as ambassador to Turkey), and the removal of Cernik from the prime minister's post and from the Presidium. The January plenum also initiated a mass screening of party members which was intended to reduce the membership substantially and to eliminate those regarded as "rightists." [48]

This unrelenting purge of public life was accompanied by an ever closer rapprochement with the Soviet Union and the other bloc members. From May 1969 on, Husak paid formal visits to each of the invading states, including four trips to the Soviet Union. At a Moscow meeting in late October, an economic agreement was reached placing Czechoslovakia in even greater dependence on the USSR. Husak used the occasion to go far beyond his previous statements on the invasion, terming it an "act of international assistance." [49]

By the spring of 1970 almost nothing was left of the democratization program, although Husak continued to pay lip service to the post-January policy. Freedom of expression had been completely curbed, and no independent organs of opinion were left. Discipline was being restored in the party, with mass expulsions used to deal with dissent. The intellectual world, especially the Academy of Sciences, the universities, and cultural institutions, were being subjected to closer party and state control. The idea of economic reform was almost dead, with a reassertion of the necessity of centralized planning and state control. The press, radio, and television were again used for ideological propaganda and conducted vicious polemics against heretical ideas and individual persons. Rehabilitation was slowed down and modified. The National Front and its constituent elements were nothing but mouthpieces of the communist party and lacked even the potentiality for independence. The federal structure remained formally intact, but its reality was whittled away by an emphasis on the need for integration of policy, by various centralizing measures, and above all, by the abandonment of the idea of federalizing the party.

VI

By mid-1970 Husak had thus achieved a kind of domestic stabilization by quashing opposition forces and by purging the party and other agen-

48. Kriegel was the first post-January leader expelled from the party, in June. Three others were ousted at the Central Committee plenum in September. Sik was expelled in October 1969, and Smrkovsky in March 1970.

49. *Rude pravo*, October 29, 1969. In his speech at the September plenum he had spoken of the presence of "counterrevolutionary forces," without, however, actually

cies. Overt opposition had ceased and political crises no longer occurred. Husak, however, lacked a firm foundation for his rule, either in widespread popular support or in a power base exclusively controlled by himself. Ultraconservative extremists, such as Bilak, Indra, and Strougal, were influential in the top leadership in Prague, and in Husak's main instruments of power – the army, the police, and the central party *apparat*. The Czech party bureau was in the hands of Kempny, appointed when Strougal was named premier in January. Even the Slovak party *apparat*, now that Husak was not first secretary, was no longer his personal instrument. Husak's chief assets were a sullen acquiescence and a developing opportunism of a tired and discouraged population, together with the self-interested support of dogmatic forces resurrected from the Novotny era. His greatest challenge was the desperate economic situation, coupled with widespread workers' apathy and serious shortages of fuel and other supplies. The plenum in January 1970, devoted to economic questions, had recommended central control, discipline, and austerity as the way out. Unless Husak could offer solutions for the critical economic problem, a more conciliatory policy at home, and a relaxation of strict Soviet supervision, none of which seemed likely, he would continue to be passively resisted by many people and regarded by others at best as a lesser evil.

After his accession to power Husak had tried to create an image of himself as a centrist. There would be no return, he said in Pilsen, in October, either to "Novotny bureaucracy" or to "Dubcek anarchy." [50] In many statements he upheld the January turn as inevitable and abjured any return to the pre-January system.[51] In particular, he ridiculed the notion that there would be a resumption of the terror of the early fifties. Arrests were indeed few and confined to lower level reform spokesmen, mainly among the intellectuals, and no political trials of reform leaders took place. In fact, however, Husak's regime was a strongly conservative one, which had abandoned or reversed most of the post-January reforms and was committed to intimate collaboration with the Soviet Union. The circumstances could best be described as analogous to those of the late fifties, prior to the relaxation and ferment of the sixties. In other words, the Novotny system had been restored, not in its earlier and worst form, but with the traits of its middle phase; its final stage, in the sixties, appeared favor-

accepting the Soviet view that there was in fact a counterrevolution. *Ibid.*, September 29, 1969.

50. *Ibid.*, October 15, 1969.

51. For instance, *ibid.*, January 20, 1970.

able in comparison to Husak's rule. An element reminiscent of the Stalinist years, however, was the resumption of direct Soviet interference and control, this time by means of military occupation. As long as Soviet troops remained and Soviet pressure continued, Husak had little room to maneuver in his relationship with the USSR and could entertain no hope of a more independent course. He had adopted a role resembling Gomulka's and showed no signs of following the model of Kadar, still less of Tito or Ceausescu. In terms of Czechoslovak history, Husak had come to resemble not so much President Hacha, a conservative but reluctant collaborator of Hitler, but rather Father Tiso, who ruled Slovakia, under Hitler's auspices, with a strong commitment to Nazi policy.

Having eliminated "rightists" and "centrists" from positions of power, Husak found that the main threat came from the "leftists," that is, the more extreme or ultraconservative forces who were dissatisfied with the degree of his conservatism and of his subservience to the Soviet Union. These elements were to be found within the very groups upon which Husak had to rely: his closest associates in the leadership and in the party apparatus, especially in the Czech bureau; editors of such journals as *Tribuna* and the Central Committee's weekly *Tvorba*; and newly appointed neo-Stalinist activists in all fields of life. The extremely difficult economic situation presented them with a strong argument for a return to centralized controls. A thinly veiled struggle between Husak and the ultraconservatives had been in progress for some time and the outcome was uncertain. The victory of the ultras would mean a regression to something close to the Stalinism of the early fifties, replete with police terror, mass arrests, political trials, complete centralism in the economy, and total conformity in cultural and intellectual life. Husak's coercive hard-line policy, although it approached this in many respects, did not yet go to this extreme.

The crucial determinant of the future was the Soviet Union. In the spring of 1969 Moscow had accepted Husak as the most suitable leader of the occupied country, capable of guaranteeing political stability at home and Czechoslovak support in all bloc questions and in foreign affairs. During his visit to the USSR in the fall of 1969, he had received a hero's welcome, and was assured of Soviet support in the solution of pressing economic problems. Having encouraged and approved the more extreme course adopted by Husak, Russian leaders may have come to the conclusion that a more radical dogmatism in Prague would produce negative results. The ultraconservative forces meanwhile provided a useful tool for pressure on Husak and could be used at any time as a lever to oust him, as Dubcek had been ousted before him. The early elevation of these elements to power would shatter the fragile stability achieved by Husak and produce an even more obdurate passive resistance. If, however, it appeared that Husak had outlived his usefulness and was no longer pliable enough to guarantee Soviet purposes, then someone else, such as Strougal, Bilak, or Indra, could be brought to power to carry out an even more ruthless coercive policy at home and a still more docile attitude toward the USSR.

The future depends, therefore, on the evolution of Soviet policy, which in turn will reflect the outcome of possible conflicts within the Kremlin leadership, of East-West relations, and of the Sino-Soviet clash. This makes it impossible to foresee whether Moscow will continue its present harsh line, or adopt an even harsher one, toward Prague, or, as seems less likely, will revert to a more moderate attitude. Yet the future also depends to some extent on the policies of other communist states in Europe, and these in turn on the uncertain and unpredictable relationship of regimes and people in each one. Events in any one state will have repercussions in the others and will also affect the policy of the USSR.

Indeed one cannot write off the possibility of surprises within Czechoslovakia itself. The eight months of democratization, the seven months of overt postoccupation resistance, and the subsequent months of silent opposition to the draconic rule of Husak have left an indelible imprint on the consciousness of Czechs and Slovaks. For some time these experiences will leave a legacy of apathy and discouragement. Under favorable and at present unforeseeable circumstances, however, these two peoples might once again step to the center of the stage in roles of substantial importance, and seek to work out new variations on the theme of national communism or a fresh version of their democratic national traditions. Nor can one be sure of Husak's own hopes or intentions. Simplified analogies with Hungary's Kadar or Poland's Gomulka are deceptive. In fact Husak is Husak, and Czechoslovakia is Czechoslovakia. The future of that country, therefore, to the extent that it depends on his will, or that of other domestic forces, will not be exactly like any of its neighbors and will remain unpredictable.

4

East Germany

BY MELVIN CROAN

"We enter the seventies full of optimism, with self-confidence and energy." So declared Walter Ulbricht in his New Year's Message marking the turn of the decade.[1] More than mere ritualized rhetoric, the sanguine note sounded by the veteran communist leader no doubt also reflected a certain measure of official satisfaction at East Germany's political consolidation at home and self-assertion in the international arena. Even the most cursory retrospective glance can serve to illuminate the basic factors making for such apparent self-congratulation.

At the beginning of the sixties, the German Democratic Republic (GDR) still appeared to be little more than an artificial political construct. Its communist political system, forcibly installed by the Soviet military occupation in the course of Germany's postwar division between East and West, seemed to lack a viable social base. In fact, East Germany's rulers constantly had to contend with widespread popular disaffection and potential unrest, cutting across all segments of society. Evidence of mass dissatisfaction was only too acutely registered in the statistics which recorded the ebb and flow of an unending tide of refugees to the West. Today, the picture is quite different. Once the Berlin Wall went up, it not only immediately arrested the damaging exodus but also set the stage for a slow and rather subtle process of enforced reconciliation between the population and the regime. And this process, almost all reliable observers agree, is now quite far advanced.[2] As for the regime itself, the East Ger-

1. *Neues Deutschland,* January 1, 1970.

2. Ernst Richert, *Das zweite Deutschland* (Gutersloh, 1964), and Wolfgang Nette, *DDR Report* (Dusseldorf and Cologne, 1968). For an attempt – albeit a methodo-

man Communist party (Socialist-Unity party of Germany [SED]) gives every present sign of being quite solidly entrenched. Under the leadership of Ulbricht and his old guard party cohorts, the SED's top cadres enjoyed long-term tenure and apparent political cohesion, unmarred by any public eruption of elite infighting. Moreover, the ranks of the top leadership have been augmented by the steady advancement of a new generation of younger men, commanding considerable technical knowledge and managerial know-how.

A decade ago, East Germany's lopsided economy, torn out of a larger national whole and still a long way from effective integration into a substitute international structure, was performing sporadically. At times its poor functioning in certain sectors conveyed the impression of an economic system doomed to chaos if not actually on the verge of collapse. To aggravate matters still further, the westward exodus carried with it some of the most productive elements of the population and, as long as the flight remained unchecked, it served permanently to becloud the GDR's economic prospects. At the beginning of the seventies, things are entirely different. For once the regime had "secured the frontier" and initiated certain economic reforms, the GDR embarked upon a period of sustained growth and development. As a result, East Germany has attained a level of productive output that makes it a major economic power, ranking ninth or tenth among the world's industrial giants. It can boast a standard of living that is the highest in the communist world and easily surpasses that of the Soviet Union. With understandable pride and a measure of shrewd psychological insight, East German commentators now point to the GDR as an "economic miracle" in its own right and that designation has been seconded by many Western students of the East German economy as well.[3]

A decade ago, East Germany's international position was utterly unenviable. Except within the communist camp, the GDR's credentials as a legitimate "second German State" went unrecognized. Indeed, at that time, the Ulbricht regime's pretensions may not even have enjoyed very widespread acceptance at home, where they were challenged by Bonn's

logically dubious one – to measure the development of this process, see Hans Apel, *DDR 1962 1964 1966* (Berlin, 1967), and the same author's less systematized observations, *Ohne Begleiter* (Koln, 1965).

3. For the official East German presentation, see Hans Muller and Karl Reissig, *Wirtschaftswunder DDR* ([East] Berlin, 1968). From the Western side, cf., Joachim Nawrocki, *Das geplante Wunder* (Hamburg, 1967), and Fritz Schenk, *Das rote Wirtschaftswunder* (Stuttgart, 1969).

counterclaim that the Federal Republic of Germany alone was entitled to represent the entire German nation. Once again, the situation has changed considerably. Although the GDR's drive for international diplomatic recognition may still be some distance from attaining its goal, real progress in the desired direction has been achieved and more is to be expected. Even short of general diplomatic recognition, the GDR's political influence has grown unmistakably. Within international communist councils, especially those still dominated by the Soviet Union, East Germany's voice has steadily gained in importance. Once Moscow's abject satellite, the GDR has turned into at least a junior partner, and possibly even more than that in the European context. Vis-à-vis its arch rival, West Germany, the GDR's competitive position has also markedly improved and, as implicit acknowledgment of that change, Bonn's once seemingly unalterable stance against East Germany has undergone modification. In sum, to paraphrase a commentary carried by the prestigious Hamburg weekly *Die Zeit* on the occasion of East Germany's twentieth anniversary, no one can realistically dismiss the GDR as merely a passing "phenomenon." [4]

This state of affairs, in itself, constitutes sufficient cause for the official tone of self-confidence emanating from East Berlin. It also helps explain the belated attention, some of it rather favorable, that East Germany has recently attracted in the English-speaking world.[5] Far from being the "major political paradox" that the present writer depicted earlier,[6] the GDR may perhaps now appear to be a paragon of progress and possibly even a model of communist political development.[7] And yet, while the progress is undeniable, the paradox persists. How else to describe a regime which, though it has become the most advanced in the communist world, economically, remains one of the most reactionary, politically? With what better word to connote a state which, for all its newfound presence in the international arena, clings tenaciously to the oldest of vestigial cold war orthodoxies?

4. Joachim Nawrocki, "Ein deutsches Jubilaum," *Die Zeit* (North American edition), October 13, 1969.

5. Among recent English language accounts, the following deserve mention: John Dornberg, *The Other Germany* (Garden City, N.Y., 1968); Jean Edward Smith, *Germany beyond the Wall* (Boston, 1969); and David Childs, *East Germany* (London, 1969).

6. Melvin Croan, "East Germany," in Adam Bromke (ed.), *The Communist States at the Crossroads: Between Moscow and Peking* (New York, 1965).

7. Zbigniew Brzezinski, "The Soviet Past and Future," *Encounter*, 34, no. 3 (March 1970), 3-16.

East Germany

I

There can be no better place to commence a closer examination of this paradoxical state of affairs than by recalling the character of the East German political leadership during the sixties. Throughout the entire decade, as for so long before, that leadership bore the indelible stamp of its ranking personage Walter Ulbricht. Throughout the sixties and, indeed, until the day he bowed out as party first secretary in May 1971, his position at the apex of the entire East German system proved so deeply entrenched as to be immune to the kind of factional challenge that had erupted several times during the fifties. Despite advanced age, he continued to display the same qualities of energy, drive, and scrupulous attention to detail that had characterized his entire career. Untainted by blood purges in the ouster of his erstwhile opponents within the SED leadership, Ulbricht's personal power developed a measure of genuine political authority enabling him to stand above and to resolve divisions of opinion within the East German ruling elite and to strike something of a pose of *Landesvater* with respect to the population as a whole.[8]

While demonstrating far greater flexibility in dealing with novel problems than might have been forecast for a sometime Stalinist subaltern, Ulbricht nonetheless continued to be intransigent on matters he deemed crucial for the survival of the SED regime. This refusal to compromise was informed by an unerring respect for the regime's intrinsic precariousness as the result of Germany's national division as well as by an uncanny sensitivity to each and every potential threat to its domestic political stability. Although the Berlin Wall served to cement Germany's partition much more tightly than ever before, it could not by itself fully allay Ulbricht's anxieties. During the second half of the sixties, two major fears were once again in evidence. These were, first, a dread that international developments beyond the SED's immediate control might lead to the political isolation of the GDR and, secondly, but no less importantly, anxiety lest internal liberalization within other communist countries might either contribute to the same result or else infect East Germany domestically and thus serve, in either instance, to undermine the Ulbricht regime.

These basic concerns helped to shape official East German attitudes toward the Eastern bloc as a whole and to determine its policies toward individual communist states and parties. As a consistently outspoken partisan of "socialist internationalism" under Soviet aegis, the SED has

8. Carola Stern, *Ulbricht: Eine politische Biographie* (Cologne and Berlin, 1963), especially the concluding chapter.

always reacted adversely to manifestations of disunity in the communist camp and to signs of erosion of Soviet political authority. With respect to the major fissure involving China, the GDR early fell into line behind the Soviet Union, although careful scrutiny of the evolution of the SED's position on the Sino-Soviet conflict reveals some interesting differences of emphasis.[9] Because of the nature of the case, Ulbricht must always have found the protracted polemics between Moscow and Peking deeply distasteful and feared the wider international ramifications of the struggle between the two communist giants. Thus, Ulbricht sought to utilize the leeway that the Sino-Soviet conflict itself afforded, if not to moderate the dispute, then at least to assure that it did not lead to any weakening of communist positions vis-à-vis the German question. Leeway for arbitrating the dispute was never very great as far as Ulbricht was concerned and it all but disappeared with the onset of Mao's Great Proletarian Cultural Revolution during which, incidentally, East German diplomatic personnel were among those physically assaulted in Peking. What remains as a symptom of the SED's basic concern, however, is the degree to which its spokesmen have warmed to the theme of an ostensible "Bonn-Peking" axis. It was therefore entirely in character for the East Germans to consider the bloody clashes that broke out on the Ussuri as a dire Chinese provocation deliberately designed to divert Soviet attention from the "menace of West German imperialism" in Europe.[10]

With respect to the situation in Europe, where vital East German interests are directly involved, the SED's reaction has been practical as well as rhetorical. While official endorsement of Soviet leadership is no less strong (as can be illustrated by countless official pronouncements, running from denunciation of Rumania's independent economic course in the early sixties to today's repeated endorsement of the Brezhnev doctrine),[11] the pur

9. See the insightful analysis by Carola Stern, "East Germany," in William E. Griffith (ed.), *Communism in Europe*, vol. 2 (Cambridge, Mass., 1966), 97–154.

10. "Aus dem Bericht des Politburos an die 10. Tagung des ZK der SED," *Neues Deutschland*, April 29, 1969.

11. Hermann Axen, "Proletarischer Internationalismus in Unserer Zeit," *Einheit*, October 1968, pp. 1203–19. For a general discussion of the defense of the thesis of "limited sovereignty" in socialist international law on the part of East German jurists, see Jens Hacker, "Die SED und die Breshnew-Doktrin," *Deutschland-Archiv*, 3, no. 2 (February 1970), 198–203. The SED's position on this and related matters has brought it into open conflict with the Italian Communist party and the League of Yugoslav Communists. In May 1969, the SED circulated a confidential memorandum to East German party functionaries which presented a comprehensive indictment of Yugoslav domestic and foreign policy. For the text, see "Zur Politik des Bundes der Kommunisten Jugoslawiens," *Informationen*, no. 31 (1969), as reproduced in

pose has always been to forge a coordinated Eastern bloc policy toward West Germany on terms thought appropriate by East Berlin. With this objective in mind, the GDR has in recent years pursued a much more active, if largely negative foreign policy, thereby also demonstrating the degree to which Ulbricht himself had outgrown his former status of Soviet viceroy in Germany.

Although the groundwork had been laid before, East German assertiveness vis-à-vis Moscow gained immeasurably from Khrushchev's political downfall in October 1964. As long as there had been a single strong man in the Kremlin, Ulbricht, out of consideration for the security of his own political tenure, deemed it inadvisable to exert untoward pressure on the Soviet leadership. Accordingly, he had to swallow his disappointment at Khrushchev's decision to relax Soviet pressure on Berlin after the Cuban missile crisis and had to content himself with a politically insubstantial friendship agreement in place of the long promised separate Soviet peace treaty. Although Khrushchev's final foreign policy venture, anticipating a personal visit to West Germany, may have loomed especially foreboding, Ulbricht's objections were carefully guarded. When Khrushchev actually fell from power, however, Ulbricht exhibited a different kind of restraint. Far from applauding the ouster or waxing enthusiastic about the new Kremlin leadership, Ulbricht remained masterfully ambiguous. In effect, he used the political transition in Moscow to serve quiet notice on the Soviet Union that henceforth the SED could be expected to be heard from much more forcefully where its own interests were involved.[12]

These interests were quite obviously at stake when the Grand Coalition Government, formed in Bonn at the end of 1966, inaugurated a new and much more active *Ostpolitik* on the part of the Federal Republic. For several years before that departure, the SED had already made a display of its special sensitivity to West German policy toward Eastern Europe by warning its allies of the ostensibly disruptive political designs behind Bonn's quest for better trade relations. Faced with the prospect of a concerted West German drive aimed at a political rapprochement with Eastern Europe, Ulbricht did not bother to wait for the Kremlin to make up its own

Deutschland-Archiv, 2, no. 11 (November, 1969). The publication of this document in the West (initially in the *Frankfurter Allgemeine Zeitung*, September 26, 1969) led to a sharp Yugoslav rejoinder to the SED and a belated (and unpersuasive) denial from East Berlin as to its authenticity. See Ilse Spittmann, "Die SED und Jugoslawien," *Deutschland-Archiv*, 2, no. 11 (November 1969), 1237.

12. Ilse Spittmann, "Soviet Union and DDR," *Survey*, no. 61 (October 1966), 165–76.

mind about how to handle Bonn's new overtures. As far as Ulbricht was concerned, they were unacceptable. His spokesmen lost no time in denouncing them as such and the GDR swung into immediate action to counter West Germany's fresh approach to the East.[13]

Demanding full diplomatic recognition from West Germany and refusing to negotiate with Bonn about anything less, Ulbricht also pressed acceptance of this demand as a precondition for diplomatic relations between the other East European states and the Federal Republic. Much to his chagrin, Rumania agreed to enter into formal relations with West Germany in January 1967 without particularly concerning itself with East German objections. To prevent any repetition of such fractious behavior, Ulbricht concentrated his efforts on reinforcing the "iron triangle" linking the GDR to Poland and Czechoslovakia and further sought to enlist the support of other East European countries to solidify the GDR's rear flank as much as possible. Toward that end, during the course of 1967 East Germany concluded a series of bilateral treaties of "friendship, cooperation, and mutual assistance" with Poland, Czechoslovakia, Hungary, and Bulgaria. Whatever the views of the individual East European signatories, East German commentators hammered home the point that these pacts were meant to constitute a solid phalanx against West Germany. Moreover, this interpretation obviously enjoyed Soviet support, especially after Rumania's demarche toward Bonn. The Karlovy Vary conference of East European communist parties held in the spring of 1967 laid heavy stress on the need to strengthen both military preparedness and political unity against the danger of West German "revanchism, militarism, and neo-Nazism" and thus signaled an unmistakable triumph for Ulbricht's position. In shelving, at least for the time being, its own previous proposal for an all-European security conference in favor of a rigid anti-West German front, the Kremlin may have been motivated by the desire to utilize the German issue to arrest fissiparous tendencies in Eastern Europe. By so doing, however, it had in effect aligned itself squarely behind East Berlin.

This alignment of interest grew even closer during 1968, both in the period of Czechoslovakia's "experiment with freedom" and in the immediate aftermath of the Soviet-led invasion. If the Kremlin reacted to Dubcek's course between January and August 1968 with increasing displeas-

13. For the general international background, see Richard Lowenthal, "The Sparrow in the Cage," *Problems of Communism* (November–December 1968), pp. 2–28, and Melvin Croan, "Bonn and Pankow: Intra-German Politics," *Survey*, no. 67 (April 1968), 77–89.

ure, Czechoslovak developments served almost from the very outset to reawaken all of Ulbricht's deep-seated anxieties concerning domestic infection and international isolation. Repeated East German charges purporting to detail the preparation of a "counterrevolution" in Prague masterminded by "West German imperialism" make this only too clear. Given such an interpretation of Czechoslovakia's reformist course, it was inevitable that relations between Prague and East Berlin should have deteriorated rapidly. Given the fears that lay behind it, it makes sense to conclude that Ulbricht himself came rather early on to press for the most stringent measures against the Dubcek regime and that his insistence upon forceful action must be accounted a significant contributory factor in the Kremlin's fateful decision to intervene in Czechoslovakia.[14]

Immediately after the August invasion, it appeared as if Ulbricht now believed that the SED had secured for itself a decisive role in socialist bloc affairs in Europe and thus also in East-West relations. Certainly, the East German leader's pronouncements concerning both international relations and domestic affairs reached a new level of schoolmasterly self-confidence. Thus, while calling for tightened international coordination and discipline under Soviet leadership, Ulbricht found repeated occasion to single out Soviet-East German economic and scientific ties and their military cooperation as shining examples of socialist internationalism in action. In addition, he took it upon himself to proclaim the necessity of constructing socialism "on the basis of one's own resources" as a doctrinal imperative. By no means did this signify endorsement of national autonomy, a concept that he dismissed as "ridiculous drivel." Rather it constituted a call to end economic dependence upon the West and to pursue closer integration among the communist states along the lines followed in relations between the GDR and the Soviet Union. Finally, with particular reference to Czechoslovakia but also as a more general rebuttal of Marxist revisionists elsewhere, Ulbricht held up the GDR (not the USSR) as a model of economic efficiency and political stability.[15]

It may well be that an intimate awareness of the Kremlin's Czechoslovak tribulations, together with a sense of exaltation over the application of its own harsh prescription for dealing with the situation, actually per-

14. This is not, however, to argue that Ulbricht was the "prime mover" behind the Soviet invasion of Czechoslovakia. See Melvin Croan, "Czechoslovakia, Ulbricht and the German Problem," *Problems of Communism* (January–February 1969), pp.1–7.

15. *Neues Deutschland*, October 25, 1968. For further discussion, see Croan, "Czechoslovakia, Ulbricht and the German Problem."

suaded Ulbricht that henceforth the GDR would share in the primacy enjoyed by the Soviet Union, at least with respect to the European theater.[16] If so, he was shortly to be proved mistaken. While Moscow could not tolerate any unilateral action toward West Germany by a liberalized Czechoslovakia, neither was it prepared to countenance a veto over its own approaches to the West by a rigidly inflexible East Germany. To overcome the stigma attached to the occupation of Czechoslovakia, the Kremlin found it useful to move toward diplomatic initiative. Accordingly, at the March 1969 Budapest meeting of the Political Consultative Committee of the Warsaw Treaty Organization, the Soviet Union revived its previously shelved proposal for an all-European security conference and considerably softened its anti–West German polemics, thereby confirming signs of a changed attitude toward the Federal Republic that had been manifest from late 1968. Indeed, in March 1969 Moscow made something of a display of improving relations with Bonn by demonstratively briefing the West German government on the Sino-Soviet conflict while simultaneously playing down the crisis in Berlin that the SED sought to provoke in connection with the convocation of the West German presidential election assembly there. By the end of the month signs of tension between Ulbricht and the Soviet leadership were incontrovertible. At a Moscow meeting held to commemorate the fiftieth anniversary of the establishment of the Third International, Ulbricht spoke out in defense of the Comintern's 1928 indictment of social democracy as the "main enemy," while the Soviet ideologist Mikhail Suslov, in company with Boris Ponomarev, CPSU secretary in charge of relations with foreign communist parties, criticized it as sectarian in character and harmful in consequence.[17]

At stake, of course, was not merely the proper interpretation of Comintern history but also the quite topical matter of the correct approach to present-day West Germany, whose Social Democratic leader, Willy Brandt, had served as foreign minister from late 1966 and was to accede to the federal chancellorship with the formation of a new government in October 1969. Persisting in his détente-oriented *Ostpolitik* and broadening it to acknowledge the existence of "two German states in one nation" (thereby effectively conceding de facto recognition to the GDR), the Brandt government received a favorable response from the Soviet leader-

16. David Binder, "The New Ulbricht Wins a Key Role in Soviet Bloc," *New York Times*, November 18, 1968. This article attracted considerable attention in West Germany and elicited favorable mention in *Neues Deutschland* (December 6, 1968).

17. See the *International Herald-Tribune* (Paris), March 27, 28, 1969, and Anatole Shub, "A Guide to Soviet Policy – 'Social Fascism' 1928," *ibid.*, March 28, 1969.

ship, as well as from Poland's Gomulka, who had broached the prospect of bilateral negotiations with West Germany as early as the spring of 1969. None of the other East European states, except the GDR, found the principle of bilateral negotiations with the Federal Republic distasteful, and by the end of 1969 Ulbricht had no real alternative but to associate himself with a change of attitude of which he disapproved.

This is not at all to suggest that, within the course of a single year, the GDR had been transformed from an active force keeping the Eastern bloc in line against West Germany into a passive pawn in Soviet-East European relations with the Federal Republic. On the contrary, while accepting bilateral contracts between individual East European states and West Germany and, indeed, entering upon top level contacts itself, as demonstrated by the Stoph-Brandt meetings at Erfurt and Kassel in March and May 1970, the GDR continues actively to pursue its own interests in a manner that bespeaks fear of a genuine détente in Europe and determination to employ all available political resources to counter it.

Much as before the East German regime continues to clamor for bloc solidarity behind its own position on the German question. In fact, Ulbricht himself actually went beyond his prior demand for full diplomatic recognition by Bonn to insist upon West Germany's renunciation of its membership in NATO and sweeping political changes within the Federal Republic as essential preconditions for any normalization of East German-West German relations.[18] Such intransigence was put to the acid test with the signing of the Soviet-West German Treaty of August 1970. Although the longer range political consequences of the agreement cannot be accurately gauged, the hopes expressed by some quarters in Bonn that it would lead directly to an acceptable Berlin settlement and a concomitant reduction of the GDR's influence on Soviet policy proved premature. Basically out of sympathy with the Soviet-West Germany Treaty, Ulbricht fought tooth and nail against Bonn's détentist view of the treaty. In so doing, he sought not merely to shield the GDR's entrenched position but to

18. Ulbricht's statement to an international press conference, *Neues Deutschland*, January 20, 1970. See also Ulbricht's remarks of March 17, 1970, on French television as quoted in Ilse Spittmann, "Deutscher Gipfel in Erfurt," *Deutschland-Archiv*, 3, no. 4 (April 1970), 432. In view of the domestic political utility of international tension over Germany and the economic advantages accruing from Western nonrecognition of the GDR (which permits trade between East Germany and West Germany to be treated as domestic German trade and thus confers upon the GDR certain EEC privileges), it can be questioned whether Ulbricht was really interested in de jure recognition from Bonn. See Joachim Nawrocki, "Viele wollen die Anerkennung – will sie auch Ulbricht?" *Deutschland-Archiv*, 3, no. 1 (January 1970), 35–37.

engineer, if possible, a major political defeat for the Brandt government in West Germany. There is abundant evidence that Ulbricht carried his fight for a German policy at once unyielding in regard to the GDR's interest and also politically offensive against the West into the highest councils of the Kremlin, where he enjoyed powerful support right up to the day of his retirement as East German party first secretary. Whether Ulbricht's successors can exercise that kind of leverage upon Moscow is a moot question. Certainly, they lack Ulbricht's stature at home and to that extent are more dependent upon Moscow for personal political support. That practical consideration aside, their own conceptions of the German question appear every bit as inflexible as Ulbricht's if not more so; this is especially true of Erich Honecker, Ulbricht's successor as party first secretary. Behind this tough international line lies an assessment of the East German domestic scene which, while officially boastful of economic efficiency and political stability, nonetheless remains fearful of the possibly disruptive consequences of a genuine relaxation of international tensions. Before venturing an assessment of the GDR's future prospects, we must, therefore, turn next to a consideration of the internal sphere.

II

There can be no mistaking the impressiveness of East Germany's economic growth during the sixties. Several key indicators will suffice to convey a sense of the overall picture. The annual growth rate of the gross national product, which had fallen to 3.7 per cent in 1961 and 3.3 per cent in 1962, attained the following levels in subsequent years: 4.2 per cent (1963), 7.4 per cent (1964), 9.5 per cent (1965), 5.5 per cent (1966), 8.3 per cent (1967), 7.1 per cent (1968). Between 1964 and 1968 industrial production increased at an average annual rate in excess of 6 per cent. Agricultural production which in the wake of the brutal collectivization of 1960 showed a negative growth rate of −1.5 per cent for 1961 and −2.3 per cent for 1962 experienced a dramatic recovery and recorded the following annual percentage increases: 12.3 per cent (1963), 13.0 per cent (1964), 11.5 per cent (1965), 10.6 per cent (1966), 6.1 per cent (1967), 6.5 per cent (1968).[19]

Considering East Germany's dismal economic performance earlier, this record could not have been compiled without some fairly major changes. The erection of the Berlin Wall in August 1961, with its stabilizing effect

19. Calculated on the basis of East German statistical annuals by Joachim Nawrocki, "Auferstanden aus Ruinen. Zwanzig Jahre DDR-Wirtschaft," *Deutschland-Archiv*, 2, no. 9 (September 1969), Table 3, p. 948.

on the labor force, was an essential condition but scarcely a sufficient one as the continued downward spiral experienced in 1962 clearly indicates. Something more was required to attain the record of growth listed above, and it came in the form of a major overhaul of previous economic practices. First introduced in 1963, these changes seemed to involve such a sharp departure from established party orthodoxy as to suggest to many Western observers the strong possibility of widespread ideological erosion and a concomitant relaxation of the SED dictatorship. Yet nothing of the sort has happened so far. If anything, political control and ideological discipline are more strongly in evidence today than at the outset of the new economic program. To understand why this is the case is also to appreciate how little the theory and practice of East Germany's economic development have in common with the ideas espoused by Ota Sik and his school in Czechoslovakia or, for that matter, with the liberalizing practices now quietly unfolding in Hungary. In fact, it is a moot question whether the East German economic program deserves to be dignified with the designation "reform" or whether it ought to be regarded as a case of rationalization and modernization.[20]

As initially unveiled at the Sixth Congress of the SED in January 1963, the East German economic overhaul owed much to the Liberman discussions in the Soviet Union. The New Economic System of Planning and Management (NES), as it was originally termed, never really sought to do away with central planning; rather, it attempted to combine planning with certain principles of market economy. With that goal in mind, the NES called for a thorough examination of the entire price system in order to take realistic account of the actual value of capital equipment and of the economic costs of all productive processes. The original East German blueprint also envisaged administrative decentralization of decision-making authority and an unprecedented reliance upon various material incentives. Both these announced objectives seemed to sanction economic practices that had long been officially castigated as "revisionist" and, perhaps for that reason, many Western observers looked to the implementation of such measures as a harbinger of the eventual relaxation of the party's ideological grip over society.

So far all such expectations have been disappointed, although it would be more accurate to report that in East Germany's case, they have never

20. Richard V. Burks, *Technological Innovation and Political Change in Communist Eastern Europe,* Rand Corporation Memorandum, August 1969, and, for a general background discussion, Michael Gamarnikow, *Economic Reforms in Eastern Europe* (Detroit, 1968).

really been permitted to come to the test. For no sooner had the pressing task of revamping the price structure been successfully completed than the regime began to reverse direction with respect to more basic structural changes in the economy. This became initially evident with regard to the degree of autonomy to be accorded to individual enterprises (VEB) and industrial branch combines (VVB). As originally formulated, the New Economic System seemed to allow a considerable degree of independence both to individual enterprises and industrial combines. As if to sanctify this novel autonomy and underscore the acceptance of certain free market principles, the VVBs were officially heralded as "socialist concerns" whose task it was to serve as "the leading economic organs," and their managers received the imposing but previously abjured title of "General Director." Yet, although precise regulations governing the rights, duties, and responsibilities of the VVB and the VEB were drawn up, they were never promulgated. Indeed, at the end of 1965, the "General Directors" of "socialist concerns" had to forfeit many of their freshly granted decision-making perquisites. The VVBs lost their financial autonomy and were once again subordinated to their respective industrial ministries. The National Economic Council, which had been initially charged with providing overall economic coordination under NES, was abolished at the same time. Its functions reverted to the State Planning Commission whose role was thereby considerably strengthened.

At the Eleventh Central Committee plenum of the SED in December 1965 Ulbricht announced a transition to the "second stage of the New Economic System." In retrospect it is clear that what he actually had in mind was the more narrowly restrictive practice aimed at the maintenance and strengthening of central direction and control of the economy. Thus, when the Seventh Party Congress of the SED, at its meeting in April 1967, rechristened the New Economic System as the Economic System of Socialism, more was involved than merely a change of name. As the economic discussions at the Seventh Congress repeatedly emphasized, the accent was henceforth upon "mastering the scientific-technical revolution." This entailed a novel imperative which the chairman of the Council of Ministers, Willi Stoph, formulated as the need "to study thoroughly and apply the newest findings in the field of cybernetics, information theory, input-output and systems analysis and other specialized fields of knowledge." [21] In other words, the purpose was to streamline central planning and economic administration so as further to improve overall eco-

21. As quoted in Nawrocki, "Zwanzig Jahre DDR-Wirtschaft," p. 950.

nomic performance, but this goal was to be initiated essentially from the top down and was to be attained in a manner that had very little to do with any prior intimation of decentralization.

If any doubt remained on this score, it was entirely dispelled by the Ulbricht regime's highly explicit reaction to the economic reforms that had been projected for Czechoslovakia. Not only did the SED leadership engage in personal vilification of individual Czechoslovak reform economists but it also subjected their doctrines to close scrutiny, all of it harshly critical. Particularly heavy abuse has been aimed at certain free market principles which the SED itself seemingly had endorsed at the outset of its own New Economic System. All such notions have now become anathema, for they are held to embrace "petty bourgeois" ideas of spontaneity, which form the part and parcel of "modern revisionism" and, as such, are detrimental to the very survival of socialism. In this connection, Ulbricht himself provided an unwitting illustration of the degree to which some of his previously expressed thoughts concerning the NES had changed. In 1964, the East German leader had spoken of the need to realize "a certain self-administration in the economic system on the basis of the plan." [22] In 1968, however, he had this to say: "So-called self-administration – or I ought to deal with the concept more exactly and say bourgeois self-administration of enterprises – embodies a renunciation of the concentrated energetic drive led by the state as a whole for the highest scientific attainment on structurally determined bases; it expresses renunciation of the aim of systematically developing the economic foundations of the freedom and independence of the socialist states." [23] The SED organ, *Neues Deutschland*, summarized the gist of Ulbricht's remarks in even blunter language, when it evoked the venerable but almost forgotten Stalinist motto: "Plan discipline is state discipline." [24]

Recent pronouncements have gone so far in the direction of extolling central planning and the politically controlled economy that one must guard against the unwarranted conclusion that actual practice has reverted entirely to the dismal experience of the pre-NES period. Despite the

22. Concluding remarks to the Seventh Central Committee plenum of the SED, December 1964, as quoted in Walter Ulbricht, *Zum neuen Okonomischen System der Plannung und Leitung* ([East] Berlin, 1966), p. 116. See Kurt Erdmann, "Das Ende des Neuen Okonomischen Systems," *Deutschland-Archiv*, 1, no. 9 (December 1968), 998–1001.

23. Walter Ulbricht, *Die weitere Gestaltung des gesellschaftlichen Systems des Sozialismus* (Report to the Ninth Central Committee plenum of the SED, October 1968 ([East] Berlin, 1970), p. 49.

24. "Plandisziplin," *Neues Deutschland*, November 13, 1968.

recrudescence of ideological appeals in place of economic laws and of recent signs of stagnation in certain industrial sectors, the phenomenal growth of the sixties remains an accomplished fact. Given the overall achievement, it is small wonder that the standard of living should have risen so steadily and that this should have contributed to the process of reconciliation between the population and the regime. Moreover, the great premium still placed upon economic expertise, administrative skill, and scientific talent serves the same purpose. By opening up new avenues of social mobility, the drive for economic growth has increasingly stamped the GDR as a "career-oriented society," something that also has served to cement popular allegiance, especially among the younger generations.[25] Finally, for all its doctrinal rigidity, the SED too has had to bow to some practical imperatives of the new economic course. It has greatly deemphasized the use of political terror toward society as a whole. Though always held in ready reserve, the means for evoking fear and terror have come to be augmented by a network of institutionalized social controls. Within the party's own ranks, no less than within other administrative structures, new scope has been provided for careers based on talent.

The latter development has been examined in great detail by a West German political sociologist whose findings led him to conclude that the GDR ought to be characterized as an example of "consultative authoritarianism" rather than as a "totalitarian" political system.[26] In his view, a managerial-technocratic "counter-elite" has arisen in juxtaposition to the "strategic clique" composed of aging party functionaries around Ulbricht. There is, of course, ample evidence to support such an argument. One needs only to consider the meteoric rise of such previous political unknowns as Gunter Mittag, now Politburo member and Central Committee secretary for economic affairs, Werner Jarowinsky, Politburo candidate and Central Committee secretary for trade and supply, George Ewald, Politburo candidate and agricultural specialist, two Central Committee members, Gunther Klieber, a data processing expert, and Walter Halbritter, a financial specialist, and the late Erich Apel, Politburo candidate and the reputed mastermind of the NES until his suicide in late 1965. These are only a few of the more prominent members of the new breed of men of high competence in their special fields who have been coopted into the top echelons of the SED. One can also point to their counterparts at lower lev-

25. Ernst Richert, *Das zweite Deutschland*, and Peter Christian Ludz, "Die Zukunft der DDR," *Die Zeit*, October 10, 1969.

26. Peter Christian Ludz, *Parteielite im Wandel* (Cologne and Opladen, 1968).

els in the party and in state bureaucracies, especially in the field of economic administration.

Yet, nothing would be wider of the mark than to suppose that such specialists form a self-conscious managerial-technocratic faction, much less that they necessarily constitute a liberalizing force. To be sure, none of the members of the "counter-elite" has shown any special concern for ideological matters. By virtue of their background, training, and, above all else, occupational responsibilities, they are always prone to neglect "fundamental ideological positions" and thus may possibly come into conflict with more narrowly dogmatic political decision-makers. Nevertheless, the Ulbricht leadership during the sixties did successfully foster the advancement of managerial-technocratic talent without surrendering one iota of the party's claim to political primacy. Indeed, given the Ulbricht regime's political psychology, it is not surprising that it has remained alert to any even implicit challenge by the "counter-elite" to the political primacy of the "strategic clique." If individual technocrats ever aspired to a greater political role, they have received a sharp rebuff because of events in Czechoslovakia. For once the Prague reformers were overwhelmed by force of arms, Ulbricht began to hammer home a point that may well have been insufficiently stressed in the GDR's preoccupation with economic growth – namely, that the party's primacy has to be vigorously exercised, if it is not to be lost. Significantly enough, it fell to Gunter Mittag, the very member of the political elite who seemed most to embody the managerial-technocratic attributes, to champion the party as "the leading force and not some kind of societal interest group representation." [27] This he did in the course of a stinging rebuke of Gunther Kohlmey, a prominent East German economist, who found himself in trouble in the fifties for a "revisionist" attitude toward political control. The larger lesson of this personal reprimand was only too obvious. Whatever their individual predilections, members of the "counter-elite" henceforth would be required to show a healthy respect for the disciplinary value of ideological guidance and political supervision.

As for the party old guard, it certainly takes its own ideological professions with dead seriousness. In this respect, as in so many others, Czechoslovak developments proved a catalyst for a sustained counteroffensive on the part of the SED. Maintaining that Dubcek and company had fallen victim to notions of convergence between East and West as well as to a host of other revisionist currents allegedly promoted by the West as a particu-

27. *Neues Deutschland*, October 27, 1968.

larly sinister form of psychological warfare against the socialist bloc, party spokesmen called for uncompromising ideological purity. To counter the appeals of "humanistic socialism," the SED has devoted considerable energy to developing its own image of the future under what is now officially termed "the developed social system of socialism." [28] Premised on a distrust of individualism and a fear of pluralism, the official concept amounts to a blueprint for an integrated network of social subsystems tied to the "economic system of socialism" with the entire elaborate monolith motored by sophisticated techniques of social control operated by the party as the repository of political authority and ideological truth. It is in view of this concept that Kurt Hager, the SED's ranking ideologist, boasted that the GDR is "correctly programmed," the "programming" being a function of political goals: "Cybernetics, systems theory, operations research, etc., are in their scientific discoveries in complete agreement with the fundamental principles of dialectical materialism. But they are not identical with the Marxist-Leninist world view and cannot substitute for its specific task. That must be most decisively asserted. *The specific task of the scientific world view of the working class cannot be replaced by any other science.*" [29]

III

To round out this picture of ideological orthodoxy linked to the mystique of technology, a word should be said about the role of official nationalism. Given Germany's national division and the psychological predisposition of many veteran SED functionaries to "proletarian internationalism," the problem of nationalism has always been a particularly touchy one. Reflecting tactical uncertainties of the moment, there has also been considerable ambiguity, even in official pronouncements, as to whether East Germany can be said to constitute a separate nation. Nonetheless, a doctrine of the GDR as the "better, truer" Germany has been heavily propagated both for purposes of additional social cement at home and as a weapon in East German's rivalry with the Federal Republic. To enlist foreign Germanophobia against West Germany, the contrast between the GDR as an ostensibly peaceful, progressive, and humane society and the Federal Republic as allegedly "militarist" and "reactionary" has sometimes been pushed to the point where the East Germans are almost depicted as not

28. See Ulbricht, *Die weitere Gestaltung des gesellschaftlichen Systems des Sozialismus.* The new official textbook *Politische Okonomie des Sozialismus und ihre Anwendung in der DDR* ([East] Berlin, 1969) is especially instructive.

29. *Neues Deutschland,* April 30, 1969.

really German at all. For domestic purposes, needless to say, the emphasis is entirely different, with great stress being placed on the historical continuity of the German state. Laying claim to all the towering figures of classical German culture as well as, of course, to its pre-Marxist and Marxist revolutionary traditions, GDR official nationalism also seeks to inculcate a pride in East Germany's own achievements of economic reconstruction and industrial development. But the most striking feature of GDR nationalism has been the incorporation of Prussian virtues into the official doctrine, to the point where its rhetoric and symbols, together with the regime's rigid authoritarianism, increasingly serve to convey the image of a distinctive Prussian brand of communism.

Nowhere has the official trilogy of "ideology, technology, and nationality" taken a greater toll than in the cultural field, where the regime has never been inclined to grant any real concessions. Even during the relatively mild period of 1963–65, the party's cultural watchdogs always remained on the alert. At the international literary conference, held at Liblice near Prague in May 1963, they fought hard to prevent the "rehabilitation" of Franz Kafka whose adherents the SED today counts among the "intellectual forerunners of counterrevolution" in Czechoslovakia.[30] At home, they banned unpalatable foreign authors, including the Soviet writer Solzhenitsyn, and pounced upon a wide variety of heterodox expression. As a result, the party declared war on East Germany's best known intellectual figures and hounded individuals as diverse as Stefan Heym, the novelist-essayist, Robert Havemann, the scientist-philosopher, and Wolf Biermann, the unconventional ballad-singer.[31] The denouement occurred at the Eleventh Central Committee plenum of the SED, the same forum at which Ulbricht announced the transition to a second, more restrictive stage of the New Economic System. Only the novelist Christa Wolf, then a candidate member of the Central Committee, rose to champion the claims of intellectual creativity; she was subsequently dropped from that body for her temerity. When the authoress of the internationally acclaimed novel *Divided Heaven* completed a new book, *Thoughts about Christa T.*, in 1969, the edition authorized for publication was so small as

30. See the remarks of Klaus Gysi, GDR minister of culture, in *Neues Deutschland*, August 29, 1968, and the three-part series, "Die geistigen Vorreiter der Konterrevolution," *ibid.*, September 10, 11, 12, 1968, as well as the remarks of Ulbricht to the Ninth Central Committee plenum of the SED, *ibid.*, October 25, 1968.

31. For a general discussion, see M. Reich-Ranicki, "The Writer in East Germany," *Survey*, no. 61 (October 1966), 186–95. On Biermann, see Margaret Vallance, "Wolf Biermann: The Enfant Terrible as Scapegoat," *ibid.*, pp. 177–85.

to earmark it entirely for cultural functionaries. Those promptly attacked its concern with the human condition as an example of the spread of "false ideological concepts." [32]

Christa Wolf's difficulties offer only one illustration among many of the official straitjacket in which the regime continues to hold East German culture. Quite apart from any question of the free expression of political dissidence, the SED now insists upon party-mindedness in the most narrowly restrictive Stalinist sense. Consider the following guideline, laid down by Kurt Hager, preparatory to the Sixth East German Writers' Congress in 1969: "The Maxist artist and scientist must not forget for a single moment that aesthetic-artistic pursuits involve ideological processes and that these ideological processes decide the essential core of a work of art and also that its 'structure' is to be determined by that fact and by its function in the societal process." [33]

To reduce the possibility of further annoyance from intellectuals more concerned with depicting the fate of the individual than with meeting ideologically determined requirements relating to "the societal process," the regime has multiplied its efforts to control cultural life. The precepts of the so-called "Bitterfeld Way," first introduced in 1959 under Ulbricht's personal imprimatur, have once again been extolled as the correct method to overcome the division of labor between intellectuals and manual workers. In practice this means that party functionaries with scant understanding of and less sympathy for the life of the mind are to take individual writers and artists in hand in order to put an end to their social isolation and sense of alienation. In line with this approach, the regime has now struck upon the novel device of "social editors" who are drawn from the production line to instruct authors on what is socially useful and what must be censored.[34]

Given so repressive an atmosphere, it is scarcely surprising that almost all critical voices have fallen completely silent. The major exception is that of Professor Robert Havemann, whose public lectures attacking dogmatism and Stalinism and calling for greater freedom of opinion, information, and criticism in East Germany caused an official scandal in 1963 and resulted in his ouster from the SED and his enforced retirement. Al-

32. "Kunstwerke entstehen nicht in Selbstlauf," *Neues Deutschland,* May 1, 1969.

33. "Grundfragen des geistigen Lebens in Sozialismus," *Neues Deutschland,* April 30, 1969.

34. For a detailed discussion and analysis of the "Bitterfeld Way" and the latest control mechanisms, see Dorothy Miller, "The East German Literary Scene," *Radio Free Europe Research,* June 4, 1969.

though subject to repeated harassment, and recently under police surveillance, Havemann has remained defiant and, remarkably enough under the circumstances, has also managed to send out to the West repeated statements of his personal beliefs. While it obviously is impossible to ascertain with any degree of precision how widespread these beliefs may be, there are good grounds for supposing that something akin to Havemann's position is shared by many other critical East German intellectuals. However this may be, Havemann's personal beliefs add up to an extraordinary profession of "modern revisionism" of precisely the kind the SED ideologues purport so greatly to fear. Already on record as having endorsed the 1968 Czechoslovak reforms as the right way to achieve "a radical and uncompromising breakthrough to socialist democracy," [35] Havemann recently elaborated upon the same basic theme. In an essay entitled "Tomorrow's Socialism," he took the GDR to task for "its political contradictions, the Wall, its tutelage of literature and its petty bourgeois puritanism" and offered the following alternative perspective: "Economic democracy, that is, popular rule over the economy, requires the realization of political democracy, that is, the transition to democratic socialism. And only this achievement will signify, politically and socially, completion of the socialist revolution." [36]

The contrast between Havemann's aspirations for socialism and the official conception currently propagated by the SED could hardly be more complete.

IV

What future, then, can one predict for East Germany? If the GDR's present domestic rigidity and international inflexibility bear the unmistakable stamp of Ulbricht's personal leadership, can major changes be anticipated now that he has departed from the scene? Certainly, there is no single successor on the horizon who seems to combine Ulbricht's tactical agility with his purposeful firmness nor is there any individual who appears powerful enough politically to lay effective claim to the mantle of Ulbricht's personal authority. Unless all present signs are misleading, East Germany after Ulbricht seems destined to have its first experience of collective leadership, most likely to be shared by Honecker, Stoph, and, perhaps, Mittag. Collective leadership invariably means weakened leadership, which is always susceptible to further impairment resulting from personal rivalries

35. *Svet v Obrazech* (Prague), May 21, 1969.

36. Robert Havemann, "Der Sozialismus von morgen," *Die Zeit*, October 10, 1969.

and factional infighting. Given the distinctive political styles of the leading candidates for the East German succession as well as the different interests they appear to stand for, disputes over domestic policy matters are a distinct possibility. If, as some signs already suggest, economic growth stagnates, latent tension between managerial-technocratic elements, exemplified by Mittag, and the professional party functionaries, led by Honecker, could well erupt into an open conflict. Yet, it would be premature to anticipate a direct challenge to the party's primacy by the managerial-technocratic "counter-elite." Members of the new elite must be presumed to have developed a full sense of vested interest in the SED regime and consequently a sensitivity to the threat to their own position which might arise from any dismantling of its authoritarian structures. For these reasons as well as by virtue of their narrow professional concerns, it would be grossly misleading to expect the "counter-elite" to emerge as a champion of "humanistic socialism," the appeals of which have been largely restricted to members of the humanistic intelligentsia. And the latter group, it should be stressed, has always been far removed from the centers of actual power. For better or worse, the perpetuation of the classical cleavage between *Geist* and *Macht* is in keeping with the tradition of the German political culture.

This is not to rule out a future extension of various "small freedoms" to the population as a whole, if only in the interest of further economic growth or else for purposes of streamlining the dictatorship at home and improving its image abroad. In a political system as tightly controlled as that of the GDR, however, a serious problem is bound to arise with respect to managing the unintended consequences of any such concessions. Contrary to the currently fashionable supposition in the West, the East German population cannot be written off as either so materially satisfied or else so stupefied and submissive as to be permanently immunized against the lure of major political change. The incalculable number of protests, undertaken at great individual risk, against the invasion of Czechoslovakia in 1968, and the more recent spontaneous outburst of popular acclaim for Brandt when he visited Erfurt testify to a climate of opinion that is potentially quite volatile. This consideration provides reason enough, from the point of view of all aspirants to power after Ulbricht, to practice the greatest restraint in tampering with existing political controls. Finally, all ranking members of the political elite realize with Ulbricht the implications of Germany's national division for their own hold on power. As long as they continue to feel insecure by virtue of the absence of a genuine national base for their rule, none of East Germany's future leaders seem likely to venture too boldly upon the path of relaxation at home.

In the final analysis, therefore, the future of intra-German relations may exert greater influence on internal East German developments than vice versa. Although progress on the German question as a whole depends first and foremost upon agreement between the two superpowers (the United States and the Soviet Union), the scope for initiative on the part of the two German states is considerable. Ulbricht employed the leeway available to him to try to block movement toward a détente. It is at least conceivable that his successors may prove more flexible or else more susceptible to pressures from Moscow, should the Kremlin deem it in its own interest to resume the diplomatic initiative toward Germany. Should that in fact come to pass, the range of possible longer term consequences is truly vast.

At one extreme, if the GDR's long-standing international demands were to be gradually satisfied and if its domestic structures were simultaneously streamlined without impairing the regime's institutional controls, a more self-confident successor leadership in East Berlin might be tempted to try to play an increasingly active role in West German political life. This might be pushed, perhaps, even to the point of advancing the GDR and its "socialist achievements" as something of a German Piedmont, from which to extend appeals for a revivified German national communism. At the other extreme, a gradual reduction of tensions between the GDR and the Federal Republic might contribute to a political rapprochement between the two German states to the point of inducing major internal changes in East Germany that might ultimately produce a political order more nearly in line with West German aspirations. In either instance, as in other, shorter term, and more plausible scenarios, the political interaction between the two parts of divided Germany seems destined to increase rather than to diminish. If, mindful of this development and, much like Ulbricht, fearful of its potentially disruptive domestic consequences, the East German leaders of the seventies resolutely oppose any inner-German rapprochement, they retain the power to obstruct its development. In the latter eventuality, an all too probable one, the East German paradox may once again appear visibly acute.

5

Poland

BY V. C. CHRYPINSKI

The downfall of Khrushchev in October 1964 must have aroused mixed reactions in Gomulka, the Polish party's first secretary, but, in all probability, this sudden removal of the Kremlin boss from the Soviet political arena did not strike him as "writing on the wall." Although publicly praising the ousted ruler,[1] privately he might not have been displeased with the occurrence. As an individual, Gomulka still might have harbored the resentment created by the initial scorn shown him by Khrushchev in October 1956; as a Polish political leader, he might have been relieved that the specter of a new Rapallo raised by the visit of Khrushchev's son-in-law, Adzhubey, to Bonn was – at least temporarily – removed. But whatever his feelings, Gomulka knew that Poland's geopolitical situation as well as his own position as Poland's leader dictated remaining on good terms with the Kremlin masters regardless of his personal like or dislike of the way in which they acquired power.

The new Soviet rulers made Gomulka's task much easier by paying him an official visit before meeting any other East European leaders. This gesture of uncommon courtesy and appreciation smoothed the way for future cordial relations which bound Gomulka, the Polish United Workers' party and, *ex necessitate rei*, Poland to the Soviet chariot even more strongly than before. This was demonstrated by the Polish leadership's condemnation of China in its dispute with the Soviet Union, their criticism of Rumania's independent behavior and their severance of diplomatic relations with Israel, and finally by Poland's participation in the Soviet invasion of Czechoslovakia.

Gomulka claimed that this was the only policy for Poland, and he ex-

1. *New York Times,* October 18, 1964, p. 1.

pected other Poles to recognize and appreciate the argument. He succeeded to a great degree, for today most Poles recognize the validity of the policy of alliance with their Eastern neighbor as a protection of their national interests vis-à-vis Germany. But Gomulka made the mistake of stressing too much Poland's dependence on the Soviet Union, because later the people came to believe that every Polish deficiency had its source in Moscow, and that Gomulka himself was but a tool in Soviet hands.

Good relations with the new Soviet leaders certainly improved Gomulka's stature in communist Eastern Europe and strengthened his hand at home, but did little to solve his – and the nation's – domestic problems. Many of the troubles were ascribed to him personally and there was a visible growing disenchantment with his halfhearted policies of liberalizing the political system and of improving economic conditions. "Comrade Wieslaw," who in 1956 had been the nation's favorite, and an inspirational communist, has become, a few years later, a spent force and an obstacle to change. Even his desirable personal characteristics, such as modesty, sobriety, and orderliness seemed now to many of his former admirers to be nothing more than attributes of a grey bureaucrat. Throughout the years there have been rumors of his failing health and of pressures on him to make way for a younger party man.

Of course, many internal problems were not of Gomulka's making and it would be simplistic to assume that he was always free to choose the methods by which to deal with them. They arose as a result of environmental pressures, some of which are beyond the control of any leader. Yet in handling them, Gomulka demonstrated a striking lack of imagination and an inability to free himself from the ideological straitjacket. Faced with grave problems and limited resources, he embarked on a course of ambivalent and often opportunistic maneuvers, accompanied by increasingly harsher administrative pressures called forth by popular and indifferent hostility. Angered and frightened when the protesters took to the streets, Gomulka fell back upon the use of naked force, which did little to endear him to the Poles or to enhance the prestige of the communist leadership.

Even sceptical observers cannot but admit that the unrest of 1968 and of 1970 demonstrated a significant erosion in the system of support enjoyed by Gomulka and his regime in 1956. The causes underlying the growth of popular dissatisfaction can perhaps best be shown by, first, analyzing the most important demands generated by the domestic environment, and secondly, by evaluating the role played by a few crucial groups in the political process and their attitudes toward the communist leadership.

But to grasp the reasons for Gomulka's downfall one must go a step further and take a look at the decision-making group itself, i.e., at the leadership of the Polish United Workers' party (PUWP), because it is in this group that the fate of Gomulka was ultimately decided. His manifested inability to cope with domestic problems and a dramatic loss of popularity exposed him to the growing challenge from other party leaders. Their major bids for power came in the wake of students' riots in 1968 and of workers' demonstrations in 1970. Gomulka managed to survive the first assault, and the Soviet invasion of Czechoslovakia temporarily reinforced his position within the party. But the second trial was beyond his endurance and he was ousted as PUWP first secretary. The era of Gomulka came to an abrupt end.

I

The retrogression from the "Polish October" (which began in the late fifties), though causing widespread disillusionment, did not lead immediately to an open defiance of the communist regime. Instead, a peculiar relationship was established between the rulers and the ruled through the sixties which became known as the "small stabilization," a sort of armed neutrality in which the people abstained from political involvement and the regime refrained from direct political socialization.

The situation was not only unusual but, in the long run, untenable. The symptoms of impending trouble could be discerned on both sides of the fence. The people were becoming restless and increasingly contemptuous of the leadership, while the leaders were showing signs of internal dissent and insecurity, and a growing disdain for the public. Progressive deterioration of the economic situation and the regime's inability to deal with it added fuel to the fire. Inevitably, the emergence of a new radical temper led to direct clashes. There can be little doubt that many of the domestic problems had their source in growing demographic pressures. The Polish population expanded from under 24 million in 1946 to 32.5 million in 1970. The increase, smaller by a million than that predicted only a few years earlier,[2] indicated a significant downtrend in the birthrate (from 19.5 per million in 1955 to 8.2 per million in 1969), but it nevertheless created a highly demanding situation in relation to other socioeconomic factors.

Accelerated urbanization was accompanied by crucial housing shortages and a crisis in available educational facilities. The rapid expansion

2. Edward Rosset, *Polska Roku 1985* (Warsaw, 1965), p. 72.

in the size of the labor force, coupled with ideological insistence on full employment, resulted in the misallocation and underutilization of manpower resources. Shortages of consumer goods, services and food, were aggravated by the regime's ideological commitment to the development of producers' over consumer's industries; there was an overall decline in real earning. The process of urbanization[3] was the result of mass migration of peasants, mostly young men and women, into the cities which started in the early fifties under the dual impulse of collectivization and industrialization. It continued, on a smaller scale, during the sixties when 1.7 million people moved out of villages; the migration total in the 1950–70 period amounted to six million persons, and, by the end of 1970, 52.2 per cent of the entire population resided in urban communities.[4] The population explosion and the transition from a traditional agricultural to an urban industrialized society, together with other equally momentous changes (such as the shift of Poland's boundaries), gave rise to new needs and demands, all of which imposed heavy burdens on the national economy.

The housing problem was probably the most vexing. Even before World War II over 50 per cent of the population lived in overcrowded quarters, and the war resulted in almost total destruction of 40 per cent of all habitable rooms in urban areas, because of military operations and the systematic demolition of Polish cities, especially Warsaw, by the Germans. Postwar efforts brought some amelioration of the crisis but the improvement, hampered by the primacy of industrial investments and the population explosion, lagged significantly behind actual needs. The ratio of persons per room decreased only slightly, from 2.02 in 1931 to 1.61 in 1966. Between 1966 and 1970, only an average 5.8 dwellings were built per 1000 inhabitants, and the fulfillment of the five-year plan of 673,000 apartments fell short by 34,000 units. In 1970 the socialized sector, which formed the backbone of the entire housing construction program, built 138,500 apartments with a total of 411,300 rooms. However impressive these figures might seem, they represent a 3.5 per cent decline from 1969.

The whole situation was rendered still worse by regional disparities, overcrowding of a significant percentage of occupied apartments, progres-

3. Stefan Nowakowski, "Procesy urbanizacyjne w powojennej Polsce," *Studia Socjologiczne*, no. 3 (1965), 43–80.

4. Czeslaw Kozlowski and Zygmunt Szeliga, "Portret Polakow," *Polityka-Statystyka*, no. 3 (March 1971), 1–4. It must be noted, however, that this statistical picture is, in part, the result of including some neighboring rural areas into the administrative boundaries of the cities as well as the granting of urban status to some villages.

sive dilapidation of old dwellings (30 per cent of all Polish housing was constructed before World War I), and – last but not least – by the small size and low standard of newly built apartments. In the circumstances, the number of people requiring better dwellings was constantly on the increase and an average waiting period was over seven years. At the end of 1969, 877,900 families awaited their lucky turn in the housing cooperatives alone; of these close to 400,000 families had paid all due charges in full.[5] In 1970, over one and a quarter million people were waiting for the allocation of dwellings.

The housing problem, more acute than in any other communist-ruled country of Eastern Europe, had strongly adverse effects on the national economy as well as on the whole development of social life. It restricted rational exploitation of the available industrial labor force, led to the economically unjustified dispersal of investment means, and imposed heavy material and social costs on the population. Young people were especially affected by this problem; their chances of acquiring better education and jobs or starting families of their own quite often depended on finding a place to live.

The solution of the problem was not easy; nevertheless, as many pointed out,[6] the emergency in this area was easier to overcome than in those areas where industrial products were in short supply. Housing construction, unlike other industries, could be greatly accelerated with the use of existing resources of building materials, equipment, and specialists, and with only a minimal expenditure of foreign currency. What was actually needed was the courage to break away from the Soviet model (followed only by Bulgaria and Poland) which describes housing construction as "nonproductive" investment, secondary to industrial investment. To ameliorate the problem the regime should have considered housing like any other commodity that was freely obtainable on the market.[7]

But Gomulka and associates were unable, or unwilling, to perceive the advantages that a changed policy could have had on the national economy, especially on the labor market and the entire structure of consumption, and, in the long run, on political attitudes. They missed the chance to ease the specter of unemployment by providing, at low cost, thousands of places for the growing army of job seekers, and to remove pressure

5. Witold Kasperski, "Spoldzielczosc mieszkaniowa," *Gospodarka i Administracja Terenowa*, no. 5 (May 1970), 19.

6. For instance Jerzy Urban, "Artykul pierwszej potrzeby," *Polityka*, no. 38 (September 19, 1970), 3.

7. *Ibid.*

from the troubled food market by redirecting private spending from foodstuffs to housing.

Motivated by their commitment to narrowly interpreted principles of Marxism and afraid that housing concessions might slow down the "building of socialism," communist leaders of Poland decided to continue their orthodox and unrealistic policy. In the name of lofty ideals, they overlooked the authentic strivings and needs of the people who after decades of war and postwar deprivations had no taste for more misery and sacrifices. Consequently, the distance between the rulers and the ruled increased greatly, and the support they might have enjoyed among the masses was significantly undermined.

Another difficult problem was education. The population explosion in Poland after World War II produced about twelve million children who literally inundated Polish schools from kindergarten to college. Since the law required that all children be given elementary education, the primary schools had to provide room, between 1964 and 1969, for over five million pupils annually, with a peak of 5.7 million in 1967–68. To accommodate these huge numbers, it was necessary to employ 207,000 teachers and maintain 26,000 schools with 140,000 classrooms, of which 11,000 were rented and many urgently required repairs or replacements.[8]

The situation in the high schools was less critical because the influx of youngsters was comparatively smaller. Nevertheless, between 1964 and 1968, about two million pupils annually attended secondary schools of vocational or college preparatory type. It was characteristic that among the students was a disproportionally small number of children from worker families whose percentage decreased from 28.9 in 1956–57 to 28.2 in 1966–67. A similar trend, only more accentuated, manifested itself in regard to pupils of peasant origin whose number dropped during the same period from 24.7 per cent to 17.7 per cent.[9] Since graduates of these schools normally form the bulk of university students and provide future leaders of society, the phenomenon appears to have pointed social and political significance.

The number of available places at Polish institutions of higher learning expanded rather slowly (from 251,900 in 1965–66 to 304,600 in 1968–69), and every year a great many frustrated candidates were denied access to one of seventy-six existing colleges. Between 1964 and 1969, the num-

8. Henryk Jablonski, "Najblizsze zadania szkolnictwa podstawowego i sredniego," *Gospodarka i Administracja Terenowa*, no. 11 (November 1968), 6.

9. *Ibid.*, pp. 4–5.

ber of qualified applicants doubled;[10] in 1969 alone, out of 100,000 applicants only 45,000 were admitted after satisfactorily accumulating the necessary number of points awarded them for high school records, for performance at the entrance examination, for proletarian origin, and extracurricular (read political) activities.

Higher capital allocations would have helped the schools to alleviate their problems, by construction of new buildings and improvement in teachers' salaries, which, at the elementary and secondary levels, were lower than those earned in industry, public administration, or the military. Communist leaders, although appreciative of the importance of education in the new socialization of youth and of the crucial importance of teachers in the process, nevertheless failed to give higher priority to educational budgets. This decision was undoubtedly made necessary, from their point of view, by the first priority demands of the industrial sector.

Another significant consequence of the population increase was the tremendous hike in the size of the productive population identified as men between 18 and 64, and women between 18 and 59. Between 1956 and 1965 the size of this group increased to 1,450,000 persons; in the next five years (1966–70) it rose to 1,600,000.[11] Most of this increase was accounted for by those born after 1945. Previously unemployed women also entered the labor market at the same time, especially in nonagricultural occupations. As a consequence well over 300,000 jobs had to be found annually to accommodate this huge, and not fully anticipated, influx of labor.

Ideologically committed to a policy of full employment, the Polish government had no other choice but to create needed jobs in the socialized sector on a mass scale. Even so, shortages of jobs appeared, caused primarily by geographic, seasonal, and occupational divergences. In the eastern and southern provinces, which normally employ 36 per cent of the national work force, the number of applicants was almost double that of the jobs available.[12] Seasonal fluctuations, related to the interdependence of the labor market with agriculture and the building trades, created big and repetitive differences which varied between 350,000 and 500,000 people

10. Ryszard Herczynski, "Rafy polityki naukowej," *Polityka*, no. 15 (April 10, 1971), 11.

11. Dr. H. Krol, "Intensive Development Versus Employment," trans. from *Trybuna Ludu* (Warsaw), February 2, 1971, *RFE, Polish Press Survey*, no. 2285 (March 19, 1971), 1.

12. Tadeusz Kochanowicz, "Zatrudnienie a sytuacja demograficzna," *Nowe Drogi*, 21, no. 5 (May 1967), 19.

every winter.[13] Vocational shortages also occurred because some branches of the socialized economy (such as the garment industry in the province of Cracow) were unable to provide enough jobs for about 50,000 graduates of vocational schools in their home areas, and because the latter were unwilling to move to other localities where openings existed.[14]

Paradoxical as it may appear, the overall success in placing a large majority of job seekers in the socialized economy had its dark side as well. New jobs created in industry at a great expense automatically reduced the means for improvements in the area of consumption and in other "nonproductive" sectors, such as education, health, housing, and social welfare. In addition, when financial resources for the task were exhausted, it was decided to resort to excessive employment, not justified by economic considerations, in existing plants. Thus, the traditional phenomenon of hidden unemployment in agriculture was replaced by concealed unemployment in industry and other sectors, including public administration. This led to a drop in the tempo of productivity, particularly in 1962 and 1963,[15] and consequently jeopardized any significant improvement in the standard of living. Hardships thus incurred affected a great many individuals and contributed significantly to the disenchantment with the political system.

Similar in scope and magnitude were corollary tensions, generated by persistent deterioration of real income caused by the growth in the cost of living, and by perpetual shortages, in quantity, quality, and assortment, of many basic goods on the domestic market. The decline, hurting all segments of society, was especially painful for the urban masses.

With the continuation of ideologically motivated policies of excessive employment and high investment in the industrial sector, wages remained unnecessarily low. After an initial growth of average gross monthly pay in industry from 1192 zloty in 1955 to 2194 zl. in 1965, the annual increase leveled off at about 100 zl., i.e., less than 5 per cent. In 1970, the average monthly gross nominal pay in the socialized sector amounted to 2455 zl. (a 3 per cent increase only over 1969). It should be noted here that some income groups showed no increase at all, or an increase at a rate lower than the average.

13. Antoni Rajkiewicz, "Zatrudnienie – problem nie tylko ekonomiczny," *Nowe Drogi,* 18, no. 6 (June 1964), 133–34.

14. Maria Jarosinska, "Spoleczne zagadnienia mlodziezowego robotniczego rynku sily roboczej," *Kultura i Spoleczenstwo,* 3, no. 1 (January–March, 1968), 175.

15. Zbigniew Madej, "W sprawie mechanizmu zatrudnienia i plac," *Nowe Drogi,* 18, no. 5 (May 1964), 4.

An examination of family budgets disclosed that monthly income per family member amounted to only 600-1000 zl. for 40 per cent of all workers and only 1000-1500 zl. for 42 per cent of all white-collar functionaries. These low figures persisted in spite of the fact that in 1969 a great many married women (60 per cent of the wives of manual workers and 70 per cent of the wives of office workers) were gainfully employed. At the same time, the cost of maintenance of a person in a four-member family amounted to 1051 zl. in the workers' group, and to 1334 zl. in the white-collar category. In order to meet expenses, people had to supplement their regular income either by overtime work, additional jobs, or pilferage in the place of employment.[16]

Quite naturally, this situation could not satisfy growing expectations of the people for a better material life; earning increases did not even meet the rising food prices, which, from 1960 to 1968, went up by an average of over 11 per cent (from a 5 per cent increment for farm butter to 18 per cent for pork)[17] and continued to increase throughout 1969 and 1970. It is no wonder that an average family used over 50 per cent of its budget for foodstuffs, their diet slanted heavily toward bread and potatoes and low protein intake.

Price increases were aggravated by shortages of some food products, deliveries of which to the market fell below planned quantities. Such was the case for meat, meat products, animal fats, butter, milk, cheese, fresh eggs, fresh and frozen fish, and salted herring. In some instances, especially with respect to imported goods, the 1970 supplies fell below the 1969 level (coffee beans and cocoa by 40 per cent and citrus fruit by almost 14 per cent). At the same time, 1970 export quotas of food products increased by more than 20 per cent over 1969.[18]

The shortage of meat was especially trying for the masses. From January to August 1970, for example, meat supply declined by 2.7 per cent, and in August of that year alone the figure dropped again by another 3.7 per cent, cutting the consumption of meat, in 1970, to about 52 kilograms per person. As a result, a per capita increase in meat consumption in the 1966–70 period amounted to 4.2 kilograms only, and was significantly lower than the growth of 6.7 kilograms achieved between 1960 and 1965. It was no secret that the Gomulka version of the 1971 plan called for a

16. Georg W. Strobel, "Vorgeschichte und Ursachen der Polnischen Krise vom December 1970," *Europa Archiv*, 8 (1971), 297.

17. *Concise Statistical Yearbook of Poland, 1969* (Warsaw, 1969), Table 11, p. 300.

18. Zofia Zwolinska, "Fulfillment of the Economic Plan for 1970," *RFE, Poland/9* (April 13, 1971), p. 9.

further reduction in meat consumption of 1.8 kilograms per person.[19] As might be expected, the prospect had political as well as economic repercussions.

Food shortages on the retail market reflected the difficulties of Polish agriculture, which resulted from the agricultural policy of the government and were aggravated by the inclement weather that had afflicted Poland for two consecutive years. The story, long and involved, touches upon a wide variety of subjects.

The existence and operation of private farms unique in Soviet-dominated Eastern Europe remained in the realm of uncertainty, which deeply distressed land-owning peasants. The 1956 decollectivization decision, while economically sound, evoked among communist leaders grave political doubts.[20] They dreaded retrogression on the "road to socialism," were horrified by a prospect of capitalistic revival, and feared the scorn of communists from other "people's republics." Consequently, they treated decollectivization as a necessary evil to be prolonged for another ten or fifteen years only. The agrarian policy, therefore, was hindered by indecisiveness, continued many of the old prejudices and restrictions, and was largely based on a stalemate of contradictions. No wonder that in the circumstances the peasants felt uneasy and showed little interest in long-range investments or in planning the future of their children around the ownership of land. But this was not all. They were also troubled by high delivery quotas, low prices for obligatory procurements, cumbersome bureaucracy, shortage of supplies, and a score of other deficiencies, among which inadequate housing and poor retail trade outlets occupied a prominent place.[21] Quite naturally, contradictions, uncertainties, and blunders in the agricultural policies of the regime resulted in considerable erosion of the political support which Gomulka had won from the peasants in 1956.

Thus demographic and economic factors figured significantly in the broad picture of a gradual widening of the gap between the people and the party through the sixties and undermined the credibility and effectiveness of Gomulka's leadership.

19. Harry Trend, "Polish Agricultural Problems and the Post-Gomulka Agricultural Policy," *RFE, Poland/11* (April 22, 1971), p. 7.

20. Wladyslaw Bienkowski, *Kryzys Rolnictwa czy Kryzys Polityki Rolnej* (Paris, 1970), pp. 26ff.

21. Eva Celt, "The Demands and Grievances of the Polish Population," *RFE, Poland/10* (April 14, 1971), pp. 19–21.

II

Although many aspects of demographic growth can be verified by traditional measurements, there are some which have no chance of showing up in statistical tables. Nevertheless, they are important in evaluating social developments. One such aspect is the mood of the people.

About one half of the Polish population consists of young people born after 1945, who are brought up under communism. The size of this group will, by 1975, surpass the number of those born before the war. One may only speculate on the consequences of this biological fact, considering the already evident differences between the younger and older generations. They are free of the defeatist inhibitions imposed on their parents by the tragic experience of war and occupation, and they demonstrate a renewed spirit of optimism and ambition.

It is characteristic of Polish youth that their attitudes are colored by strong patriotic sentiments. This can be seen in their keen interest in Poland's history, including the highly romantic period of the nineteenth-century struggles for independence against three invaders, one of whom was Russia. In the sixties, these emotions came to the surface several times, beginning with the publication of a book by Zbigniew Zaluski, *The Polish Seven Deadly Sins*, which presented a most eloquent defense of the Polish romantic past, and ending with the showing of the film *The Ashes*, which, adhering strictly to the realist tradition, condemned the Polish cult of heroism and Poland's romantic history. The debates ensuing on those occasions demonstrated quite strongly the degree of ascending nationalism.[22]

Poland's communist leaders did not hesitate to use this nationalistic revival for a variety of purposes. The so-called "partisan" group within the PUWP, led by General Moczar, skillfully utilized it in intraparty struggles to dislodge their rivals. Party ideologists, alarmed by the spiritual estrangement of the youth, decided to employ nationalism to refurbish the image of their party. Consequently, they ordered a major revision of the history of the Polish communist movement that would portray it in more patriotic colors, by emphasizing that its program and activities were always inspired by Poland's national interest.[23]

The ruling elite even turned to nationalism to carry on its struggle with

22. Adam Bromke, "History and Politics in Poland," *Problems of Communism*, 15, no. 5 (September–October 1966), 65–71.

23. Adam Bromke, "Polish Communism: The Historians Look Again," *East Europe*, 16, no. 12 (December 1967), 20–27.

the Catholic Church. As was to be expected, however, the assault upon the Church, led from the nationalist position, was doomed to failure. The identification of Catholicism with Polish nationalism, built up over centuries of a shared lot, was much too penetrating to be eradicated by twenty-odd years of communist efforts. The 1966 commemorations in observance of the millennium of Poland's Christianity and nationhood vividly demonstrated this fact. It was in the course of millennial celebrations that the Church once again proved it possessed the moral strength and intellectual foresight to fulfill its great historical role. The occasion arose in connection with Polish-German relations, when Polish bishops addressed an invitation to their "German brothers in Christ" to "forgive and forget" the past and to join the Poles in the millennial jubilee. This gesture of goodwill and act – as future events proved – of great statesmanship exposed the Church to severe trials. The German hierarchy, while expressing its willingness to come to the celebration, decided to use this opportunity to stress the plight of Germans expelled from the territories annexed by Poland after World War II and to assert these peoples' bonds with their "ancient homes." [24] Many Poles, including not a few clergy, with the memories of war and occupation still fresh in their minds, bitterly resented the exchange of letters and questioned the wisdom of the bishops' initiative. The regime furiously attacked Cardinal Wyszynski and tried to the fullest to exploit the resentment shown by some of the faithful.

Not unexpectedly, it was the rural population that primarily gave support to the Catholic Church. Despite intensive atheistic propaganda, the great majority of the peasants (83.3 per cent) professed religious beliefs,[25] and recognized the Church as an intrinsic part of their lives. Their deep faith, imbued with the inseparable mixture of emotionalism and nationalism, committed them to the Church, which, in turn, relied on the peasantry for its existence and activities.

A similar outlook pervaded the communist party in its relationship with the urban proletariat. The party claimed its authority to govern by affiliating itself with the workers whose importance as a class was then stressed as a matter of ideological and practical necessity.[26] It goes without saying that in this relationship the proletariat became the adjunct of the party, not the party the servant of the proletariat. Outwardly this method gave

24. Both texts in *Oredzie Biskupow Polskich do Biskupow Niemieckich* (Warsaw, 1966).

25. Stanislaw Markiewicz, *Sprzecznosci we Wspolczesnym Katolicyzmie* (Warsaw, 1964), p. 129.

26. For example, Wladyslaw Gomulka, *O Naszej Partii* (Warsaw, 1969), p. 684.

an appearance of unity and power. Inwardly, however, the bond between the masses and their self-proclaimed leaders was weak and constant efforts were required to keep the workers' loyalty.

But the communist leadership, with a surprising lack of realistic insight into the situation, weakened its own endeavor by paying more attention to theory than to real issues. Instead of concentrating on reasoned arguments, they either engaged in abstract debates about "the building of socialism" or indulged in emotional quarrels over who was more patriotic. The workers were convinced that socialism was, in some large sense, for their ultimate benefit. But this awareness was severely tested when they discovered that the communist leaders often adopted pragmatic policies at odds with the principles they preached.

In the first place, the workers realized that the creation of a socialist state and their own professed elevation to the status of the "ruling class" have not radically improved their position in the structure of the society, or given them a dominant voice in the operations of governmental bodies and of the national economy. Despite constant recitations of the ideological role they were supposedly to play, their function was limited merely to that of manpower. The nationalization, which apparently made them co-owners of the means of production, left them in the old place of hired hands subordinated to a management in which they had no direct participation. The institutions, manifestly created for the realization of their class needs and aspirations, became "one-way transmission belts," submissive to political bureaucracy and totally incapable "not only of defending the interest of the workers, but even of mediating in conflict" [27] between the masses and the ruling elite.

Secondly, the workers discovered a dismaying neglect of their living and working conditions. Like the rest of the population, they suffered from overcrowded housing, high prices, and deficient supplies. A representative poll conducted among the workers revealed that a majority of them (62 per cent) felt that the national income was not justly distributed.[28] In addition, they were deeply hurt by low wages, unjust distribution of premiums and bonuses, bad organization and unrealistic norms of work, poor quality of work safety and hygiene measures, as well as other shortcom-

27. Franco Fabiani in *L'Unita*, February 24, 1971, as reported by Kevin Devlin, "Italian Communists Analyze Polish Crisis," *RFE, Italy: Party Affairs* (March 1, 1971), p. 2.

28. Jan Wojtaszek, "Struktura klasowa w swiadomosci spolecznej," in Stanislaw Widerszpil (ed.), *Socjologiczne problemy przemyslu i klasy robotniczej* (Warsaw, 1966), p. 189.

ings. It soon became evident that the working masses were falling into a general mood of frustration and resentment. Clearly, the communist leaders had failed where they were most convinced of success and where they needed it first. Consequently, they found themselves in great danger where they had felt most secure.

Such a review of problems, though only touching upon a few selected areas, clearly indicates that societal tensions existed and that open conflicts were inevitable. The most dramatic of these conflicts were the student riots in March 1968 and the workers' revolt in December 1970.

The 1968 crisis began with the intellectuals. Ironically, these were the men who in 1956 had paved the way for Gomulka. Later, however, Gomulka disassociated himself from their "revisionist" ideas and reimposed stringent yokes on their creativity. The curbs exercised by unimaginative and suspicious bureaucrats, often the remnants of the Stalinist period, had caused a deep sense of frustration and insecurity. In addition, but contrary to official claims, many intellectuals had been unable to secure an income adequate to meet the demands of decent existence.

The protests of intellectuals against the political stagnation and ideological sterility of Gomulkaism were very important in rallying dissident students. Whether or not the youngsters shared the views of their elders, they fully equaled them in their restiveness. The causes of the students' unrest were complex. Many of them, even if only for the sake of self-interest, pressed for meaningful economic reform. Many, reflecting the desires of the intellectuals, demanded the democratization of the political system. Almost all of them desired changes in the system of college admissions and in the distribution of stipends and scholarships. They wanted also the improvement of professional opportunities for university graduates and better financial compensation for people with college degrees.

Their protest took various forms, from freewheeling discussions to the formulation of political programs, the most symptomatic of which was the "Open Letter" circulated by Kuron and Modzelewski in 1966. Critically evaluating the party from within, these two young communists blamed their party for the "class rule" of communist bureaucracy and called for its replacement by "workers' democracy." [29]

The authorities met the students' challenge, like that of the intellectuals, by resorting to repression. The outcome, however, was not what the party wanted to achieve. On the contrary, the repressive measures only resulted

29. Text in George Lavan Weissman (ed.), *Revolutionary Marxist Students in Poland Speak Out (1964–1968)* (New York, 1968), pp. 15–90.

in bringing closer together two lines of dissent: that of the intellectuals and of the students. The situation became highly explosive.

The fuse was lit when the authorities banned further public performance of the nineteenth-century Mickiewicz play *Forefathers' Eve*, which had certain anti-Russian overtones. In protest, the intellectuals passed resolutions condemning the "excesses" of censorship and accusing the party of ruining Polish cultural life; the students took to the streets, at first in Warsaw and then in other university cities throughout the country.

One cannot escape the impression that Gomulka was seriously concerned about the possibility of workers joining hands with the students. If they had, the situation might well have gotten quickly out of hand. To prevent such a development, Gomulka adopted repressive violence and incredible tricks, including the "anti-Zionist" witchhunt, which ultimately succeeded in keeping these two groups apart and in containing the rioting students.

At the same time, a long mounting power struggle within the party came to the fore and split the communist leadership into contending factions. The Polish communist party was faced with the greatest crisis since 1956.

III

In 1968 the facade of the Polish United Workers' party looked very impressive. Its membership had risen from a 1959 low of 1,023,000 members and candidates to a new height of 2,030,000. In the last four years alone 700,000 new recruits were added to the party roster, among them 383,000 workers and 118,000 peasants. The rapid growth of membership, however, created a number of ambiguous benefits.

As the party expanded, its ranks were swelled with the newcomers who now clearly dominated the 390,000 old-timers who had been members before the 1948 "unification" with the socialist party. Many of the new recruits joined the party for utilitarian reasons, such as authority, career, or economic advantages. Consequently, they were less concerned with the party's ideological objectives than with the preservation of its power position in order to advance their own interests. It is no wonder that the party was riddled with cynicism, opportunism, and corruption. The extent of these vices is best illustrated by the fact that in a six-month period in 1966, 17,000 members and 14,000 candidates were expelled from the party, mainly for "economic crimes," ranging from petty thefts to huge swindles such as the notorious "meat scandal" in Warsaw.

The lack of ideological zeal was no obstacle to advancement within the party. In fact, the nonidealists formed the mainstay of the party and the backbone of its apparatus, especially at the middle level. Interested in the success of the party as a vehicle of personal aggrandizement, they were in the eyes of the party leaders more reliable and trustworthy than the idealists with their supersensitivity to ideological overtones and their inflexibility in pragmatic matters. But in return the party had to absorb this group, heavily loaded with conservatism, prejudices, and resentment to all innovations. In addition, the educational level of many members was rather low,[30] contributing to the parochialism and the anti-intellectual bias of the party as a whole.

The social composition of the party lost its proletarian character with the decline of manual laborers from 60 per cent in 1949 to 40.2 per cent in 1968. This happened as a result of two coinciding occurrences. Despite strenuous efforts and recent successes, the party failed to attract the masses of workers. The failure was particularly marked, since industrialization has brought about a considerable increase in the proportion of workers in the population. At the same time, with economic and administrative tasks overriding the political role of the party, party leaders had to recruit into the party, and subsequently into the party apparatus, better educated individuals, especially from among young engineers, technicians, economists, business administrators, and social scientists. The extent of their success was illustrated by the steady rise of white-collar workers from 17.3 per cent in 1949 to 43 per cent in 1968. But success had its drawbacks as well: it not only spoiled the proletarian makeup of the party, but it also injected into the party apparatus an element of possible trouble, for the better educated might not pay the same unquestionable obedience to the party leaders as had their less qualified predecessors.

Nor was this all. The numerical growth of the party resulted in its rejuvenation. During the first quarter of 1966 alone, over 46,000 members and candidates were admitted, and 40 per cent of these were under the age of twenty-five. By contrast, the top party leadership remained in the hands of old, prewar communists, with the average age of the Politburo members being sixty. Quite obviously this generation gap, aggravated by differences in education, provided a fertile ground for internal frictions and factional activities.

Life at the top was strongly competitive. The highest leaders, while more or less united in basic values and common interests, were constantly involved in a power struggle to take over the place occupied by Gomulka.

30. Only 7.5 per cent of members are university graduates and 26.4 per cent completed high schools. Czeslaw Herod, "Struktura spoleczno-zawodowa PZPR," *Nowe Drogi*, no. 2 (261) (February 1971), 82.

As far as one can infer from outward signs, two men offered themselves as alternatives to the old leader. One was Edward Gierek, the first secretary of the party in Silesia and a Politburo member. The other was General Mieczyslaw Moczar, an alternate member of the Politburo and one of the nine secretaries of the Central Committee in charge of security and the armed forces.

Gierek's power base was in Upper Silesia. This province was, in economic terms, the most important region of Poland, turning out about one-fifth of the total industrial production. Although the area occupied only 3 per cent of the state's territory, it was inhabited by 11 per cent of the population. In Poland's specific situation, it was very important that Gierek controlled the province with the highest concentration of workers in the country and – what was of even greater significance – that the provincial party organization of Upper Silesia, with over a quarter-million members, was the largest in Poland. Gierek was personally credited with economic successes in the province which allowed its inhabitants to enjoy a higher than average standard of living. Consequently, he was quite popular among the Silesian population as well as among many workers throughout the country. He was also respected by the technocrats who had a high opinion of his economic and organizational abilities. In matters political, such as democratization, nationalism, and relations with the Soviet Union, his views were not much different from those of Gomulka.

Moczar had a heterogeneous, loosely knit following. Its inner cadre was formed by the so-called "partisans," bound primarily by the old ties of comradeship forged in the wartime underground, by similar dislikes of intellectuals and liberals, and by a common appetite for power which was denied them by the "muscovites," i.e., the communists who had entered Poland with the Soviet army. Since many among the "muscovites" were Jews, Moczar took a strong anti-Semitic line, hoping to fill resultant vacancies with his own men. In his bid for increased authority, Moczar counted on his comrades in the army and in the security apparatus who occupied many important posts. He was also favored by the lower and middle echelons of the bureaucracy whose members felt an affinity with Moczar because of his proletarian background and because his drive for power promised them a chance of personal advancement. In addition, Moczar built his own popular base in the Union of Fighters for Freedom and Democracy which included ex-servicemen, old revolutionaries, political prisoners, members of the anti-Nazi underground, and former inmates of Hitler's concentration camps who were of both communist and noncommunist leanings. To unite these diverse people into an effective operational instrument, Moczar sought to consolidate their attitudes by the injection of heavy doses of patriotism and nationalism.

Growing tensions within the country provided both factions with an opportunity for a direct challenge to Gomulka. The "partisans" were the first to act.

IV

More proof is needed to support the thesis that General Moczar and his "partisans" had provoked the students' unrest in March 1968. The banning of the *Forefathers' Eve* might have been caused by the intervention of the Soviet Embassy, irritated by public reactions to the play; the step might have been taken by other authorities of their own volition. One cannot, however, dismiss the possibility that the censor's decision and the highly provocative behavior of the militia, mysteriously called to disperse the protesting crowd, were deliberately aimed at creating a "crisis atmosphere" [31] in which a group ready for action could attempt to gain control of the party. Since it was the "partisans" who synchronized their launch for power with student unrest, it may well be assumed either that they concocted the whole affair, or – at least – that they were aware of the developments leading to the outburst. It is very likely that Moczar, as the head of the security police, was able to get information to which no one else had access.

The main tactical device of the "partisans" was the phantom of Zionist conspiracy. Gomulka swallowed the bait and with his blessing alleged plotters were expelled from the party and the state apparatus. As might be expected, the culprits were sought not only among the Jews, but also among other real or suspected rivals, including "liberals" and ex-socialists.

Shortly afterward, however, Gomulka realized that the anti-Jewish campaign was tied up with the intraparty struggle for power and that its outcome had scarcely strengthened his position. Thus he decided to interfere and to moderate the anti-Zionist theme. At about this time, Gierek, who at first also had jumped on the anti-Zionist bandwagon and for a while had presented himself as an independent contender for power, came around and sided with Gomulka. Finally the Russians also threw their support behind Gomulka. This was the turning point. The scales were tipped in Gomulka's favor and he made full use of the chance to reconsolidate his authority in the party. The Soviet-led invasion of Czechoslovakia further strengthened his position.

31. A. Ross Johnson, "Poland: End of an Era?" *Problems of Communism*, 19, no. 1 (January–February 1970), 32.

It would be wrong to assume that Polish participation in the invasion of Czechoslovakia was merely an outcome of the domestic power struggle. Certainly it was not. It was primarily an expression of Poland's dependency upon the Soviet Union and a proof of the Polish leaders' loyalty to the Kremlin. It also reflected Gomulka's genuine concern with the Czechoslovak crisis. He feared that the Czechoslovak communist party had lost its leading position, and, if this were true, the future of socialism in Czechoslovakia would be seriously jeopardized. He also suspected – no matter what his rationalization might have been – that Czechoslovakia was being infiltrated by West Germany, thus exposing Poland to the same danger of encirclement that had been so fatal to national survival in 1939. Of course, whatever the reasons, Gomulka was not the man to let the opportunity of strengthening his position go by.

The confirmation of Gomulka's success came at the Fifth Party Congress in November 1968. Gomulka was praised by all speakers, including the chief Soviet guest Mr. Brezhnev, and was reelected first secretary. At the same time other changes took place in the highest party bodies, apparently reflecting Gomulka's wishes, but, in fact, indicating that his victory at the Congress was achieved at a definite price. First of all, he had to give in to the pressures from below and to permit the inclusion of younger *apparatchiks* in the top party leadership. Symptomatically, they were not only younger, but they also represented a new style of leadership. They were much better educated, and, although hardly "liberals," they were less dogmatic. Because they were more aware of the complexity of Polish problems and were more inclined to seek their solutions along new lines, they became known as the "pragmatists."

The post-Congress period once again revealed the complexity of the Polish situation. On one hand there appeared some signs of hope in domestic and foreign relations. There were indications that the strained Church-state relationship was undergoing quiet improvement. Cardinal Wyszynski was again allowed trips to Rome, and several articles [32] were published in the official press emphasizing the community of interest between believers and nonbelievers in Poland and even indicating that a papal visit to Poland might now be possible.

There is little doubt that the governmental decision to open negotiations with Bonn, which ultimately led to the signing, on December 7, 1970, of the treaty sanctioning Poland's western boundary and normalizing Polish-German relations, can also be considered an example of positive develop-

32. For example, Andrzej Tokarczyk, in *Glos Pracy*, May 22, 1969.

ments. For Poland, as well as for the rest of Europe, nothing but good can come of this important act. Of course the problem is not, as yet, ultimately solved. West Germany could facilitate the process by ratifying without delay the treaty. Poland could do the same by taking a less rigid approach to the German question, especially to intra-German relations and, above all, by lifting a heavy burden of past mistrust and prejudice.

Despite these indications of hope, there were a number of disturbing occurrences. The harsh measures taken against the intellectuals and students continued unabated, accompanied by an intense campaign against "revisionism," "liberalism," "bourgeois escapism," etc. The most outspoken critics among the writers were purged, and the most rebellious students were expelled from colleges, conscripted into the army, or sentenced to prison terms in a wave of show trials, which have continued into the seventies. Over one hundred faculty members at Warsaw University and many more at other colleges throughout the country were dismissed from their posts. The traditional autonomy of academic institutions was abolished and ideological education at colleges has been intensified. A new admissions and scholarship policy was formulated favoring allegedly "reliable" candidates from worker and peasant families.

Characteristically, the use of administrative measures toward ideologically nonconformist individuals and groups was — as it appears — approved by all factions at the top. Of course, it did not mean that their differences in other areas were eliminated, or that the rivalries for power abandoned. On the contrary, the reshuffling of the leadership at the Fifth Congress only added a new competitive element to the circle of old contenders.

Perhaps it was the euphoria of diplomatic success that blunted Gomulka's awareness of the realities at home. Perhaps the party apparatus at the center failed — for a variety of reasons — to impress upon him the gravity of domestic developments and in particular of the growing mood of despair among the workers. Perhaps he felt secure behind the shield of the Brezhnev doctrine. Whatever the reasons, the decision to radically increase the prices of foodstuffs, fuel, and many other goods acted like the proverbial match thrown into a barrel of gunpowder. The explosion violently shook the entire Polish political system and marked the end of the Gomulka era.

The increases, which were announced ten days before Christmas 1970, as if deliberately to provoke a reaction, triggered a chain of disorders that started with riots in the Gdansk shipyards, leaped to other cities along the Baltic coast (Gdynia, Sopot, Elblag, Slupsk, and Szczecin), and gradually spread, by such various methods as petitioning and sit-down strikes, to many industrial centers in the country, including Warsaw where a general strike was scheduled for December 21. What Poland then faced was not just isolated disturbances centered on local grievances, but a nationwide breakdown involving issues which affected the broad mass of the population.

The crisis was marked by a number of significant characteristics, the first of which was its unquestionable political nature. This was due not only — as Marxists might argue — to an innate relationship between economics and politics, or to the fact that in Poland, as in all socialist states, the communist party is directly and wholly responsible for all economic decisions, but above all to clearly political demands raised by the protesting workers. The protesters asked for equal treatment of all citizens regardless of their views, for broader cooperation between the party and the society, for the proper division of jurisdiction between the party and the state administration, for a more effective functioning of the parliament, for freely elected workers' councils, and for a number of similar actions. But, there were no publicly expressed demands for the abolition of the socialist system, nor were anti-Soviet sentiments voiced openly.

Another interesting feature was the essentially proletarian character of the outburst. It started with the shipyards hands and dockers, and most workers rallied around them in the following days. Other social groups, especially the intelligentsia and the students, on the whole remained aloof. Perhaps the repressions of 1968 were still fresh in their minds, or perhaps they were isolated from the working class by deeper reasons.

In any case, the workers' rebellion demonstrated that this class had successfully absorbed the influx of postwar rural newcomers and had once again achieved a high degree of unity and group consciousness. It also revealed the political maturity of the workers who were able to call into existence their own form of organization and their own channels of communication and command. Obviously, the lessons of history had not been lost on them, and they were aware of the possibilities offered by the creation of "dual power." [33]

The crisis of 1970 also demonstrated the extraordinary weaknesses of Poland's political system. Among these deficiencies were the following: the striking blindness of the communist rulers to the plurality of interests in modern society; the "downright incapacity of the Polish Party to create . . . an authentic mass basis";[34] the unreasonable concentration of po-

33. Leopold Labedz, "From Poznan to Gdansk," *Interplay* (March 1971), p. 23.

34. Giuliano Procacci, in Devlin, "Italian Communists Analyze Polish Crisis," p. 23.

litical power in the hands of a small oligarchy, which was weakened by the struggles of the cliques and was prone to domination by a "charismatic" leader; and, the highly authoritarian and repressive methods used on all levels of an excessively large and ossified bureaucracy. The crisis exposed the basic truth observed by Milovan Djilas that every form of communism breeds its own Stalinism.[35]

The December events made clear the tactics used by the ruling communist elite when confronted with a crisis. At first, the authorities responded to the emergency with threats and repressions as well as with the usual rhetoric declaring that the unrest was caused by "hooligans" and other "anarchistic and criminal," or "unpatriotic" elements. When, however, the attempts to terrorize the workers failed, some party leaders decided to appease the angry masses by putting the blame on Gomulka and by eliminating him from the decision-making circle. One can easily imagine that Gomulka and his associates (Kliszko, Spychalski, Strzelecki) were not too happy with this solution, but they were powerless against the Gierek-Moczar forces who joined hands and pushed through their stratagem. It is still impossible to obtain information complete enough to ascertain the true course of events; there are rumors of an anti-Gomulka conspiracy, of his house arrest, of Moscow's refusal to intervene on his behalf, and many others. Whatever the case, on December 20, 1970, an extraordinary meeting of the Central Committee relieved "Comrade Wieslaw" of his post as first secretary and replaced him with Gierek.

The new era did not begin in the most enviable situation. The problems Gierek had to face were many and major. Paradoxically, not a few of them were the product of policies in which he had directly participated in the past.

In the first place, Gierek had to restore order in the Baltic provinces and get the strikers back to work. One must admit that he handled these immediate tasks with admirable zeal. Not only did he lift the state of emergency, lower prices, increase the wages of the lowest paid workers, shelve the controversial wage scheme, and order an inquiry into the incidents, but he went personally to the Szczecin and Gdansk workers, admitted to them that they were right to voice their dissatisfaction, and pledged to give them a real say in public affairs.

Secondly, Gierek also has moved to gain the support of the peasantry. A more imaginative program aimed at overcoming the difficulties in agriculture by restoring the confidence of private farmers was undertaken.

35. Milovan Djilas, "Wnioski z polskiego grudnia," *Kultura* (Paris), no. 3 (1971), 51.

The abolition of unpopular compulsory deliveries of grain, potatoes, and livestock, effective from January 1972, was announced. At the same time the improvement of health and other social services in the rural areas was promised.

But this is not all. With the sensitivity of a subtle politician, he allowed the rebuilding of the old royal castle in Warsaw and made concessions to the Catholic Church. Without question, both moves were bound to create a favorable impression on the Polish population as a whole and to regain some of the support lost by the ruling elite during the December crisis.

At the same time, Gierek came a few steps nearer to the consolidation of his power within the Politburo. In the post-December shake-up, he got rid of all of Gomulka's close associates, with the exception of Jozef Cyrankiewicz, a perennial opportunist, who was kicked upstairs from the position of prime minister to the primarily honorific office of chairman of the State Council, and of Stefan Jedrychowski, the minister of foreign affairs. He also chipped away at the position of General Moczar whose apparent illness was used to strip him of his responsibility as director of the army and security forces. The event aroused widespread speculation that this may mark the end of Moczar as a serious contender for power.

So far, Gierek has been cautious in enlarging his own group, which consists of a few older conspirators (Kruczek and Jaroszewicz) and a number of younger *apparatchiks* (Babiuch, Olszowski, Szydlak, and Tejchma) who lent him their support against Gomulka. It may be expected, however, that the next party Congress, called for December of 1971, will provide a chance for Gierek to further improve his position. The stage for this major coup has been set with the creation of the pre-Congress Commission, whose members are usually elected to the Central Committee, which in turn appoints the Politburo. Among the ninety-three members of this body, there are a great many men whom Gierek elevated after December to important posts in the central and provincial party apparatus.

Yet it would be premature to assume that the factional power struggle is over. The decline of Moczar may cause some disarray in the ranks of his supporters, but it will not put an end to their ambitions. They still occupy a fair share of influential positions, especially in the army and security forces, and they have a broad base in the Union of Fighters for Freedom and Democracy, which has over 350,000 members and whose activities enjoy considerable popularity among the Polish people. It is hard to believe that being so strong the group will just fade away.

There is also a possibility that the Stalinist faction, which was reduced after 1956 to a political nonentity, may use Gomulka's downfall for a quiet comeback. The inclusion of Zenon Nowak, once a powerful leader of this group, in the official delegation to the Twenty-fourth Congress of the Communist party of the Soviet Union as well as his appointment to an important ambassadorial post in Moscow, might be taken as an indication of the Stalinist revival. The rumors [36] of a new faction being built up around Wladyslaw Kruczek add fuel to this speculation. This sixty-year-old member of the Politburo, who is also the boss of trade unions, was closely linked to the Stalinist group in 1956 and is known for his obsession with revisionism.

But of paramount importance is the presence in the Politburo of a bloc of younger *apparatchiks* whose support may be a crucial factor for Gierek. Some of them, like Tejchma, were brought to the top by Gomulka, but became disillusioned with his performance and consequently deserted when the December crisis offered an opportune moment. Others, such as Babiuch, advanced to the summit in reward for supporting the anti-Gomulka drive. These *apparatchiks* do not form a unified group, but represent the same managerial type of political activists and have a similar pragmatic approach to socioeconomic problems. Coming from the middle echelon of the party, they are familiar with the entrenched apparatus at all levels and might possibly gain influence among the lower functionaries remaining under the spell of Moczar. Their age (between thirty-seven and fifty) puts them in a most advantageous position since time is on their side. Meanwhile, they could work in unison with Gierek or, as a matter of fact, with anybody who will respect their abilities and aspirations. Barring the unexpected, their chances for intraparty victory look very promising indeed.

But capturing control of the decision-making structure in a factional struggle and ruling over a nation are two completely different propositions. Governing the Polish people in the seventies will be a very difficult task, and success will depend ultimately on the ability of the masters to legitimize their leadership in the eyes of the masses. To achieve this end, the leaders must dispel widespread apathy, raise the standards of living, solve outstanding economic problems, and improve Poland's position vis-à-vis the Soviet Union. All these goals are not easy to reach.

For many years, the conviction has been growing among the Polish people that their communist rulers are failing to take full advantage of all potential possibilities offered Poland by her resources and by international configurations. Some ascribed this inertia to the personal shortcomings of Gomulka and his coterie; others – perhaps a majority – questioned the

36. *Economist*, May 22–28, 1971, p. 37.

capabilities of the political system. The net effect was the same: passivity, stagnation, and a degrading moral atmosphere. The mood of resignation spread to all segments of Polish society and grew with each consecutive year. Even the younger generation has not been free from its effects, especially since March 1968.

However justified, the situation is dangerous not only to the careers of communist rulers, but to the future of Poland as well. Gierek seems to understand the peril and has made great efforts to overcome it, to mobilize the society, and to release its energy: hence, his promise of a "dialogue" with the people, as well as the party's attempts to start a "campaign for truth" and to forge "links with the masses"; hence, the canvassing of the country by party leaders and the unending consultations with the workers and farmers, intellectuals and students, and even the bishops. To a certain extent, Gierek has succeeded and has induced some positive feelings toward his leadership. But the attitude was far from the enthusiasm that had greeted the coming of Gomulka in 1956. The people have remained sober; Gierek must earn their support not by words, but by deeds.

When one considers Gierek's attempts to create a new climate and to draw forensic veils over the past, one is inclined to wish he had selected a better target for such zeal. The promised investigation of the tragic December events has not materialized and the much talked about "personal responsibility" has never been invoked. The democratization which was emphasized so eagerly has been reduced to "correcting mistakes" in the system. A functional separation between the party and the government, discussed earlier, remains in the sphere of generalities and the leading role of the party is stressed as strongly as ever. Institutional guarantees in the form of freely elected bodies, especially workers' councils, once again have become only empty promises. It is small wonder that the people retain doubts about the actual willingness of Gierek's leadership to institute popularly supported reforms and to introduce any significant change in the political system.

The people, however, pass judgment on the rulers primarily on the basis of economic well-being. In this area, there are promising signs that Gierek already has started moving in a desirable direction, and it is quite certain that the regime will make life more tolerable for the people. The traditional excessive investment in heavy industry has been diverted toward consumer goods and housing, and ten specialist "task forces" study various subjects to prepare recommendations which, it is hoped, will improve the effectiveness of the economy. The purpose of these measures is to produce more in quantity as well as in quality. To do it, however, is not a simple matter. In Poland, as in other communist-ruled countries, a specific economic structure was created which makes the introduction of a more viable model very difficult.[37] In general, the change would require considerable investments for which domestic capital is scarce. In many cases, it would call for the closing down of some enterprises, or even for the elimination of certain branches of industry. In addition, it would demand the shifting of resources and labor, a move extremely unpopular among the workers, and significant increases in labor productivity, which cannot be accomplished without the import of advanced technology from the West.[38] This, again, could not be done without gaining greater freedom from the Soviet Union.

It is a characteristic peculiar to the Polish situation that domestic issues are always overshadowed by foreign politics.[39] Since the end of World War II, Poland's relations with the Soviet Union have weighed heavily upon internal developments. This dependency is acutely felt by the Polish people, who resent the status of a satellite, although they appreciate Soviet protection vis-à-vis Germany. Gierek would tremendously increase his popular appeal if he could receive from the Soviets a guarantee of greater freedom.[40] The years to come may improve the chances for such a demand, since the Soviet Union has an urgent interest in the stabilization of the regimes it has established in Eastern Europe. And, the growing Sino-Soviet conflict may provide an additional push in the same direction.

Failure to achieve significant gains in the domestic and foreign spheres may be fatal not only to Gierek (or whoever rules Poland in the future) and to the nation, but to the international environment as well. It would increase the tempo of retrogressive instability, and should the conditions become unbearable, another eruption may take place with unpredictable consequences. As past experience has shown, serious internal disruption in the socialist world could lead to grave setbacks in the process of international détente and to a renewal of an ominous arms race. The future is assuredly fraught with danger.

37. Z. M. Fallenbuchl, "From the Extensive to the Intensive Strategy of Economic Development in the Soviet Union and Eastern Europe," paper read at the April 1970 conference of the Michigan Academy of Arts and Sciences.

38. Richard V. Burks, *Technological Innovation and Political Change in Communist Eastern Europe* (Santa Monica, Calif., 1969).

39. As persuasively argued by Adam Bromke, *Poland's Politics: Idealism or Realism* (Cambridge, Mass., 1967).

40. For the impact of the workers' outburst in 1970 upon Polish-Soviet relations see, Adam Bromke, "Beyond the Gomulka Era," *Foreign Affairs*, 49, no. 3 (April 1971), 480–92.

6

Hungary

BY FERENC A. VALI

The dramatic ouster of Nikita Khrushchev in October 1964 gave rise to a more acute alarm in Hungary than in any other Soviet bloc country of East-Central Europe. The Soviet leader was considered the "founding father" of the communist regime which came to power after the Revolution of 1956, a regime popularly known in and outside Hungary as the Kadar regime after its eponymic leader, Janos Kadar. It was Khrushchev who had chosen Kadar to become the head of the party and government in the Soviet city of Uzhgorod during the climactic days of early November 1956. It was this government which had "asked" for the second massive Soviet intervention and was eventually installed by Soviet forces in Budapest in mid-November.[1]

Khrushchev had been Kadar's mentor from then on. During the following seven years he visited Hungary several times, more often than any other country of the Soviet commonwealth. The Soviet premier's last visit to Budapest was in the spring of 1964. Most characteristically for the aims of the Kadar regime, he told workers that it was incorrect to believe that revolution was the only thing of significance. Instead, he said, "the important thing is that we should have more to eat – good goulash – schools, housing and ballet. . . ." [2] We may also assume that the same recipe for the successful building of socialism in Hungary was imparted by Khrushchev to his disciple Kadar; if used correctly, this recipe could forestall the need for another comradely assistance to Hungary by her Soviet protectors.

Following Khrushchev's removal from office the Hungarians feared

1. See Ferenc A. Vali, *Rift and Revolt in Hungary – Nationalism versus Communism* (Cambridge, Mass., 1961), pp. 369–73.

2. *New York Times,* April 2, 1964.

that the position of Kadar and the postrevolutionary leadership would be affected by the upheaval in the Kremlin. The people were apprehensive that the change might herald a return of pro-Stalinist elements, including Matyas Rakosi, the Hungarian Stalin, a Soviet resident since his ouster in 1956 who was known to have been bombarding the Soviet leadership with memoranda suggesting how to control Hungary.

However, Kadar, upon returning from Warsaw where he had learned of his political godfather's eviction, was able to reassure his adherents and the Hungarian public that his policies would be continued.

I

After the Revolution of 1956, Kadar was the most hated man in Hungary, for he had betrayed the revolutionary movement to which he had given his word and had executed Imre Nagy, the revolutionary prime minister. It is certainly ironic that, after only eight years, Kadar has become associated with the more liberal type of communism which Hungary has been allowed to enjoy since the early sixties.

Indeed, Kadar had passed through a number of metamorphoses during his career, transformations which may variously be considered as evidence of mediocrity and weakness of character, or of flexibility or duplicity. Kadar's many changes may also be explained by the special character of the Hungarian scene after the 1956 revolt and by the Soviet desire to prevent similar outbreaks in the future. Finally, Kadar can be regarded as a contrast to the ugly forces represented by Rakosi, just as Khrushchev was at pains to create an image of himself which was different from that of Stalin. Although Kadar lacks the vanity and sadism of Rakosi, he nevertheless is ambitious and opportunistic. However, he does listen to advice. As a leader he possesses no charisma and makes no pretension of practicing the "cult of personality."

The experience Kadar undoubtedly has acquired during the ups and downs of his career (he was jailed by Rakosi from 1951 to 1954 and suffered torture) taught him to follow three political guidelines: never to oppose the Soviet comrades; never to allow the undermining of party power; and, subject to these two primary requirements, to seek a popular base of support. In the wake of the Revolution of 1956 and upon Soviet advice, he applied terror and cruel oppression.[3] Subsequently, however, and again following Soviet advice and his own common sense, he began to "human-

3. For the hesitant and subsequently cruelly oppressive attitude of the Kadar regime see Vali, *Rift and Revolt*, pp. 390–99.

ize" the regime, as far as such "humanization" was compatible with the party rule and acceptable to Moscow. He was prudent enough to be led by his counsel of associates which held moderate views and fought both the Stalinists and the revisionists.

Kadar was able to rid himself of some members of his original clique: demagogues like Gyorgy Marosan, incompetents like Istvan Kossa, and outright terrorists like Imre Dogei.[4] He systematically tried to surround himself not only with men who generally shared his views, but also with technical experts, some of them old party members, some new converts to the party, and some even nonparty specialists.

The first secretaryship of the party (the Hungarian Socialist Workers' party, as the communist party was renamed during the revolution) remained in the hands of Kadar, but the post of chairman of the Council of Ministers was, except for short periods, left to one of his trusted lieutenants. One of these, Ferenc Munich, was phased out because of old age; another, Gyula Kallai, proved too moderate a success and was shunted off in April 1967 to the more innocuous presidency of the National Assembly. He was replaced by Jeno Fock, the party's managerial expert.

The changes in posts in April 1967 also involved Istvan Dobi, the chairman of the Presidential Council (titular head of state), a perennial puppet who had sworn in all the governments before, during, and after the revolution. A former member of the Smallholders party, then admitted for his "merits" into the communist party, Dobi was known for his devotion to excessive drinking. He died within a year of his replacement by Pal Losonczi, a former minister of agriculture. Of peasant stock, Losonczi, like Dobi, represents the peasant element in the top leadership. It is worth remembering that the government has retained its official name adopted in 1956: the Revolutionary Worker-Peasant Government.

The principal acolytes of Kadar, whether filling high party or governmental posts, are almost all economic, managerial, or *agit-prop* (agitation-propaganda) experts. Besides Kadar, the prominent Politburo members include Fock, Losonczi, Bela Biszku (formerly minister of the interior, later second secretary of the Central Committee, and cadre specialist), Rezso Nyers (former minister of finance, then the top economic expert of the party), Lajos Feher (an agricultural expert), Antal Apro (once a Stalinist, and after 1956 the Hungarian contact with Comecon), Zoltan Komocsin (the ideological expert), and Sandor Gaspar (the Trade Union leader).

4. All three persons were present when the original Kadar government was formed in Uzhgorod.

Kadar is relatively young (having been born in 1912). Despite constant rumors that his health is shaky, no ominous crisis of succession seems to threaten the Hungarian party, at least not for the time being, as it does several other Soviet bloc parties. It appears, nevertheless, that the second man in command and therefore Kadar's potential successor is Biszku, who is not much younger than Kadar himself.

Kadar inherited the *apparat* trained under Rakosi and has still to operate with many Stalinist-type functionaries, especially on the middle and lower party organization levels. Most of these old-time *apparatchiks* can be regarded as "dogmatists," and the present leadership has had to wage a subtle, but constant struggle against their attempts to oppose or to slow down some of the innovations initiated by experts or more liberal-minded leaders.

Kadar has emphasized several times that he has had to conduct a "two-front struggle" against both leftists and rightists of the party. His last utterance to this effect was in a December 1969 interview with Giuseppe Boffa, editor of the Italian communist newspaper *L'Unita.*[5]

On February 5, 1961, a three-line communiqué by the Hungarian Telegram Agency revealed that Rakosi had died at Gorky at the age of seventy-nine. He had been permitted to return to Hungary in 1969, but soon he returned to Russia for medical treatment where he died in hospital. The Hungarian leadership preferred to pass over his death without further comment.

Some of the former pro-Rakosi Stalinists were, however, allowed to return to leading positions, although after the revolution Kadar had stated that they would never be admitted to directing posts. Naturally, the leadership examined each individual case to see whether the person in question would prove reliable. Thus Bela Szalai, who together with the other Stalinists spent more than two years in exile in the Soviet Union, staged a comeback as deputy minister of foreign trade.

Another and more paradoxical case is that of Rakosi's prime minister, Andras Hegedus, who also had taken refuge in the Soviet Union during the 1956 revolution, but who, upon his return to Hungary, devoted himself to academic preoccupations, primarily to the study of sociology. Surprisingly, he revealed himself as an ardent "revisionist," the "sin" for which he was several times reprimanded; he still manages to retain his party membership.[6]

5. The interview was also published in *Magyar Hirek*, December 13, 1969.

6. On Andras Hegedus and his views see *Studies in Comparative Communism*, 2,

Although some former Stalinists were permitted to return to leading positions, the Kadar regime continues to distrust former sympathizers of the revolutionary Prime Minister Imre Nagy because they are considered anti-Soviet. Even if readmitted to the party, they are given only low positions.

While denying power to all those who did not follow Kadarism, that is, the centrist road, the regime has – as in the case of Hegedus – shown considerable tolerance of the expression of quasi-revisionist views. Accordingly, some oral and even printed deviationist opinions are being expressed with relative impunity even though the culprits may be censured or may find further promotion blocked.[7] But anti-Soviet or "counterrevolutionary" attitudes or "conspiracies" (and the term is still given a very broad interpretation), whether "imperialist" or "pro-Chinese," not only are condemned, but their protagonists are prosecuted. In 1965 members of a "counterrevolutionary" organization with the alleged purpose of restoring the Catholic Democratic People's party were sentenced to long prison terms. On the other hand, members of a pro-Chinese student group, led by Gabor Revai (son of Jozsef Revai, left-wing ideologist under Rakosi), were also sentenced.[8]

The security police, still very active though more discreet, is strictly controlled by the party. Political trials, though less frequent than in Rakosi's time and after the revolution, are still held *in camera*, and Kadar himself admitted that despite the much heralded amnesty of 1963 there remained "several hundred" political prisoners serving sentences.[9]

Second to the principle of strict obedience to Moscow is Kadar's determination to uphold party control. He learned this lesson while witnessing the disintegration of the communist party during the last days of October 1956. He has resolved "never to give up power," and to uphold this resolution, he is ready to fight against the right and the left, both against "revisionists" (most of the intellectuals in the party may be considered to belong to this group) and against those who advocate a return to a "true, militant, hardfisted leadership."

no. 2 (April 1969), 121–52. See also William F. Robinson, "Hungary's Turn to Revisionism," *East Europe*, 16, no. 9 (1967), 14–17.

7. In more severe cases, however, expulsion from the party follows. Three staff members of the Philosophical Institute of the Hungarian Academy of Sciences were ousted from the party because they had signed a declaration condemning the invasion of Czechoslovakia by forces of the Warsaw Treaty Organization at a philosophical conference in Yugoslavia. *Partelet*, December 1968.

8. *New York Times*, January 27, 1970.

9. *East Europe*, 15, no. 9 (1966), 56–58.

Kadar's authority within the party has never been absolute. He is no dictator in the sense that Rakosi had been. His prestige has to rest on the confidence which he continues to enjoy even after Khrushchev's ouster. His influence is maintained by the inner-party clique of moderates who rightly believe that its position is closely linked to Kadar's. Furthermore, Kadar is supported by a number of influential nonparty experts and other intellectuals who, for opportunistic reasons, cling to his person.[10] To a more limited extent, he is also backed by large segments of the people who are inclined to believe that the Kadar regime is the best communist government they can expect. But even these doubtful supporters consider him a Soviet-imposed, if benevolent, satrap. Should Kadar's position become jeopardized, or his popular policy change, his betrayal of the revolution and of his past collaborators will be easily recalled by everybody.

Laszlo Rajk, the innocently executed communist leader, was the "skeleton in the closet" of Rakosi's later years in power. Kadar has to face two such "skeletons." The first is the same Rajk, a friend whom he deceived. Kadar was minister of the interior when Rajk, his collaborator in the Hungarian wartime communist underground, was arrested. Kadar was sent by Rakosi to his friend's cell to persuade him to "confess" at his trial in exchange for his life. Rakosi arranged that this conversation be taped and subsequently used the tape to make Kadar submissive.[11] The second "skeleton" is Imre Nagy in whose cabinet he served, whom he then abandoned, and in 1958 led to the gallows, probably under orders from Moscow. Nagy continues to be treated as an "unperson," while Rajk is openly commemorated as a martyr to Stalinism; but Kadar's role in his tragedy is not mentioned in print. It must have been painful to Kadar when Nagy's martyrdom was celebrated on the tenth anniversary of his death by the Czechoslovak press during the short-lived Prague spring.

Since the reconstitution of the party in the postrevolutionary period, its membership has constantly risen. In November 1970, at the time of the Tenth Party Congress, it was announced that the Hungarian Socialist Workers' party numbered 662,000 members, that is 6.4 per cent of Hungary's population. Kadar earlier insisted that the number of "nonparty communists" in the country is much larger and includes all those who support the regime's building of socialism and thus may be considered communists "short of holding party cards." Evidently, the Hungarian leaders

10. Foreign journalists visiting Hungary maintain regular contact with these intellectuals; hence, the relatively favorable press reports about Kadar which often depict him as a most popular leader.

11. See Vali, *Rift and Revolt*, pp. 62, 227.

either consciously or unconsciously delude themselves into believing the oft-repeated Kadarist slogan: "He who is not against us, is with us." [12]

The nonparty specialists (and those who have been admitted to the party since 1956) are mostly opportunists who, nevertheless, serve the regime with enthusiasm partly because of the benefits they derive from such collaboration and partly because they like their work. They allay their bad consciences, if any, by telling themselves that Hungary now has no other choice than to serve Soviet purposes; thus everybody should make the best of a bad situation.[13]

II

Under the Soviet hegemony, Hungary has become prominent in the area because of her far-reaching economic reforms. Along the line of relative liberalization in literary publications, the theater, and travel restrictions, the New Economic Mechanism (NEM), as the new approach to economic management is known, is probably the most advanced experiment of its kind, excepting of course that of Yugoslavia.

The NEM claims to be the instrument for the democratization of the economy. Its purpose is to speed economic and technological development and to stimulate trade, especially foreign trade, in order to activate the economy which had been operating in low gear because of declining productivity, unrealistic economic targets, and prices unrelated to costs.

The NEM seeks to decentralize cumbersome management, to adopt the "socialist market-principle" in relations between state enterprises, and to establish cost consciousness with the introduction of "real" price levels. The government continues to provide a general plan and to supervise the market economy, but otherwise the enterprises are allowed to act as autonomous entities.[14]

Hungary, poor in raw materials, but relatively densely populated, is more dependent on foreign trade than any other country of the Soviet bloc. About 40 per cent of its national income is derived from trading with the outside world (a figure exceeded in Europe only by Belgium, the Netherlands, and Norway). In 1968 a 1 per cent increase in its national income

12. Kadar originally made this statement in December 1961 before a meeting of the People's Patriotic Front. Rakosi had once said, "Who is not with us is against us." Both have paraphrased from the New Testament ("He that is not with me is against me; and he that gathereth not with me scattereth." Luke 11:23).

13. Information based on conversations carried on by this writer.

14. See article by Rezso Nyers in *Tarsadalmi Szemle*, July 1967. See also Joseph Szabados, "Hungary's NEM: Promises and Pitfalls," *East Europe*, 17, no. 4 (1968), 25–32.

required a 1.5 per cent rise in imports. For Hungary it is essential to become more competitive in the international (including, of course, Western) markets in order to secure a genuine hike in the standard of living for its people.

The NEM went into operation on January 1, 1968. At the time of writing it is still premature to speculate whether the experiment has been successful or whether, as alleged by some critics and outside observers, the new system will result in a confused situation necessitating a return to the rigid planning methods.[15] However it may be, it is the political implications of the NEM which are of particular interest.

The NEM project was worked out by economic and managerial experts on a purely rational and pragmatic basis. It seems certain that the authors of the reform were neither thinking of Marxism-Leninism, nor did they care to follow its guidance. The party itself (Politburo member Rezso Nyers was one of the chief architects of the program) gave its blessing without inquiring whether the new system would prove compatible with orthodox socialist principles.

Originally, the NEM did not have an ideological base, but theoreticians of the party have since tried to provide one. Thus we find explanations describing it as "socialistic," despite its adoption of market relations. The market economy – we are told – is not per se incompatible with true socialism; a distinction has to be made between the macroeconomic (the national) and the microeconomic (relations among enterprises) levels. The principle of supply and demand is permissible at the latter level, but not at the former. It is also stated that the difference between "Marxist market relations" and "capitalist market relations" is that Marxism would never consider labor as a "commodity."

One can only conclude that economic necessity and expediency have tended to erode Marxism-Leninism, resulting in a signal departure from the doctrine. A tendency to treat Marxism as irrelevant from the economic point of view is likely to lead many to look at the political aspects of Leninism as also irrelevant. While in Hungary and elsewhere in the communist camp the regimes have been able to make important strides on the road to economic development and modernization, the system so far has proved to be incapable of bringing about political development and modernization. The NEM may well prove to be the Pandora's box in promoting demands for political democratization, the restoration of the rights of

15. For the preliminary results of the NEM see the interview with Rezso Nyers in the Czechoslovak paper *Hospodarske Noviny*, July 25, 1969.

elected bodies, the replacement of mere "voting" by genuine elections, and other elements of real participatory democracy.[16]

III

The weakest point, indeed the Achilles' heel, of the regime is its manifest dependence on Soviet support and direction. The invasion of Czechoslovakia in August 1968 recalled once more to the Hungarians their own traumatic experiences of 1956. The public and the more liberal elements in the party had ardently hoped that the democratization of the Czechoslovak regime would be crowned with success and that the Czechs, unlike the Hungarians, "would get away with it."

Kadar's role was not unlike the one he had played at other critical occasions. He tried to persuade, to mediate, and to mislead – on behalf of Moscow.[17] Hungarian participation in the occupation of Czechoslovakia was a surprise and was considered shameful not only by the average Hungarian but also by the average Hungarian party member. In view of Hungary's invasion by Soviet forces in 1956, it had not been easy to explain the participation. After two months of silence, Kadar broke the ice on October 25, 1968, by giving a simple and this time candid explanation of the Hungarian part in the assault on Czechoslovakia: "It is the fundamental principle of our foreign policy to cooperate with the Soviet Union. . . ."[18]

As might have been expected, the Hungarian Communist party warmly endorsed the Brezhnev doctrine – the official announcement of the principle of "limited sovereignty" for members of the socialist commonwealth.[19] After all, the doctrine already had been applied to Hungary, and the Kadar regime owes its existence to its application.

The Hungarian-Czechoslovak analogy may lead to an additional parallelism: Kadarism may serve Prague as an example of how to combine loyalty to the Soviet Union with limited liberalization. It is already being rumored that Gustav Husak, Dubcek's successor as first secretary of the Czechoslovak Communist party, was briefed by Kadar on how to reconstitute and stabilize the party rule.[20]

16. About "socialist democracy" and its prospects in Hungary see the interview with Bela Biszku in *Nepszabadsag*, March 8, 1969.

17. It is known that Kadar met Dubcek on August 17, 1968, almost on the eve of the invasion, presumably with the consent of the Kremlin.

18. *Nepszabadsag*, October 26, 1968.

19. See, among others, the declaration of Hungarian Foreign Minister Janos Peter, *Magyar Nemzet*, December 12, 1968.

20. *New York Times*, November 22, 1969.

To use Kadarism as a prototype implies, however, an ominous note. It would mean the use of oppressive measures, similar to those employed in Hungary for the liquidation of the "counterrevolution" of 1956. An obviously inspired article published in *Tarsadalmi Szemle*, the Hungarian ideological monthly, shortly after the Prague coup analyzed the necessity of suspending "democracy" until the workers' power was fully restored.[21] It is of course impossible to foresee whether the developments in Czechoslovakia, where conditions are somewhat different, will copy the Hungarian pattern.

What Kadar euphemistically called "cooperation" with the Soviet Union is, in fact, subservience to the basic policy pursued by the Kremlin. Unlike the domestic developments (evidently tolerated by the Soviet leadership), the scope of an independent Hungarian foreign policy is tragically narrow. In this respect, as well as in defense matters, Hungary has to toe faithfully the Soviet line. This can be clearly seen in the stance Hungary has taken on such recent issues as the Arab-Israeli conflict and the Sino-Soviet dispute and in its attitude toward the German Federal Republic.

Although the great majority of Hungarians (if only to oppose Moscow's stand) felt sympathetic toward the Israelis and rejoiced over the Arab defeat in 1967, the government has severed diplomatic relations with Tel-Aviv, though maintaining important trade contacts with the country. On the other hand, in contrast to certain trends in the Polish and Czechoslovak policy, no domestic anti-Semitism has been practiced in Hungary.[22]

If anybody in Hungary cherished hopes that the Soviet occupation forces would withdraw voluntarily, such hopes were dissipated with the invasion of Czechoslovakia and the stationing of Soviet troops within its borders. The Hungarian public is fully conscious that the presence of Soviet troops, unlike that of foreign military contingents in the NATO countries, serves less to protect their country against an outside enemy than to preserve Soviet control and communist rule over the area. Reports concerning a further integration (under Soviet command) of the forces of the Warsaw Treaty Organization were received with consternation in Hungary; rumor had it that these forces might one day be employed against the Chinese.

With regard to the conflict between Moscow and Peking, Budapest has fully endorsed the Soviet condemnation of Maoism on every possible oc-

21. Article by I. Pozsgai on the problems of the development of socialist democracy, *Tarsadalmi Szemle*, October 1968.

22. Such a policy would be even more disastrous in Hungary than in Poland; many of the leading experts, party or nonparty, are of Jewish origin.

casion. Unlike the Rumanian neutralist posture, the Hungarian attitude toward Peking has not diverged in the slightest from the Soviet position. There is no doubt that while the Hungarian leadership would be happy to display some independent pose in respect to this and other issues, to do so would be to infringe upon the limits of Soviet toleration.

Hungary's political leaders, as well as its people, have been envious of Rumania's relative independence, and the visits of General de Gaulle and of President Nixon to Bucharest have been viewed with jealous eyes. Budapest plays host to Soviet bloc conferences only and to visits by the heads of state of minor powers.[23]

Apart from considerations of prestige, Hungary is directly interested in developments related to Germany. Although Budapest, mainly for reasons of commercial and tourist relations, would prefer to follow the Rumanian lead and establish full diplomatic contacts with the German Federal Republic, the Hungarian government has proceeded with utmost caution and in harmony with Soviet advice in its relations with West Germany. Needless to say, this attitude at times has provoked the wrath of Ulbricht. In 1969 the permanent trade mission of Bonn in Budapest was raised to the level of a consulate general (though not called so) with the right to issue visas; identical privileges were extended to the Hungarian mission in Cologne.

To improve relations with West Germany, Hungarian Foreign Minister Janos Peter traveled to Bonn in 1969. In his conversations with the German leaders Peter acted as a protagonist of the European Security Conference which had been previously proposed by a meeting of Soviet bloc countries held in Budapest.

Hungary has been eager to strengthen its ties with all the countries of the Western world, primarily with the United States. After a deadlock lasting for several years, Budapest has been able to achieve a resumption of full diplomatic relations with Washington, which had been left on a de facto level since the revolution. In 1964 the American and Hungarian chargés d'affaires were replaced by ambassadors. Five years later some of the outstanding financial issues between the two countries were settled by agreement.[24] The question of war damages and indemnity for nationalized American property, however, remains unsolved. The stalemated affair created by Cardinal Mindszenty's stay in the American Embassy of Buda-

23. In 1969 the state visit of Urho Kekkonen, president of Finland, was hailed in Budapest as a major milestone in foreign policy. Kekkonen allegedly discussed the European Security Conference to be held in Helsinki.

24. *New York Times*, August 16, 1969.

pest since November 1956 was suddenly solved when the seventy-nine-year-old cardinal, with the consent of the Hungarian government and under the instructions of the pope, traveled to Rome in late September 1971.[25]

The prestige of the Hungarian regime, at a low ebb since its installation by the Soviet forces, has gradually risen in the United Nations. The seat in the Security Council occupied in rotation by one member of the socialist bloc countries fell to Hungary in 1969 – an event which Budapest tries to exploit as a triumph and as a recognition of its achievements.

Because of Hungary's need – like that of all countries – for hard currency, the government makes great efforts to attract tourists from the West. In the last ten years Budapest has become a kind of a showplace in the communist orbit. But while entertainment and other luxuries are offered to foreigners, they remain mostly beyond reach of the Hungarians.[26]

IV

The relative freedom of decision-making practiced by the Hungarian regime in internal affairs is conspicuously at variance with the constraints existing in foreign policy and in defense matters. During the sixties Hungary has followed a separate path "toward socialism" in its domestic concerns only.

In foreign affairs Hungary completely fails to enjoy the benefits of what is known as polycentrism in the communist orbit. Moscow and Peking are centers of the communist movement and, to a more limited extent, so are Belgrade and Bucharest. But Budapest is not. Nevertheless, even the strictly Soviet bloc countries, such as Hungary, have been able to pursue different internal developments in economics, in culture, and also in domestic politics, in general. Polymorphism prevails in these countries, but no sign of polycentrism is so far discernible.

Still, national feeling in all these countries, primarily perhaps in Hungary, demands a national foreign policy for reasons of prestige as much as for the safeguarding of national interests. The people of Hungary (except the few party devotees) ridicule the official thesis that there is complete identity between Hungarian and Soviet interests. It is even more repugnant to most people when the love of the Soviet Union is declared to be the hallmark of true Hungarian patriotism. Such grandiloquent slogans

25. *Ibid.*, September 28, 1971. For Cardinal Mindszenty's status see Ferenc A. Vali, "Hungary," in Adam Bromke (ed.), *The Communist States at the Crossroads: Between Moscow and Peking* (New York, 1965), pp. 81–82.

26. For a good characterization see *New York Times,* November 15, 1969.

as "Who turns against the Soviet Union becomes opposed to the whole humanity" are indigestible for the Hungarian people and add to existing anti-Soviet sentiments.

The official view, as expressed by Kadar and others, identifies nationalism with anti-Sovietism (only that "patriotism" is lauded which in the official vocabulary means loyalty to Moscow).[27] This attitude is more harmful to the regime than even economic hardships or the lack of democratic forms because it denies it the support of the traditions of Hungary's past. Unlike Gomulka, who until December 1970 successfully invoked the German danger to help stabilize his power, or Ceausescu, who can refer to Rumania's Latin heritage, the Hungarian leadership is in no position to appeal to Hungary's history. Such an appeal would foster anti-Russian sentiments as well as the latent irredentist feeling intolerable to all Hungary's communist neighbors. There are more than three million Magyars outside Hungary's borders, not much less than one-third of its present population. Discrimination practiced against Hungarians in Transylvania has already caused many headaches to the party leaders in Budapest.[28]

The latest attempt at transmuting Hungarian national sentiment for the purposes of the regime centered upon Hungary's much venerated first king, Saint Stephen (officially referred to as Stephen I). Stephen was born in 969 A.D., but official circles in Hungary decided that he was born in 970 in order to commemorate his millenary in 1970, the date which, strangely enough, coincides with the twenty-fifth anniversary of Hungary's "liberation" by the Red Army, as well as with the centenary of Lenin's birth. By synchronizing Saint Stephen's celebration with the landmarks of communist and Soviet power in Hungary, the leadership wished to create in the mind of the people a link between the "new progressive era" introduced by the Soviet occupation of Hungary and the country's christianization under the rule of its first king. It is, however, unlikely that such a transparent strategem can even partly succeed. The religious masses and those imbued with traditional patriotic sentiments are bound to view such attempts as more blasphemous than convincing.

Thus, despite the evident achievements of the regime, especially in the area of economic advancement, and despite certain accomplishments or

27. For a detailed analysis of nationalism (patriotism) and anti-Soviet sentiment in Hungary see Ferenc A. Vali, "The Regime and the Nation; Resistance and Coexistence," in Tamas Aczel (ed.), *Ten Years After* (London and New York, 1966), pp. 137–52.

28. See Ferenc A. Vali, "Transylvania and the Hungarian Minority," *Journal of International Affairs,* 20, no. 1 (1966), 32–44.

liberties achieved or tolerated in certain cultural fields, the regime still lacks genuine normalcy and stability. It remains "provisional" and is in need of a generally recognized legitimacy. It is in disarray with its own people; it is ideologically confused within itself; and it cultivates a false image of itself – posing to have independence which in fact it does not possess.

7

Bulgaria

BY MICHAEL COSTELLO

In the early seventies the character of Bulgarian-Soviet relations is outwardly very much as it was before Stalin's death. Still politically the most loyal of the Kremlin's allies, the Bulgarian communists have also pursued economic policies that seem destined to result in the near complete integration of Bulgaria's economy with that of the Soviet Union. The centrifugal forces in the bloc have not yet touched Sofia. An anomaly in the region that has clearly emerged as the graveyard of monolithic communism,[1] the Bulgarian Communist party (BCP) leadership has distanced itself from the positions of other Eastern European rulers, whose deference to Moscow has neither taken the Bulgarian form of slavish obedience nor prevented them from developing some unique policies of their own.

There are many possible explanations for the nature of Bulgaria's feasance to the Soviet alliance, ranging from historical and cultural factors to the BCP's traditional devotion to the Soviet party.[2] In the past decade, however, the most important single determinant of Sofia's dependence on Moscow has been the weakness of the Bulgarian regime, and particularly of its leader, Todor Zhivkov.

This weakness and consequent dependence have taken many forms since Zhivkov's accession to the post of party first secretary in 1954. Confronted by rival factions during his early years in power, Zhivkov managed to survive only by total reliance on Soviet (i.e., Khrushchev's) sup-

1. For an incisive study of nationalism and communism in the Balkans, see Paul Lendvai, *Eagles in Cobwebs* (New York, 1969).

2. These explanations have been examined at great length by J. F. Brown, whose *Bulgaria under Communist Rule* (New York, 1970) has filled a long-standing gap in the literature on Bulgaria.

port. Yet, even following the consolidation of his personal position in 1962 (when his two main challengers, Chervenkov and Yugov, were ousted and Zhivkov himself took over the premiership), he has been unable to implement a consistent program of any kind. His unimaginative and hesitant policies have neither generated genuine popular support within Bulgaria nor contributed significantly to the country's economic development.

Zhivkov has thus been forced to seek Moscow's continued political support, as well as enhanced economic cooperation with the USSR, which has, in effect, meant Soviet economic domination. In return Zhivkov has ruled Bulgaria as a model satellite, with his domestic and foreign policies finely attuned to Moscow's example and interests. For its participants, this arrangement has undoubtedly been a successful one. Zhivkov's longevity in power is reaching epic proportions; for the Soviet leadership, harassed by major problems at home and abroad, and reminded almost daily of its diminished authority within the international communist movement, Sofia's loyalty has been (and probably will continue to be) well worth the price, which in economic terms should not be underestimated.

I

Khrushchev's ouster in October 1964 provides a convenient takeoff point for an assessment of recent developments in Bulgaria. The official Bulgarian reaction was a telling indication of the BCP's satellite status. The party Central Committee's declaration on the changes in Moscow contained not even a nod to Khrushchev (unlike the reaction of several other Eastern European parties), but instead conveyed Sofia's immediate transfer of loyalty to the new leadership.[3]

In a more personal sense, the demise of Khrushchev cast a shadow on the political future of Zhivkov, whose loyalty to and identification with the Soviet leader was exceeded in Eastern Europe only by that of Hungary's Kadar. That the Bulgarian leader was able to weather the initial shock of his mentor's downfall is probably more attributable to the new Soviet team's desire for stability and calm in Eastern Europe than to the obsequious manner in which Zhivkov abruptly shifted his allegiance. Indeed, although Zhivkov was subsequently to be challenged, the threat came not from a Soviet reappraisal of his usefulness but from within Bulgaria, in the form of a military-political conspiracy in April 1965.

Because the attempt to overthrow the Zhivkov regime was uncovered

3. The Central Committee declaration was published in *Rabotnichesko Delo,* October 21, 1964.

before it had a chance to begin and because of the official effort to belittle the episode, there are many aspects of the conspiracy that may never be known. On the basis of the evidence that does exist, however, several facts and some speculative conclusions are worth mentioning. First, among the ringleaders themselves, there was obviously a common bond, based on wartime partisan experience and subsequent political activity in the Vratsa district of Bulgaria. Moreover, of the nine conspirators brought to trial (excluding the leader of the group, Central Committee member Todorov-Gorunia, who committed suicide to avoid arrest), five were at the time or had once been connected with the military, the most important being Major-General Anev, the commander of the Sofia garrison.

The primary motive for the plot was dissatisfaction with Zhivkov personally and with his record of subservience to the USSR. While the evidence suggests that a more independent (though not explicitly anti-Soviet) foreign policy was the chief goal of the conspirators, there is far less certainty as to what kind of model they may have wished to follow. Despite the official portrayal of them as "adventuristic supporters of the Chinese line," the conspirators probably sought to establish a more national communist regime, based partly on relevant applications of the Yugoslav and Rumanian examples.

The plot appeared timed to take advantage of the unexpected situation produced by the October 1964 reshuffle in Moscow. The conspirators may have reasoned that, given the rather uncertain atmosphere still prevailing in the Kremlin, the new Soviet leadership might not object to the removal of a leader so closely associated with Khrushchev. In this sense, the ouster of Zhivkov's mentor had a direct influence on the abortive conspiracy against the Bulgarian leader.

There was, however, another, potentially more important link between the events of October 1964 and April 1965. While Zhivkov's immediate reaction in both instances was to reaffirm his loyalty to the Soviet Union, there were signs that he began to feel that exclusive dependence on Moscow was a doubtful or, at best, an impermanent source of salvation. What may have started as a nervous reaction to the threats to its survival developed into a clear-cut attempt by the Zhivkov regime to broaden its base of popular support.

On two previous occasions – in 1956 and 1961–62 – there had been reform movements in Bulgaria which had led to varying degrees of internal relaxation or improvement in the political, cultural, and economic spheres. In both cases, however, these movements closely paralleled similar thaws in the USSR initiated by the Twentieth and Twenty-second congresses of the CPSU. In effect, the de-Stalinization issue proved to be a double-edged sword for Zhivkov. While it served as an effective instrument with which to discredit and finally oust his vulnerable rivals, the attendant relaxation resulted in unacceptable ferment. This latter danger was accentuated by the continuing opposition to Zhivkov at the middle-cadre level, from the left and the right. Thus, both waves of liberalization were disappointedly short-lived and quickly gave way to periods of reaction.

The invigoration of Bulgarian policy in 1965 seemed to offer considerable promise. Unlike the earlier reforms, this one was far more comprehensive in scope, combining domestic reforms with greater activism in foreign affairs, and was more directly responsive and attuned to Bulgarian rather than to Soviet needs. Without being too schematic (since the origins of certain initiatives preceded this period in time), it is clear that, taken together, the fall of Khrushchev and the April 1965 conspiracy served as catalysts in inducing the Zhivkov regime to adopt more pragmatic, even "national" policies.

In the domestic sphere, perhaps the most important single reform was the New Economic Mechanism (NEM). After more than three years of discussion and selected experimentation, the official Politburo "Theses" on economic reform were published in December 1965.[4] As approved by a BCP Central Committee plenum in April 1966, the basic features of the NEM were as follows: considerable decentralization of economic decision-making, with greater responsibility assigned to associations, or trusts, and to individual enterprises; wider application of the profit motive as a spur to productivity and quality; a system of wages tied to production results; and more extensive use of economic levers, such as profit, prices, credit interest, and taxes. Other major aspects of the reform included the reduction of centrally determined compulsory indices, the introduction of a three-price system of categories – fixed, variable, and free – the formation of "production committees" to facilitate worker participation in decision-making, and the granting of greater freedom of action to foreign trade enterprises.

On paper, the NEM seemed to be a surprisingly advanced reform blueprint for one of the least developed communist states in Europe. Indeed, opposition to the new system produced some strange bedfellows, such as conservative party *apparatchiks*, who viewed reform of any kind with alarm, and several noted Bulgarian economists, who regarded application of the NEM as premature. Moreover, concern was expressed that incon-

4. *Ibid.*, December 4, 1965.

sistencies in the economic blueprint would impede the implementation of the reform. There was substantial evidence to support this latter point. Thus, while the "Theses" referred to improved planning from below, the institution and role of central planning was never seriously questioned. Within the official framework of "combining centralism with the increased independence of the enterprise," [5] the regime retained a great number of economic levers and controls in its own hands. In addition, considerable hesitation was evident in the leadership's approach to the crucial question of price reform.

In summation, these problems notwithstanding, the NEM did incorporate a number of relatively "liberal" features. Given the fact that the need for reform was clearly not as pressing in Bulgaria as in several other East European countries, the regime's apparent determination to ensure a more flexible and responsive economic system was a welcome step forward. Despite consistently impressive growth rates, the Bulgarian economy had its share of problems – particularly in the areas of production efficiency and quality – that warranted attention. In recognizing these weaknesses and, in certain instances, seeming to anticipate the consequences of continued reliance on the classical system of planning and management, the Zhivkov regime displayed an unwonted degree of foresight.

Signs of a new approach were also evident in the regime's cultural policies. Unlike the earlier periods of relaxation in 1956 and 1961–62, when the party had given the intellectuals their head and then found itself being quickly outrun, the leadership now sought to place itself in a position to direct the reform movement. While Zhivkov himself steered a relatively middle course between the conservative and the liberal factions in the cultural community, it was apparent that the bulk of the concessions made to win the cooperation of the intellectuals favored the liberals. These concessions included a general relaxation of censorship, the infusion of younger persons into responsible positions on cultural bodies, broader possibilities of publication for young writers, and greater availability of Western literature in Bulgaria. Although the cultural reins remained firmly in the party's hands, and the measures it passed can at best be called "controlled reforms," the barometer in late 1965 and early 1966 was pointing toward thaw.

Regarding the question of personal freedom, an extremely difficult situation to gauge, there does seem to have been a new cycle of relative relaxation. Even though security precautions were taken in the wake of the

5. *Ibid.*

conspiracy, it is true that police repression was less an internal factor than ever before. Far greater numbers of Western tourists visited Bulgaria,[6] and there were small but noticeable increases in the number of Bulgarians given the opportunity to travel abroad. The debate over the economic reform seems to have been infectious, as the press became livelier in its criticism and public discussions on other issues showed less restraint and less obvious signs of orchestration.

Moreover, the legacy of the April conspiracy, directed as it was against the neglect of Bulgarian nationalism, made itself felt in the regime's cultivation of national feelings. This is not to say that the official blessing of patriotic sentiment merely bespoke the party's sensitivity to the pride of the population. Indeed, the sudden resurrection of Bulgarian history prior to the communist take-over and the ensuing patriotic education campaign were in part intended to counter the growing problem of "national nihilism," especially among the youth. And while attempting to identify itself with the national aspirations of the Bulgarian people, the regime clearly set limits on the parameters of historical interpretation, as could be seen for example in the communist and pro-Russian bias in the celebration of certain national anniversaries. Nevertheless, the acknowledgment and commemoration of important personalities and events from Bulgaria's past did strike a responsive chord in the population. But evoking reverence for the past was no substitute for the example of the present, particularly where Bulgaria's relations with the USSR and the rest of the world were concerned. It is in this sphere that the regime demonstrated most strongly the determination to stand on its own.

II

Besides providing impetus for internal change, Khrushchev's downfall also spurred the Zhivkov regime to more "individual" action abroad, a shift only accelerated by the April 1965 conspiracy. In contrast to earlier periods, when Bulgarian foreign policy had been little more than a synonym for relations with Moscow, there seemed to be both the interest and the will in Sofia to emerge from international isolation and to pursue diplomatic objectives considered advantageous.

It was in the Balkans, a natural arena of Bulgarian interests, that the regime registered its first solid diplomatic successes.[7] The most impressive

6. Bulgaria's conspicuous success in developing its tourist industry was reflected in the steadily rising numbers of foreign visitors – from approximately 414,500 in 1963 to 1,480,000 in 1966.

7. For a more detailed account of Bulgaria's relations with its Balkan neighbors, see

advances occurred in relations with its southern neighbors, Greece and Turkey. In July 1964 a number of agreements with Greece were signed, including the settlement of the vexing problem of war reparations. These accords, signed in Athens by Foreign Minister Bashev in an atmosphere of cordiality unthinkable only a few years before, paved the way for a marked upswing in trade and for greater cooperation in the spheres of communications, cultural exchanges, and tourism.

With Turkey, the first cautious steps toward a rapprochement were made in 1965. As in the case of Greece, there were major obstacles, historical as well as ideological, barring the way to an improvement of relations between Sofia and Ankara. Moreover, the problem of the more than 750,000 ethnic Turks in Bulgaria (approximately 10 per cent of the total population) was a major stumbling block. A climate of mutual trust gradually developed, however, as the result of an exchange of high-level visits and the signing of several economic agreements. By August 1966, the two governments were able to announce that negotiations were under way on the sensitive issue of repatriating to Turkey certain categories of Bulgaria's Turkish minority.

There was also room for improvement in Bulgaria's relations with its communist neighbors, and, here too, Sofia took several initiatives and responded favorably to those emanating from Bucharest and Belgrade.[8] The most intriguing development was the ardent courtship of Zhivkov and Ceausescu following the death of Gheorghiu-Dej in March 1965. Zhivkov went to Bucharest to attend his funeral and returned in July 1965 for the Ninth Rumanian Party Congress. Gheorghiu-Dej had not visited Bulgaria since 1957, whereas, between August 1965 and November 1966, Ceausescu journeyed to Sofia on five different occasions. Although the visits encouraged a plethora of exchanges at lower levels, the success of closer relations was clearly dependent on these exercises in summit diplomacy. The match between the pro-Soviet Bulgarian leader and the Rumanian maverick was, at best, an unlikely one, but by late 1966, the much traveled route between Sofia and Bucharest seemed to be paved with far greater Bulgarian understanding, if not support, for Rumania's position.

The strains in Bulgarian-Rumanian relations were minor, however, in comparison with the legacy of enmity between Sofia and Belgrade. Ideological differences after 1948 only added a new element to the traditional

Michael Costello, "Bulgaria's Cautious Balkan Policy," *East Europe*, 17, no. 8 (August 1968), 2–5.

8. In relations with Albania, there has been little perceptible improvement since the Soviet break with Tirana in October 1961.

hostility engendered by the Macedonian question. Yet, here too, Bulgaria made a serious effort to improve relations, the success of which seemed to be marked by Tito's trip to Sofia in September 1965, his first official visit to the Bulgarian capital in eighteen years. Although the visit resulted in no verbal or written agreements, President Tito revealed subsequently that many bilateral problems, including Macedonia, had been discussed – an advance in itself.[9] Apparently, the meeting did help to clear the air; press polemics decreased and the possibilities for closer economic and (on certain issues) political cooperation seemed more viable than at any time since 1948.

Foreign policy initiatives were not solely confined to the Balkan stage. Concurrently with its regional diplomatic activity, Bulgaria also moved to expand sadly neglected political and economic contacts with Western Europe.[10] High-level visits were exchanged with numerous countries, Bulgaria usually being represented by Ivan Bashev, its young and able foreign minister. The most spectacular gains were made in relations with France, whose then Foreign Minister Couve de Murville visited Bulgaria in April 1966, setting the stage for a visit to France by Zhivkov in October.

While interesting in themselves and a major factor in the attempt to refurbish the Bulgarian image in Europe, these political contacts were less significant than the improvements in economic relations with Western Europe. Trade with developed Western countries rose substantially in 1965 and 1966, reflecting Bulgaria's demand for imports of high quality industrial products and technology.[11] In addition, several production agreements with foreign firms were signed, and official spokesmen affirmed the country's readiness to grant facilities to Western companies investing in and helping to develop Bulgarian industry. Finally, as has been noted, the regime itself invested heavily in other types of facilities – those for the Western tourists visiting Bulgaria in ever-increasing numbers and serving as a source of invisible earnings, which partly offset unfavorable trade balances with the West.

Of all the important initiatives abroad that marked the 1965–66 period,

9. *Tanjug*, September 28, 1965.

10. Bulgaria's emergence from relative isolation was most noticeable within this European context. While concurrent initiatives were taken on other continents, these were of neither the same magnitude nor importance.

11. The most spectacular increase was in trade with the FRG. By 1966, West Germany had become Bulgaria's fourth largest trading partner and ranked second (after the USSR) as a source of imports. Total trade in that year amounted to 172.1 million dollars.

the most striking and potentially significant was Bulgaria's relations with West Germany.[12] Not only did these relations steadily improve, but, more surprisingly, they did so at a time when the Soviet attitude toward the Federal German Republic was one of overt hostility. Although Sofia's receptiveness to the new Eastern policy of the Erhard (and subsequently the Kiesinger) government was primarily conditioned by economic factors, advances on this plane were not without impact on relations at other levels, including the political. Thus, whereas the USSR and several other countries responded negatively to Erhard's March 1966 "peace note" to East European governments urging a new beginning in their relations with Bonn, Bulgaria (and Rumania) published no official reply.

Bulgaria's silence was correctly interpreted in the West German government as being necessitated by political considerations, since a Bulgarian response would have voiced an opinion opposite that of the Soviet attitude. This was subsequently reflected in the West German exhibition at the September 1966 Plovdiv International Fair and the concomitant visit of State Secretary Rolf Lahr. After meeting with Foreign Minister Bashev and other senior Bulgarian officials, Lahr reported that both sides had expressed the desire for a normalization of relations, to be reached "step by step." The state secretary further noted that the then Bulgarian Foreign Trade Minister Budinov would probably accept an invitation to visit the Federal Republic. If, by the end of 1966, Rumania seemed ready to establish relations with Bonn, then Bulgaria was not too far behind. In retrospect, this was one major international issue on which the position of the Bulgarian leadership differed quite significantly from that of Moscow.

That this occurred – indeed, that Sofia had been able to wield such freedom of action in foreign policy – was primarily the result of the new leaders in Moscow not exercising any positive control over their allies. The Kremlin chose not to force any issues that might demand a show of solidarity, thereby enabling the Eastern European countries to take initiatives that otherwise might not have been attempted. In any event, there was little in Bulgaria's policies to which the Soviet Union might have taken exception. For example, the improvement in relations with its Balkan neighbors coincided with Soviet policy in the area. Only in the case of Sofia's attitude toward West Germany was there a clear dichotomy between Bulgarian and Soviet interests, and that dichotomy was not to last long.

12. Bulgaria's interesting relationship with West Germany during the 1965–70 period has been dealt with in depth in Michael Costello, "Self-Interest Versus Orthodoxy: A Study of Bulgaria's Relationship with the Federal Republic of Germany," *Radio Free Europe Research*, May 4, 1970.

III

As J. F. Brown has noted, "Having stepped out of her shell in 1965 and 1966, Bulgaria retreated back into it in 1967." [13] For a variety of reasons, it has, with few exceptions, remained there. The retreat began and has been sustained chiefly because of the reassertion of authority by a more confident (or, one might argue, beleaguered) Kremlin in late 1966. Moscow's resumption of polemics with Peking and its related revival of the idea of a world conference of communist parties were immediately echoed in Sofia. Not only did the Bulgarian leadership hasten to organize its own propaganda campaign against the Chinese, but, at the Ninth Congress of the BCP in November 1966, Zhivkov himself launched the conference proposal by claiming that "conditions are ripening more and more for the convening of an international conference of the Communist and Workers' Parties." [14]

Indicative as these actions were of continued fealty to the Soviet alliance, they were not as detrimental to Bulgaria's foreign policy advances and interests as those necessitated by subsequent Soviet pressure. The most obvious involved the question of relations with West Germany, which, following Rumania's establishment of relations with Bonn in January 1967, became an important focus of Soviet concern. Under the combined pressure of Ulbricht and Gomulka, and anxious to prevent the divisive effect of a repetition of the Rumanian move, Moscow finally made a rejection of West German overtures a condition of loyalty to the alliance. Bulgaria immediately complied; at the Karlovy Vary conference of European communist parties in April 1967, Zhivkov delivered the first major Bulgarian attack on the *Ostpolitik* of the Grand Coalition in Bonn.[15] What is more, Sofia demonstratively subordinated an improvement of Bulgarian-West German relations to the interests of the Warsaw Pact extremists, the "inevitable" conditions being Bonn's renunciation of its "revanchist" policies and recognition of the German Democratic Republic and the status quo in Europe.

The West German issue was but one of several that were to have an adverse effect on Bulgaria's relations with Rumania. Despite the personal intimacy between Zhivkov and Ceausescu, it became evident during the course of 1967 that on specific questions of policy, the gulf between Sofia and Bucharest remained as wide as the contrast in the two countries' at-

13. Brown, *Bulgaria under Communist Rule*, p. 286.

14. *Rabotnichesko Delo*, November 15, 1966.

15. *Ibid.*, April 26, 1967.

titude toward the USSR. Taken together, Rumania's defiance of Moscow on such issues as the German question, the dispute with China, and the Arab-Israeli War and Bulgaria's total support for the Soviet position within the Warsaw Pact and Comecon spelled an end to the close relations that had existed in 1965 and 1966.

Coincident with Zhivkov's visit to Rumania in September 1967, an article written by him appeared in the Soviet party daily *Pravda* asserting that "we cannot take the position of a kind of neutrality, as if this concerned ordinary differences between two parties."[16] As was reflected in this telling statement that political priorities place Balkan cooperation below the demands of loyalty to the USSR, Bulgaria's subsequent attitude toward its northern neighbor has not been neutral, but rather has closely paralleled (or followed) Moscow's policy. Thus, the signing of a new twenty-year agreement on friendship, cooperation, and mutual aid – to replace the pact that had expired in January 1968 – was delayed until after the conclusion in July 1970 of a similarly overdue treaty between the Soviet Union and Rumania. The Bulgarian-Rumanian accord was then signed in November, but, despite a rise in press atmospherics and despite the fact that the occasion brought Zhivkov and Ceausescu together for the first time in three years, the bilateral relationship remains only formally "correct."

There were other disappointments as well for Bulgaria's proclaimed "peaceful policy in the Balkans." The April 1967 military coup in Greece considerably restrained the progress already achieved toward a normalization of relations. However, despite an initial period of polemics, Bulgaria did not move to break off connections with Greece, and its ambassador was one of the first communist diplomats in Athens to indicate that "working relations" with the ruling junta would continue. This has indeed been the case. A number of agreements, including a five-year trade protocol, have been signed, and Foreign Minister Bashev and Foreign Trade Minister Avramov both made stopover visits in Athens in 1970. Of even greater significance, Bulgaria has recently proposed a comprehensive eight-point plan for economic cooperation with Greece.[17] Although these initiatives conform with Soviet objectives vis-à-vis NATO's southern flank, they also seem to confirm Sofia's interest in the earlier gains of her patient diplomacy.

Far less interest was evident in the Bulgarian leaders' attitude toward

16. *Pravda,* September 30, 1967.

17. See *The Times* (London), February 15, 1971.

Yugoslavia. Sofia's espousal of and support for the international conference once again highlighted the divergent ideological orientations of the two countries. Of greater seriousness, however, was the outbreak of renewed hostility over the Macedonian issue. Despite an exchange of high-level visits – the Macedonian party leader Crvenkovski to Sofia in May 1967 and Zhivkov to Belgrade the following month – periodic mutual recriminations mushroomed into a sharp dispute as the ninetieth anniversary of the San Stefano treaty on March 3, 1968, drew near.[18]

In the past, the Macedonian question has been regarded as an accurate barometer of Soviet intentions toward Yugoslavia – that is, any return to the issue by Bulgaria has been inspired by or at least sanctioned in Moscow. The validity of this thesis aside, available evidence tends to indicate that the revival of this sensitive topic in 1967–68 was directly related to the Zhivkov regime's patriotic education campaign and that the "nationalistic" aspect of Bulgaria's quarrel with Yugoslavia was a source of concern to the Kremlin. During this period, much of the controversy revolved around Bulgaria's glorification of events and heroes considered in Sofia to be part of the Bulgarian national heritage, but claimed in Belgrade and Skoplje to be Macedonian in origin. Regarding the Soviet attitude, it would not seem coincidental that during his visit to Sofia in February 1968, Soviet Foreign Minister Gromyko pointedly failed to pay tribute to Bulgaria's Balkan policy.

In any event, the temporary lull in the feud following the San Stefano anniversary was broken in April 1968, when a fresh wave of polemics arose over the Macedonian "dialect" and the celebration of other historic dates. The issue has clearly affected further attempts to negotiate an improvement of relations, all of which have ended in failure.

The consequences of these setbacks for Bulgaria's foreign policy paled, however, in comparison with those accompanying its participation in the Soviet-led invasion of Czechoslovakia. If Zhivkov's response to Soviet demands for solidarity in 1967 did much to sap Bulgarian foreign policy of its earlier momentum, Bulgaria's "internationalist" attitude in August 1968 laid bare the credibility of that policy. In the Balkan region, relations with Yugoslavia and Rumania sank to a new low; given the implications of the Brezhnev doctrine, the specter of a Soviet Trojan horse in the area only exacerbated existing tensions.

Bulgaria's crude attempt to justify the Warsaw Pact action in terms of

18. The San Stefano treaty provided for the creation of an autonomous "Greater Bulgaria," including most of Macedonia. The treaty was subsequently modified, and Bulgaria's frontiers were contracted by the Berlin treaty of June 1878.

West Germany's alleged interest in the "counterrevolution" in Czechoslovakia absolutely confirmed the complete reversal of Sofia's attitude toward Bonn. Alleged examples of West German interference in Czechoslovakia's internal affairs were linked with the more active economic and cultural West German involvement in East Europe and were portrayed as indicative of "the revanchist desire to sever Czechoslovakia from the socialist community." As for the Federal Republic's so-called strategic-military interest in Czechoslovakia and its relevance for Bulgaria, the press advanced the ludicrous argument that "we cannot be indifferent toward Czechoslovakia . . . [for] we know that the Hitlerite hordes trampled over Czechoslovakia and then went on to the Balkans." [19]

The experience of 1966, when Bulgaria found itself exposed on the German question, has had an effect on its attitude toward the Eastern policy of the Brandt government. While present circumstances (i.e., an atmosphere more conducive to negotiation as a result of the Soviet and Polish agreements with West Germany) seemingly would allow Sofia greater flexibility to promote its own interests vis-à-vis the Federal Republic than it enjoyed in 1966, the Zhivkov regime has neither modified its rigid stance nor made any concrete effort to define its own approach toward West Germany. Thus, in opting to err on the side of caution in its response to the current *Ostpolitik*, the BCP leadership is again out of step with its allies, but in a far safer way.

Relations with other Western European countries were also disadvantaged by the events of August 1968. The initial consequence was the cancellation or postponement of several scheduled high-level visits and of economic and cultural exchanges. A less tangible, but for Bulgaria a far more important result was the erosion of confidence in the rationale of its foreign policy initiatives. The closer relations which Bulgarian representatives had for several years sought to establish were thereby severely compromised. Even if such initiatives may now be less credible than they once were, Bulgaria has not retreated into isolation. Though with less flair and vigor than before, it has sought with some success to restore contacts with Western European capitals. This activity has coincided with the communist attempt to gain Western acceptance of the convocation of a European security conference. Here again, Bulgaria's total commitment to the Soviet position on the format for such a conference has done little to repolish its image in Western Europe.

By the late sixties, another problem in Bulgaria's relations with the West

19. *Otechestven Front*, January 8, 1969.

had begun to surface – that is, its inability, as a small state, to trade effectively and pay for the technology it so obviously desires. There is no sizable Western market for the products of Bulgaria's light and heavy industries, because of the latter's substandard quality and various trade restrictions. And its agricultural exports are not able to defray the high costs of industrial and technological imports. In 1966, Bulgaria's trade deficit with West Germany alone amounted to ninety million dollars. That experience and the example of Rumania (whose deficit with the West is approaching dangerous proportions) appear to have been major factors in Bulgaria's decision to reduce its trade with the West in general and the Federal Republic in particular, and to achieve favorable trade balances by placing limitations on imports.[20] Correspondingly, the percentage of trade with the Soviet Union has risen to a record level (approximately 55 per cent in 1970) and is expected to reach almost 60 per cent by 1975.

IV

Along with the setbacks in foreign policy, the signs of invigoration and reform on the domestic front also proved to be short-lived. Here too the Zhivkov regime was unable (or unwilling) to sustain the momentum of 1965 and 1966. There was no single reason for the reversal; nor was it precipitated by a particular event. Indeed, the regime did not revert overnight to the all too familiar policies of control and manipulation. Instead, Zhivkov chose to minimize the potential repercussions of a widespread confrontation by attempting to insulate particular trouble spots and then deal with them one at a time, a choice of tactics that clearly demonstrated the regime's limitations. The best explanation for the shift was that Zhivkov, lacking strength in the party and support from the population, was forced to make concessions to more conservative elements in the BCP. Relatedly, his insecurity made such policies of compromise all the less tenable, especially when they did not prove effective in achieving the regime's orthodox goals. Finally, the example of the Prague spring was not lost upon the Bulgarian leadership. Although the domestic retreat had begun prior to the Czechoslovak experiment and its tragic aftermath, the entire episode was to make the party even more conscious of the primacy of its role.

20. No specific details of the decision were published, but it has been referred to in the press. In *Ikonomicheski Zhivot*, April 8, 1970, First Deputy Minister of Foreign Trade Ivan Nedev mentioned the "successful implementation of the Party CC's instructions for a correction in the correlation between exports and imports and for the realization of an active trade balance."

In view of the promising situation in 1965–66, many Bulgarians – and Western observers – believed that the Ninth Party Congress in November 1966 would lend official sanction to the changes under way and would chart the direction for future reform, one inevitable prerequisite for which was the rejuvenation of the Politburo and the Central Committee. These hopes were dashed as Zhivkov's declaration of doctrinal orthodoxy regarding domestic and foreign affairs set the tone for the Congress. The results of the party elections were even more surprising. Not only were Boian Bulgaranov (then age seventy) and Ivan Mihailov (sixty-nine) retained in the Politburo, but Tsola Dragoicheva (sixty-eight) and Todor Pavlov (seventy-six) were added to it. The nature of this concession to the older generation of party *apparatchiks* inherent in these choices was also evident in the composition of the new Central Committee, which embodied neither the youthful dynamism nor the expertise that a comprehensive reform would have required.

As was subsequently to be disclosed, Zhivkov's maneuverability was circumscribed not only by the resistance of the older cadres, but by certain other dissident elements as well. The most startling revelation was made at a plenum of the Vratsa district party committee in April 1968 by Ivan Abadzhiev, a candidate member of the Politburo who had been appointed party first secretary in Vratsa the previous September. In Zhivkov's presence, Abadzhiev admitted that the April 1965 conspirators had been an active and influential group in the Vratsa district party and, more significantly, that there were "traces [of this influence] that still have not been eliminated." [21] This disclosure posed interesting questions regarding Zhivkov's political and popular support in Bulgaria's twenty seven other district party organizations. Between April 1965 and June 1968, eleven out of twenty-eight district party first secretaries were relieved of their duties, confirming the suspicion that things were not as quiet as the party press would have it.[22]

Zhivkov's inability to assert his authority over various elements among the BCP rank and file was undoubtedly one of the factors that prompted him to exact absolute conformity from other segments of the population. The cultural community was among the first to feel official pressure; in institutional terms, the reorganization of the Committee for Culture and Art

21. The full text of Abadzhiev's speech was published in *Otechestven Zov* (organ of the Vratsa district party committee), April 18, 1968. The parts of the speech referring to the conspiracy were not reported in the Sofia press.

22. In only two of these cases did the change involve a clear promotion for the secretary in question.

in September 1966 strengthened its control over the various creative unions. And in May 1967, the First Congress of Culture ushered in a new era in the party's attempt to regulate and guide cultural affairs in Bulgaria. Since then, the policy of tighter control has hinged on three basic elements: an effort to centralize cultural institutions, with the Committee for Culture and Art exercising greater responsibility as an instrument of coordination; emphasis on the "constructive" role that culture must play in the development of Bulgarian society, accompanied by a crackdown on both thematic and stylistic experiments and by reprimands to recalcitrant artists; and, relatedly, an intensification of the campaign against the alleged threat of Western bourgeois influence, with the cultural front serving as a watchdog to unmask such dangers. The results of these efforts have not been conspicuously successful. Despite Zhivkov's personal intervention to harangue various artistic groups and the promulgation of a special Politburo decision in October 1969 dealing with "the further development of Bulgarian culture and literature," the attempt to "politicize" cultural life has met with an indifferent response.

Bulgaria's youth has also been a target of the official drive for regimentation and control. The regime's mounting preoccupation with the alienation and apathy of the younger generation came to a head in late 1967 and early 1968. The publication of Zhivkov's "Youth Theses" on December 1, 1967, triggered an extensive discussion regarding institutional reform and the revitalization of party policy toward youth.[23] Subsequently approved at a special Central Committee plenum later in December and at the Eleventh Komsomol Congress in January 1968, the theses attested to a deep-seated official concern. But, despite the acknowledged inefficacy of previous policies and the smattering of good intentions, the approach outlined in the "reform" document was basically conservative in its philosophy and administrative in its method.

Aside from the renewed emphasis on patriotic education, the most innovative aspect of the theses was the "radical reform" of the Komsomol organization, envisaged "to raise its role and authority in the overall economic, political, and cultural life of the country and to make it a true representative of the all-round interests and aspirations of Bulgarian young people." Those who might have welcomed such a reform were soon to be disappointed since this goal was to be reached by making the Komsomol the *only* representative of youth. Henceforth, all those organizations and activities, such as the Sports and Tourist unions, premilitary training, and

23. *Rabotnichesko Delo,* December 1, 1967.

cultural activities, that were outside the Komsomol were to be brought under its jurisdiction. Moreover, a Committee for Youth and Sports was created in February 1968 and entrusted with the task of "coordinating and controlling" the work of those state and public organizations involved in youth affairs.

To judge by recent evidence, the party has registered slight progress in its attempt to mobilize the younger generation by centralizing youth organizations and activities. In March 1971, the Politburo deplored that "the favorable conditions which had been created for rapidly achieving a turning point in the work of the Komsomol and among youth had not been fully utilized," [24] while a month earlier, Politburo member Boris Velchev openly acknowledged that "a large number of young people are completely apolitical." [25]

Referring in his "Youth Theses" to Bulgarian history, Zhivkov bluntly delivered what can only be construed as a self-indictment: "Not only do we not use it, but there is hardly any other state which allows such an underestimation and even belittling of its historic past." Within fourteen months, however, the Bulgarian leader was to lower the curtain on the patriotic education campaign, thus removing one of the last vestiges of the earlier reform movement. In a speech to the Sofia Komsomol organization on March 14, 1969, Zhivkov announced that "the intensification of patriotic education has been successfully completed." He then went on to say, "We cannot rely only on a patriotism based on the historic past," adding the shibboleth that "the essential criterion of patriotism and internationalism has been, is, and will remain the attitude toward the CPSU and the Soviet Union." [26]

It is difficult to imagine that in the course of those fourteen months, the BCP managed to correct an imbalance which has characterized the party's fifty-year history. More plausibly, the curtailment of the patriotic education campaign stemmed from several other factors. On previous occasions, the regime had expressed its dismay that the field of history had become an apolitical outlet for artists declining to adhere to the party's guidelines for contemporary art. Moreover, in preparation for the celebration in September 1969 of the twenty-fifth anniversary of communist rule, Zhivkov was clearly interested in spotlighting recent achievements and, official rhetoric on these advances to the contrary, comparisons with the more distant

24. *Ibid.*, April 4, 1971.

25. *Dunavska Pravda*, February 28, 1971.

26. *Rabotnichesko Delo*, March 16, 1969.

past were not very flattering to the present leadership. Initiated as it was at a time when the Zhivkov regime had begun to display newfound confidence and vitality both at home and abroad, the patriotic education campaign became increasingly anachronistic as the regime perceptibly slid back into its shell.

During the period between 1965 and 1971, the party's most conspicuous reversal took place in the sphere of economic reform.[27] As has been noted, the original economic "theses" of 1965, although never denouncing central planning and management, were in spirit as well as in several component features comparable to the more advanced reforms being undertaken elsewhere in Eastern Europe. However, it soon became apparent that, despite press reports on experiments with and refinements of the NEM, many important parts of the new system were not being applied at all. One of the first indications of this was provided in a November 1967 official decree "On Increasing the Profitability of the Economy."[28] Although intended to supplement the original principles of the reform (and in minor cases revise them), the decree attested that very little had indeed been accomplished.

In July 1968, the BCP Central Committee met and decided that the period of vacillation and experiments had ended. However, instead of implying that the NEM would finally be introduced, the decisions taken at the meeting revealed that the party's attitude toward economic reform had changed appreciably. Under the pretext of "perfecting" the system, the July plenum opted for greater central planning and control of the economy. Zhivkov's denunciation of "planning from below" and the creation of a Committee for Economic Coordination, with broad powers to regulate planning "from above," presaged a corresponding reduction in the autonomy of the associations, or trusts, and the individual enterprises.[29] The expansion of centrally determined compulsory indices, limits, and norms, as well as new regulations strengthening government supervision over financial transactions and foreign trade activity, were to have the same effect.

27. For a more detailed presentation, see L. A. D. Dellin, "Bulgarian Economic Reform – Advance and Retreat," *Problems of Communism*, 19 (September–October 1970), 44–52.

28. *Darzhaven Vestnik,* November 10, 1967.

29. Enterprise antonomy was further cut back as the result of a reorganization of the economic associations in early 1971. The latter's number have been reduced from 120 to 64, while the enterprises grouped in them have lost their "legal and economic independence." See *Darzhaven Vestnik,* December 11, 1970, and January 19, 1971.

This, then, was the vastly altered economic "reform" that was introduced throughout the country on January 1, 1969. In attempting to explain the abrupt shift back to the "command" model, it does seem plausible to exclude two possibilities. If we are to believe the statistics initially cited by the regime (for example, at the Ninth Party Congress in November 1966) on the progress achieved by enterprises operating under the new system in 1966, then it is difficult to conclude that the experiments with NEM had been a failure and that Bulgaria, for whatever reasons, was not ready for reform. Nor would it appear that the reversal was motivated by the leadership's evaluation of the dangers inherent in the Ota Sik variety of market socialism. Although, after August 1968, the Bulgarians were among the harshest critics of the Sik (and the Yugoslav) reform model, the decision to plot a course in the opposite direction was apparently taken far in advance of the enforced return to orthodoxy in Czechoslovakia.

The official rationale for central management and control is to be found in the scientific-technical revolution, which, according to Zhivkov's remarks at the July 1968 Central Committee plenum, "makes it possible under socialist conditions to administer the economy in such a way as to prevent any break in the chain, to avoid duplication, and to reach full coordination of functions and activities among the individual units."[30] Science and technology may somewhat facilitate the current goal of a centrally administered, coordinated, and controlled economy; however, the ultimate motive for the adulteration of the original reform design lies not in the newly discovered advantages of the scientific-technical revolution but in the all too familiar fears of a politically oriented and insecure leadership that refuses to recognize the legitimacy of interests (especially in the economic sphere) other than its own, and that views with considerable apprehension the emergence of a technically inclined, independently minded managerial class.

The prospect of computerized central planning in a technically backward society like Bulgaria appears hardly feasible. Yet, to dismiss this possibility out of hand may be a mistake. In September 1969 the party Central Committee once again met to discuss the "concentration of production, scientific-technical progress, and the new system of management of the national economy." The party newspaper *Rabotnichesko Delo* reported that the plenum had "outlined programs on modernization and complex automation, on setting up, by 1975, automatic systems of man-

30. *Rabotnichesko Delo,* July 25, 1968.

agement on a nation-wide level and in structure-determining concerns and enterprises." These programs were subsequently hailed as of "enormous political and economic significance." [31] Further on, the article stated that one of the practical effects of the plenum's decisions would be "to draw Bulgaria closer in all respects to the Soviet Union." It is not inconceivable that the USSR may have agreed to underwrite, at least partly, computerization in Bulgaria, thus profiting from a convenient pilot experiment.

Whether by computers or not, the Bulgarian leadership has eagerly pursued a policy of comprehensive integration with the Soviet economy. The July plenum's conclusion "to link our economy with that of the Soviet Union through specialization and co-operation in production" has been embodied in the series of sweeping economic agreements signed in Moscow in May 1969 and August 1970, as well as in Zhivkov's statement in September 1969 that the expanded coordination of the Soviet and Bulgarian national economic plans would allow them "to gradually move on to joint planning in a number of branches." [32] These developments will clearly heighten Sofia's already considerable economic dependence on Moscow.

V

If the Ninth Congress of the BCP in November 1966 augured an end to the short-lived period of reform, the proceedings of the Tenth Congress in April 1971 confirmed the return to orthodoxy since that time. In a move that exceeded even the most pessimistic pre-Congress estimates, all eleven full members of the Politburo were reelected. Though this group is certainly long on experience — the average age being sixty-three — it hardly contains the competence or dynamism necessary to bring about the party's goal, as proclaimed in the new BCP program adopted at the Congress, of creating a "developed socialist society."

This striking example of stability — or stagnation — of leadership was paralleled by the lack of any significant discussion during the six-day session. In the main report, Zhivkov reiterated the basic tenets of the regime's conservative internal policy, leaving little doubt that enhanced party control and influence are viewed as the principal mechanisms for dealing with Bulgaria's socioeconomic problems.[33] The official slogan "care for man" notwithstanding, the directives for the 1971–75 economic plan provided for a higher percentage increase in heavy industrial production than in

31. *Ibid.*, October 25, 1969.

32. *Ibid.*, September 27, 1969.

33. *Ibid.*, April 21, 1971.

consumer goods output.[34] As for foreign policy, Zhivkov's initial reference to the "sacred friendship" between Bulgaria and the USSR foreshadowed his totally conformist review of the international situation. That the Bulgarian Congress had been rescheduled [35] to follow rather than to precede the CPSU Congress (held in late March–early April) dramatized the BCP's subservient position vis-à-vis the Soviet Union.

One of the few highlights of the Tenth Congress was the presentation of the amended draft of a new constitution to replace the one adopted in 1947.[36] Taking into account "present realities," the document defines the Bulgarian Communist party as "the leading force" in the country and explicitly commits Bulgaria to "develop and strengthen friendship, co-operation, and mutual assistance with the USSR and the other socialist countries." Of more fundamental significance, the constitution envisages the replacement of the Presidium of the National Assembly by a State Council (similar to those set up in East Germany and Rumania in 1960 and 1961). This new body, whose creation was suggested at the July 1968 plenum, is invested with important executive and legislative functions. It is expected that Zhivkov – the only Warsaw Pact leader still holding the posts of both first secretary and premier – will relinquish the government position to become the chairman of the State Council. Given that the powers of the State Council appear in some instances to eclipse those of the Council of Ministers, his influence will hardly be diminished.

This factor alone suggests that, for the near future, demands for development will continue to be subordinated to the values of a leadership which is essentially concerned with maintaining its own power and is wedded to a political ideology largely inimical to innovation. The periodic cycles of advance and retreat under Zhivkov's rule have plainly demonstrated his inability to carry through a consistent program of reform. As happened after the 1956 and 1961–62 reform movements, stagnation and even retrogression have also followed the reform movement of 1965–66. Although some of the earlier initiatives have not been affected – e.g., the impressive expansion of the tourist industry and a notable improvement of relations with Turkey [37] – and the party has shown an innovative capacity

34. *Ibid.*, April 28, 1971.

35. According to the valid party statute, the Congress should have been held in November 1970, four years after the last one.

36. Subsequently approved in the National Assembly and in a popular referendum, the constitution was officially promulgated on May 18, 1971.

37. Approximately 2.5 million people visited Bulgaria in 1970. As for relations with

in certain areas, such as agricultural policy,[38] the overall ledger is heavily weighted on the side of retrenchment in both domestic and foreign policy.

Itself a disappointment in view of the considerable promise of the earlier advances, the present situation lends credence to the assumption that a lasting transformation of Bulgarian policy can come only from a change of leadership. Here, the prospects for the near future appear dim. The challenge to Moscow posed by the growing forces of nationalism, modernization, and liberalism in Eastern Europe has impelled the Kremlin to prop up the ever loyal, albeit ineffective, regime in Sofia. Zhivkov's acquiescence to Soviet demands for solidarity has been motivated partly by concern for the effect of those forces in his own country. This, however, offers little excuse for such humiliating deference in word and deed to Moscow. Bulgaria's traditional importance as a strategic outpost in the Balkans has increased now that it is the Soviet Union's only real remaining ally in the area. And, particularly at the present time, its positions within the Warsaw Pact and Comecon are a valuable source of support to the USSR.

Nevertheless, there is little evidence that Bulgaria has sought to take advantage of these bargaining points in relations with the Soviet Union. The failure to do so only strengthens the hypothesis that its pro-Soviet policies have stemmed not from a calculated assessment of self-interest but from the weakness and failures of the Zhivkov regime. Reliance on the Soviet crutch has been necessitated by Zhivkov's lack of domestic strength, thus obviating his opportunity to bargain from a quid pro quo position.

This weakness, in combination with the BCP's traditional dependence on doctrinal orthodoxy,[39] has manifested itself internally in the regime's essential conservatism on the key question of the role of the party. Whereas by 1968 the Yugoslav, the Czechoslovak (pre-August), and, to some extent, the Hungarian societies were exhibiting pluralistic tendencies,

Turkey, the repatriation agreement was signed in 1968, and the emigration of limited numbers of Bulgarian Turks began in 1969.

38. The most remarkable example of Bulgarian willingness to experiment in this field has been the creation of agro-industrial complexes, a move finally decided upon at the April 1970 Central Committee plenum. Averaging twenty to thirty thousand hectares in size, the complexes are seen as a means of encouraging "specialization and concentration of production," and as a mechanism for developing cooperation between industry and the rural economy.

39. The history of the BCP before its assumption of power has been excellently covered by Joseph Rothschild, *The Communist Party of Bulgaria: Origins and Development, 1883–1936* (New York, 1959), and by Nissan Oren, "The Bulgarian Communist Party, 1934–1944" (Ph.D. dissertation, Columbia University, 1960).

Zhivkov had already turned his back on the notion that antagonistic interests might exist under communism. The direction of developments in Czechoslovakia undoubtedly confirmed his own estimation of the dangers inherent in any limitation of the party's primacy. Gomulka's recent fate has not altered that thesis. Despite several signs of official concern with the invigoration of the trade unions, long the epitome of the classical "transmission belt," neither the basic policies nor the style of the Zhivkov leadership has thus far seemed influenced by the Polish crisis of December 1970.

In effect, the Bulgarian communists have clung to the monolithic theory of the state and the society, in which the power of the party should be not only maintained but increased. Through its own actions and through such vehicles of central control as the Committee for Economic Coordination, the Komsomol, and the Committee for Culture and Art, the BCP shows every sign of continuing to translate its theory into practice.

8

Rumania

BY GABRIEL FISCHER

The emphatic assertion of Rumanian independence, including the often spectacular changes in Rumanian foreign policy, has been one of the most interesting and significant phenomena on the international scene in the last decade.

The crushing of the Hungarian uprising was followed by a strong Stalinist backlash in Rumania. It seemed then that the Rumanian party had decided to preclude any kind of developments which could be identified with the Hungarian syndrome. Paradoxically, however, the profound impact of the events of 1956 had gradually been assimilated into the particular Rumanian political context, and eventually found full expression in the new emphasis on nationalism. In reacting to 1956, it became clear to Gheorghiu-Dej that to be accepted and supported by the people communism had to become national in character, as well as in aims and policies. He appreciated the importance of nationalism as the vehicle for generating genuine support for the party and the government and as the medium of communication between the rulers and the ruled. Hungarian leaders were swept away in 1956 because they were "aliens" who did not and could not understand the Hungarian people.

Thus the basic lines of the new Rumanian policies already had been drawn up by Gheorghiu-Dej. These general guiding principles were the priority of the idea of nationhood and of the national framework, the role of traditions in the process of socialist upbringing, and the search for an independent foreign policy and for a new role in the international arena. The authoritarian centralist political system remained as the third basic cornerstone of the new policies, without, however, the worst distortions of the Stalinist model.

Gabriel Fischer

The personality of Nicolae Ceausescu, the present secretary general of the Rumanian Communist party and the chairman of the State Council of Rumania, has played a significant part in the implementation and institutionalization of these principles and in their synthesis into a novel and reasonably coherent model of national communism.

Ceausescu came to power in March 1965. At that time, to use the expression of a French Kremlinologist, Bernard Feron, he was a man "without biography." Western news media were quite embarrassed by the scarcity of data concerning his life and personality, and accordingly Western accounts of him were vague. However, almost all agreed that Ceausescu was a one-dimensional party activist and an authoritarian with strong Stalinist proclivities. His peasant origins and "non-Muscovite" upbringing were accentuated as well as his career within the Rumanian Communist party apparatus, his lack of any political or cultural contacts with the outside world, and his provincialism. A typical *apparatchik*, he lived, acted, and advanced within the national framework and outside the mainstream of international communism. His background and activities formed a firm base both for his commitment to an authoritarian party system and for his Rumanian ethnocentrism.

Ceausescu's relationship with Gheorghiu-Dej was a complicated one, reflecting a kind of a "dauphin" complex. His devotion to Gheorghiu, to whom he owed his rise and his position, is considered to have been beyond doubt especially since his personality and character did not seem to qualify him for the leadership. By all accounts, Ceausescu lacked charismatic qualities, and because of a certain roughness in behavior and poor performance on the platform, he was not popular in the party. To assure that Ceausescu did not emerge as a likely rival, Gheorghiu made it a practice to give him unpopular tasks and assignments. Nevertheless, for Ceausescu the activity in Gheorghiu's shadow was a good political education, training him in the necessary qualities of adjustment, self-discipline, caution, perseverance, and patience and teaching him how to survive in dangerous situations and how to take advantage of opportunities in order to attain and to consolidate power in an East European communist system.

It was obviously Gheorghiu's will that Ceausescu should follow him as the leader of the party. The succession was both smooth and balanced. The older members of the Rumanian Presidium were not considered able to govern by themselves; Ceausescu, young and already in command of some very important levers of power, was considered the most suitable to ensure the continuity of the regime and to serve as the new leader. At the same time his relative isolation in the party and his general obscurity throughout the country guaranteed that it would be difficult if not impossible for him to become a real dictator. It was believed that because he would need the advice and support of the old guard, a genuine collective leadership would be established.

I

In the first phase of Ceausescu's leadership the accent was clearly placed on continuity. At the Ninth Congress of the Rumanian Communist party held in July 1965, the leadership appeared united and collectively responsible for the continuation and consolidation of Gheorghiu's legacy. Its composition remained, by and large, unchanged. In particular, there were no alterations in the makeup of the ruling Presidium.

Gradually, however, Ceausescu proceeded to strengthen his position in the government and in the party, particularly among the middle cadres. His followers and collaborators entered the Secretariat and were elected as alternate members of the party's Executive Committee. From the very beginning and with considerable skill, Ceausescu attempted to conciliate groups which had been offended by Gheorghiu: the intellectuals, the former Grivita faction,[1] the old party members (many of them Jews or members of other national minorities), Spanish Civil War veterans, and last but not least, the peasants. He also tried to impose a strict puritanical style and a new morality on the leadership and on society; the policy was reflected in such measures as the legislation against abortion and divorce and the campaign against corruption. As a parallel measure he took steps to increase the standard of living of the population. The new and undoubtedly progressive pension law was an example in this field.

It is only the second phase of Ceausescu's rule that ushered in the real Ceausescu era. Its official inauguration dates from the National Conference of the Rumanian Communist party in December 1967; its best moment was the Czechoslovak crisis in the summer and fall of 1968; and its apotheosis was the Tenth Congress of the Rumanian Communist party in August 1969. The idea of continuity no longer appeared important. The main elements of the Ceausescu image included dissociation from the past

1. The Grivita group was composed of the participants in the great railway strikes in Bucharest during the first months of 1933. Gheorghiu-Dej, who wanted to assume all the merit for the organization of the strike, charged other participants with deviations and eliminated most of his former co-fighters from Rumanian political life. Under Ceausescu some of them came back to the political scene. One, Dumitru Petrescu, became vice-chairman of the State Council and a member of the Executive Committee and of the permanent Presidium of the party. He died in the fall of 1969.

and from many aspects of Gheorghiu's policies, and a new emphasis on Ceausescu's ability to guide the country on the path of gradual integration into the system of advanced societies. Rumania is considered in many aspects to be an underdeveloped society; the creation of the necessary conditions for the Rumanian people to catch up with the economically and culturally advanced countries while avoiding the type of sacrifices which Stalin had forced on the Soviet people became one of the essential aims of the leadership.

The Ceausescu era has been characterized by a feverish reform activity encompassing the whole of Rumanian society. The new penal code and the code of penal procedure, the administrative reform (which restored the traditional Rumanian administrative unit – the *judet*, or county), the reemergence of organizations of national minorities (Hungarian, German, Ukrainian, and Serb), the increase in the minimum wage, and the introduction of the automobile with all its consequences are examples of how Ceausescu's imprint has become manifest in the whole social and economic life of the country.

The negation of the past was epitomized in the dismissal of Alexandru Draghici, who together with Gheorghiu was responsible for past abuses, and in the elimination of the majority of the old guard, men such as Chivu Stoica, Gheorghe Apostol, Alexandru Birladeanu, and Dumitru Coliu. They were removed because they opposed at least some aspects of Ceausescu's foreign policy, as well as the new emphasis on the cult of personality. Ceausescu publicly charged that the discharged leaders were unable to comprehend the needs of a modern socialist society: "We appreciate and respect all those who in the past made their contribution to the development of the society in different domains of activity, but nobody can live on the merits of the past, everybody has to work with all his efforts at present, for the creation of the future." [2]

Openings made by the departure of the old guard were filled by Ceausescu's closest collaborators and supporters of his policies, such as Paul Niculescu Mizil, Ilie Verdet, Gheorghe Pana, Manea Manescu, Vassile Pantelinet, Mihai Gere, and Petre Lupu; they entered the leading organs of the party and occupied key positions in the government. The take-over by the Ceausescu team has become a more or less fait accompli.[3]

2. *Scinteia*, October 1, 1970. Western news media commenting on the elimination of Chivu Stoica mentioned that he seemed to have opposed President Nixon's visit to Bucharest, especially because it was scheduled on the eve of the Tenth Congress of the Rumanian Communist party.

3. Maurer, Gheorghiu's prime minister, who still occupies the same position, seems

The Czechoslovak crisis was undoubtedly the most significant factor in the strengthening of the Ceausescu regime. The moral and political weaknesses of the present Soviet leadership were demonstrated clearly by the Soviet intervention in Czechoslovakia, which, while it led to the collapse of the reform movement, failed to reach its goal in all respects. The intervention strengthened and consolidated the domestic position of the Rumanian leadership (as well as that of Yugoslavia), and increased popular commitment to and identification with the regime and its leaders, because of the need for common defense of the country's independence.

Ceausescu skillfully took advantage of the possibilities offered by the Czechoslovak crisis. He let the Soviet leaders know that Rumania would offer resistance to invasion. Such a resistance by Rumanian army units and the restoration of patriotic guards at the gates of Rumanian factories, even if only of a token character and for a short period, would have been extremely painful for the Soviet leaders. The shedding of the blood of Rumanian workers was something which the Soviet Union wanted to avoid in the framework of its interventionist policies.

Ceausescu also apparently informed the Kremlin that he planned cooperation with Yugoslavia in case of an armed intervention. The common frontier with Yugoslavia would have provided refuge for members of the highest organs of the party and state and for a substantial part of the army, an awkward situation in view of the de facto coverage given Yugoslavia by NATO. In addition, legislation was adopted in Rumania designating as traitors all those who collaborated with the Soviet Union and declaring a priori any such collaboration to be null and void. It must be assumed that Yugoslavia was ready to approve such Rumanian intentions. Contacts between high officials of Rumania and Yugoslavia were quite frequent at the time of the crisis; they have continued into the present as well.

Rumanian diplomacy also actively sought American support in discouraging possible Soviet interventionist intentions. Actually, President Johnson did speak out against "unbridled aggression" and the dangers of the Soviet Union "unleashing the dogs of war"; such pronouncements, under the circumstances, seemed to provide the Rumanians with necessary reassurance.

Finally, the Rumanian leaders have used the Sino-Soviet differences to their own advantage. It appears that China promised to help, if Rumania

to be well integrated into Ceausescu's team. Before his serious car accident in 1970, he served as a kind of "super foreign minister" assigned to delicate international missions.

were invaded, not only by stepping up anti-Soviet propaganda but also by increasing the activity at the Sino-Soviet frontier.[4] The Rumanian public is convinced that such Chinese pressure was and still is in the realm of political realities.

Some Western commentators have underlined the tactical aspects and importance of Ceausescu's attitude. For example, an editorial in the *Christian Science Monitor* stated that "President Ceausescu was odd man out in the Russians' attempt to make the 1968 invasion of Czechoslovakia seem a Warsaw Pact – and not a Russian – operation. If he had gone along with the Russians, Mr. Ceausescu knew that he would have been concurring in a precedent that could be used against himself, should Moscow decide to get rid of him." [5]

It must be stressed that Ceausescu's condemnation of Soviet intervention in Czechoslovakia was utterly sincere and went beyond tactical considerations. It stemmed from the conviction that Soviet action was harmful not only to the Czechoslovaks and possibly to the Rumanians and Yugoslavs, but also to the whole international communist movement, including the Soviet Union. Perhaps, from a tactical point of view, Ceausescu overstepped permissible bounds in the harshness of his condemnation of the Soviet actions in August and September 1968, as some Western commentators assert, and that he overrated the strength of a possible international reaction to the intervention. Among the Rumanian people, however, this attitude obviously strengthened his credibility and his appeal. That the Soviet invasion of Rumania did not materialize was interpreted by the public as a sign of Rumania's toughness and skill and as proof that it was possible to defend the country's independence by policies of defiance. The leadership wanted to create the impression (and has done so with some success) that such a policy could succeed, but only if the party and the leader behaved with circumspection and avoided any traces of revisionism, "antisocialism," or an excess of liberalism in their domestic policies. Domestic orthodoxy would make Soviet intervention in Rumania look like a clear assertion of Russian imperialism rather than evidence of fraternal "care." It is interesting to note that after the invasion of Czechoslovakia, Hungarian commentators contended that the conditions necessitating intervention in Czechoslovakia did not exist in Rumania, and so the application of the Brezhnev doctrine in the latter country would not have been valid.

4. There were rumors of Soviet-Rumanian frontier incidents in August 1968 on a smaller scale than the Sino-Soviet confrontations.

5. *Christian Science Monitor*, March 9, 1970.

During the Czechoslovak crisis and immediately thereafter, Ceausescu succeeded in establishing closer contact with representatives of other communist parties and in defending the correctness of the Rumanian position. The leitmotiv of his reasoning was that Soviet hostility toward the Rumanian leadership was a threat not only to the leaders personally but also to the stability of the regime itself.

The Tenth Congress of the RCP, with all its political pomp and circumstance, proved to be a clear expression of the consolidated Ceausescu era. Not only had the rivals been eliminated, but Ceausescu was being identified with the party – and vice versa – as the symbol of national dignity. The slogans of the Congress, such as "Ceausescu – R.C.P.," or "Ceausescu and the people," or simply "Ceausescu, Ceausescu," exemplify this trend.

Moreover, the leadership emerged from the Congress as a coherent body, representing more or less the same generation and possessing similar aims and outlooks. Chances are good that it will remain united, providing there are no major failures in internal or foreign policies.

Every speaker at the Congress highly praised Ceausescu. Janos Fazekas, for example, a Hungarian member of the Executive Committee and vice-chairman of the Council of Ministers declared: "I have known Nicolae Ceausescu for 25 years. In this period, long enough in the life of a man, I have had countless occasions – due to the nature of my work and to the tasks assigned to me by the party – to ascertain directly his exceptional human qualities, his particular theoretical ability and working capacity, his unlimited dedication to the cause of socialism and communism. I can assert with full conviction that his whole being is identified with the strivings of the Communist Party, of the people, of the working men. I want to emphasize his great love for the homeland which is organically connected with proletarian internationalism, which in turn stems from the immortal teaching of Marxism-Leninism, from the feeling of respect towards all the workingmen regardless of nationality." [6]

Clearly Ceausescu has encouraged the growth of the "cult of personality" around himself. Its fundamental thrust has remained unchanged since the Tenth Congress even though the tone has been moderated. For example, the fight against the devastating floods in the spring of 1970 and the celebration in May 1971 of the fiftieth anniversary of the Rumanian Communist party were used to enhance Ceausescu's stature and prestige. Telegrams, letters, resolutions of meetings, and pledges made on these occa-

6. *Scinteia*, August 9, 1969.

sions were always addressed personally to Ceausescu, as the leader of the party and the nation. Of course such a cult not only extols Ceausescu but also condemns all who are or may be opposed to the Ceausescu line.

At home and abroad the Ceausescu image has gradually changed from that of a "ruthless," "rigid," "defiant," "reserved," "suspicious" party hack to that of a "youthful and energetic," "courageous," "determined," "sincere," "self-secure," and "persevering and consistent" leader.[7]

II

The three basic principles which Ceausescu inherited from Gheorghiu-Dej have been enlarged and adapted to his personality and to Rumania's recent experience on the path of independent policies. Ceausescu's early aversion to theoretical exercises had undergone significant transformation as it became increasingly necessary for him to justify in theory the essential features of his policies, especially when confronted by Moscow. Such continuous confrontation, regardless of the underlying motive, requires a supply of theoretical arguments which blend into the patterns and the jargon of Marxism-Leninism.

Ceausescu's theoretical arguments still have certain Stalinist features cast in the Lukacs mold; under Stalinism theory did not guide revolutionary strategy and tactics, but pragmatic and tactical considerations inevitably determined and provoked theoretical debates. For example, the need to strengthen Rumania's position against the theoretical justification for Soviet interventionist policies caused Ceausescu to proclaim that socialism in Rumania is so well entrenched that it cannot be seriously endangered by either internal or external forces: "Does there exist indeed in Rumania, where the socialist relationship triumphed completely and where the exploiting classes were liquidated forever, the danger of restoring capitalism in one form or another? No, there is not such a danger." [8]

To accept the opposite view implies overrating the strength of the im-

7. Some of the American opinions on Ceausescu's personality are worthy of note. The following appraisals were made after his visit to the United States in the autumn of 1970. American businessmen, bankers, and industrialists, who met Ceausescu, found him: "shy, soft-spoken and savvy," but also "authoritative and treated by his aides with the utmost deference." One New York businessman remarked: "It is obvious that he doesn't have to run for office." Another noted that Ceausescu was tough, but he manifested "a certain openness of intellect." An executive added that the Rumanians "were not what you'd call a warm and gregarious group of people." On the other hand, a housewife in a model home visited by Ceausescu in Reston, Virginia, stressed that the Rumanian president "seemed very down-to-earth." *New York Times,* November 13, 1970.

8. *Ibid.*, October 18, 1968.

perialist forces and underrating the forces of progress and socialism. In a strictly orthodox wrapping, this thesis is clearly directed against the Brezhnev doctrine which makes the necessity of "common defense" of socialist achievements dependent on the Soviet judgment as to when and where this "common defense" is needed. However, Ceausescu's argument is not only cast in orthodox terms but also assumes an offensive: Whoever refutes it is automatically liable to be accused of lack of confidence in the forces of progress and socialism.

The Polish events of December 1970 produced a new, more analytical, more profound, and more sincere approach to this kind of argument. In general the rioting of Polish workers had a strong impact on Ceausescu and the Rumanian communist leaders. The Rumanians realized that those who toe a hard ideological line are bound to use the Polish developments as proof of the danger of underestimating the strength of hostile forces present in every socialist society. But courageously Ceausescu has thrown the ball back: the thesis of the definitive victory of socialism continues to stand firm. There are still a few isolated hostile elements, remnants of the former owner classes in Rumania as well as in other socialist countries; yet neither they, nor external opposition, can provoke a powerful outburst of popular dissatisfaction. Such a social conflict occurs only if the ties between the party and the workers are significantly weakened, if a communication gap develops between them. Meanwhile the Rumanian party stated that it had not – at least not under Ceausescu – committed the errors of its Polish colleagues and that it will continue to solve social conflicts only by methods which correspond to the democratic nature of the new system.

How has Ceausescu enlarged and developed Gheorghiu-Dej's guiding ideas? He is obviously skillful at what Demichev, one of the Soviet leaders, labels as "nationalization of socialism." National diversity, according to Ceausescu, is "the inevitable and irreversible framework" of the activity of the communist parties because even under socialism a national framework endures as the lasting structure of society.

It is socialism in fact which, at least in Eastern Europe, makes a whole community realize its national character and generates conscious national life among the people of the country. Apparently Ceausescu's view is that nationalism is not only the product of the past as transmitted by the older generation but it is generated by the emergence of new and numerous middle strata and, above all, by the important growth of the intellectual elite.[9]

9. Ghita Ionescu's statement seems to be exaggerated, especially when applied to the present: "In many a young Rumanian it is possible to see a patriotism devoid of na-

According to Ceausescu, the nation is the basic reality of the present phase of world development regardless of the social system, and real social progress can be achieved only through full satisfaction of national demands. Therefore, self-determination is not a value secondary to socialism, but on the contrary, socialism and self-determination are corollaries and mutually reinforcing values.

The unconditional defense of national independence and sovereignty does not mean nationalism, argue the Rumanian leaders. "National" and "nationalist" are concepts which stand separately: concern for and promotion of a national personality lead to respect for national independence and to categorical rejection of interventionist policies. Thus it is not the so-called nationalism, but the interventionist policies which constitute the real danger to the unity of the socialist system and to the successful building of socialism in individual countries. Finally only those who live within a national framework and are fully integrated and dedicated to it can comprehend the national particularities and interests of their country and only they have the right and the knowledge to make decisions concerning the vital issues of the community.

Consequently, the Rumanians argue that the successful construction of socialism in one's own country, predicated on the support of the people in response to national demands and needs and determined by national traditions, is the best expression of internationalism and the most efficient propaganda for the cause of socialism. No model of socialism, derived from the experience of only one country, can apply to all communist countries, even if this one country is the Soviet Union. To impose alien models, which will ultimately be rejected by the population as being contrary to its traditions and character, is to endanger socialism in its natural framework.[10] Consequently, a unique national model of socialism for each country is not only a possibility, but also an essential prerequisite for success.

Given this uniqueness of national form, it can be seen that differences in the economic and social structure of the socialist countries are not only inherited from the past but are also generated by current distinctions. Differentiation is thus a continuous and actual process in Rumanian eyes, and the equalization of the level of development of the socialist countries is a utopian idea.

The demand for absolute sovereignty for the socialist states is extended

tionalist excess and tempered by geo-political realism, which only a romantic would call into question." *Communism in Rumania* (London, 1964), p. 348.

10. The Rumanians quote Engels that the existing national state, at least at the beginning, will be the natural framework of socialist construction.

also to the communist parties. Each party is independent in determining its policies and the means to achieve them. No party, say the Rumanians, can be the sole "supreme guardian of Marxism-Leninism" or the "infallible depository of Marxist truth." [11] Acting within well-defined national structures, *each* party has to achieve the necessary synthesis between general rules and specific conditions. This formulation supports the Rumanian emphasis on the role of particular national conditions in the building of socialism.

This emphasis on the national sovereignty of socialist countries and their communist parties, however, does not preclude international cooperation between them. Such cooperation is necessary, and any misunderstandings can and should be eliminated. Meaningful association and coexistence can survive only between states of different socialist models in conditions of "immense diversity and variety." This, in a nutshell, is the Rumanian variant of the idea of "unity in diversity."

The idea of the primacy of national interests even under socialism also extends to the need of each socialist country to build its own independent economic structure – a principle which refutes any kind of economic integration. Further, because an advanced society must have its own scientists and researchers who can adjust the needs of science and technology to particular national conditions, autonomous scientific and technical research has to be developed by each socialist country.

III

Ceausescu's personal touch has left its imprint on Rumanian foreign policy, which is now more relaxed, more imaginative, and more courageous than it was under Gheorghiu. Because of the strictly centralized system, it has not lost all its rigidity, but in the five or six years during which independent policies have been stressed, the decision-makers have acquired important experience and greater flexibility.

The Rumanian leader's expectation was that the eventual success and survival of the Czechoslovak reform regime would alleviate Rumania's relative isolation within the socialist system and that the country would be able to liberate itself, to some extent at least, from the "Russian obsession." However, the Soviet intervention in Czechoslovakia put an end to these reckonings, and Rumania had to return to its already "traditional" tight-

11. See among others Paul Niculescu Mizil's speech at the National Conference of the party in December 1967, or the article in the theoretical organ of the party, *Lupta de Clasa*, January 1970.

rope policy toward its powerful neighbor. "Independence, not defiance"[12] has become the slogan of Rumania's low-key policy toward the Soviet Union.

Obviously, Rumania does not want to provoke the Soviet Union unnecessarily. Although it has no illusions about Soviet intentions and feelings toward the Rumanian leadership, it considers that at present there are still some political and even moral difficulties which prevent the Soviet Union from making a complete break with Rumania. Rumania's task is, of course, to use and underline these difficulties, through intelligent maneuvering. Almost every Rumanian foreign policy action pursues this aim. Rumania's insistence that the United Nations reassert the principles of sovereignty, independence, and nonintervention as the basic rules governing the relations between member states, its repeated proposal for the interdiction of military exercises by alien armies on the territory of sovereign states, and its stand against bloc policies and against foreign military bases are all clear examples of these tactics.

Economic and military integration are rejected equally by the Rumanians, and it seems that they are invariably reluctant to accept a standing Warsaw Pact force — in one form or another. In his sharp reply to General Shtemenko's hints at the process of integration within the framework of the Warsaw Pact, Ceausescu emphasized that only the orders of the Rumanian party and government and of the Supreme Command of the Rumanian Armed Forces can be implemented in his country.[13]

The Rumanians also oppose any kind of territorial extension of the scope implied in the new Soviet-Rumanian Treaty of Friendship, Cooperation, and Mutual Aid, which was finally signed on July 7, 1970, after long procrastination on both sides. They stressed repeatedly that the treaty was to be a safeguard against the "imperialist" threat and under no circumstances was to be applied against a member state, or any socialist state. But the text of the treaty does not limit its application to Europe, and the Rumanians were not fully satisfied in this respect. The definition of aggressor as "any force of imperialism, militarism and revanchism" is flexible enough to cover the interpretation of both signatories. However, and this is very important, the Brezhnev doctrine and the possibility of its implementation — so much in the foreground of the Soviet-Czechoslovak pact of spring 1970 — is absent from the Soviet-Rumanian treaty. And the

12. *New York Times,* April 19, 1970.

13. *Scinteia,* February 6, 1970. Stressing his country's loyalty to the Warsaw Pact, Ceausescu nevertheless added that Rumania wants to cooperate with armies of all the socialist countries. This includes, of course, China and Yugoslavia.

word *integration* is also missing from the paragraph concerning the Comecon.

The tension between Rumania and the Soviet Union is ever present and at times has created more or less open crises. Increasingly a chronic state of affairs in the relationship between them has developed, with more or less acute periods, alternating with intermittent ceasefires – thus reflecting the wishes of the two countries either to temporarily avoid new complications or simply to express their inability to achieve more radical solutions. Economic pressure, the long delay in signing the Soviet-Rumanian treaty, the repeated demands for Warsaw Pact maneuvers on Rumanian territory, and the continuous insistence on greater integration within the Pact and within the Comecon are all clear expressions of Soviet policies toward Rumania. The "Rumanian issue," even if it is not specifically referred to, is hinted at in every major utterance of the Soviet leaders. In Budapest on April 3, 1970, for example, Brezhnev warned against the danger of nationalism, stressing that ". . . no national interest of the socialist countries should be asserted to the detriment of the international interests of socialism." [14]

Soviet speeches, articles, and books stress the scope of "the permanent internationalist aid" which the Soviet Union has granted to Rumania for the "consolidation of its independence," and for its socialist regime and economy. Khrushchev's threat, "If you do not come with us we go ahead without you," is often reiterated. However, one wonders if Soviet decision-makers really want to go ahead with Rumania under the present leadership which in the Soviet view may become, especially in a crisis, a potential Trojan horse. At present the pressure on Rumania to integrate into the Soviet-dominated system may be considered a deliberate policy to weaken the Rumanian leadership. For its part, the Rumanian effort is concentrated on avoiding a situation which would leave the country isolated and defenseless.

Thus, a basic tactical objective of Rumania is to gain time. The emphasis on initiatives favoring the preparation of a European security conference reflects this preoccupation. If the conference proposal becomes the subject of concrete and serious negotiations, the chances of survival of the present Rumanian policies are improved for it is unlikely that the Soviet Union would risk a new open intervention at such a time.

Rumania's plans to maintain and to strengthen its independent status fit well into the current situation of the Sino-Soviet confrontation in which

14. *Pravda*, April 4, 1970.

there are no open hostilities, but also no signs of reconciliation and in which there is a gradual but continuous Soviet-American détente, accompanied by a general thaw in East-West relations on a bilateral as well as a multilateral basis. In this context one may understand the positive appraisal given by the Rumanians to the improvement in Chinese-American relations. Apparently Rumania has served as a mediator in bringing about this development. Its ambassador to Paris, Constantin Flitan, without confirming or denying the Rumanian contribution to the Sino-American thaw, significantly said, "We are proud of the role which has been assigned to us." [15] The arrival of China on the international scene, marking the trend toward multipolarity, is supported by the Rumanians, as opening up to them scope for diplomatic maneuver. On the other hand, the development of greater rigidity in the foreign policies and the mutual relations of the superpowers may seriously endanger Rumania's position.

In spite of the permanent Soviet menace, the basic assumption of the Ceausescu leadership is that there will be an inevitable and gradual erosion of bipolarity in the field of foreign policy. Gheorghiu-Dej viewed the world system as dominated by the rules of bipolarity and tried to act accordingly. His successor recognizes the weight and influence of the great powers, but does not sympathize with them, not even with China. Politically and even emotionally he is committed to the affirmation of the rights of middle and small powers in the international arena. Under his leadership Rumania as a middle power has asserted itself on a regional and a world level.

In the last six years Rumania has succeeded in creating its own special image in the international system. In 1967 the Foreign Minister Corneliu Manescu became the first East European chairman of the General Assembly of the United Nations. De Gaulle's visit in the spring of 1968, the behavior of the country during the Czechoslovak crisis, and Nixon's visit to Rumania in the summer of 1969 focused the attention of world opinion on Rumania and raised the country's international prestige. Ceausescu's visits to the United States, France, and other countries were aimed at achieving the same objective and, indeed, they expanded the opportunities of the Rumanian leaders in the field of foreign policy. In general Rumania no longer had to emphasize that its stance was different from that of the Soviet Union as it had done at the time of the Middle East crisis or at the opening of diplomatic relations with the German Federal Republic.

Of course there are still moments when doubts appear, both in the West and in the East, about Rumania's ability to defend its independent line in

15. *Le Monde*, May 6, 1971.

foreign policy. For example, in the first months of 1971 some Western newsmen referred to Rumania's effort to normalize its relations with the Soviet Union and to align itself more closely to the Soviet position on many important issues. Rumania's decision to join the Comecon Investment Bank, after its initial refusal in May 1970, its participation in one of the recent Comecon ventures in the field of chemistry (Interchim), in the Warsaw Pact Defense Ministers' Committee, as well as in Warsaw Pact maneuvers (in May 1969 in the Soviet Union and in October 1970 in the German Democratic Republic), and finally its indurate criticism of the Israeli position were all regarded in the West as expressions of a more "orthodox" standpoint. But in essence the Rumanian position has not changed. Rumania still opposes integration within Comecon; according to Ceausescu, Comecon must be open to all socialist states and must be able to attract nonsocialist ones as well. Moreover, in 1970 the share of all socialist countries in Rumanian foreign trade was 54 per cent, which is less than corresponding figures for the other socialist countries of Europe except Yugoslavia. At the same time the new Foreign Trade Law opens up possibilities for Western investment and industrial cooperation. Rumania has also successfully avoided having Warsaw Pact maneuvers on its own territory. Its economic and tourist ties with Israel are still expanding. Finally, Ceausescu's visit to China in the summer of 1971 is obvious proof of Rumania's intention to continue to build up its relations with China even if this cooperation arouses the ire of the Soviet Union. The basic precepts of independence, sovereignty, nonintervention, equality, and reciprocal benefits were quite emphatically reaffirmed by Ceausescu on the fiftieth anniversary of the Rumanian Communist party: "I was asked at different interviews if Rumania intends to renounce the upholding of these principles. In fact we consider that in certain respects these principles are for human society today, for friendly relations throughout the world, as water and air are for the existence of man. How could we renounce water and air? It would mean the renunciation of life. No, we can not renounce these principles, because they constitute the preconditions of the independent and free life – the preconditions of the independent and free life of all nations of the world." [16]

Officially the axis of Rumanian foreign policy is friendship and cooperation with all the socialist countries. However, this does not exclude a strong emphasis on Rumania's desire to develop political and economic relations with all the countries of the world. These two aims are frequently

16. *Scinteia*, May 8, 1971.

proclaimed within the same sentence, for Ceausescu and his colleagues want to stress that they think and act in world dimensions, and that in many fields they do not differentiate between the socialist and capitalist systems. There is a theoretical justification for that. Socialism can be built only on the basis of the most up-to-date scientific, economic, and technical developments, which are present in the most advanced capitalist countries but are absent in the Soviet Union and other socialist countries, according to the Rumanians. The demand for modernization requires close economic and scientific contacts with the West so that the existing technological gap might be narrowed. In addition, the principle of eclectic assimilation of everything that is most valuable for a modern society is cautiously but resolutely extended to the noneconomic fields of culture, art, education, psychology, sociology, and aesthetics. Tourism and personal contacts with the West are also encouraged.

Ceausescu and his companions appear not to be afraid of these contacts. They would like, however, to extend Western influences in Rumania gradually, being careful to keep them under control in order not to disturb the national evolution and the political status quo. They appear convinced that in the long run the West in general and the United States in particular will accept national models of communism, especially if socialist states assert their independence vis-à-vis the Soviet Union. This opinion stems not only from the intentions of the American decision-makers, but from the sheer fact of the great geographical distance between the United States and Eastern Europe. In Bucharest, Nixon reassured the Rumanians in this respect, declaring that people can come to an understanding on earth if they have already reached the moon: "If we want to progress towards this understanding which requires continuous efforts, we have to see the world as it is: a world with different social orders: a real world where many interests divide people and many interests bring them closer." [17]

Ceausescu and his comrades clearly believe, more now than some years earlier, in the convergence of different social systems, the convergence which is spontaneous as much as it is artificially induced. The international (not only socialist) division of labor, for example, is accepted by the Rumanian leadership as an essential reality of the international system. Also understood as a general truth is the idea of the ability of each nation to contribute to the cultural and scientific values of the world. The need for an interchange of these values seems to Ceausescu to be morally accept-

17. *Ibid.*, August 3, 1969.

able as well as politically expedient. The striving for modernization and convergence is thus complementary.

IV

Watching closely the evolution of the East European socialist systems, Ceausescu has come to the conclusion that changes and improvements are needed in Rumania. However, these must come through a gradual, cautious, and always controlled process of development. All reforms must be initiated from above by the leadership and not as the result of pressures from below. Popular satisfaction, in Ceausescu's opinion, remains satisfaction even if it results from changes inspired by different groups of the society but implemented by an alert, responsive, and farseeing leadership. In Rumania, where democratic traditions are weak, particularly in comparison with those in Czechoslovakia, the leadership views its role as the essential element for successful and uninterrupted socialist progress, without major troubles and disorder. The socialist "law and order" concept implies a benevolent dictatorship which avoids terror and prefers to control through warning and persuasion rather than through suppression or categorical interdiction.

Within these limits, the Rumanian leaders strive to create an image of modernism for their political model (called officially a "multilaterally developed socialist society"), by comparing it with the Soviet model which they consider obsolete. A new style adopted by Ceausescu reflects this emphasis on modernism. Unlike the Soviet leaders, he tries to recognize and to accommodate new trends wherever they may appear. The growing importance of the student movement not only in the West but throughout the world is, for example, often underscored in his public utterances – although the existence of such a movement in Rumania is recognized only formally. Just as de Gaulle's ideas had influenced Gheorghiu-Dej's political thinking, the former French president's visit to Rumania has left its imprint on Ceausescu too, with many elements of de Gaulle's personal style, such as the "immersion in the masses" technique, having been integrated into Ceausescu's pattern of public behavior.[18]

In search for new models, there is also a trend among Rumanian leaders toward a certain degree of assimilation of Western political institutions.

18. It is also noteworthy that Mao Tse-tung's authoritarian style has had a strong impact on Ceausescu who apparently would like to adopt some of its features. This influence is evident in his handling of cultural issues and youth problems, for it was in these areas that the party line hardened after his visit to China in the summer of 1971.

Ceausescu obviously used some features of an American electoral campaign before and during the Tenth Congress of the Rumanian party. His election to the post of secretary general was proposed by local party organizations, supported by mass organizations and professional groups, and carried out not by the new Central Committee of the party, but by the plenary session of the Congress itself.

Another expression of Ceausescu's insistence on modernization is his desire to impart a scientific character to decision-making. Decisions in economic problems, for example, are preceded by studies, polls, surveys, and soundings; local party organizations, ministries, people's councils, and managers of enterprises do research and prepare special studies on ways and means of implementing the decisions of the party and the government in their respective areas of authority.

For genuine modernization, however, the Rumanian model of socialism needs changes in content rather than in form, and it should reduce its centralism in favor of democracy. Though it is true that nationalism can be a powerful unifying and driving force for a society, especially in the face of external danger, it cannot satisfy the diverse needs of the population in the long run and it may prove difficult to control.

The Yugoslav evolution since 1948 is a living reminder to Ceausescu that independence and the assertion of national interests cannot be separated indefinitely from democratization and decentralization. The delicate but necessary task of reforming the economy in the direction of gradual decentralization illustrates the difficulties faced by the Rumanian leadership.

Currently, a tri-level industrial structure is being introduced with industrial administrations and combines interposed between enterprises and economic ministries. Although the role of the ministries is being somewhat reduced, the outcome of the experiment is uncertain, because of the retention of centralized planning. Central organs can thus keep the base of their former prerogatives in the field of foreign trade and international decision-making. The transition may be long and painful, especially because the leaders, with their commitment to centralism, often seem to vacillate in their economic policy. After the National Conference of the party in December 1967, for example, the direct guidance of the economy at the central level was entrusted mainly to the government, and party leadership lost its primary and immediate responsibility in this area. At the local level, however, party committees and economic commissions have been given direct responsibility for economic activities. The central party role in economic planning was restored by the December 1969 plenum of the Central Committee which created new economic commissions headed by top party leaders. This development suggests that the leadership of the party, obviously anxious to correct deficiencies in the Rumanian economy, wants to reimpose its direct control over economic policies.

Despite these and other signs of the continuation of centralist tendencies, Ceausescu takes considerable pride in the regime's "continuous expansion of socialist democracy," and boasts of its main achievement, the establishment of permanent and direct contact between the leadership and the people.[19] He frequently visits different provinces, inspecting enterprises, cooperative and state farms, universities and research institutes, and even market places, and he meets with different groups of intellectuals. On such occasions Ceausescu himself explains the policies of the party and the government, stressing legality and humanism and defending the victims of injustice or abuse. He emphasizes that the leaders and the people must achieve direct communication, and he attempts to project an image of a good and understanding national leader who is genuinely sympathetic to his people and their wants. Still he accents the need for responsibility and discipline among the citizens in a socialist democracy, rather than their right either to criticize or to oppose the regime.

It is true that the Rumanian public is kept better informed now than ever before on the international situation in general and on the internal and foreign policies of its government, but the information is regarded as an essential premise for participation, and not the participation itself; in Rumania the one-way flow of influences, from the ruler to the ruled, continues to prevail. Labeled a dialogue by Ceausescu and other leaders, the process is in fact still mainly a monologue. The Front of Socialist Unity, the mass organizations, the professional groupings of the intellectuals, and the semestral general meetings of the workers and employees in the enterprises reflect all the characteristics of pseudo-participation at least for the time being.

As far as the scope and the activity of mass organizations are concerned, they continue as "conveyor belts," in theory and in practice, and the lead-

19. In his important study, "Rumania Today," *Problems of Communism*, 18, nos. 2, 11 (January–February, and March–April 1969), 32–38, 8–17, J. F. Brown asserts: "After twenty years of sterility, inhibition and at times terror . . . Ceausescu has sought within the limits of his philosophy to inspire genuine mass participation and real communication between rulers and ruled, particularly since the National Conference of December 1967 when he felt that his power was safely consolidated." This affirmation, which seems somewhat optimistic when applied to the present situation, is concluded by a statement that some of Ceausescu's domestic policies "have left in their wake latent resentments which may lead to upheavals and eventually force a reassessment of the whole philosophy on which these policies are based."

ership is careful not to allow these organizations to become transformed into real interest or pressure groups. In this respect the case of the trade unions is relevant. Early in 1971 Ceausescu, at a session of the Central Committee of the party, complained that the trade unions do not fulfill their tasks. (Only one participant in the discussion spoke of the defense of the workers' interests as the trade unions' main task.) Changes in the activity and organization of the trade unions were then worked out by the party and implemented by the Congress of the General Union of the Rumanian Trade Unions. The Congress also elected as its new chairman Virgil Trofim, who had formerly been secretary of the Central Committee. Ceausescu stressed that the party leads the mass organizations and helps them to develop the ability to solve their own problems. In practice, however, the trusteeship of the party does not help the mass organizations to act on their own. In a system where the party is omnipresent and assumes a leading role, there is little room for the autonomous development of interest groups. There have been no real changes in the electoral system or, despite some expansion of the role of the National Assembly and its standing committees, in the Rumanian power structure. The rights of people's councils at both the county and municipal levels have been expanded to some extent, but these changes affect the executive committees of these organs rather than the councils themselves. Although the regime needs active support of the population in its confrontation with the Soviet Union, it actually discourages any significant increase in popular participation.

If democratization is to take place in the East European countries, the development of inner-party democracy is a necessary, a priori prerequisite. In Rumania the party still clings to "democratic centralism" as its guiding operational principle and remains monolithic. The formation of factions is prohibited not only for tactical reasons as a defense against possible Soviet endeavors to split the party, but also because Ceausescu strongly believes in the idea of strict party unity. The party, namely the leadership, is always right and members merely carry out the decisions and the instructions of central organs.

No criticism is allowed of either the political line of the party or of the decisions of the leadership. Critical scrutiny is allowed only if mistakes and distortions occur in the actual policy implementation. And even within these limits, *Scinteia*, the organ of the Central Committee and a kind of collective ombudsman in Rumania, is cautious in concrete criticism even of local party organizations for fear that the prestige of the party as a whole may suffer. Such criticism is normally absent from the local news media.

At present the leading role of the party in every aspect of society is carefully preserved. The powers of local party organizations to control social, economic, and political activities were even extended. At the Tenth Congress these powers were made applicable to the universities and schools and to medical institutions and hospitals, in addition to the customary survey of economic enterprises. Despite a now greater degree of tolerance toward the intellectuals (including writers and artists), the party can still assert its exclusive ownership of the mass media and its right to maintain strict control over all manifestations of cultural life.

Party and state functions are in many respects merged. The first secretary of the Communist Youth, for example, is ex officio the minister for youth. The chairman of the Trade Unions Council is, de jure, a member of the Council of Ministers, and first secretaries of party organizations in cities, towns, or counties are at the same time mayors or administrative chiefs of their respective units. Ceausescu himself combines the duties of secretary-general of the party, chairman of the State Council, supreme commander of the Armed Forces, and chairman of the Front for Socialist Unity. Within this framework it is the party and its apparatus that exercise the real decision-making powers. The party also guides foreign policy formation and ideological activity, and controls directly both security services and the armed forces. Promotion and appointments are still closely dependent on party membership of the candidates.

Nevertheless a gradual change has taken place in the nature of the party. It now has more than two million members, and the only requirements for membership is that anyone who is considered "useful and valuable" should join the party. The candidacy stage for membership has been abolished, and the issue of social origin no longer plays a role in admission. The duties of members are less onerous, with outward manifestations of allegiance and support considered generally sufficient. There are fewer party meetings and few tasks for members to fulfill. According to the new rules, local level organizations have only one meeting a month and hold elections every two years; the county and municipal organizations convene conferences only once in four years. The characteristics of a typical party functionary have also changed; most of the central and local leaders can be considered technocrats, experts in their field of activity; many of them have university degrees and take definitely pragmatic positions on issues. All these are signs of a degree of depoliticization of the party which means also a degree of deemphasis on ideological considerations.

In the face of this evolution, the party and its apparatus continue to dominate Rumanian society from above and still provoke and foster a sense of alienation among the Rumanian citizens. Centralized structures and operational methods signify that there is a continuous danger that the leadership will become isolated and its ability to respond at a given moment to popular pressures will weaken. This possibility is all the greater because as yet there are no institutional or participatory patterns which would further the democratization of the regime. For the time being, progress is dependent mainly on the personality and goodwill of the leader and on his conviction that the clock cannot be turned back.

In spite of the many contradictory features of the Ceausescu era, the Rumanian developments have an obviously positive meaning. Khrushchev thought that after the intervention in Hungary, the Hungarian experiment would not be repeated; a similar conviction of Brezhnev and company led to the intervention in Czechoslovakia. However, it is precisely this Soviet policy which is bound to occasion in socialist states new efforts to seek other than Soviet forms and to search for ways to assert greater independence. Rumania is now building a different model of socialism in an East European context, and the experiment represents a link in the continuous chain of de-Stalinization, as Raymond Aron calls it.

It is clear that the distinctive features of the Rumanian model will multiply, develop, and acquire even more definitive contours. The chance of survival exists – in spite of the continuous Soviet menace – and there is a hope that the present leadership and Nicolae Ceausescu will endeavor further to improve their communication with the people and to recognize their wishes in the future building of the Rumanian model. As Andre Fontaine says, "Rumania may hope that with time its originality will become, as did Yugoslavia's neutrality an element of the *status quo*." [20]

20. *Le Monde*, January 2, 1970.

9

Yugoslavia

BY JOHN C. CAMPBELL

Mentioning some plain and well-known facts may help to explain at the start Yugoslavia's unique position. Yugoslavia is wholly independent in its domestic and its international policies. It is not in any East European bloc. It is not a member of the Warsaw Pact or of the Council for Mutual Economic Assistance (Comecon). It does not follow any line laid down in Moscow. Disarray in the communist world began with Yugoslavia's declaration of independence in 1948. On the other hand, Yugoslavia is, or says it is, a socialist country. It has a one-party political system, and the one party is the League of Communists. Its leaders – and notably Marshal Tito, the supreme leader – speak of its role in the international workers' movement and in the world's march to socialism. But when this workers' movement holds a conference in Moscow, Yugoslavia is conspicuously absent.

It is this anomalous position that enables Yugoslavia to be of the East (mainly ideologically) and of the West (mainly economically) and at the same time to glory in its leadership of the nonaligned; to associate itself in special status with the Comecon in Moscow and with the Organization for Economic Cooperation and Development (OECD) in Paris; to repudiate the Brezhnev doctrine, but to rally the socialists and progressives of the world against the menace of Western imperialism. Thus, when comparing events in Yugoslavia with those in Poland, Hungary, and other East European countries, we have to keep reminding ourselves of this special context. Developments which seem parallel may not be. Others may seem totally at odds, and yet be similar.

This context is relevant to the question of Yugoslav leadership and example in the communist world. Yugoslavia is rightly cited for its separate road, its market socialism, its workers' councils, and its political reforms. Yet, we have to take into account that no Dubcek or Kadar or Ceausescu has been in the fortunate position of Tito. He and his lieutenants, in deciding how much freedom to allow the press or how to vote in the United Nations, have only their own position to consider. They do not have to look over the shoulder to see what fate may be brewing for them in the Kremlin. The Yugoslavs were lucky enough, or courageous enough, to have their break come early, in the same year in which the Soviets completed their take-over of Eastern Europe by engineering the coup in Czechoslovakia. The Warsaw Pact was not concluded until seven years after the great divide of 1948.

Once Stalin hesitated, the game was won. And once Tito cut the umbilical cord, Yugoslavia has moved in ways that reflect the historical forces, tensions, and pressures which make up the complex society of that country. We have not only an experiment in socialism and some lessons for other socialist societies, but also a number of other factors: national temperament, conflict among component nationalities, and economic backwardness – all of which are simply part of the local scenery. They remain there whether Yugoslavia is building socialism or something else.

I

Let us look at the period of the last five years by beginning somewhere around the middle of it, specifically in 1968 when Eastern Europe, and indeed all of Europe, was shaken by the crisis over Czechoslovakia. For the Yugoslavs, as for the Czechs and Slovaks, there was the same sequence of exhilaration and hope as the great transformation took shape during the first half of the year, and then incredulity and letdown when Soviet troops brought it to an abrupt end in August. Those feelings were heightened by two special circumstances.

First, Tito and his friends had been convinced that the time was past when the Soviet Union would act as it did, despite the evidence of political pressures and a military buildup to do just that. Like many in the West, they had taken the signs of détente in the past few years at close to face value and had convinced themselves that liberalization was the prevailing wind in Eastern Europe, and that the Soviet Union would not use force to stop it, even though they were not entirely happy about it. Nineteen fifty-six, the year of Hungary, seemed a long time ago.

Second, there is a special bond between Czechs and Yugoslavs which evolved long before there was a Czechoslovakia or a Yugoslavia. It survived the Stalin period (during which official Czechoslovakia joined Stalin in the campaign to bring down Tito) and in the late 1960s it was flowering again. In 1968 there was talk of a revived Little Entente as both Yugoslavia and Rumania were openly sympathetic to Dubcek and the new regime in Prague. Tito visited Moscow in April and bluntly told his hosts that intervention would be a catastrophe. That Tito and Ceausescu were received with great public enthusiasm in Prague the week before the invasion of Czechoslovakia bore witness both to their own feelings and to the reason for Soviet concern over the rise of a new grouping of East European states which, though socialist in name, would be in fact anti-Soviet.

Although the Soviet leaders had not been saying much about Titoism lately, they had been annoyed at Yugoslavia's negative attitude toward the world conference of communist parties they were trying to organize. And Tito, when the Warsaw Pact troops moved into Czechoslovakia, was apparently genuinely alarmed that his own country might be attacked next. Hence the hurried changes of military dispositions and the public preparations for partisan warfare. Tito made it quite clear that Yugoslavia would fight if attacked. And he also looked to the West, not for military guarantees, but for some assurance that the United States was not without interest in Yugoslavia's maintenance of its independence. The atmosphere was more like that of the early fifties than of the late sixties. The Brezhnev doctrine was nothing other than what Stalin and the Cominform had asserted, that is the right to suppress national independence in the name of socialism. Perhaps we can use this moment of truth in 1968 as a gauge to evaluate Yugoslavia's foreign policy and internal affairs before and after this crucial event.

Yugoslavs are wont to interpret their country's foreign policy record since 1948 as one of consistency. But above the bedrock of insistence on independence, some rather marked oscillations have taken place between defiance of the Soviet Union and entente with it; of course, there have been matching similar oscillations on the Soviet side. The crisis over Czechoslovakia was the third time — they seem to come at ten-year intervals (1948, 1958, 1968) — that Yugoslavia was put under great pressure and danger of attack. In between have been periods of normal relations and even more than that: of collaboration between the two states and between the two communist parties.

From 1968 one need look no further back than a year. In 1967 the major world crisis was in the Middle East, where the Soviet Union and Yugoslavia had close relations with the radical Arab states, notably with the United Arab Republic. It was a time when both Moscow and Belgrade seemed mesmerized by a theory that American imperialism was unleashing an offensive against socialist and nonaligned states, witness Vietnam, Indonesia, the Dominican Republic, and (closer to home) Cyprus, the coup in Greece, NATO maneuvers in the vicinity, and finally the attack by the West's surrogate, Israel, on "progressive" Arab countries like Egypt and Syria. Tito rushed off to Moscow to meet with Soviet and East European leaders and to issue a joint statement, the first time he had taken such a step since the break with Stalin.

Or one need look no further ahead than a year. In September 1969 Tito was receiving Gromyko in Belgrade and later told the world, "We arrived at the common conclusion that it is best to forget the past and cooperate on those things which are of common interest to us." [1] What assurances Gromyko may have given him we do not know. One thing he did not do was to state publicly that the Brezhnev doctrine did not apply to Yugoslavia.

These shifts should teach the West a lesson it should have learned long ago – that Yugoslavia, as long as Tito is there, will not stay pushed to one side or the other. He will not go back, but neither will he come over. He will stand firm against Soviet threats in time of crisis but will always take up again the search for a normalization of relations as long as it includes respect for Yugoslav independence. The long-term calculation is still that the Soviet leadership will have to understand, in time, that only on this basis can socialist states live and work together.

In the Yugoslav attitude toward Russia there is a combination of attraction and distrust which has its roots not only in the communist movement and communist ideology and in Tito's own experience, but also in the historical past. Somehow the relationship with Russia has remained at the center of Yugoslav international policy. Yet never since 1949 has Tito left his country alone face to face with Russia. Yugoslav foreign policy has displayed a versatility and flexibility which has enabled the country to play an international role well beyond its size and resources. "Nobody can isolate Yugoslavia," Tito declared at the Ninth Party Congress in March 1969, boycotted by the Soviet Union and all the Eastern European parties except the Rumanian.[2] And he was right.

From the United States he had received the assurance he wanted when

1. Press conference, Kranj, October 4, 1969.

2. Closing speech, Ninth Congress of the League of Communists of Yugoslavia. Excerpts from speech in *Yugoslav Facts and Views*, Yugoslav Information Center, New York, no. 52, March 16, 1970. For enthusiastic reception of the statement, see *New York Times*, March 16, 1969.

the U.S. ambassador to Yugoslavia, Burke Elbrick, emerged from a White House conversation with President Johnson in October 1968 to say that the president had made very clear his continuing interest in Yugoslavia's independence, sovereignty, and economic development.[3] Tito then completed the game by stating publicly that Yugoslavia did not feel threatened by the Soviet Union and was not asking for help from anyone.[4] President Nixon's visit to Yugoslavia in the fall of 1970 was a logical sequel to these events. America demonstrated its interest and its support without making a precise commitment, which neither side wanted.

With Western Europe, Yugoslavia's relations improved markedly after the shock of the Czechoslovak affair. President Saragat of Italy visited Belgrade in October 1969, and the Yugoslavs have welcomed Willy Brandt's coming to power in West Germany. The real problems in relations with Western Europe are economic: how to sell Yugoslav goods in the Common Market and how to secure Western capital goods and technology on terms Yugoslavia can afford. In February 1970 Yugoslavia concluded a three-year trade agreement with the Common Market, at a time when trade with the Eastern bloc was showing no gains.

After the Czechoslovak crisis Yugoslavia also took a new look at China, at the very time that the Chinese began to show a revived interest in Eastern Europe. The Yugoslav record of relations with that country has had two major themes: First, early hopes after 1948 that China as a great independent communist state would be a natural ally against the Soviet Union, hopes which were dashed when China took Stalin's side. Second, bitter Chinese denunciation of Yugoslavia, when the Sino-Soviet conflict developed in the 1960s, as being even more revisionist and more guilty of the restoration of capitalism than Moscow itself. The Yugoslavs responded in kind, but always with a feeling of regret that things had deteriorated through China's pigheadedness.[5] Tito's rapprochement with Moscow during this period made it natural that he should find Mao's "dogmatist" and "Stalinist" views as obnoxious as Khrushchev did.[6]

3. *Department of State Bulletin,* November 11, 1968, p. 497.

4. Press conference, Jajce, November 30, 1968.

5. John C. Campbell, "Yugoslavia and China: The Wreck of a Dream," in A. M. Halpern (ed.), *Policies Toward China: Views from Six Continents* (New York, 1965), pp. 368–88; A. Ross Johnson, "The Sino-Soviet Relationship and Yugoslavia" (paper prepared for meeting of American Association for the Advancement of Slavic Studies, Denver, March 1971), pp. 1–3.

6. Sonja Dapcevic-Orescanin, *Sovjetsko-Kineski Spor i Problemi Razvoja Socijalizma* (Belgrade, 1963), pp. 7–12, 179, 211–15.

Then suddenly, in the spring of 1969 when the Soviets were feverishly preparing their world conference of communist parties which neither China nor Yugoslavia would attend, Tito sent a trade mission to China. Taking the line so successfully followed by Rumania, the Yugoslav press began to assume a neutral position in the Soviet-Chinese border dispute and printed material reflecting China's view of it. The Chinese saw the opening, and the two countries have since concluded trade agreements and restored full diplomatic relations. In May 1970 Bogdan Orescanin presented his credentials in Peking, where there had been no Yugoslav ambassador since Vladimir Popovic had left the chilly and hostile atmosphere of that capital in 1958.

Parallel events took place closer to home, in relations with Albania. Fear of Yugoslavia and a long-standing territorial dispute had a great deal to do with Albania's ride on Stalin's bandwagon after his break with Tito in 1948, and on Mao's after Khrushchev made up with Yugoslavia and got into a quarrel with China. Then toward the end of the sixties the press in Tirana and in Belgrade began to talk about Balkan solidarity instead of revisionism and Maoism. Prime Minister Ribicic declared Yugoslavia open to suggestions for the improvement of relations and a willingness to make some itself.[7] Finally came the agreement to restore full diplomatic relations, reduced to the token level for twenty years. The Czechoslovak affair thus sparked a rather remarkable diplomatic revolution in Yugoslav-Albanian relations, though the change is not likely to be permanent since the causes of conflict between the two states, notably a latent territorial dispute, remain.

Another anchor to windward for Yugoslavia is its now well-established practice of cultivating the world of the nonaligned. Nonalignment has been a most useful policy in avoiding commitment to either side in Europe and in gaining prestige and diplomatic support from the third world.[8] But the Yugoslav-initiated drive for a new summit conference of the nonaligned in 1970 generated less enthusiasm than those of Belgrade in 1961 and Cairo in 1964. Tito, after his latest trip through Africa early in 1970, told the Federal Assembly that the policy of nonalignment had proved its worth, nobody except enemies of peace dared to challenge its correctness, and the necessary task for the future was agreement on a program of com-

7. Tanjug International Service, May 2, 1970.

8. Alvin Z. Rubinstein, *Yugoslavia and the Nonaligned World* (Princeton, N.J., 1970), *passim.*

mon action.[9] Yet the showy conference in Lusaka later that year, for all its resounding talk and resolutions, was without impact on world politics.[10] The fact of the matter is that the messages of those prior meetings (anti-colonialism, support for economic development, and distrust of the big powers) are not exactly novel now. And with the disappearance from the international scene of many of the leaders of that earlier day (Nehru, Sukarno, Nkrumah, Ben Bella) and the shifting relationships among powers both great and small, the nonaligned as a group are a fading force in world affairs. Each has its own priorities.

In the late sixties Tito and Nasser were the two remaining stalwarts, but what happened to their solidarity when Israel invaded Egypt and the Soviet Union invaded Czechoslovakia? Yugoslavia had backed the UAR's cause against Israel, but Tito was ill placed to play a real mediating role in the Arab-Israel conflict, as both Nasser and his successors saw plainly that their cause was in the hands of the great powers, not in those of third-world leaders. As a result Nasser found his position in the Middle East so dependent on Soviet support that he could not bring himself to object to what happened to Czechoslovakia.[11] Nor did Mrs. Gandhi, in her efforts to avoid offending the Soviets, provide India's old companion in nonalignment with any comfort.[12]

Finally, Yugoslavia kept up its steady practice of full participation in the work of the United Nations, doing everything possible to make a reality of the rights of small states and the duties of large ones. Not wishing to seek security in alliance with great powers, it has preferred to stress the universal rights and obligations of the U.N. Charter and their validity for relations between socialist states as well as between all others. Perhaps not the most solid rock on which to rest a nation's security, the United Nations is important in the total pattern of Yugoslav foreign policy as background to the several strands which link it in varying degrees of mutual interest and confidence with the East, the West, the nonaligned, and especially with its immediate neighbors. Yugoslavia may again come into a time of peril, but as Tito has said, it cannot be isolated.

9. "Tito's Report to the Federal Assembly," *Review of International Affairs* (Belgrade), 21 (April 5, 1970), 15–20.

10. For final documents of the conference see special supplement to *Review of International Affairs*, 21 (September 20, 1970).

11. The UAR government made no official statement, and Cairo radio, using reports from TASS and *Pravda*, took the Soviet side in its broadcasts.

12. Mrs. Gandhi, who could do no more than muster up "profound concern,"

II

Yugoslav relations with the Soviet Union, of course, go beyond the bilateral dimension. The adherence of all East European states to Marxism and the Soviet theory that there can be but one "correct" translation of its principles into practice have turned every national dispute into an ideological struggle. Thus Stalin after 1948 mobilized all his satellites in the campaign to crush Tito, the traitor to Marxism-Leninism, and found Titoists wherever he found opponents or potential opponents. Thus Tito, even though claiming that Yugoslavia's separate road was strictly its own, inevitably became a symbol of hope or of hate to all communists in Eastern Europe, depending on their satisfaction with the Stalinist system. The interplay of action and reaction mixed up ideology with questions of security, nationalism, economic reform, political reorganization, and a host of other things. So long as Yugoslavia remains independent, its very existence as a socialist state making its own decisions stands as a challenge to Moscow and affects the other states of Eastern Europe. Perhaps more than any other outside influence, Titoism defined in almost any terms has contributed to the disarray of the Soviet empire in Europe.

How much influence has Yugoslavia really had in Eastern Europe? Enthusiasts often exaggerate. The effort to find new principles and institutions, not uniformly successful by any means, has been above all a response to conditions in the country itself, not a universal prescription for all socialist states. The revisionist philosophers and the practical politicians who wanted change in Poland, Hungary, or Rumania have not seen in Yugoslavia a model wholly suited to the forces at work in their own societies. Yet particular Yugoslav reforms have been studied and sometimes copied in the other countries. The idea of the workers' councils found expression in Hungary and Poland in 1956 and in Czechoslovakia in 1968. Yugoslav debates on relations between party and state and the people have had more than one echo beyond the frontiers to the east.

Characteristically, it was a political and economic crisis in Yugoslavia itself that led to the adoption of bold measures of reform in the mid-sixties.[13] In many ways they cut through the indecisiveness of the past and put the prestige of the regime on the line in favor of freer economic relations both internally and with the outside world. By running well ahead of

blocked a resolution in Parliament condemning the Soviet invasion *New York Times*, August 23, 1968.

13. Rudolf Bicanic, "Economics of Socialism in a Developed Country," *Foreign Affairs*, 44, no. 4 (July 1966), 633–50.

the pack, even at an uncertain pace, Yugoslavia became the symbol of the "liberal" trend in dealing with the types of problems they all (including the Soviet Union) faced in one form or another. The controversy within Yugoslavia went on as before, but from 1965 onward the official weight was behind the campaign for decentralization, market economy, material incentives, freeing of the currency, participation in world economic institutions, and a changing and probably declining role for the party as opposed to the centralism, strict party control, and the "bureaucratism" of its own old guard, which did not differ much from those of orthodox stripe throughout Eastern Europe.

Because the Soviet Union's system, despite some limited economic reforms, was the most centralized and rigid of all, Moscow and Belgrade were at opposite ends of the poles in the controversies which took place as each East European country wrestled with the question of what to do. Economic reforms in this or that country were not in themselves considered subversive of the established order. Those adopted in Czechoslovakia began to be put into effect in 1966, well before the pro-Soviet leadership of Novotny was overthrown. In Hungary a potentially far-reaching reform was put into effect in January 1968 by Kadar, the most cautious of leaders in dealings with the Soviet Union. Even Bulgaria had its smaller scale experiments. Yugoslavia, however, was a country acting freely and on its own, and its economic reforms were accompanied by a political crisis which shook the top leadership of the League of Communists. The issue of new forms of economic life could not be divorced from the issue of new forms of socialism, or from that of national independence for each socialist state.

Czechoslovakia provided an example of this mixing of internal with international questions. Its experience had a special significance for the Yugoslavs as a test whether a relatively advanced socialist country could dismantle Stalinism, as their less developed one had, and could develop a more productive and at the same time more human type of socialism. The Yugoslavs in 1968 were under no illusions that the Czechs would look to Belgrade for leadership – it might well be the other way round – but here at least was the first major break since 1956, which would show that the Yugoslavs had been right on the big issue posed in 1948 and contested ever since. The Czechoslovak spring seemed to be the beginning of a new era in Eastern Europe in which Yugoslavia would have some company as other communist states began to make their own reforms and go their separate roads. The only troubling questions were how fast the process would go and whether the Russians would permit it at any speed.

"When the Russians rape the Czechs, the Yugoslavs scream," so goes the saying. The events of August 1968 left the Yugoslav people stunned but also determined to defend themselves. The Rumanian reaction was the same. Although the immediate crisis passed for both countries, they still present to the Kremlin, from outside and inside respectively, a challenge to the control of its security zone in Eastern Europe. Yugoslavia is the more difficult problem for the Russians, both because its reforms have progressed much farther and because it is less subject to pressure. If the Russians are going to dispose of the Yugoslav challenge, they are probably going to have to do it from the inside. That point raises some questions where our analysis is on less firm ground, for they are partly speculative in that they involve the future and partly obscure in that they involve purposes and policies which depend upon secrecy. However, this is one way in which to get into the complexities of Yugoslavia's internal affairs.

III

Vladimir Bakaric, one of Tito's principal lieutenants and the elder statesman of the party in Croatia, said a few years ago that Yugoslavia had two main problems – the economic reform and the nationalities question – and that if the first could not be solved, the second would immediately move to the fore as problem number one.[14] His meaning was that the country could stand some setbacks in its economy if it were only a matter of wages and prices and rates of growth, but that the antagonisms between nationalities were such, and were so tied up with economic issues, that any deep economic crisis was bound to bring into question the very existence of the federal state.

This is not the place for any long disquisition on Yugoslavia's nationalities problem, undoubtedly the most intricate in Europe. We shall have to content ourselves with a definition and a few historical facts. Yugoslavia has been informally and not inaccurately described as a state with six republics, five South Slav peoples, four languages, three religions, two alphabets, and one political party. In contrast to most of the rest of Eastern Europe, the vital issues are not between the Yugoslav majority and national minorities, but as in Czechoslovakia, between the branches of the Slav family, especially the Serbs and the Croats (who share the same language but in their more nationalistic moments are not prepared to admit it). This antagonism clouded the national movement before there was a Yugoslavia and proved to be a fatal flaw in the interwar Yugoslav state, preventing its

14. *Borba,* March 6, 1966.

dealing with other problems and contributing to its eventual collapse in 1941.

In the years immediately after the Second World War the conflict was dampened by horror over the massacres that had taken place in the name of Croatian or Serbian nationalism during the war, by the appeal of the communist-led partisan movement for the reconciliation and equality of nationalities, and by the tough policy of the new rulers in subordinating these old disputes to the new tasks of establishing their own power and the foundations of socialism.[15]

No regime, however, could indefinitely repress or ignore feelings and forces which reflected the reality of Yugoslavia, especially after that regime lost the anchor of Soviet support and had to depend on all the people of the country to pull together with their leaders in the hour of peril. Tito had to relax some of the severe pressures on the population and to appeal to their patriotism. They did support him strongly, for they liked Stalin a great deal less, and in that sense it was a display of nationalism against foreign domination. But they did not thereby create or demonstrate a sense of Yugoslav nationality different from or superseding their separate nationalities as Serbs, Croats, Slovenes, and so forth. "Yugoslavism" has been a theory put forward from time to time before the Second World War as well as in the communist period, but it has not yet become a reality.

As Yugoslavia, after the break with Stalin, began to develop its own political and economic institutions, and especially as economic decisions had local consequences in one part of the country or another, differences based on nationality began to be evident within the party and the agencies of government. The more democratic and decentralized the country became, the larger the differences loomed. Divergences in historical tradition – Slovenia was for centuries part of Austria, Croatia was associated with Hungary, Serbia and Montenegro had their long and very different history of living and fighting with the Turks and winning their independence, Bosnia developed into a divided land of Muslim Slavs, Orthodox Serbs, and Catholic Croats, and Macedonia remained under Turkish rule until the Balkan wars and was fought over by others long before and ever since – these divergences had persevered as a cultural barrier running right through the country, a line which for centuries had divided the world of Central Europe from that of the East.

Tito's communist regime could not change that situation merely by pro-

15. Frits W. Hondius, *The Yugoslav Community of Nations* (The Hague and Paris, 1968), pp. 137–209; Paul Shoup, *Communism and the Yugoslav National Question* (New York and London, 1968), pp. 101–43.

claiming socialism. For that historic line, in a rough sort of way, divided the country into advanced and backward regions, with the average Slovene enjoying an income about three times as high as the average inhabitant of Macedonia or Montenegro.[16] When the government tried to pump capital into the poorer republics, it ran into Slovenian and Croatian objections to paying taxes for the benefit of inefficient industries elsewhere and to the detriment of the economy as a whole. The investment program became a kind of competition between the separate republics, so that decisions on the location of railways, ports, and highways became bitterly contested matters of national prestige as well as economic advantage.

In Slovenian and Croatian complaints there was often a hint of separatism. In the poorer republics there was a strong sense of a right to call on the federal treasury to help them toward an equal status with the others. And in Serbia, though the idea of domination in prewar style was not seriously entertained, many had the feeling that the Serbs, the largest nationality, had the duty to hold the country together, for there is meaning in the fact that Belgrade, the federal capital of Yugoslavia, is also the historic and present capital of Serbia.

Add to these nationality divisions the divergent views within the leadership on the subjects on institutional change and foreign orientation – liberals versus conservatives, reformers versus old-style partisans, decentralizers versus centralizers, those who look to Western Europe and those who look to Moscow – and you have all the ingredients of a country pulling itself apart, especially when views on the future of the system often divide along that same national-cultural-economic line between north and west on one side and south and east on the other. All this is an oversimplification, of course, for there are conservative Croats and liberal Serbs, and some of the leading reformers come from the more backward republics. The infinite complexities of Yugoslav politics, however, do not cushion the collisions that in a given set of circumstances could produce a full-blown crisis.

The interaction of problems one and two, economics and nationality, has been evident in the struggle over reform in the past five years. At the Eighth Congress of the League of Communists in 1964 a cleavage already existed between the forces of liberalization and reform on the one side and those of conservatism and centralism and "bureaucratism" on the other.

16. See Joseph T. Bombelles, *Economic Development of Communist Yugoslavia* (Stanford, 1968), Table 48, p. 158.

It took a strong personal effort on the part of Tito to keep the dispute from breaking out into the open.[17]

Although it was not really resolved, the liberal forces with Tito's support had the strength to push ahead with the far-reaching economic reforms of 1965, which continue to be the charter of the Yugoslav economy today. The main idea of the measures was more rational organization and a sounder base for growth by giving greater play to market forces and to competition, so that enterprises would have to rely on themselves rather than on subsidies. The day of the "political factories" was over. It meant the end of detailed central planning and of centralized control of investment. But it definitely did not mean the end of socialism, as the Yugoslavs define it, for the ownership of enterprises was vested in the society as a whole, and the principle of social self-management, built on the workers' councils, remained at the center of the official ideology.[18]

Internationally, the purpose of the reforms was to force the Yugoslav economy to make its way in the world economy through devaluation of the currency, reduction of trade barriers, and the development of a strong financial position with an eventually convertible dinar. In this context "the world economy" means essentially the noncommunist world, the world of private trade and capital movements, of the General Agreement on Tariffs and Trade (which Yugoslavia has joined), of the World Bank and the International Monetary Fund, and especially of the European Common Market where Yugoslavia has to sell so large a part of its exports and obtain its capital goods and technology. Thus the new economic measures – and this the reformers knew very well – would, if successful, turn the country away from any large-scale meaningful economic collaboration with a closed economic bloc in the East; and significantly the volume of trade with Comecon countries has fallen since 1968 from about one-third to one-fourth of all its foreign trade.[19]

Few people in Yugoslavia missed the political significance of the economic reforms, national or international, especially as they were accompanied by talk of a new role for the League of Communists, to infuse it with new blood, sharpen its educational functions, and reduce its control.

17. John C. Campbell, *Tito's Separate Road: America and Yugoslavia in World Politics* (New York, 1967), pp. 133–35. For Tito's speech at the Congress see *VIII Kongres Saveza Komunista Jugoslavije* vol. 1 (Belgrade, 1965), 311–64.

18. Branko Horvat, *An Essay on Yugoslav Society* (White Plains, N.Y., 1969), pp. 79–121, originally published as *Ogled Jugoslavenskom drustvu* (Belgrade, 1967).

19. IMF, IBRD, *Direction of Trade, Annual 1963–68*, pp. 359–60; OECD, *Overall Trade by Countries*, March 1971, p. 29.

The conservative forces (old partisans and party warhorses, local functionaries with power and patronage they wanted to keep, doctrinaires who wanted the party to restore discipline and rule as it did in the past) were vaguely trying to sabotage the reforms, hoping that Comrade Tito would see the light, or perhaps looking forward to the time when Comrade Tito would not be around.

The question of political succession was in people's minds well before 1966, even if it went unmentioned in public. Not that anybody thought Tito could have a successor in the unique position of power and prestige that he enjoyed. But there would be pieces of political power to be had – the presidency, the control of the party apparatus, the levers of economic control, command of the army and of the police – and who would be on hand to pick them up? Aleksandar Rankovic was certainly a leading contender. He was the vice president of Yugoslavia. He controlled the security services, which had their men in all the agencies of party and government. He had been with Tito since before the war and was always near the center of authority. He was the most powerful Serb in the regime. And he was known to be the Soviet Union's choice for the succession.[20]

Inevitably, the forces opposed to reform looked to Rankovic. Inevitably, the reformers distrusted him. Just how the so-called Rankovic plot developed is not easy for an outsider to discover. He certainly had ambitions for the exercise of power after Tito. He may have been merely incautious enough to act too soon. At any rate, his alleged planting of microphones in Tito's villa – just as if it had been the American Embassy – was hardly the hallmark of a master plotter. The immediate consequence was the famous Fourth plenum of the League's Central Committee, held at Brioni in July 1966, at which Rankovic was exposed and expelled. This event was another watershed comparable to the economic reform. It lead to a reorganization of the League of Communists. No longer did the conservatives have any chance of rallying round a major leader.

IV

It is not wise to leave this affair as a closed book, partly because not everybody in Yugoslavia is content with the way things have been going since. The economic reforms have gone forward and there is now no turning back to centralism. But they have hardly been a roaring success. Inequalities remain; there is inflation with unemployment and a lag in productivi-

20. During a visit Rankovic made to the Soviet Union in 1965 his hosts showered honors and signs of favor on him.

ty. Only the phenomenal growth of tourism and the emigration of several hundreds of thousands of Yugoslav workers to Germany have saved the country from serious unrest and a disastrous gap in the balance of payments. Much of the youth is disaffected, or seriously questioning the system for a variety of reasons.

The student rebels of Belgrade University, who rioted in 1968 and were temporarily mollified by President Tito's personal appeal and promises, never got any real redress for their grievances with respect to university life and organization. Some of the young intellectuals have a kind of puritanical leftist view which condemns the chase of the almighty dinar in which almost everybody, from party chiefs to university professors, is engaged. Some complain that freedom is still too restricted and democratic progress too slow. Through all the thinking of the student movement runs a strong current critical of things as they are.[21] Tension and dissent in the society inevitably are reflected in the nationality question and in the interaction between internal and external influences. This point brings us back to Rankovic, who, incidentally, was never tried and was allowed just to fade out of public life. The Serbian nationalism which he was taken to represent, rightly or not, could feed on these difficulties and the discontent they have created. Even those tendencies of anticommunist nationalism always present in Serbia have shown signs of new life as potential allies of the old guard communists. And in Croatia the party leadership takes on more and more the color of its national base as it defends Croatian economic and cultural interests.

There is a theory that Serbian alienation is a card the Soviets can play if a crisis arises over the succession to Tito. When Rankovic was still a powerful figure, it used to be said that Croatia and Slovenia would never accept him as the leader of Yugoslavia and might be prepared to break up the country to avoid it. Now that Tito is likely to be succeeded by some form of collegial leadership,[22] possibly with the reformers and non-Serbs in the driver's seat, the question is whether the powerful Serbian party will

21. Dennison A. Rusinow, "Anatomy of a Student Revolt," pts. I and II, *American Universities Field Staff Reports,* Southeast Europe Series, 15, nos. 4–5 (August, November 1968); Lev Detela, "The Jugoslav Student Revolt: An Attempt at Interpretation," *Review* (London), no. 9 (1970), 768–88.

22. In a speech at Zagreb, September 21, 1970, Tito proposed the creation of a presidium to replace the single president of the Republic. In June 1971, twenty-three amendments to the 1963 constitution were adopted, including provision for a collective presidency consisting of three from each republic and two from each autonomous province (twenty-two in all). See Anton Vratusa, "Jugoslavia, 1971," *Foreign Affairs,* 50, no. 1 (October 1971), 148–62.

accept that, and whether the Soviets would find an opening with a bargain: Soviet support in return for a Serbian-dominated Yugoslavia. Another rumor has it that Moscow will back a large independent Croatian state as a means of establishing Soviet power on the Adriatic. These theories lack plausibility because they tend to overrate Russia and to underrate Yugoslavia. That is not to say that the Soviet leadership would not attempt to subvert Yugoslavia, just as Stalin tried from 1948 until his death five years later, or perhaps to dismember it.

Another and more alarming prospect must be considered within the realm of the possible. The Soviet leaders of the seventies may be more daring than Stalin was if they judge the need for action pressing. If Yugoslavia should become in their minds the same kind of threat to their security in Eastern Europe that Czechoslovakia was, they might resort to the naked use of force. After all, the Brezhnev doctrine, which Yugoslav officials and commentators have not ceased to denounce as incompatible with the rights of sovereignty, is not confined to Russia's allies in the Warsaw Pact. It refers to any socialist state anywhere, and that definition could include Yugoslavia, China, or Albania; an armed attack on Yugoslavia might follow a Soviet take-over of Albania which, with the Soviet fleet in the Mediterranean and Soviet troops stationed in Hungary, would put the Yugoslavs in a vise.

The intention of the Soviet leaders to solidify their bloc by tightening both the Warsaw Pact and the Comecon has caused concern in Rumania, and no doubt has been discussed in the increasingly frequent exchanges between Rumanians and Yugoslavs. The two countries form a potential barrier which could reduce the Soviet position in the Balkans to a semi-isolated Bulgaria. The forward Soviet policy in the Mediterranean and the Middle East may indicate a new view in the Kremlin of the strategic importance of the Balkans, which in the past has definitely taken second place to Eastern Europe's northern tier: East Germany, Poland, Czechoslovakia, and Hungary.

A Soviet attack on Yugoslavia, whose leadership could be charged with corrupting socialism as easily as Dubcek and his colleagues were, would be fraught with danger to world peace, and for that reason the Western European nations and the United States should be doing some hard thinking. More important than what they would actually do in the event of attack may be what they can do to deter it. The West might be able to avoid the test of will by meeting the prior test of ingenuity.

The more likely circumstance is that the Soviet leadership will not be so foolhardy as to risk a world war over Yugoslavia, and that that country's fate will depend on its own ability to hang together. Actually, there is no real alternative for its peoples (except perhaps for the Albanians who live in the area adjacent to Albania). Slovenes or Croats may occasionally dream of secession, but they have no place to go. They need Yugoslavia, as Yugoslavia needs them. The federal state comes to look more and more like a confederation, but one in which the essential minimum of central authority (defense, foreign policy, common currency, and market) are retained.

Under Tito the country has established two principles of policy, or of conduct, which transcend his personal role and the limits of any ideology or system. The first is that Yugoslavia will not allow itself to be dominated from outside, whether the external environment is one of cold war or of détente. The second is that the institutions forming the "system," no matter what name you give them, have come more and more to reflect the society, not just the will of the ruling few.

There is still a key problem which has not been resolved: the role of the party in a decentralized, self-managing society. For the most part the communists want to retain a monopoly of political power. But they have created these other institutions which strive for power because of their very nature. Some want to hold back, others want to go ahead and carry democratization further. A meeting of the Presidium of the party debated this very question in December 1969, putting considerable stress on the need for discipline.[23] More recently, as the centrifugal forces have continued to make themselves felt, Tito has castigated disruptive elements, insisted on discipline, and threatened a purge.[24] Yugoslav society is in many respects dynamic, while the party seems puzzled and indecisive. It is a bold but perhaps justified conclusion that Yugoslavia has passed the point where the monopoly of power can be maintained, although the pendulum will keep swinging for some time to come. A party which is increasingly a grouping of national communist parties, moreover, finds it ever harder to assert itself from the center.

A decade ago I put the question of the future of southeastern Europe in this way: Would the revolution that began at the end of the Second World War eventually result in the socialization of the Balkans or the Balkanization of socialism? [25] The latter proposition seems to be history's answer, and Yugoslavia is the country which has shown the way.

23. *Komunist*, December 11, 1969; *Borba*, December 16, 1969.

24. Speech at Pristina, April 14, 1971, released by Tanjug, April 15, 1971.

25. John C. Campbell, "The Balkans: Heritage and Continuity," in Charles and

John C. Campbell

The specifics of the Yugoslav model of socialism are a fascinating subject for study — the workers' councils, the socialist self-management, the complex federal arrangements, the relationship between party and government; to say nothing of its less attractive features — the scramble for status and prestige by the "new class," the gap between doctrine and reality, the squabbling of nationalities, and the sheer weight of Balkan tradition which makes it so difficult to put even the most logically conceived reforms into practice. Some of these specifics go to the essence of man as a political animal. Some are but provincial idiosyncrasies. They all add up to a separate road which by its existence denies the unity of the communist world.

The Yugoslav system is not a model at all because it keeps changing. It is still an experiment and perhaps always will be. But that is precisely why it remains a challenge and a danger to the Soviet empire, a major influence on Eastern Europe, and a hope for the evolution of a freer and closer association of all the nations of Europe, in the East and in the West and in the middle.

Barbara Jelavich (eds.), *The Balkans in Transition: Essays on the Development of Balkan Life and Politics since the Eighteenth Century* (Berkeley and Los Angeles, 1963), p. 396.

10

Albania

BY PETER R. PRIFTI

The fall of Khrushchev in October 1964 was both a victory and a defeat for the Albanians: a victory because their arch enemy and the debunker of their idol, Joseph Stalin, had been consigned to the dustbin of history; a defeat because Khrushchev's demise did not result in a change of course for the USSR. The Albanians' jubilation over the fall of the Soviet premier was thus somewhat restrained by the uncertainty of what would follow in the Kremlin. There is evidence that the hope of the Albanian communists was that Khrushchev's successors would reorient the Soviet Union to a pre-1956 domestic and foreign policy. Therefore, in their initial comments on the power shake-up in Moscow, Albania's leaders generally limited themselves to pointing out its significance for the struggle against revisionism and against the general line of the USSR since the Twentieth Congress of the CPSU.

Albania's position on the Kremlin shake-up did not crystallize until November 13, 1964, when *Zeri i Popullit*, the party's daily organ, published a lengthy polemical article on the Testament of Togliatti, the Italian Communist party, and the CPSU. Originally scheduled for publication in mid-October, the article had been delayed by Khrushchev's fall. However, since the new CPSU leadership was continuing substantially the same policies, a kind of Khrushchevism minus Khrushchev, it was published without changes. The interval between mid-October and mid-November was a momentous one for Tirana, for a change of course in the Soviet Union could have meant a change of course for Albania as well – a shift of the country's political center of gravity from Peking back to Moscow.

Yet in the end, the partial victory the Albanians had won with Khrushchev's ouster failed to moderate their hostility toward the Soviet Union, and in fact incited them to intensify the struggle and widen the breach still more between Moscow and Tirana. In this "struggle to the end," Albania labored at a disadvantage. Lacking economic, political, and military power, it could not realistically hope to wage a successful battle against the mighty Soviet Union, and had to rely largely on polemics as a substitute. The awareness by the leaders of the Albanian Party of Labor (APL) of this unequal contest, of their ambitious ideological aspirations, and most of all, perhaps, of the nearly successful economic, political, and "military" blockade which the Soviet Union mounted in the early sixties to topple them from power accounts to a large extent for the fury of their polemics.

However, a cultural factor — that of the Albanian character — also contributed to the dispute. Albanian tradition did not allow for a middle position between friend and foe. This was reflected in political alliances, which the Albanians tended to perceive in human terms. Take, for example, the remark made by Premier Mehmet Shehu in October 1967, when he sought to explain Albania's loyalty to China. "We Albanians," he said, "love our friends with all our hearts, and we hate our enemies with all our hearts." [1] Secondly, the Albanians achieved liberation by means of a successful guerrilla struggle; hence they were less inclined to submit to Moscow's authority and more prone to resent Soviet attempts to dominate them — a fact which contributed much to the bitterness of their feud with the USSR.

Albania's totally uncompromising position toward Khrushchev's successors revealed the depth of Soviet-Albanian enmity and also the strength of Tirana's alliance with Peking. By this time, three years after its break with the Soviet Union, Albania shared a nearly uniform foreign and domestic policy position with China. Unlike the USSR and East Europe, it rejected a détente with the West in favor of an all-out ideological, political, and economic battle between the socialist camp and the West; dismissed the doctrine of peaceful coexistence as dangerous and counterrevolutionary; belittled the threat of atomic war; saw Asia, Africa, and Latin America as the centers of revolutionary storms; and was confident that by waging a militant contest against capitalism, imperialism, and reaction, Marxism-Leninism would emerge victorious and socialism would triumph throughout the world.

On the domestic front, Albania, like China, hailed the dictatorship of the proletariat as a vital and indeed indispensable institution in a truly socialist country; rejected economic and cultural liberalization in favor of

1. *Bashkimi*, organ of the Democratic Front of Albania, October 11, 1967.

strict party control over all facets of social and economic life; and remained vigilant against the penetration and spread of bourgeois and revisionist ideology among the population. In short, Tirana seemed thoroughly wedded to the Chinese version of Stalinism. However, it is vital to remember that in political life content is sometimes even more important than form. Albanian Marxism is undeniably Chinese in form, but it remains Albanian in style and content – a fact that is too often ignored by analyses focused exclusively on Tirana's role in the international communist movement. Therefore, let us first look at the country's internal developments.

I

The period from 1965 to 1970 was marked by a number of events and developments in Albania which had extensive influence in shaping the country's life, as well as in determining its role in international affairs. During this period Albania embarked on its fourth Five-Year Plan, held the Fifth Party Congress, observed the five hundredth anniversary of the death of its national hero, Scanderbeg, and the twenty-fifth anniversary of its liberation. Above all, in a move superficially if somewhat deceptively resembling developments in China, it launched its own version of the Cultural Revolution, with the avowed aim of "revolutionizing" every aspect of Albanian life and of turning the country's face irrevocably toward socialism and communism.

In his celebrated speech of November 7, 1961, Enver Hoxha, first secretary of the APL, said that the causes of the Soviet-Albanian split were "entirely ideological and political" in nature.[2] True, there were both ideological and political considerations involved, but analytically emphasis should be placed on the political aspects and most importantly on the role of Albanian nationalism in these events. For a close look at Albania's actions and statements by its leaders, especially with regard to the USSR, Yugoslavia, and Greece, leads to the conclusion that beneath the surface the causes of the split were more nationalistic than ideological in nature.

In recent years nationalism also has been a major force in internal Albanian affairs. In literature, the theater, song and dance, folklore and artifacts, the government encouraged the use and development of national themes, including such traditional patriotic virtues as heroism, self-sacrifice, and love of freedom and independence. The government also honored such prominent national and literary figures of the Albanian Ren-

2. *Zeri i Popullit*, November 8, 1961; W. E. Griffith, *Albania and the Sino-Soviet Rift* (Cambridge, Mass., 1963), Document 14, p. 263.

aissance as Mihal Grameno and Bajram Curri, two noted patriots; Petro Nini Luarasi, a leading educator; and the poets Cajupi, Naim Frasheri, De Rada, and others. As one Albanian publicist put it, "Never before has the period of the Renaissance been so highly appreciated, and the works of its heroes so widely publicized as in the years of the people's power." [3]

Thus, it is not surprising that during 1968–70 Albania observed with considerable fanfare the anniversaries of four milestone events in its history: the ninetieth anniversary of the League of Prizren (established in 1878), which sparked the Albanian national movement; [4] the sixtieth anniversary of the Congress of Monastir (1908), which adopted the alphabet currently in use in Albania; [5] the fiftieth anniversary of the Congress of Lushnja (1920), convened to save Albania from dismemberment by its neighbors; [6] and above all the Scanderbeg anniversary, which was celebrated for an entire week, from January 11 to 17, 1968, and was attended by scholars from the West and East Europe, including Yugoslavia, though curiously not from China.[7]

The Albanian leadership took advantage of the Scanderbeg festivities not only to bolster nationalist sentiment, but even more to build up the party image and promote the party line. "Our party," wrote *Bashkimi*, "as the worthy heir of the patriotic and revolutionary traditions of our people, raised to a higher level the unbounded love for the Fatherland, for freedom and for independence." [8] Speaking at a commemorative meeting in Tirana, Mehmet Shehu, premier of Albania, said that the legendary struggle of the Albanian people against the Turks in the fifteenth century inspired Albanians even today in their struggle against the imperialists and the revisionists.

In fact, nationalism operated both as a cause and as an effect on the development of Albanian politics. Acting as a cause, it pushed the Albanian leadership — out of concern for the country's sovereignty and independence — to break first with Yugoslavia in 1948 and then with the USSR in 1961, thereby effectively isolating Albania from East Europe. The resulting isolation, in turn, induced the leadership to foster nationalism as a

3. Zija Xholi, "Dialectical Materialism — Our Guide in Education, Culture and Science," *Mesuesi*, March 22, 1968.

4. *Zeri i Popullit*, June 4, 1968.

5. *Ibid.*, November 14, 1968.

6. *Bashkimi*, January 21, 1970.

7. *Ibid.*, January 12, 13, 16, 17, 20, 1968.

8. *Ibid.*, January 20, 1968.

means of strengthening the country's defenses and of promoting the party's program for socialist construction.

Yet, while fostering national traditions and national pride, the APL continued to profess total loyalty to proletarian internationalism and to the teachings of Marxism-Leninism, as interpreted by Peking and Tirana. To be sure, Albania practiced national communism, but in this case nationalism was used to reinforce communism rather than as an alternative to it. In other East European countries still under the influence of Moscow, nationalism as a force had tended to erode the power and authority of the communist party.[9] In Albania, the communist leadership, being relatively free of outside control, appeared more and more to be using nationalism for ideological ends; in particular, to advance the goals of the ideological and cultural revolution within the country. For example, Ramiz Alia, a member of the APL Politburo, and widely recognized as Albania's cultural commissar, has said that the major preoccupation of the party now was "to cleanse the superstructure of [Albanian] society of everything alien to it. . . ."[10]

Such was the general background of the Albanian cultural revolution, which was launched in strength early in 1966. According to the Albanian leaders, this revolution was but the latest phase of what they called the "uninterrupted revolution," whose beginnings reached back to the Second World War, and whose end lay far in the distant future. This revolution was marked by three phases: the first, political, was the phase of national independence and the consolidation of communist power; the second, socioeconomic, related to the building of the economic base of socialism; the third, ideological and cultural, was the ongoing revolution whose aim was the destruction of bourgeois ideology and the complete construction of the socialist society. The central idea of this revolution, and the chief mechanism for its implementation, was the class struggle, which was conceived as being far more than opposition to the class enemy abroad and to the former exploiting classes within. In his report to the Fifth Party Congress, held in November of 1966, Enver Hoxha defined the class struggle as follows: "Class struggle means struggle against . . . putting comfort, self-interest and personal glory ahead of the general interest, against bu-

9. In this respect, Albania and Yugoslavia fall in a category different from that of the other East European countries, for both of them achieved their liberation through their own armed struggle. Yet, interestingly, communism in the two neighboring Balkan countries took different and mutually antagonistic directions, though both countries shared a common experience in their quarrel and break with Moscow.

10. *Zeri i Popullit*, November 19, 1969.

reaucratic manifestations, against religious ideology . . . and backward customs, against underestimation of woman and refusal to grant her equal rights in society, against the bourgeois way of life, against idealism and metaphysics." [11]

Going a step further, Hoxha refined his definition of class struggle to the point of making every man an object of the all-inclusive struggle. Speaking in almost purely moral and theological terms, he said: "Let no man think that he is safe from evil . . . The conscience of every man is a battlefield of the sharp struggle between the socialist and bourgeois ideology." [12] Every man must therefore see himself as in a mirror, and as he washes his face, so must he cleanse his conscience daily.

The first rumblings of Albania's "uninterrupted" revolution were heard as early as the summer of 1964 – well before the Chinese Cultural Revolution began – at the Second National Song Festival, when Albanian composers and musicians were attacked for failing to write national music and for abandoning themselves to the influence of decadent Western music. The tempo picked up in April 1965 when *Drita*, the weekly organ of the Albanian League of Writers and Artists, accused three young writers of departing from socialist realism in their most recent works.[13] Not by accident, the same issue of *Drita* made a strong attack on Soviet art, focusing in particular on the writings of Yevtushenko and Solzhenitsyn. In fact, the "evils" of Soviet society, brought on by revisionism, whether in art, political institutions, morals, education, economics, or religion, were consistently held up as negative examples to the Albanian public throughout the course of the ideological and cultural revolution.

It is not surprising, then, that artists, writers, and intellectuals in general became the first targets of the developing revolution. In the eyes of Hoxha, artists and intellectuals – because they do not engage in direct physical work, and hence are removed from close contact with the masses – make up the weakest link in the socialist society and are therefore the most vulnerable targets of bourgeois and revisionist propaganda. Thus, the first concrete implementation of Albania's drive for the "revolutionization of the entire life of the country" occurred in late January 1966 when forty members of the League of Writers and Artists "took the decision," at a

11. Enver Hoxha, "Report on the Activity of the Central Committee of the Albanian Party of Labor," *Fifth Congress of the APL* (Tirana, 1967), p. 136.

12. *Ibid.*, p. 137.

13. *Drita*, April 18, 1965.

meeting in Tirana, to go into the countryside and live and work among the people.[14]

The decision marked the Albanian leadership's first attempt at the rectification of artists and intellectuals. Later that year, at the Fifth Party Congress, Hoxha remarked that in socialist Albania art and culture must be "socialist in content and nationalist in form." Since then, Albanian literature has increasingly reflected the principle enunciated by Hoxha. Yet there was evidence of a considerable and potentially serious gap between the party leadership on the one hand, and the intellectual community and the public on the other, in their respective understanding of socialist realism and the manner in which it should be applied in the realm of art.[15]

The dispatch of intellectuals to the countryside was the prelude to a novel and, for a while, puzzling political development the following month. On February 10, 1966, Radio Tirana announced that twelve high-ranking party officials, including Politburo members Gogo Nushi, Manush Myftiu, Rita Marko, and Haki Toska, were assigned to different regions of the country to do grass roots work for an unspecified length of time. Contrary to rumors at the time, the transfers did not signal a governmental or party shake-up, provoked by disappointment with Chinese economic aid, since the officials affected by the move retained their full rank. More likely, the motive for the "decentralization" measure was to increase the party's control at the regional level, stimulate economic productivity, and rebuff in a rather dramatic way Soviet and East European attempts at the time to wean Albania away from China.[16] More importantly, from the viewpoint of the unfolding ideological revolution, the move was designed to bring party officials "back to the masses," as well as to teach them the virtues of physical labor — two cardinal principles of the revolution.

It was not until March 1966, however, that the cultural revolution began to affect other significant sectors of society. On March 4, 1966, the Sixteenth Party plenum met to discuss measures for dealing with bureaucracy, "strengthening and modernizing the army," and reorganizing the party and state apparatus. The results of the plenum became known the next day through the publication of the "Open Letter to the APL Central Committee" to "communists, workers, soldiers and officers of Albania." The letter revealed that measures had been taken to lower salaries of high

14. *Nendori*, 13, no. 3 (March 1966), 3–7.

15. See especially *Zeri i Popullit*, November 2, 18, 1969, March 18, 1970, in connection with the Albanian theater.

16. *New York Times*, February 12, 1966; *The Times* (London), February 15, 1966.

officials, eliminate ranks and insignia in the army, and reintroduce political commissars within the armed forces – a throwback to the period of the War of National Liberation. The letter was harshly critical of party and government functionaries who had been infected by bourgeois vices, had lost contact with the masses, lacked self-discipline, and behaved like petty tyrants. It was the first time that a major party statement called attention to the problems it was facing with its own members and apparatus, and to the urgency of dealing with them.

The changes resulting from the reorganization of the state apparatus were made known by Premier Shehu on March 17, 1966, at the conclusion of the Ninth Legislative Session of the Popular Assembly. He revealed that the number of ministries had been reduced from nineteen to thirteen, and that the ministers affected by the measure had been assigned to new posts. The move to streamline the government was part of the drive to curb the widespread bureaucracy, combat the economic malaise, and – in line with the objective of the unfolding cultural revolution – raise the political and ideological level of the cadres and the masses. This last point took on added meaning with the announcement at the Assembly that the Minister of Foreign Affairs Behar Shtylla had been replaced by Nesti Nase, former Albanian ambassador to Peking.

Subsequently, a massive campaign was started to send cadres and functionaries to the production line. During the next six to seven months, the campaign involved some fifteen thousand administrative personnel, plus additional thousands of intellectuals and youth. Although it would have been vehemently denied in Tirana, this mobilization drive had some resemblance to Khrushchev's attempts to force students to work in farms and factories for the betterment of their ideological perspective and the economy. At no time did the Albanian cultural revolution go much deeper than the traditional self-criticism among party cadres. The practice of public humiliation of functionaries conducted by the Red Guards in China did not occur in Albania.

The Fifth Party Congress, held November 1–8, 1966, was intensely preoccupied with the country's ideological and cultural revolution. Hoxha's report to the Congress was in large part an appraisal of the revolution since its inception in January and an outline of its future course. He called on every Albanian to place reliance first of all on his own forces and to put into practice "the great slogan" of the party – "think, work and live like revolutionaries." He stressed the danger of the "degeneration" symbolized by the CPSU and explained that this occurred "as a consequence of its bureaucratization . . . which gradually stifled its revolutionary spirit and drive."[17]

The next high point in the march of the revolution came on February 6, 1967, when the first party secretary delivered his programmatic speech, "For the Further Revolutionization of the Party and the Power."[18] Subsequently, the speech assumed a status in Albania equal to, if not greater than, the documents and decisions of the Fifth Party Congress and initiated what may be considered the second phase of the ideological revolution. It showed Hoxha's exasperation with the bureaucrats and the concern of the party leadership over the growing alienation of the people from the government.

This time Hoxha appealed directly to the people, inviting them to criticize openly and without fear all bureaucrats and reactionaries who were violating party norms, socialist legality, and the spirit of the revolution. The appeal resembled in some respects Mao's "Hundred Flowers" call back in 1957. The reaction was an immediate, widespread, powerful, and in some instances explosive – if not totally spontaneous – outpouring of pent-up emotion and resentment on the part of the people, especially women and youth. Wall posters, attacking bureaucratic practices and anachronistic social phenomena, made their appearance; in some cases there were public denunciations of the offenders; women en masse clamored for their rights; and a movement against religious beliefs and practices, first started by students of the "Naim Frasheri" public high school in Durres, Albania's chief seaport, began to spread through many parts of the country. There is no doubt that much of the resentment was genuine. However, the form it took and the objects of attack were strictly controlled from above to accomplish the regime's objectives – mobilization of women into the labor force and the elimination of a potentially alternate center of power in the Albanian church.

There followed a three-pronged drive for "the emancipation of women," and against "religious beliefs" and "backward customs." The government saw the latter as serious obstacles to its program for economic development, the elimination of all vestiges of feudal and bourgeois institutions, and the creation of the new communist man, equipped with a new consciousness and a new morality. Religion as an institution was long suspect in the eyes of the party leaders, in part because they considered it mystical and parasitic, and alien to Albanian culture, and in part – it may be as-

17. Enver Hoxha, "Report," p. 89.

18. *Zeri i Popullit,* February 7, 1967.

sumed — because belief in God posed to the people an alternate object of supreme loyalty, as against the party. Accordingly, on November 22, 1967, a government decree abolished "the material basis" of religion; i.e., it legalized the closing of all churches and mosques in the country.[19] The religious establishment thus became the first major victim of the ideological revolution, and Albania earned the distinction of being "the first atheist state in the world." [20]

The government action stirred resentment among the older generation, as well as among some communists; consequently, the party leadership sought for ways to fill the void in the people's lives created by the disappearance of the religious establishment. In practice this meant substituting national holidays for the forbidden religious celebrations. Victories won during the partisan war became feast days. Deaths of local heroes or other events with historical significance to a village or region were almost religiously commemorated.

Another major focus of the drive to revolutionize Albanian life was educational reform. Sparked off by Hoxha in a speech to the APL Politburo in March 1968, this move was elaborated upon in two major addresses by Premier Shehu in April 1968 and June 1969.[21] Shehu called for "a qualitative leap" in education to rid Albanian schools of all harmful vestiges of Soviet influence and to create a "truly revolutionary and socialist" intelligentsia that would be "loyal to the end to the Party's cause." The new system was to rest on a tripod comprising theoretical learning, productive work, and physical and military training. Chinese influence in the new system was underscored by Shehu's remark that the works of Mao Tse-tung would be included in the program of Marxist-Leninist studies, alongside the works of Marx, Lenin, and Stalin.

By the summer of 1968, the revolutionary ferment had reached the judicial system. As a result of action taken by the Popular Assembly on June 24, 1968, the court network was decentralized in favor of the establishment of popular courts at the village level, the aim being to bring the masses closer to the judicial organs and enable them to "participate in the judicial process."

19. *Gazeta Zyrtare*, November 22, 1967.

20. *East Europe*, 16, no. 11 (November 1967), 35.

21. Enver Hoxha, "For the Further Revolutionization of Our Education," *Information Bulletin* (of APL-CC), 20, no. 2 (1968), 3–24; Mehmet Shehu, *Information Bulletin*, 20, no. 2 (1968), 25–62, and *Zeri i Popullit*, June 29, 1969. For a detailed discussion of education in Albania, see John I. Thomas, *Education for Communism* (Stanford, Calif., 1969).

As for the economy, the years 1965–66 marked the end of the third Five-Year Plan (1961–65) and the beginning of the fourth such plan, as the APL leadership intensified its efforts to turn Albania from an agrarian-industrial society into an industrial-agrarian one. According to Premier Shehu, the fourth Five-Year Plan (1966–70) was drafted in consultation with the largest number of working people ever to take part in economic planning in Albania, in line with the principle of relying on the masses as the surest means of avoiding the pitfalls of bureaucracy. Nevertheless, the problem of bureaucratic cadres and low productivity, especially in agriculture, persisted.

In 1968 the party responded by instituting "working class control" in the economy, a mechanism designed to check the power of the cadres by enlarging the workers' initiative and by making them the final arbiters in matters pertaining to the economy.[22] Organizationally, working class control was implemented by setting up workers' control committees, as distinguished from state control committees, to supervise – in effect, audit – daily operations of the enterprises. Workers' committees represented control from below, while the state committees represented control from above. In theory the two types of control complemented each other, but it was expected that the efficient exercise of supervisory power by the workers' committees would in time render superfluous the state committees.

As of this writing, there have been numerous complaints in the Albanian press about exploitation of workers' committees by the state bodies amounting to attempts to coopt the new focus of authority. It is therefore too early to determine the effects of "working class control" on the Albanian economy. The communist leaders of Albania, however, seem convinced that central planning and direction of the economy are a sine qua non for the successful construction of socialism. They constantly attacked the free market economy as anarchic and the profit motive as debasing. It was, in fact, in the area of economics that Albania attacked Yugoslavia most strongly and most often, charging Belgrade with the abandonment of socialist gains and the restoration of capitalism.[23]

The Albanian leadership seemed bent on building a collectivized, egalitarian society, and toward this end worked steadily for "the gradual nar-

22. Enver Hoxha, "The Control of the Working Class," speech delivered at the meeting of the party Secretariat on April 9, 1968, but not distributed abroad.

23. Besim Bardhosi, "The Marxist-Leninist Theory of Planning – A Target of the Attacks and Distortions of the Modern Revisionists," *Ekonomia Popullore*, no. 2 (March–April 1965), 69–83.

rowing down of differences between the working class and the peasantry, between city and town, between industry and agriculture, between mental and physical labor." [24] For a country hampered by an underdeveloped economy, as well as the vestiges of nearly five centuries of subjugation by the Turks, it was an ambitious goal. Nevertheless the party pushed forward in concrete attempts to equalize wages and to require that students and intellectuals spend some time working in factories and on the farms. These efforts were complemented by periodic mass campaigns whereby thousands of factory workers and urban youth were sent to the countryside to help with agricultural work. The underlying rationale for this reshuffling was that if the various segments of the population mingled with one another on the work front, there would be a simultaneous social interaction, and the resulting exchange of knowledge, skills, and experience would favor the elimination of differences among them. Again caution is suggested in attempting to evaluate success. However, in line with this goal, Albania completed the collectivization of agriculture early in 1967, introduced collective work norms in place of individual norms, made new moves to convert agricultural cooperatives into commune type organizations, and enacted a law to transform artisan cooperatives into state enterprises.

In the course of the fourth Five-Year Plan, Albania experienced a number of failures, especially in its efforts to solve the endemic problem of bureaucracy, but it did bring about major changes, particularly in industrialization. Industrial development included textile combines, chemical fertilizer plants, cement factories, food canning plants, and factories for the processing of metals. Advances were also made in lumber processing, oil refining, and railroad construction. Plans were underway for the electrification of the entire country by 1971, and as of November 1969, the government had eliminated direct taxation of its citizens – thus becoming the first communist nation to abolish the income tax.[25] A year later, on November 4, 1970, the party announced that the program for the electrification of the country had been completed, and October 25, the day on which power was installed in the last village, was proclaimed a national holiday, henceforth to be commemorated as the "People's Festival of Light."

The special characteristic of the fourth Five-Year Plan was that it occurred concurrently with the development of the ideological and cultural revolution, and as such the successes and failures of the plan were also a

24. Enver Hoxha, "Report," p. 49.

25. *Zeri i Popullit*, November 13, 1969; *New York Times*, November 19, 1969.

measure of the successes and failures of the revolution. Compared with the Chinese Cultural Revolution, the Albanian variety was moderate, orderly for the most part, and at all times under the direction and control of the party. Moreover, unlike the Chinese Cultural Revolution, which was basically political in nature and involved a fierce intraparty struggle, Albania's revolution was — in effect, if not in rhetoric — a technique of economic and social mobilization, viewed by the APL leadership as a necessary step toward the larger and more ideological end of building a communist society in Albania. To understand that end, it is now necessary to look at Albania's relationship with the rest of the communist world.

II

The importance of China has been an overriding fact of political life for Albanian relations with other communist states and parties. In Peking the Albanians found a protector that not only could save Tirana from being swallowed by Belgrade — a long-standing Albanian fear reactivated by Khrushchev's rapprochement with Tito — but could confront Moscow on more or less equal terms. As Hysni Kapo, the third ranking member of the Albanian hierarchy has put it, "If someone were to ask us how many people do we have, our answer is 701 million." [26] Moreover, the fact that China is far away is to Albania's advantage, since distance is not an insignificant consideration to a small state seeking powerful allies.

In the years following Tirana's break with Moscow, China's economic and technical aid proved indispensable to the survival of the Albanian communist leadership. It is a fact that Hoxha is unlikely to forget. The party leaders have described those years as the most difficult period since the war of liberation. In June 1965, China reportedly advanced a 214-million-dollar loan to Albania to finance the fourth Five-Year Plan,[27] and in November 1968, an Albanian trade delegation to Peking concluded what Enver Hoxha enthusiastically called a "brilliant" economic agreement, which ostensibly included the largest amount of credit China had ever given to Albania, although no actual figures were disclosed. Since then, the two countries have signed several additional economic and other agreements. The most important of these was concluded on October 16,

26. *Peking Review*, 9, no. 19 (May 6, 1966), 3. Kapo's remark brings to mind the attitude of the Montenegrins before the Second World War, who said that a correct estimate of their strength had to take into account the combined populations of Montenegro and Russia.

27. Jan S. Prybyla, "Albania's Economic Vassalage," *East Europe*, 16, no. 1 (January 1967), 9–14.

1970, when a high-level Albanian economic delegation, headed by Politburo member and President of the State Planning Commission Abdyl Kelezi, signed a five-year trade agreement in Peking, at the end of a two-month visit in China. *Zeri i Popullit* (October 17, 1970), described the agreement as "a powerful support" to the Albanian people during the period of the next Five-Year Plan (1971–75).

The Albanians distinguished sharply between Soviet and Chinese motives in giving economic aid. Chinese assistance was "disinterested," while the Soviets used such aid to pressure Albania into supporting Moscow's line. This is probably an exaggeration of the truth, yet the Chinese did profit from the Soviet Union's heavy-handed manner of dealing with the poor but proud and independent-minded Albanians, and took care to respect them and treat them as equals.

Despite their dependence on Peking and their initial praise for the Great Proletarian Cultural Revolution, the Albanian leadership may well have been confronted by a tense situation created by certain aspects of China's cultural upheaval. During 1968 Albanian interest in Chinese domestic affairs appeared to wane, for reasons not clearly known at this time. One might speculate first that the Albanians feared that the inward nature of the Cultural Revolution would tempt Peking to view its foreign commitments less seriously. Secondly, Red Guard activity had its disquieting, chaotic side. Hoxha believed in "uninterrupted revolution" controlled from above, and he could easily have felt threatened by such spontaneous initiatives from below even when they were channeled by a somewhat organized group. That such actions frequently meant severe humiliation of party cadres could have had perhaps more serious implications for Albania than for China.

To illustrate the point, it may be useful to consider the composition of the delegates to the Fifth Party Congress. Statistics show that out of a total of 834 delegates, 374 or about 45 per cent were in the 40–50 age bracket, and that 72 per cent of the delegates had been party members before 1951.[28] The party was aging, and as a consequence job security had become a matter of concern to large numbers of cadres. This "generation gap" became a major cause of friction within the party ranks, as the APL leadership sought to replace the older cadres with younger and better trained people. Given the ferment of the developing revolution, the situation could have gotten out of hand, unless the leadership maintained order during the period of transition in power and position. Therefore it

28. *Fifth Congress of the APL* (Tirana, 1967), p. 346.

is not surprising that the Red Guard phenomenon did not become a true feature of the Albanian counterpart to the Chinese Cultural Revolution.

The difference, however, in the approach and style of the Chinese and Albanian cultural revolutions apparently did not damage state relations between Tirana and Peking. The Albanians extended warm greetings to the CCP leaders on the occasion of the Ninth Party Congress in April 1969 and reacted with great indignation to the Sino-Soviet border clashes in the spring and summer of the same year, placing the entire responsibility for the conflicts on the USSR. When Sino-Soviet talks on the border issue began on October 20, 1969, *Zeri i Popullit* took note of the event, but made no comment; nor did it cease its violent attacks on the Soviet Union in the weeks that followed. Perhaps this could have been an indication that the Chinese were not serious about the negotiations. Yet it could equally well have meant that such negotiations were unacceptable to Tirana, for a dangerous situation could have developed as its ally sat down to talk to its enemy.

During the following year, Albania's relations with China were marked by uncertainty and ambiguity, apparently because of the increasing Sino-Soviet contacts and the resulting limited détente between the two communist giants. Thus, Albania failed to report the developments of the Sino-Soviet talks on the border question. Tirana also maintained silence on Peking's renewed diplomatic and trade activity with the Soviet Union and East Europe. Tirana's reaction to these events suggested a certain strain in the Sino-Albanian entente. Although outwardly there were no signs of disagreement between the two allies, there is reason to believe that China's reactivization had prompted Tirana to review its relations with Peking, thus introducing — at least in principle — an element of instability in the seemingly immutable alliance.

For the most part, Chinese and Albanian policies coincided on all the major issues in the years 1965–70. But it would be a mistake to think that Albania was merely a mouthpiece of Chinese policy, with no initiative for independent action or no capacity to influence Peking. To a certain extent, there seemed to be reciprocal influence between the giant of the East and the tiny nation on the shores of the Adriatic. Thus, Albanian policy mirrored China's position on Japan, India, North Korea, North Vietnam, and even Cuba — with which Albania had the most cordial relations before the emergence of Sino-Cuba differences in 1966. But it is equally true that China's policy toward Yugoslavia, Greece, and Bulgaria invariably took into account Albania's position with respect to these countries. Here again the Chinese profited, by negative example, from the Soviets who generally disregarded Tirana's conception of its interests and role in the Balkans. The very fact that Albania was China's only ally during this period enabled it to exercise a measure of control over China – when Tirana's interests were concerned – which would not otherwise have been possible. There was some justification, therefore, for Albania's denial of the Soviet and Western thesis that it was a mere satellite of China.

III

The foremost constant in Tirana's foreign policy in the second half of the sixties, and the controlling factor in its relations with East Europe, was its implacable opposition to the CPSU leadership. The rule applied by Albania was simple: whatever policies the Soviet Union espoused or put into practice, Albania opposed and attacked. For example, Albania attacked all Soviet moves for a rapprochement with the United States, on the ground that they were nothing but Moscow-Washington plots for world hegemony. Likewise, Albania branded Soviet proposals for disarmament as treacherous maneuvers intended to lull the peoples of the world into a false sense of security. In cases where Soviet and Albanian policies objectively coincided, as in their support of Vietnam against the United States, or the Arabs against the Israelis, Albania either belittled the aid given by the Soviets or questioned Moscow's motives for giving such aid, and warned its recipients that they were being betrayed.

In addition to public polemics, the Albanian leadership avoided all contact with the Soviets and spurned all initiatives for an improvement of relations with Moscow. On February 2, 1965, Albania rejected a Polish invitation to attend a meeting of the Warsaw Pact countries. The invitation reportedly was a friendly gesture to Albania on the part of the new CPSU leaders, which may have opened the way to a Soviet-Albanian reconciliation. In January 1966 the USSR and its East European allies invited Albania to take part in a conference of socialist countries to map a "united action" strategy for helping Vietnam. Again, Tirana turned down the invitation, accused the Soviets of supporting American aggression against Vietnam, and served notice that Albania would not participate in any meetings of East European countries if the Soviets were involved in them.[29] The following month the USSR supposedly made a formal attempt to resume diplomatic ties with Albania. Shortly before the opening of the Twenty-third Congress of the CPSU, Moscow asked the Albanian Party of Labor to send a delegation to the Congress, but again met with a rebuff

29. *Zeri i Popullit*, February 12, 1966.

from Tirana.[30] Subsequently, the Soviets made additional efforts to improve relations with Albania. Perhaps the most significant and striking attempt occurred in April 1970, on the occasion of Lenin's centenary in Moscow, when Brezhnev noted that the USSR was in favor of restoring relations with all "socialist countries." Tirana brusquely declined the offer, and instead vowed never to stop polemics against Moscow. It seemed clear that as long as Hoxha remained in power, there was practically no chance of a reconciliation between Albania and the Soviet Union, barring radical changes in Soviet politics.

Indeed, not only did the Albanians spurn all Soviet attempts to break the Sino-Albanian alliance, but they repeatedly called for the overthrow of the "Brezhnev-Kosygin clique," and claimed that revolutionary groups already existed within the Soviet Union.[31] Convinced that the dialectic of history was on their side, Albania and China worked energetically to promote factionalist activity within the USSR and the international communist movement. Since 1966, Albania has served as a base of operations for a Polish, anti-Gomulka communist party, headed by Kazimierz Mijal, a former minister of communal economy in Poland.[32] At the Fifth Party Congress, the APL leadership announced with pride that thirty-one Marxist-Leninist communist parties and groups were present at the Congress. Again, in November 1969, during Albania's celebration of the twenty-fifth anniversary of its liberation, no less than twenty-two "Marxist-Leninist" parties and groups were in attendance. Several of them, including the Dutch, Swedish, and Danish delegations, highly praised the APL and Albanian socialism. The Dutch, for example, said that ". . . the Albanian people and its Party of Labor [are] the greatest example of inspiration for all Marxist-Leninists in the world." [33]

Meanwhile, Tirana intensified her broadcasting activities in support of factionalist aims. A Polish source in London reported in September 1966 that Albania had begun broadcasting in the Polish language. The program was said to be under the direction of Kazimierz Mijal.[34] And in October 1967, on the occasion in honor of China's eighteenth anniversary, Albania

30. *Die Zeit*, February 22, 1966; *Zeri i Popullit*, March 22, 1966.

31. *Zeri i Popullit*, December 20, 1966.

32. *Ibid.*, December 4, 1968; "Call to Communists, All Honorable Men of the United Polish Labor Party," *Rruga e Partise* (monthly organ of APL), 16, no. 9 (September 1969), 73–79.

33. *Zeri i Popullit*, December 4, 1969. Pro-Albanian communist parties, as distinct from pro-Chinese parties, reportedly were active in Austria and Belgium in 1969.

34. *Dziennik Polski* (London), September 8, 1966; RFE, September 12, 1966.

inaugurated two new radio stations with the avowed purpose of furthering the aims of world revolution.

At the same time, Albania strongly opposed the holding of an international conference of communist parties, and when such a conference was finally held in Moscow in June 1969, *Zeri i Popullit* called it "a yellow international" and commented: "The current conference of the revisionists will seal their betrayal of communism, and effect the final split between Marxist-Leninists and revisionists." [35] Tirana was confident, however, that centrifugal forces within the revisionist camp were driving it to its inevitable destruction.

Albania's attitude toward the Soviet Union also determined its policy toward East Europe. The yardstick of Albania's relations with the East European countries was the degree of their collaboration with the Soviet Union; i.e., the warmer their relations with Moscow, the cooler Tirana's attitude toward them. Accordingly, Albania found itself at odds with all the East European countries – with the possible exception of Rumania – until the Czech invasion. As for Yugoslavia, the APL leaders had long ceased to consider it a socialist country, and they heaped scorn on "the treacherous leaders of the Soviet Union who rehabilitated Tito's clique . . . and held out the Yugoslav way as a model that should be followed by others." [36] By August 1968, Rumania was the only country in East Europe with which Albania maintained both state and party relations – the result mostly of Rumania's pursuit of a course within the socialist camp that was largely independent of the Soviet Union. Nevertheless, Tirana was not happy with Bucharest's neutrality in the ideological war between the USSR on the one hand and China and Albania on the other, or with Bucharest's expansion of political and economic relations with the West. The Albanians also criticized the Rumanian leadership for allowing President Nixon to visit Bucharest in July 1969, declaring that the visit was incompatible with Rumania's declared position on the struggle against imperialism.

IV

The invasion of Czechoslovakia by the Soviet Union and four Warsaw Pact countries came as a shock to the Albanians, and resulted in a limited realignment in Tirana's international position. Hoxha did not expect the

35. "Open Fire on the Revisionist Betrayal," editorial in *Zeri i Popullit*, June 10, 1969.

36. "Mirror of the Degeneration and Failure of Tito's 'Self-Administration,'" *ibid.*, July 6, 1968.

USSR to use force against the Czechs. On September 12, 1968, Albania formally withdrew from the Warsaw Pact which, according to the Albanians, had been transformed "from a defense pact against imperialist aggression into an aggressive pact against the socialist countries themselves." [37] China was quick to approve Tirana's move, and in a telegram to the Albanian leaders indirectly warned the Kremlin that an attack on Albania would meet with disaster.[38]

Meanwhile Tirana halted temporarily its polemics against Yugoslavia, and in a move intended apparently as a signal to Belgrade, charged that massive Soviet military forces had been stationed on Bulgarian soil, thus posing a direct threat to the Balkan peoples. The Chinese backed up Albania's accusation, even though there was no reliable evidence of Soviet troops in Bulgaria.

Presumably these developments were the result of a deliberate decision by Tirana to reappraise its relations with Belgrade. Although Belgrade had adopted a policy of friendship and cooperation with Albania following the fall of Rankovic in July 1966, Tirana had failed to respond in any meaningful way before the Czech invasion. Albania continued, however, to expand trade relations with Yugoslavia, and showed some interest in developing contacts with the Albanian-populated province of Kosovo in southwestern Yugoslavia. In May 1968, several Albanian scholars from the Tirana State University traveled to Pristina, the capital of Kosovo, to take part in a commemorative conference on Scanderbeg. Communication between publishing houses in Tirana and Pristina resulted in agreements for the exchange of books, periodicals, and educational materials. The fall of 1968 witnessed a series of violent demonstrations in Kosovo by the Albanian nationals; yet despite such happenings, trade and cultural relations between Albania and Yugoslavia continued unhampered.

That the Kosovo incidents were surmounted with such relative ease can be credited largely to the repercussions of the Czech invasion in the Balkans. For in the aftermath of the Soviet attack a new trend began to appear in Albanian-Yugoslav affairs, which suggested the beginning, perhaps, of a new era in their relations. From all indications, this trend was the direct result of Tirana's increasing fears of Soviet aggression against Rumania, Yugoslavia, and Albania. This uneasiness was augmented by the Sino-Soviet border clashes and the growing Soviet naval activity in the Mediterranean during 1969. Tirana, therefore, moved to meet the appar-

37. *Information Bulletin* (of APL-CC), 20, no. 3 (1968), 22–48.

38. *Zeri i Popullit,* September 19, 1968.

ent Soviet threat by forging what seemed to be tacit defense alliances with its neighbors.[39] Toward that end, in April 1969, Albania publicly offered to assist Yugoslavia and Rumania against Soviet aggression, and a year later an editorial in the party's daily not only reaffirmed Tirana's pledge of assistance to Belgrade, but went so far as to praise Yugoslavia's National War of Liberation, "led by the communists." [40] It was a big concession for Albania to make to the heretofore despised Yugoslav communist leadership. For its part, Yugoslavia welcomed Tirana's efforts to improve relations. An article in the Zagreb daily *Vjesnik* (April 25, 1970) took note of Albania's favorable evaluation of the Yugoslav partisans' struggle, saying that "our papers have . . . correctly appraised it as the expression of a new and more positive attitude toward Yugoslavia." The article, entitled "Our Neighbor Albania" and signed "B.M.," expressed the hope that the two countries "will . . . find the solution to all major questions existing between them."

Albanian-Yugoslav relations continued to develop favorably, and in February 1971 full diplomatic relations between the two countries were established. The event was greeted with much enthusiasm in Belgrade, and was reported immediately by the Chinese news agency, an indication presumably of Peking's approval of this development. An improvement in Sino-Yugoslav relations some months earlier (in the summer of 1970) probably influenced Tirana's decision to follow suit. But by far the main factor which pushed Tirana toward a rapprochement with Belgrade was its constant distrust of Moscow and fear of Soviet aggression. As a further step toward realigning its position in the Balkans, Albania improved markedly its relations with Turkey and went so far as to establish diplomatic ties with Athens in May 1971, even though Greece has considered itself technically at war with Albania since the Second World War.[41] The normalization of relations with Greece and increased contacts with Turkey were in fact part of Albania's new stance toward the West. This modification of policy led to an expansion of relations with various West European countries, particularly in such areas as tourism, air communications, trade, and diplomacy. By the end of 1970, for example, Albania had established diplomatic relations with ten West European nations. Tirana's intense activity vis-à-vis the West at this time signaled the start of what

39. L[ouis] Z[anga], "Albania's Uncommonly Friendly Soundings Towards Yugoslavia," RFE, April 9, 1970.

40. *Zeri i Popullit*, April 5, 1970.

41. *Ibid.*, May 7, 1971.

may be called Albania's "opening to the West," and noticeably changed the country's political landscape.

These alterations in Albania's position were accompanied by a steady stream of attacks on Soviet "social imperialism" and on the "Gustav Husak clique" which supinely submitted to Soviet occupation. Faithful to the doctrine of revolutionary struggle, Tirana kept calling on the Czech people to rise in armed rebellion against the Soviet occupiers and the traitorous Czech leaders, for that was the only way they would gain their freedom, save their nation, and restore true socialism in Czechoslovakia.

V

Five years after Khrushchev's fall, and nearly fifteen years since the Twentieth Congress of the CPSU, Albania has succeeded in disproving the domino theory as applied to the communist world. A Stalinist country practicing a militant type of communism, it has withstood the "revisionist wave" that has swept over East Europe since the 1956 thaw. It has successfully resisted the pressures for liberalization, generated by the far-reaching political, economic, social, and cultural changes in other Eastern European countries. Instead, Tirana has emphasized reform from above without political liberalization. This pattern differs from the Stalinism of the late twenties and thirties in that the APL leadership has shown considerable concern that increases in the standard of living and in industrialization rise in a parallel progression. The attitude is that modernization should not occur at the expense of human welfare, and an increasingly significant part of the Albanian budget has been devoted to housing, education, and health care.[42]

The de-Stalinization program in the Soviet Union – symbolized in Tirana's eyes by Khrushchev – and its powerful repercussions in East Europe, plus of course the new, internal developments in China set off a counterresponse in Albania. They triggered the ideological and cultural revolution which, in the late sixties, became the major political fact of life in Albania's domestic affairs. Confronted by the new political realities in East Europe and the ferment in China, the Albanian leaders inevitably had to launch the cultural revolution, first of all to justify to their own people their policy vis-à-vis the revisionists, and thus consolidate their position; secondly, to complement the domestic developments in China in order to show their solidarity with Peking; and thirdly, to inspire the Al-

42. *Bashkimi*, January 14, 15, 16, 1969.

banian people with the vision of a society and a way of life far superior to the one they knew.

Yet, stripped of its ideological rhetoric, Albania's effort to revolutionize the country's life was in effect a bold, energetic, haphazard, and risky attempt to bring about needed economic and social changes in Albanian society, which in many respects was still feudalistic, oriental, clannish, and patriarchal. In attempting such a massive social experiment, the Albanian leaders faced a paradox, for the very seclusion and isolation of their people – which was thought to be necessary for the experiment to succeed – cut them off from the more advanced societies of the West and East Europe and tended to perpetuate many of the backward features of Albanian life. On the threshold of the seventies the results of Albania's experiment seem inconclusive, but there is little doubt that the leadership intends to press forward.

As is the case with all revolutionary movements, the ferment caused by the intensification of the "uninterrupted" revolution in Albania disaffected certain segments of society, including bureaucrats, religious elements, and significant portions of the intelligentsia and the farming populations. However, the discontent did not appear to pose a major threat to Hoxha's power, since he apparently had the support of the army, the loyal cadres, the youth, and the industrial workers. Other factors in his favor were the rise in the people's standard of living, a tradition of authoritarian rule in the country, and an efficient state security system. Perhaps most important of all were the powerful nationalist sentiments which he continued to symbolize in the eyes of the population, in large part because of his role as leader of the country's National War of Liberation.

The ideological and cultural revolution was part of Albania's overall revolutionary stance. In line with this policy, Albania became the leading exponent of revolutionary propaganda in Europe and the nerve center for the factionalist activity of the pro-Chinese communist parties of Western Europe. Such a role perhaps was useful to the Albanians as a means of overcoming their sense of isolation, but the prospects for success in extending their political power and influence in Europe are limited. Moreover, their openly hostile position invites retaliation and makes Albania a natural target of attack by its enemies in the Kremlin and East Europe, as well as in the pro-Soviet communist parties of the West. Here again Tirana's role within the communist world seems paradoxical, since its actual capacities are not commensurate with its revolutionary aspirations. On the face of it, the commitment of Albania – a small, weak, and isolated country – to a revolutionary role would seem futile, if not ludicrous, except that it is allied with a militant and powerful China. That fact, coupled with a growing rebellious mood in many parts of the world among students, youth, and various disadvantaged groups, gave Albania's revolutionary stance a measure of respectability and credibility. In any case, by the end of the sixties the austere Tirana communists were firmly committed to the doctrine of revolutionary change in Albania and the world.

Externally, the major political event which had an especially strong impact on Albania's foreign policy was the invasion of Czechoslovakia. The invasion had a traumatic effect on Albania's leaders and made them fully conscious of the geopolitical realities in the Balkans and Europe. In part, the sense of shock was the product of their having misread the Kremlin's intentions and the true aspirations of the Czechoslovak people.

The Czechoslovak crisis brought to the fore the national reflex in the Albanian leadership, particularly in view of the observation made by the Soviets, following Albania's withdrawal from the Warsaw Pact, that they could not rely on China for help in case of national emergency. Apart from the question of its validity, the remark was a veiled threat which the Albanian leaders could not afford to ignore. Accordingly, Albania moved gradually to deemphasize its ideological and political differences with its neighbors and to seek a modus vivendi with them, in the interest of national security. Only extreme concern for Albania's independence could induce Hoxha to draw closer to Tito's Yugoslavia or to the "fascist military clique" in Athens.

Albania's overall response to the Czech invasion was to develop its ties both with China and its Balkan neighbors. And as long as Sino-Soviet tensions continue, and the Brezhnev doctrine is in force, the prospects look good for a steady improvement of relations, at a state level, between Albania and its Balkan neighbors, as well as the West. On the threshold of the seventies, it appears that Albania will maintain its special relationship with China, but at the same time expand its connections with other countries, particularly in the direction of the West. Albania's renewed interest and activity in its natural and historic-geographic environment seem almost certain to affect the character of the Sino-Albanian entente and to lessen Chinese influence on Tirana during the decade of the seventies.

11

External Forces in Eastern Europe

BY ANDREW GYORGY

The old Latin phrase *fluctuat, non mergitur* (it fluctuates but does not submerge) characterizes the new assertiveness of the ancient forces of political and economic nationalism in Eastern Europe, an area never particularly noted for peace and harmony.[1] Thus, the developments in the region and the fortunes of its one hundred and thirty million people are to be largely determined by the delicate interplay of an externally imposed communist ideology and the indigenous forces of political nationalism. The continuing tug of war between communism and nationalism seems to have evolved a specific equilibrium, assigning "spheres of influence" to each. For example, domestic relations allow greater freedom to nationalist determinants than do foreign affairs.

The increasingly significant concept of "domesticism" denotes an internal area of economic and political leeway in which the traditional patterns of Eastern European nationalism can be asserted even in the context of a communist society. The ability to develop one's own initiative and momentum in domestic matters is a meaningful factor in contemporary Soviet-East European relations. Yet, the domestic sphere ends literally at each individual nation's borders. When the endemic vigor of nationalistic

NOTE: The author of this chapter is indebted to Colonel Alfred Pabst of the United States Army for research assistance. Col. Pabst is a doctoral candidate at George Washington University preparing a dissertation on *Ostpolitik*.

1. Adam Bromke's early penetrating remark "It is clearly not Communism but nationalism which is . . . the major political force in Poland" can be applied to all of Eastern Europe in the 1970s. "Nationalism and Communism in Poland," *Foreign Affairs*, 40 (July 1962), 641.

forces extends beyond the national boundaries and threatens the "collective" (as did Dubcek's Czechoslovakia), then direct intervention is used to restore the equilibrium.

In external matters, on the other hand, the ideological dictates of international communism take over and maintain their monopoly. Nationalism is deemphasized to the point where it almost disappears, particularly in the three salient and closely related spheres which affect the interests of the "collective": common military matters; economic relations; and foreign policy. The Warsaw Treaty Organization especially and Comecon impose the most severe limitations on national aspirations. Within this context "domesticism" is allowed an approximate 50 per cent of the internal *Lebensraum* in which the national leadership can operate with relative freedom, on condition, however, that in the external sphere it undeviatingly follows the line of obedience to and compliance with communist bloc policies.

To appraise the complex interplay of communist and nationalist forces, this chapter will first survey the major cohesive external factors in East European communism and then balance them with an analysis of domestic aspirations which at times have culminated in genuine polycentric trends.

I

The complicated interrelationship of East European communist states is reflected in the two important treaty networks binding these countries to the USSR. Described here as "cohesive factors," these are the Warsaw Treaty Organization (WTO) on the military side and Comecon in the economic and commercial sphere. Together they ensure the continuation of the predominant position which the Soviet Union has played in the area since the end of the Second World War. The Warsaw Pact or Warsaw Treaty Organization was launched informally in 1949, but was not formally signed until May 14, 1955. Through a multilateral military design WTO has attempted to establish and to keep secure the Soviet Union's postwar strategic safety zone in Eastern Europe. There is nothing mysterious in this modern imitation and communist version of the traditional nineteenth-century Western concept of spheres of influence. Viewed in historical terms, WTO is essentially the Soviet expression of the age-old Czarist ambitions to secure the flanks of Russia, to bolster militarily its exposed and vulnerable westernmost boundaries, and to develop an imperial *cordon sanitaire* all its own. As such it has been centrally relevant to the troubled status of postwar Europe.

The Soviet military safety zone in Eastern Europe serves a double purpose. In a negative sense, it excludes the Western enemy (North Atlantic Treaty Organization, the United States, etc.) from the region by denying its use and control to all noncommunist forces. A related positive function is the inclusion of the region into the Soviet aggressive military blueprints, which comprise the launching of offensives from Eastern European bases, the planning of weapons and food caches for strategic points, the control of airfields, and the deployment of highly trained Soviet divisions prepared for battle. For the ten years following the end of the Second World War, Red Army troops were stationed in almost all the Eastern European countries. Between 1955 and 1958 these forces were gradually withdrawn from Rumania and Bulgaria, and partly from Poland, but East Germany, Hungary, and, since August 1968, Czechoslovakia have continued to serve as bases for the Soviet military.

The official signing of the Warsaw Pact formalized an already existing set of fourteen bilateral treaties tying the countries of Eastern Europe to the Soviet Union (see Figure 1). It also served to induct East Germany, a former enemy state, into the Soviet's military network in a manner similar to the inclusion of the German Federal Republic within the framework of NATO. In 1956 and in 1968 the WTO was used as a vehicle to keep Hungary and Czechoslovakia, respectively, in the communist bloc. The presence of Soviet troops, or the possibility of their rapid introduction should the need arise, has bolstered the various Eastern European communist regimes, but at the same time has imposed limits on their policies by making sure that they do not transgress the tolerable limits of "domesticism."

The Council of Mutual Economic Assistance (Comecon) was founded in 1949. Comecon's original objective, like that of the Warsaw Pact, was

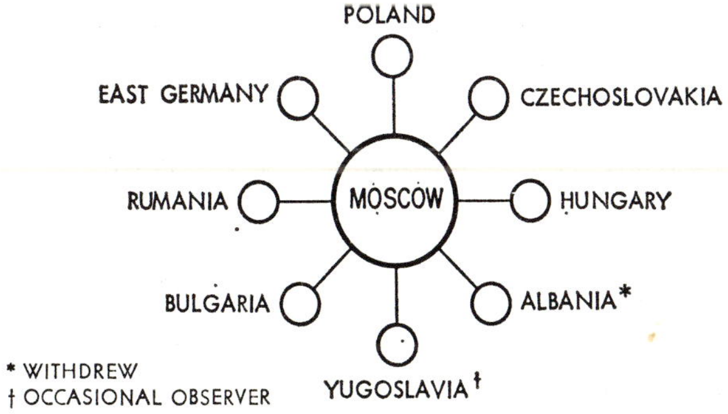

Figure 1. Bilateral aspects of CEMA and WTO.

defensive. Just as WTO was essentially designed to offset NATO, Eastern Europe's economic organization was instituted with the hope of counteracting the growing success of the European Economic Community in Western Europe and of preparing the ground for a similar integration in the East. Particularly since 1955, Comecon's frantic activities have increasingly reflected the twofold intention of the Soviet leadership: namely, to unite Eastern Europe firmly with the Soviet Union by a skillful exploitation of economic resources and division of labor; and to keep the satellite economies in fair-to-prosperous shape, thus guaranteeing the cooperation of the people and hopefully preventing a recurrence of the revolutionary upsurge of the 1953–56 period.

The organizational purpose of Comecon is to serve as an agricultural, industrial, capital- and labor-market focus for Europe's communist countries. To accomplish this objective economic intrabloc relations are organized on three parallel levels: multilateral arrangements within the Council itself, bilateral trade pacts between each member and the Soviet Union, and bilateral economic agreements between individual East European countries. The first arrangement binds all members to each other and to the dominant central authority of the USSR. Bilateral trade pacts directly link individual East European states to Moscow, usually in the form of a five-year agreement promptly renewed at the end of each term. Agreements of the third type create direct connections between the countries concerned, without directly involving the Soviet Union (see Figure 2). It is extremely difficult to appraise in statistical terms the overall intrabloc economic orientation of each of the member states. The major share of

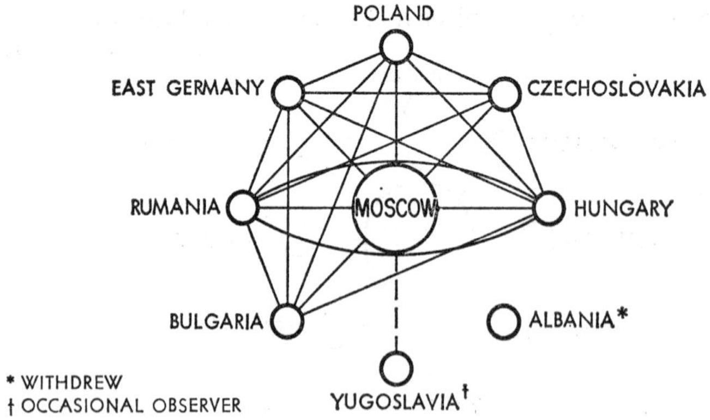

Figure 2. Multilateral aspects of CEMA and WTO.

each individual country's volume of foreign trade, estimated at around 60 to 65 per cent of the total, is conducted with their fellow communist states.

Several major areas of weakness have appeared recently within the structure of Comecon. In particular, manifestations of economic nationalism have become evident as certain countries have either voiced their dissatisfaction with the Soviet-imposed economic order or have actively challenged it. Rumania has openly and successfully defied Comecon policies since 1964. The Rumanians were the first to oppose directly the Russian views on the balanced economic development of member nations within Comecon, which assigned to Rumania a permanent role as an agricultural resource base, while other socialist countries were to industrialize. This accusation reflected a rapidly emerging sense of Rumanian nationalism and escalated to the point where it acquired a distinctly anti-Russian flavor.

In operational terms, intrabloc foreign policy-making has been among the major cohesive forces holding together the USSR and its East European allies. Although domestic expressions of nationalism may be increasingly tolerated in the conferences of the European communist states, there is little leeway for nonparticipation in or even abstention from these meetings. With the exceptions of Yugoslavia (which is not vulnerable to Soviet dictates) and Rumania (which frequently refuses to sign the communiqués issued by such conferences), all other countries are compelled to follow the common foreign policy line, be it European security matters or anti-Vietnam declarations.

On the practical level this foreign policy linkage between bloc ideology and bloc discipline has asserted itself primarily in the various European regional organizations such as the ECE. Recently it has also increasingly emerged in the global international organizations, i.e., in the United Nations, the International Monetary Fund, the World Bank, and the General Agreement on Tariffs and Trade in which Poland and Czechoslovakia are already members, and Hungary and Rumania are expected soon to be admitted. Generally bloc voting prevails in all these situations, and Soviet signals are obediently followed, again with the exceptions of nonaligned Yugoslavia and occasionally recalcitrant Rumania.

Bloc unity and discipline have been considerably tightened since the Warsaw Pact seizure of Czechoslovakia in August 1968. Toward the end of that year a new Soviet doctrine was officially pronounced (or, rather, an old one was resurrected) to rationalize and to justify retroactively the military intervention. Quickly dubbed the Brezhnev doctrine by the West, this concept introduced the notion of limited sovereignty for socialist countries. According to the Moscow ideologues, the real sovereignty of Czechoslovakia demanded that the "fraternal socialist countries" protect it from those who threatened to undermine "the very foundations of [its] independence and sovereignty." A term used in the Khrushchev era, the *Socialist Commonwealth*, was appropriately revived suggesting that the central or core country of such a commonwealth (the Soviet Union) had the right to intervene in the internal affairs of any of its member states — as it did in Czechoslovakia. Sovereignty for such commonwealth members, Brezhnev explained, could not be accepted as an "abstractly understood" concept but would have to be limited by the dictates of a "counterrevolutionary" situation or, more accurately, by the external and unilateral decisions of Soviet policy-makers.[2]

II

"Polycentrism" in the context of this discussion is defined as a factor influencing Soviet-East European relations in a negative or divisive manner, potentially disrupting the cohesion imposed by the USSR on its satellite nations. Of the several polycentric forces which have recently asserted themselves on the Eastern European political stage, two have been of particular significance: the Sino-Soviet dispute and the German question.

Since 1961 the Sino-Soviet dispute, a disruptive power and ideological conflict between the two communist giants, has directly affected every East European nation. Its impact has contributed to the creation of at least four national or group subcategories which, with one exception, can be considered here as forces that are weakening the overall Soviet power position. The Eastern European countries have been presented, in effect, with four options or alternatives. They can, first, support communist China unequivocally to the point of precipitating an open break with the USSR. This choice was made only by Albania, which severed relations with the Soviet Union in the early sixties. Secondly, they may seek a position of political maneuver and material advantage by playing off one major ideological antagonist against the other. This was attempted in a modest way by several of the East European countries but exploited only by Rumania,

2. For a valuable recent analysis of communist international organizations in general, and Comecon in particular, see Richard Szawlowski, "The International Economic Organizations of the Communist Countries, Parts I and II," *Canadian Slavonic Papers*, 10, no. 3 (1968), 254–78, and 11, no. 1 (1969), 82–107, and Boris Meissner, *Die Breshnew Doktrin, Dokumentation*, 2nd ed. (Cologne, 1970), p. 190.

which has played the bribery-bargaining-exploitative game with acrobatic skill and great national satisfaction.[3]

The third alternative is to pledge complete loyalty to the Soviet Union in the hope of gaining sizable political rewards and economic concessions; the majority of the Eastern European satellites selected this course. Although there were some differences in the extent to which the bloc countries supported the Soviet Union in the period from 1962 to 1970, it can be said that Bulgaria has backed the Soviet Union most loyally across the board, and Hungary, East Germany, Poland, and Czechoslovakia (though with different degrees of enthusiasm at various stages of its recent turbulent history), have echoed Soviet policy in its military, economic, and diplomatic aspects, insisting in turn on a "most favored satellite" treatment from the Muscovite leadership. The abjectly and totally pro-Soviet line has frequently forced those countries into overexuberant, and thus embarrassing and unpopular, protestations of friendship with the USSR, but it is clear that by the seventies they have either directly or indirectly profited from the communist camp's internecine power struggle.

The fourth course of action, that of independent isolationism, was possible only for Tito's Yugoslavia. Its foreign policy posture can only be described as a "plague on both your houses" approach to the problem, punctuated with occasional pro-Soviet noises, but with an essentially aloof attitude toward the day-by-day vicissitudes of the Sino-Soviet dispute itself. Although Yugoslavia nominally favors the Soviet side, its diplomats are primarily intent on going through the correct motions of support rather than taking a substantive side in the conflict. Its attitude is essentially neutralist, antibloc in regard to both NATO and WTO orientation, and both anti-Soviet and anti-Chinese whenever the issue of actual diplomatic or political involvement emerges. Thus, Yugoslavia can be described as de facto nonaligned.

In sum, the future impact of the Sino-Soviet dispute on the eight countries is in the direction of erosion and a greater latitude of polycentric communism with most of these nations deriving benefits from its fractionalizing influence.

III

The so-called German question affects Eastern Europe profoundly. Its spectrum is a complicated one, ranging from Pankow's dogmatic internal

3. For a more detailed treatment of this subject, see an earlier version of this chapter in *Nationalism in Eastern Europe*, by A. Gyorgy, Research Analysis Co. Report, January 1970, esp. pp. 58–64.

policies on the one end to Bonn's flexible *Ostpolitik* on the other. To gain a proper perspective of the complexities of the German question, several different policy situations must be considered in some detail. The problem of the continuing existence of the two German states must be viewed as the most basic fact affecting the future of Germany and, in broader terms, of the entire European continent. The chances for unification are minimal in the foreseeable future. The longer the division is maintained, the more rigid will be the lines of separation irrationally dividing East from West in Germany.

The growth of East German nationalism received relatively little scholarly attention because of the usual assumption that the GDR was simply a Soviet occupation zone (*Sovietische Besatzung-Zone*, in West German terminology). In the past few years, however, several sociological studies have pointed out that East Germany has been attempting to create its own national image, beginning approximately in 1952, when the "Two Germanies" doctrine officially replaced the policy of German unification under communist aegis.[4]

The GDR's nascent nationalism is based on the stabilization of political, economic, and social life, and on a rapidly accelerating East German popular interest in the country's politics and economics. It is characterized, above all, by a firmly antagonistic posture toward Bonn. As the most common expression of East German nationalism, the anti-West German orientation is not in itself a startling development. Its most surprising feature, however, is the degree of popular identification "one finds among citizens of the GDR with their government and with the new society which is emerging. Young people particularly express approval for the German Democratic Republic, and ask accusingly why the West refuses to recognize it. 'It is our state, after all,' many say, 'and by refusing to deal with it you are really hurting us.' Identification with Bonn has lost its appeal, for the Berlin Wall makes it abundantly clear where life must be spent." [5]

The Berlin issue is inextricably interwoven with the separate national-

4. Notably Peter Christian Ludz, *Parteielite im Wandel* (Cologne and Oplanden, 1968).

5. Jean Edward Smith, "Limitations of Political Persuasion: The German Democratic Republic and Soviet Policy in Central Europe." A summary of a paper presented to the American Political Science Association at its New York session, September 10, 1966. Smith also analyzes the East German's growing revulsion to Bonn's claim to represent all of Germany and to speak in the name of the citizens of the GDR. A less biased and more restrained view of East Germany's nationalism is presented by Welles Hangen, "New Perspectives behind the Wall," *Foreign Affairs*, 45 (October 1966), 135–47.

ism of the two Germanies and with the gloomy perspective of the East Berliners as they view the divided and enclosed city. Berlin, whether East or West, cannot be separated from the Soviet role in Eastern Europe or from the greater problem of a direct East-West confrontation. The two Berlins are the focal points of several ideological forces, namely, the East Germans' sense of nascent nationalism; a specifically West Berlin nationalism expressed in both the *Lokal Patriotismus* (localized nationalism) and the continued support of the Bonn government, which places a great deal of symbolic emphasis on the need to maintain a free West Berlin [6] and is engaged in highly sensitive negotiations with the USSR and with the East German regime to ease the tensions in and around the beleaguered city; the resolve of Western Europe, NATO, and the United States to stand fast in West Berlin; [7] and major ideological and nationalistic Soviet commitments in Berlin. For the Soviet Union, East Berlin has both a symbolic and a military importance. It is essential to maintain Moscow's dominant position not only in East Germany, but, indeed, in all Eastern Europe. The dismantling of the Berlin Wall would have a symbolic significance, for it would bolster hopes of freedom throughout the entire area.

In view of the explosive and relentless crosscurrents affecting Berlin, continued friction over this divided city seems practically inevitable. Moreover, the Berlin issue is both insoluble and permanent. Since Western retreat is impossible and the "wall of shame" is not likely to come tumbling down, the ideological-diplomatic-military deadlock will stretch into the future, hopefully without major crises, but also without much chance of resolution.

The most important element of the present German question is the Federal Republic's *Ostpolitik*. During the period of the Kiesinger-Brandt coalition, this policy gathered momentum in its first two years of operation but slowed down appreciably after the August 1968 invasion of Czechoslovakia. Since 1969 the Brandt-Scheel coalition government has followed its own *Ostpolitik* along three parallel and chronologically synchronized levels: first and directly with the USSR; subsequently with Poland; and fi-

6. Occasionally the stress is more than symbolic and becomes provocative. The decision to hold the Federal presidential elections in West Berlin on March 5, 1969, promptly triggered a renewed "Berlin crisis" in retaliation for what the East Germans and the Soviets considered an "act of provocation."

7. The present deployment is approximately 5500 U.S. troops, 2700 U.K., and 2000 French, for a total of 10,200. These statistics were given to the author in an unclassified briefing in Bonn, at the Ministry of Defense of the Federal German Republic in February 1969.

nally in multilateral and highly sensitive negotiations concerning the "Berlin Question."

In its direct negotiations with the USSR, the Brandt government has paid careful attention to the "step-by-step" or "stage-by-stage" process of improving relations with its powerful neighbor to the East. An important element of Bonn's relations with Moscow was related to the timing of political events. For example, the election of a new president of the Federal Republic was scheduled for March 1969. The East German government was unable to persuade the Soviets to prevent this election from taking place in Berlin. From a current perspective it appears that the Soviets were not interested in sacrificing other aspects of their policy in Europe for the sake of an East German gain in Berlin. Russia was probably more concerned with three facets of its foreign policy which could have been affected adversely by a breakdown in relations over Berlin: a dialogue with West Germany which might lead to Bonn's signing the Nuclear Non-Proliferation Treaty; a resumption of the SALT talks which were suspended after the invasion of Czechoslovakia; and a desire to keep the Western flank in Europe secure in view of the deterioration in Sino-Soviet relations. The Federal Republic's signature on the Non-Proliferation Treaty in November 1969 signaled to the Soviet Union that it was ready for serious negotiations on a bilateral treaty involving the renunciation of force. Moreover, it was an encouraging sign for the Soviets' much sought after goal of convening a European security conference.

Negotiations with the Soviet government picked up momentum in 1970. Apparently the most significant of these discussions was a thirty-six hour meeting between Gromyko and Brandt over an eight-week period in which all the problems affecting the two countries were explored. The result was the signing of the West German-Soviet treaty in Moscow in August 1970. The treaty focused on two points: a declaration not to use force against each other; and an acknowledgment of the geopolitical realities which now confront them and are likely to do so for some time to come.

More important than the treaty's substance for the West Germans was the fact that it paved the way for negotiations on the other two levels of the *Ostpolitik*. Poland apparently was given the green light to begin bilateral negotiations with West Germany. The first secretary of the Polish Communist party, Wladyslaw Gomulka, in a speech in May 1969, had extended an invitation to Bonn to open talks with a view of improving relations between the two nations. Bonn accepted that invitation in November 1969. The following February the first round of meetings took place in Warsaw. Several others, held alternatively in Warsaw and Bonn, ensued.

West German-Polish talks ceased during the summer of 1970, while West German negotiations with the USSR were in progress, but they were resumed in the fall. In November 1970 the West German Foreign Minister Walter Scheel and Polish Foreign Minister Stefan Jedrychowski, who were the primary negotiators, announced agreement on the treaty, which was signed by Chancellor Brandt in Warsaw in December.

For the German Federal Republic the pact maintained the overall momentum of *Ostpolitik*, while for the Poles it primarily signified a recognition of the Oder-Neisse boundary. The treaty confirmed the "inviolability of the existing frontiers, now and in the future," and pledged "to respect unreservedly the territorial integrity of both parties." It also signaled progress toward an all-European security conference. For both West Germany and Poland the treaty meant a giant step toward a normalization of relations, both diplomatic and economic.[8] As Bonn and Warsaw announced their agreement, preparatory talks between West Germany and Czechoslovakia were also being publicized.

The third level of negotiations outlined in West German *Ostpolitik* has been carried out with East Germany. There is a deliberate vagueness in Bonn's policy with respect to the principle, established in the Paris Agreements, that the West German government was the sole legitimate representative of the German people in international affairs.[9] This vagueness and the gradual modification of the Hallstein Doctrine provide some ground for negotiation between Pankow and Bonn. The Soviet Union probably desired that the West Germans talk with the East Germans, while the Federal Republic's aims were twofold: to prevent a further deepening of the gulf between the two parts of Germany in the hopes of possibly even bridging it; and to secure guarantees for Berlin. Consequently Brandt accepted Willi Stoph's offer of a meeting and the two met in Erfurt in March 1970 to open the first discussions ever held between the leaders of the two Germanies.

This meeting was followed by a second at Kassel in May 1970, where Brandt offered a twenty-point program which included these principal items: (1) renunciation of force; (2) exchange of high commissioners with Cabinet rank; (3) mutual respect for their independence, in domestic as well as foreign affairs; (4) full observance of Four Power agreements on Berlin and the two Germanies, and acceptance of the Federal Repub-

8. For an evaluation of the Warsaw Pact see Adam Bromke and Harald von Reikhoff, "The Polish-West German Treaty," *East Europe*, 20 (1971), 2–8.

9. E. H. Albert, "The Brandt Doctrine of Two States in Germany," *International Affairs*, 46 (1970), 296 et seq.

lic's ties with West Berlin; (5) easing of travel between East and West Germany; (6) free exchange of information; (7) continuation of all present trade regulations; and (8) a solution to the question of the international recognition of the GDR.[10]

On the critical issue of Berlin, Four Power negotiations began in March 1970. To date no progress has been reported despite occasional brief glimmers of hope for a major breakthrough in the tangled and seemingly insoluble Berlin issue. Pankow, of course, has remained the chief stumbling block. Moscow, on the other hand, at least has appeared to be willing to continue negotiations on the Berlin problem.

IV

The Federal Republic of Germany began a search as early as 1963 for a foreign policy that would reflect the changes which were occurring in superpower politics. This process has culminated in the efforts undertaken by the Brandt-Scheel coalition government. Bonn perceives in *Ostpolitik* a possibility of enhancing its security through a lessening of tensions with the Soviet bloc. There is little doubt that it feels it can adapt to changes in the direction of normalization of relations more readily than can the communist states. However, this situation works to its advantage in the bargaining process and enables it to retain flexibility on the most critical issues. The Federal Republic believes that essentially the Soviet Union determines the policies of the communist countries, and consequently, if mutually satisfactory agreements could be achieved first with the Soviet Union and then with Poland, the Soviets would then pressure the East German regime to negotiate a suitable agreement with Bonn.

In the long run, a great deal will depend on the course of relations between East and West Germany. Unless they improve in the near future, and unless Pankow ceases to react hysterically to "Eastern" initiatives by Bonn, the Federal Republic will find it increasingly difficult to probe more deeply into Eastern Europe. East German protests have usually triggered increased Soviet pressure on the country involved. In such circumstances there is little prospect for a viable *Ostpolitik*. Bonn cannot effectively negotiate directly with Budapest, Prague, or even Warsaw if active displeasure voiced by Pankow brings about a Moscow veto, or at least a considerable slowdown in negotiations.

10. Josef Korbel, "West Germany's *Ostpolitik*: I, Intra-German Relations," *Orbis*, 14 (Winter 1970), esp. 1061 et seq. See also Anatole Shub, "Soviets Say Big Four Talks on Berlin Moving Forward," *Washington Post*, March 10, 1971, and Joe Alex Morris, "Brandt Seen Hurt in Berlin Voting," *Washington Post*, March 15, 1971.

Andrew Gyorgy

The legacy of Adolf Hitler's National Socialism still lingers on the East European scene as a historic force exacerbating the lines of division. Anti-German feelings are widespread in Eastern Europe, and bitter memories of military oppression, Nazi brutality, and mass genocide are most pronounced in Czechoslovakia, Poland, and, of course, the Soviet Union. A quarter of a century is a long stretch of time, but not long enough to forgive or forget the incredible wartime record of the Third Reich. This fear of Germany persists in several of the Eastern European countries and makes true reconciliation extremely difficult.

Some of the internal developments in West Germany are also a source of concern to Eastern Europeans. There is a fear that the National Democratic party, which has been winning 5 to 10 per cent of the regional votes in the Federal Republic, may yet prove to be the direct successor to Hitler's National Socialists. The reluctance of the former Kiesinger government to outlaw the NDP heightened the feeling among East Europeans that a repetition of history was not impossible. The economic success of West Germany and its great "economic miracle" have created envy and even alarm on their part, contributing further to their "Colossus Again" complex. A shaky coalition government heads this prosperous economic system, adding to Eastern European apprehensions.

Some aspects of the Federal Republic's foreign policy have been no less disturbing in the eyes of the Eastern Europeans. One of them was Bonn's initial unwillingness (before the December 1970 treaty with Poland) to recognize formally the Oder-Neisse boundary, settled de facto by the mass expulsion of the Germans after the Second World War and by twenty-five years of Polish reconstruction, but still a source of potential contention. The other problem has been the controversy over the Czech-controlled border province of Sudetenland.

Anti-German feelings are periodically rekindled by communist propaganda. The Soviet Union skillfully plays on the anti–West German, anti-Nazi, "antirevanchist" sentiments of the vulnerable northern tier countries – Poland, Czechoslovakia, and, to a lesser extent, East Germany and Hungary – which are the key elements of the Soviet WTO and Comecon networks. In this propaganda, however, an impression is carefully created that all the Nazi legacy is to be found in the Federal Republic and none in East Germany.

For the Eastern Europeans there is also the persistent fear of a "second Rapallo," i.e., a possibility of another agreement between Germany and Soviet Russia on the pattern of the Rapallo Conference of 1922. An exclusive rapprochement between Bonn and Moscow would be considered a near disaster by Eastern Europeans – a sellout of some of their legitimate interests by the Soviets to a resurgent West Germany. Khrushchev's attempts to negotiate directly with Bonn (in 1962 and 1963 through Bonn's ambassador in Moscow, the late Heinrich Kroll, and in September–October 1964 through his son-in-law Adzhubei) provoked hysterical reactions, not only from Pankow, but also from Prague and Warsaw. Many Eastern Europeans were genuinely relieved when Khrushchev was removed in 1964 and his ill-fated "Rapallo" experiment collapsed.

The German question, then, in its manifold complexities, profoundly affects, and in all likelihood will continue to influence, the situation in Eastern Europe. Because of Eastern Europe's juxtaposition to Germany, developments in Eastern Europe, and particularly in the northern tier, form a part of the East-West confrontation in the heart of that continent, and will eventually have a considerable impact on Soviet-American relations.

V

This brief analysis of the interplay between the forces of communism and nationalism in the European communist states would be incomplete if it did not stress the impact of two important background factors, one largely economic, the other of international political significance.

Each nation of East-Central Europe is gripped by its own version of a revolution of rising expectations. The masses of people, especially the younger generation, demand improvements in the standard of living, more material goods, and a better economic performance instead of vague promises of a glowing, but remote, future. Although reflecting a set of globally existing phenomena, this vigorous economic revolution has only emerged in Eastern Europe in the course of the past decade. It has a national flavor in each country, and it pressures national leaderships to develop domestic plans, programs, and "new economic mechanisms" aimed at satisfying pent-up popular needs and demands. In many situations, as for example in the Poland and Hungary of the early seventies, this trend has emphasized the primacy of a national economic orientation over international ideological concerns. Thus, in the long run, it will exert a fractionalizing, polycentric, and "antibloc" influence, since communism and popular mass aspirations conflict rather than coincide in ultimate purpose.

Another potentially important force, the widespread political interest in and concern with an all-European security system, must also be noted. Deriving originally from the Rapacki Plan of 1956–57, this essentially Polish- and Soviet-sponsored movement has been enthusiastically debated throughout East-Central Europe in the past few years. It would express itself first in an all-European security conference, then in a gradual de-emphasis on and eventual dismantling of the Warsaw and Atlantic pacts, with an atom-free zone guaranteed for Central Europe. These various projects frequently move along abstract lines, neglecting such major loopholes as the Berlin issue and the role of power politics concerned with nuclear weapons on the part of the United States and the Soviet Union. However, as a gradual attempt to develop a regional alliance system, the European security drive should not be minimized. In the future it may even prove capable of radically changing the situation in the area by simultaneously curbing the twin excesses of communism and nationalism. By creating a supranational, politically independent organization,[11] it may enable the Eastern European countries to join an all-European community.

11. Of the growing literature on modern nationalism, the following are particularly relevant to Eastern European nationalism: Louis L. Snyder, *The New Nationalism* (Ithaca, N.Y., 1968); Kurt London (ed.), *Eastern Europe in Transition* (Baltimore, 1966); and R. V. Burks (ed.), *The Future of Communism in Europe* (Detroit, 1968). For up-to-date discussions of closely related issues, see also "Czechoslovakia 1968," *Canadian Slavonic Papers,* 10, no. 4 (1969), 409–591, and Viktor Meier, *Neuer Nationalismus in Sudosteuropa* (Opladen, 1968), esp. chaps. 1 and 2, on Rumania and Yugoslavia. The economic aspects of Eastern European nationalism are explored in a scholarly historical perspective in Peter F. Sugar and Ivo J. Lederer (eds.), *Nationalism in Eastern Europe* (Seattle, 1969). See especially the excellent essay by Sugar, "External and Domestic Roots of Eastern European Nationalism," pp. 3–54. On recent developments in the broad field of European security, the two most useful studies are Timothy W. Stanley, *A Conference on European Security, Problems, Prospects and Pitfalls* (Washington, D.C., 1970), and *Détente Diplomacy: United States and European Security in the 1970's* (with Darnell M. Whitt) (New York, 1970).

12

Outer Mongolia

BY PAUL F. LANGER

At the height of their power, centuries ago, the Mongolians ruled an empire encompassing both China and Russia. Today, the descendants of Genghis Khan no longer pose a threat to their neighbors. Two-thirds of the ethnic Mongolians now live under Chinese or Russian rule and the remainder, barely more than one million, lose themselves in the vast, empty spaces of the Mongolian People's Republic (MPR).[1] Precariously sandwiched between the USSR and the PRC[2], the sparsely populated and economically undeveloped MPR must somehow find ways of preserving a measure of independence in the face of conflicting pressures exerted by its two powerful communist neighbors.

Historically, the Chinese rather than the Russians have been viewed by the Mongolians as the principal threat to their survival as an ethnic group. For hundreds of years, the area which is today the MPR – Outer Mongolia – was a mere Chinese dependency. Only in recent times has Russian (Czarist and then Soviet) military intervention against China enabled some Mongolians to regain independence from Chinese control. Thanks to Russian power, the Mongolians escaped the fate of losing their identity under a mounting tide of Chinese immigrants. But the fate of their brothers in Chinese-ruled Inner Mongolia, which is rapidly being submerged by

1. According to the MPR Bureau of Statistics, the country, as of January 1, 1970, had a population of 1,227,800 inhabitants on a territory of more than 600,000 square miles – twice the size of Texas. Some half million people of Mongol stock live in the Soviet Union, mostly in the Buryat Autonomous Soviet Socialist Republic (formerly the Buryat-Mongol ASSR). The major Mongol *irredenta*, however, is in China, where the Inner Mongolian Autonomous Region has 1.5 million Mongol inhabitants.

2. Outer Mongolia's borders total some 4400 miles – about 39 per cent run along Soviet territory, 61 per cent are shared with China.

the swelling Chinese population, serves as a constant reminder of the continued presence of a Chinese ethnic threat. The Chinese communist government has sponsored a continuous immigration of ethnic Chinese colonists, who now total more than 11.5 million. Thus, the Mongolians of Inner Mongolia have been reduced to minority status. Peking also has redrawn the boundaries of the Inner Mongolian Autonomous Region in order to include more Chinese peoples and thereby dilute the once predominant Mongolian ethnic group.[3] A Moscow broadcast in Mongolian on April 25, 1970, is typical of the manner in which Soviet propaganda exploits this issue and keeps Mongolian fears of the CPR alive. The broadcast accused Peking of enslaving the Mongolian minority population of China and of pursuing a policy of extermination. Similarly, only two days later, another Soviet broadcast declared that the Soviet Union continues to be the real friend of the Mongolians and that the day will come when the Inner Mongolians will be able to enjoy socialism to the fullest – an implicit Soviet threat against China. Another Moscow broadcast (September 6, 1971) directed toward the Mongolian population of Chinese Inner Mongolia, suggested that there is serious friction between the local population and the Chinese garrisons, stating flatly, "The Inner Mongolian people hate the Peking leadership and the army."

In Ulan Bator, the capital of Outer Mongolia, it is remembered with gratitude that Bolshevik intervention in 1921 made it possible to install a sovereign Mongolian regime. But under the domination of the Red Army, the new republic had to accept the status of a Soviet satellite and was hermetically sealed off from all contact with the noncommunist world, including relations with China. Although this state of total isolation and complete dependence on Soviet power continued substantially unchanged until the end of the Second World War, the Soviets allowed the Mongolians at least a degree of cultural autonomy so long as this did not conflict with the goal of "building socialism" on the Soviet pattern. Nor did the Soviets pose an ethnic threat as had the Chinese – no attempt was made by Moscow to colonize Outer Mongolia with Russian settlers. Meanwhile, the extremely undeveloped and militarily weak new country benefited from its association with the Soviet Union in a number of important ways: the Soviets furnished economic and technological assistance – on a modest scale – and provided protection against foreign encroachment, notably against expansionist Imperial Japan whose forces were severely defeated

3. For further details on the status of the Mongolians under Soviet and Chinese rule, see A. J. K. Sanders, *The People's Republic of Mongolia – A General Reference Guide* (New York, 1968).

in eastern Mongolia in 1939 by an essentially Soviet military effort. Again, thanks to Russian pressures, the Nationalist government of China reluctantly agreed in 1945 to recognize the Mongolian Republic as an independent state, an agreement which was subsequently reaffirmed by the Chinese communists.

The advent of a communist regime in Peking opened up new vistas for the Mongolian government. The Soviets relaxed their tight control over the Republic at least insofar as the Chinese were concerned. For a number of years after 1949 Moscow appeared to be willing to concede to the Chinese communists at least a secondary role in Ulan Bator. It is not clear whether this departure from traditional Soviet policy in Outer Mongolia was a response to Chinese pressures or whether the Soviet leaders saw in the MPR an opportunity to demonstrate without much risk their trust in Sino-Soviet cooperation, a relationship in which Moscow meant to play the leading part. At the time, this policy was welcomed by the Soviet-sponsored Mongolian leaders. The opening of the country's southern borders and the promise of Chinese aid could provide them with obvious material advantages as well as with greater leeway in dealing with the Soviet Union.

The signing in October 1952 of a ten-year economic and cultural agreement between China and the MPR symbolized the beginning of a new era in Outer Mongolia's foreign relations. But as early as 1954, it had become clear in Moscow – and Ulan Bator – that the Chinese communists were unwilling to let Soviet predominance in the Mongolian Republic go unchallenged. When Khrushchev visited Peking in 1954, Mao Tse-tung raised the issue of Mongolia's Soviet-dependent status, pressing for true independence – thereby enhancing Chinese opportunities – in Ulan Bator.[4] Although disturbed by these Chinese moves, the Soviet Union did

4. In July 1964, Mao Tse-tung told Japanese visitors that he had asked the Soviet Union to restore true independence to Outer Mongolia. The Soviets apparently interpreted this suggestion as reflecting a Chinese desire to free Mongolia from Soviet domination so as to be able to reintegrate it all the more easily into the Chinese sphere of influence. Since then the Soviet Union has sought to keep Outer Mongolia's fears of China alive by insisting that it has clear evidence of Peking's evil intentions. M. Sladkovsky (ed.), *Developments in China* (a Soviet book published in English in 1968 under the auspices of the USSR Academy of Sciences), has this to say: "Mao Tse-tung adopted an openly chauvinistic attitude in the territorial question. As early as the nineteen thirties, he told Edgar Snow that the Mongolian People's Republic would be part of China. The demand for the MPR's incorporation in China was made by the Maoist leadership also after the Chinese People's Republic was proclaimed, in particular in talks with a Soviet Party and Government delegation in Peking in 1954" (p. 66). Similar accounts can be found in other Soviet sources, and there is little doubt that the Mongolian leadership has been made aware of the Soviet interpretation of Chinese policy toward the MPR. It must also be recalled that on September 29,

not react immediately. The Chinese communists were allowed to build a railroad link between Peking and the Mongolian capital which was completed in 1956. That same year, the MPR signed a new economic assistance agreement with the Chinese communists. A few months later, the Soviet Union countered with a more substantial aid agreement and voluntarily relinquished to the Mongolians the joint Soviet-Mongolian companies controlled by the USSR.

As Sino-Soviet relations went from bad to worse, Chinese efforts to increase Peking's leverage in Outer Mongolia must have caused concern in Moscow. This concern was no doubt accentuated by symptoms of rising Mongolian nationalism allied to pro-Chinese elements. Mongolian fears of China were allayed when, in 1960, Peking offered a Treaty of Friendship and Mutual Assistance to the MPR and, two years later, signed a border agreement which was generally favorable to the Mongolians. By that time, the Soviets apparently felt it was necessary to mobilize their not negligible assets in the MPR in an attempt to contend with China's growing influence there. Though the details of the story remain to be clarified, we know that those in the MPR power structure who were pro-Chinese – or rather nationalists – either were removed or quickly saw the portents of events. As could be expected, the Mongolian premier and party leader Yumjagiin Tsedenbal, who owed his position and rise to Soviet support, openly sided with Moscow in the Sino-Soviet conflict and strongly criticized Peking. His ruling Mongolian People's Revolutionary party (MPRP) endorsed without reservation the decisions of the Twenty-first and Twenty-second congresses of the CPSU, the MPR joined the Soviet-sponsored Council for Mutual Economic Aid, and Mongolian ideological statements assumed a distinctly anti-Chinese tone. By the mid-sixties the thousands of Chinese workers who had been active on aid projects in the MPR, at Chinese expense, had been repatriated.[5] Their place was taken by workers and specialists from the neighboring Soviet republics. Meanwhile, substantial Soviet forces moved back into the MPR to bolster its defenses; Peking subsequently protested that this action was a glaring example of the "brutality of the Soviet revisionists."[6]

1965, the then Chinese Foreign Minister Chen Yi, at a press conference, had stated: "After its founding new China succeeded to this commitment [of Chiang Kai-shek to recognize Mongolia's independence]. . . . There are Han chauvinists in China who have always refused to recognize the MPR. We are opposed to such Han chauvinism."

5. Sanders, *The People's Republic*, estimates the peak number of such Chinese workers in Mongolia to have been 13,150 in May 1960, although other sources give figures as high as 40,000.

6. See the joint editorial in *Jen-min, Jih-pao*, and *Hung-ch'i*, March 18, 1971.

Outer Mongolia

In the past several years, Chinese influence has been systematically eliminated in Outer Mongolia. Absolute loyalty to the Soviet Union has become once more the sine qua non for positions of responsibility in the MPR, as had been the case until the advent of the Chinese communist regime in 1949. By 1971, this process had transformed the Mongolian People's Republic into a Soviet forward position bristling with weapons and military readiness. Chinese leverage built up during the 1950s has been drastically reduced and relations between Peking and Ulan Bator have seriously deteriorated. These relations, however, have recently improved somewhat – reflecting the change in Moscow's and Peking's strategy in their conflict – but the Mongolian leaders made it very clear at the Twenty-fourth Congress of the CPSU and elsewhere that they remain firmly in the Soviet camp.

The blue-uniformed Chinese labor battalions have not returned to Mongolia. Nor has the Chinese economic aid program, discontinued in 1966, been revived. Peking's hostility toward the Mongolian regime has been evident in many ways. When, in 1968, blizzards, floods, and other natural disasters wrought havoc on the Mongolian economy and the communist world volunteered relief, China refrained from participating in the rescue action. Although a trade agreement was concluded between the two countries in the summer of 1969 and was renewed in 1971, the value of commercial exchanges between Outer Mongolia and China has dwindled to negligible proportions. Mongolia's foreign trade (presumably in 1968–69) with the Comecon countries accounted for 96 per cent of the total turnover, thus leaving a mere 4 per cent for China and the noncommunist countries. In 1971 it was reported that 97 per cent of the MPR's trade was with the socialist countries. Recent Soviet sources indicate that the Soviet share alone of the MPR's trade is about 84 per cent.[7] The Mongolian students have left Peking and the Chinese language is no longer taught in the MPR, not even at the country's only university. Meanwhile, a series of purges have removed all Peking-oriented nationalist elements from the MPRP. The background of these purges in the 1960s and the role the Chinese factor played in them are still unclear. Harrison Salisbury, who visited the MPR in 1969 and has had a long-standing interest in the country, contends that "in 1962 the Chinese almost certainly attempted a coup against the Russian-oriented Mongolian government." [8] North Vietna-

7. N. Torbenkov, *International Affairs,* Soviet (English language) journal (Moscow), November 11, 1969.

8. Harrison Salisbury, *War between Russia and China* (New York, 1969), p. 125. The central issue of some of the purges of Mongolian nationalists appears to have

mese and North Korean communists continue to attend the functions of the Mongolian party, but not the Chinese. Either they are not wanted in Ulan Bator or they prefer to boycott such conferences so long as the MPRP insists on advertising its identity with the views of the Soviet party.

Paralleling the deterioration of Sino-Soviet relations, there have been repeated reports of incidents ranging from anti-Chinese riots in the Mongolian capital to attacks on Mongolian diplomats in Peking to the harassment of trains running between China and Outer Mongolia. Still more serious, in recent years, a number of military clashes have occurred along the tense 2600-mile border separating the two countries. The Soviets have left no doubt about their readiness to defend their position in the MPR. Soviet President Podgorny, in 1969, cautioned Peking that the Soviet armies would defend the MPR's territorial integrity against China as resolutely as they had done, thirty years earlier, against Imperial Japan.[9] The CPRC, however, has given no indication that it wishes to embark on such a military venture.

During the past several years, the Mongolian leaders have consistently supported all Soviet ideological and foreign policy positions and have not hesitated to engage in debates with their Chinese neighbors. The tone of these mutual recriminations has faithfully reflected the language used by the Soviet Union in its conflict with Peking.[10] Thus, the high level of tension between Moscow and Peking during 1969 and much of 1970 was mirrored in the sharp manner in which the Chinese rebuked the Mongolians and the equally blunt replies which came promptly back from Ulan Bator. As Chinese strategy changed in 1971 and Sino-Soviet relations entered a new phase of persistent but less vitriolic hostility, the Mongolian

been their glorification of the Mongol conqueror, Genghis Khan. The eight-hundredth anniversary of his birth was celebrated in 1962, and the Russians quite understandably disapproved of attempts to idealize the Mongol national hero since this could only lead to a heightening of nationalistic and anti-Russian sentiments. This concerned the Soviets all the more because the Chinese communists in Inner Mongolia were organizing anniversary celebrations for Genghis Khan, no doubt with the intention of embarrassing Mongolian-Soviet relations. For a detailed discussion of this episode in Sino-Soviet-Mongolian relations, see Paul Hyer, "The Re-evaluation of Chinggis Khan: Its Role in the Sino-Soviet Dispute," *Asian Survey*, 6 (December 1966), 696–705.

9. See the article in *Pravda*, August 19, 1969, by colonels V. Klevtsov and M. Novikov.

10. It was noted, for example, that in 1965 Mongolia suspended polemics against the CPR at a time when the Soviet leaders made efforts to improve relations with Peking. See M. T. Haggard, "Mongolia: New Soviet Moves to Bolster the Ruling Group," *Asian Survey*, 6 (January 1966), 13–17.

leaders also toned down their comments on Peking policies without, however, abandoning their anti-Chinese stance. The Mongolians have accused Peking of pursuing a policy of "great power hegemony," have referred to the Chinese leaders and their followers in such terms as "Maoist toughs," and have described their policies as "reckless" – evident enough in their "innumerable miscalculations and failures" – and as a repudiation of "proletarian internationalism." [11] On March 5, 1970, a broadcast in the Chinese language beamed toward Peking from Ulan Bator attacked "Mao and his ilk" and severely criticized the Cultural Revolution for having inculcated chauvinistic thinking in the minds of Chinese youths. Later that month, on the occasion of the visit of Czech President Ludvik Svoboda to Ulan Bator, Sambuu, the chairman of the PMR Great Hural (corresponding to the Supreme Soviet in the USSR), took the Chinese to task for their "great power chauvinistic and anti-Soviet course." At the Sixteenth Congress of the MPRP, Tsedenbal, in his opening speech on June 7, 1971, expressed a desire to normalize relations with China, but also stated that his party was on principle opposed to the "anti-Marxist political line of the Chinese leaders."

Tsedenbal was also the only Asian communist leader at the Twenty-fourth Congress of the CPSU to attack Peking openly for its "divisive activities" and its "anti-Soviet propaganda" and to warn that the MPR would continue to stand by its Soviet ally.[12] The close relationship between the MPRP and the CPSU was repeatedly stressed by Tsedenbal and Soviet party leader Brezhnev. In a meeting which took place in Moscow in April 1971, they announced that there was a "complete unity of views between the CPSU and the MPRP." [13] In his report to the Twenty-fourth Congress, Brezhnev already had pointed to the "strong and tested friendship" which had endured between the two parties for half a century. The theme of firm Soviet-Mongolian friendship was again stressed when on June 17, 1971, at a ceremony in the Kremlin, Tsedenbal was decorated with the Order of the October Revolution and President Podgorny on the occasion declared that "not the smallest cloud" was darkening the horizon of Soviet-Mongolian relations.[14]

Because of these close ties between the USSR and the MPR, the Chinese

11. "What is behind the 'Ninth Congress of the CPC,'" *Information Bulletin*, 13/14, 1969 (Supplement to the Soviet-sponsored *World Marxist Review*).

12. See Tsedenbal's speech, *Pravda*, April 3, 1971, and his lengthy article, *ibid.*, March 1, 1971.

13. See *ibid.*, April 17, 1971.

14. See *ibid.*, June 18, 1971.

communists ever since 1967 have labeled Tsedenbal a "traitor" and a "pro-Soviet revisionist" for supporting faithfully Soviet positions. Typical is an editorial in Peking's official organ, the *Jen-min Jih-pao* (People's Daily) on March 4, 1969, which accused the Soviet Union of threatening China by massing troops along the Sino-Soviet (and Mongolian) border and of having occupied Outer Mongolia and turned it into a Soviet colony. This latter allegation is persistently voiced by the Chinese in the hope of arousing anti-Soviet nationalist sentiments among the Mongolians. For example, one of the most important statements issued from Peking in recent years ("Leninism or Social-Imperialism?") repeatedly refers to the harmful Soviet role in Outer Mongolia. A characteristic passage reads: "Once its political power is usurped by a revisionist clique, a socialist state will either turn into social-imperialism, as in the case of the Soviet Union, or be reduced to a dependency or colony, as in the case of Czechoslovakia and the Mongolian People's Republic." [15]

As China has temporarily been compelled to withdraw from competition with the Soviet Union in Mongolia and as Peking's relations with Ulan Bator have become strained, the prewar Soviet monopoly of power has been reestablished. A brief review of the Soviet position and of Soviet tangible and intangible assets in the MPR verifies that in 1971 Outer Mongolia was firmly – and apparently quite willingly – in the Soviet orbit.

I

Outer Mongolia has modeled itself in all respects after the Soviet Union. In its efforts to "build socialism through bypassing the capitalist stage of development," it has consistently sought to introduce and to develop Soviet-style political, economic, and cultural institutions. The Mongolian People's Revolutionary party takes its cue from the CPSU ("Lenin's own party," as the Mongolians like to say) and follows the organizational and operational code of its bigger brother. According to Ts. Dugersuren, a member of the Politburo of the MPRP, in 1969 the party had 2,193 primary units and more than 50,000 members (58,048 members and candidate members as of April 1, 1971). Dugersuren also commented that "the ideological work of our party is directed toward educating the working masses to be completely loyal to the fatherland, [to have] loyalty and respect for the Soviet Union and other nations of the socialist camp . . ." [16]

15. The official English version of this document appeared in *Peking Review*, 13, no. 17 (April 24, 1970), 9.

16. *Namyn Amdral*, no. 2 (1969). English translation, *Joint Publications Research Service*, no. 49336, November 26, 1969. Hereafter cited as *JPRS*.

It is also noteworthy that while the Soviet Union is constantly mentioned in MPRP policy statements (such as the documents of the Fifteenth and Sixteenth congresses held in 1966 and 1971, respectively), the CCP is generally ignored when it is not singled out for criticism. The MPRP's May Day slogans for 1969 included "warm and fraternal greetings to the great Soviet people engaged in a successful construction of Communism in their fatherland!" and "warmest, fraternal greetings to workers and specialists from the Soviet Union and other socialist countries, taking a personal part in our socialist construction!" There was no mention of China. On the occasion of the MPRP's fiftieth anniversary, Tsedenbal declared that his party "has based itself and continues to base itself on support and on organizational help from the CPSU. . . . The MPRP has marched and will continue to march in a single formation with the CPSU." [17]

Mongolian leaders are as much at home in the Soviet Union as in the MPR. Tsedenbal, for example, studied economics and finances at a Soviet institute, and Sambuu served as envoy in the USSR from 1938 to 1946. MPRP officials often tour the neighboring areas of the Soviet Union and have discussions with their Soviet counterparts. For example, in July 1968, a group of Mongolian central and local government officials spent some ten days studying Soviet administrative practices in the Chita Oblast. The younger generation of leaders is, of course, even more familiar with the Soviet Union than their elders of prerevolutionary vintage. Mongolians are taught Russian when they are children, and Russian serves as the second language for much of the Mongolian population. The most gifted students go West to Moscow for their advanced education. And the relations between the Soviet Union and Outer Mongolia are further strengthened by strong contacts between Russia and the Mongolian population as a whole. Residents of Ulan Bator could watch the proceedings of the Twenty-fourth Congress in Moscow on their television screens and were given the opportunity to listen to the report of CPSU Secretary-General Brezhnev. The citizens of Outer Mongolia learn the correct line of thinking by reading *Unen*, which, not surprisingly, means "truth," as does *Pravda* in Russian. In fact, the ideological and political articles in both papers offer almost identical viewpoints and opinions. In furthering their propaganda tactics, the Mongolians assert "the wealth of experience accumulated in this field in the Soviet Union must be studied and copied." [18]

17. *Pravda*, March 1, 1971. English translation, *Current Digest of the Soviet Press*, March 30, 1971.

18. *Namyn Amdral*, no. 9 (1968). English translation, *JPRS*, no. 47256, January 15, 1969.

Soviet influence is also reflected – and facilitated – by the common use of the Cyrillic script (significantly, the Chinese communists in Inner Mongolia have turned to the Latin script to impede cultural relations between Mongolians on both sides of the border). Books, periodical literature, motion pictures, television and radio, and a continuous succession of exhibits and lectures concerned with events in the Soviet Union constantly expose the inhabitants of the MPR to Soviet thinking and influence. These contacts are based on a cultural-scientific work plan agreed on annually between the two countries. Much of the resulting activity is organized and sponsored by the Soviet-Mongolian Friendship Association, which also arranges visits of Soviet cultural, scientific, and economic delegations to Outer Mongolia. Frequently, Soviet military and high-level political representatives are sent to Ulan Bator to reinforce Soviet-Mongolian ties and to strengthen the bonds of cooperation between the two countries. Such visits have increased in recent years, reaching a high point in 1969 and early 1970 when intensified Sino-Soviet friction encouraged the Soviets to pay even greater attention to their Mongolian ally. In May 1969 Podgorny visited the MPR, using the occasion to lash out against Peking. In July 1971 Premier Kosygin went to Ulan Bator to attend the fiftieth anniversary celebrations of the Mongolian regime. Among the military delegations was one headed by Colonel-General A. V. Gerasimov, deputy chief of the staff of the Soviet Armed Forces, in March 1970, preceded by a mission under Marshal V. I. Chuikov in October 1969. More recently, in March 1971, a Soviet military delegation under Colonel-General V. D. Sozinov visited Ulan Bator. The Mongolian People's Army is trained by Soviet officers and patterned after the Soviet model. Its top leaders have been awarded the Order of Lenin and attend as observers the military exercises of the Warsaw Pact powers. For example, General Batin Dorj, defense minister of the MPR, was present at the "Brotherhood in Arms" exercises in East Germany in October 1970.

Much of the Soviet Union's all-pervasive influence in the MPR is, of course, a result of the important contributions it makes to the development of the backward Mongolian economy. "Ample economic aid from the Soviet Union and other fraternal countries continues to bear fruit for the Mongolian people, . . ." stated Tsedenbal in his January 1970 report to the Central Committee of the MPRP. In contrast to other communist movements and regimes, the MPR does not stress self-reliance as a basic policy theme. On the contrary, it emphasizes the need for outside aid. Thus, Tsedenbal in an article in *Pravda*, written on the occasion of the Lenin celebrations in the USSR, pointed out that in undeveloped Outer Mongolia "everything had to be created anew, relying on the selfless aid of the Soviet people." [19]

The already fairly substantial Soviet aid program of the 1950s was stepped up further about 1960 when competition with Peking prompted the Soviet Union to increase its assistance to Mongolia. Ever since, the economic aid the Soviets have poured into the MPR has vastly exceeded the economic benefits they derive from Mongolia.[20] The MPR's last Five-Year Plan (1966–70) relied almost entirely on Soviet investments for the modernization of the Mongolian economy. Soviet aid during this five-year period is estimated at 1.1 billion dollars, making Mongolia one of the world's "most aided" nations on a per capita basis.[21] It is interesting to note that the original Soviet commitment (in 1965) was only 550 million dollars, and that, in late 1967, probably in response to the sharpening Sino-Soviet conflict, the commitment was doubled. Although dozens of new projects were built with Soviet assistance during 1966–68, the MPR remains a predominantly underdeveloped agricultural and livestock-breeding economy.[22] In 1967, industrial goods accounted for a mere 30 per cent of the total national product. According to Tsedenbal's report to the Sixteenth Congress of the MPRP, their share was expected to reach only 33.5 per cent by 1970.[23]

Soviet help also rescued Outer Mongolia from starvation during the several recent natural catastrophes. With Soviet assistance, Ulan Bator is being transformed into a modern city, although in 1967, R. A. Hibbert, former British charge d'affaires in Ulan Bator, reported that over half of the capital's inhabitants were still living in tented suburbs.[24] New urban-industrial complexes (of military significance), started in October 1961, are being developed at Darhan (or Darkhan) and more recently at Choibalsan, which is particularly important as a base against China. In 1968 the

19. *Pravda*, April 20, 1970. A Mongolian participant in a *World Marxist Review* round table discussion also stressed, as do virtually all MPRP leaders, that Mongolia's passage from feudalism to socialism without having to go through capitalism "is inconceivable without all-round cooperation with the Soviet Union and other socialist countries." *World Marxist Review*, 14, no. 4 (April 1971), 107.

20. See Robert A. Smith, "Mongolia: In the Soviet Camp," *Asian Survey*, 10, no. 1 (January 1970), 25–29.

21. *Ibid.*

22. *Unen*, January 15, 1969. *Namyn Andral*, no. 1 (1969).

23. A report published in *World Marxist Review*, 14, no. 7 (July 1971), 33, put industry's share in the MPR's gross social product at 34.1 per cent.

24. R. A. Hibbert, "The Mongolian People's Republic in the 1960s," *World Today*, 23 (March 1967), 122–30.

first secretary of the Darhan Party Committee reported on the progress at "the city of friendship," where Mongolian soldiers were working with skilled construction workers from the Soviet Union and from Eastern European countries. On the occasion of the conclusion of an economic agreement between the MPR and the USSR on April 19, 1965, Premier Kosygin in his speech in the Kremlin stressed the significance of the Darhan projects in these terms: "The construction program at Darhan has become a symbol of socialist internationalism and mutual assistance. Mongolian, Russian and Czechoslovakian specialists and workers work there together in an atmosphere of friendship." [25]

Soviet specialists, many of whom come from the bordering regions of the USSR, are everywhere in the MPR. Despite Chinese criticism, the MPR joined the Comecon in the early 1960s, and East European members of Comecon are now increasingly important factors in the Soviet effort to give Outer Mongolia a modest industrial base and to develop its usefulness for the eventuality of a Soviet conflict with China. In September 1963 a Comecon conference was held in Ulan Bator to coordinate the MPRP's twenty-year development plan. Actually, the Mongolian Five-Year plans are drawn up with the principal assistance of Soviet State Planning Committee officials. In short, Outer Mongolia is being integrated into the wider framework of Soviet foreign economic policy.

The ideological complexion of the MPR faithfully reflects the Soviet model. At a time when relations between Moscow and Peking had severely deteriorated, *Namyn Amdral* (Party Life), the MPRP Central Committee journal for political and ideological education, inveighed against the Chinese contention that the "national liberation movement" in Asia, Africa, and Latin America constituted the main zone of the anticapitalist struggle. Soviet propaganda directed toward Asia seeks to present "the experiences of the MPR" – meaning its close cooperation with the Soviet Union – as a model to be followed by the developing countries of Asia, Africa, and Latin America. Furthermore, it accused Peking of distorting Marxist-Leninist theories and of pushing the revolutionary movement onto an adventurous road while refusing to recognize the opportunities for a peaceful transition to socialism. For example, Kosygin, addressing a meeting in Ulan Bator on July 10, 1971, stated, according to a Soviet broadcast (as monitored by *FBIS* on July 12, 1971), that many Asian and African countries are backward and feudal and have a theocratic government like prerevolutionary Mongolia. He went on to argue that the gap separating these countries

25. English translation, *JPRS*, no. 48540, August 4, 1969.

from the advanced ones could be spanned, as was done by the Mongolians, without passing through the capitalist stage, by relying on the aid of the Soviet Union. Like the Soviet leaders, Tsedenbal and the rest of the MPR hierarchy warned of the dangers of nuclear war and stressed the emergence of a "world socialist system" as the decisive factor for socialist victory.[26]

Beginning with the decisions of the Twentieth and Twenty-first congresses of the CPSU, and as recently as its Twenty-fourth Congress, the Mongolian party has consistently sided with the Soviet Union in all matters involving controversy with Peking. This has been true of the Albanian and Yugoslav issues, the Chinese attack against India, the Cuban missile crisis, and the question of peaceful coexistence and nuclear weapons (the MPR promptly ratified the Nuclear Non-Proliferation Treaty). The Mongolian leaders, like their Soviet counterparts, have appealed for communist unity in support of the communist struggle in Indochina and they have praised as exemplary the Soviet position on the "national liberation movements." [27] They have endorsed the holding of an international communist conference, which had been strenuously opposed by the Chinese, by pro-Chinese, and even by independently minded communist parties. Repressive Soviet actions in Czechoslovakia found strong backing among the Mongolian leaders, who have endorsed the Warsaw Pact as well as the concept of regional security systems in Europe and Asia, a Soviet proposal which Peking has found highly objectionable. The Mongolian leadership thus repays the Soviets for their aid and protection by providing them with the only communist voice in Asia willing to defend their policies against Chinese attacks. At this time, when other Asian communist parties either lean toward Peking or take a neutral stand in the Sino-Soviet controversy, the Mongolians make a significant contribution to the Soviet Union's claim of being both a European and an Asian nation.

Outer Mongolia's national security has always rested on its military alliance with the Soviet Union. In early 1946, the USSR concluded a twenty-year Treaty of Friendship and Mutual Assistance with the MPRP. Before its expiration, Ulan Bator was visited by Brezhnev, who was accompanied by Soviet Foreign Minister Andrei Gromyko, and Defense Minister Rodion Malinovsky. Out of these Soviet-Mongolian talks came a new treaty

26. *Namyn Amdral*, July 1964. English translation, *JPRS*, no. 26407, September 16, 1964.

27. *Unen*, December 24, 1968, for example, stated: "It is necessary to point out that the CPSU, the great party of Lenin, always discharged its internationalist obligations before the international communist movement with honor, and it is continuing to do so. The CPSU has become a model of dedication to socialism, Communism, freedom of peoples and progress."

of alliance (signed on January 15, 1966), which reconfirmed Soviet responsibility for the defense of the Mongolian Republic. The treaty is widely believed to contain secret military clauses. A number of high-level Soviet military personnel have since visited the Mongolian capital, large numbers of Soviet troops have moved into the MPR, and indications are that Outer Mongolia has been turned into a (probably nuclearized) Soviet rocket base for war against China. Harrison Salisbury describes how he encountered Soviet rocket and missile forces, artillery men, airmen, and tank forces in the MPR. He estimates the total of Soviet forces in Mongolia to be about 100,000 to 200,000, and other sources speak of five divisions (approximately 75,000 to 150,000 troops). According to the United States Arms Control and Disarmament Agency, the total of MPR armed forces, regular and paramilitary, has fluctuated during the sixties between 30,000 and 33,000 men.[28]

II

During the first half of its existence dating from 1921, i.e., before the advent of the communist regime in Peking, communist Outer Mongolia lived as a Soviet dependency in complete isolation from outside influences. The pattern of its social, economic, political, and ideological development was determined during those years by a communist leadership which owed everything to the support of the Soviet Union. Close institutional ties developed, therefore, between the two regimes. As has already been mentioned, during the 1950s a new era began for Outer Mongolia when Sino-Soviet cooperation allowed the Chinese to participate in the development of the MPR. By playing their Chinese cards right, the Soviet satellite eventually might have been able to gain a degree of independence from the Soviet Union. But the growing estrangement between Moscow and Peking soon precluded such an option for the MPR. Too weak and vulnerable to play a balance-of-power game between the two communist giants, the Mongolian leaders were confronted with an "either-or" choice. That they sided with the Soviet Union is hardly surprising. Quite clearly China was the weaker of the two powers, and at the same time, as viewed from Ulan Bator, Chinese national aspirations must have seemed more dangerous.

There are other reasons which favor a Soviet orientation in Ulan Bator. Unlike communist China, North Vietnam, or North Korea, the MPR does

28. Salisbury, *War between Russia and China*, pp. 151–53, 171. See United States Arms Control and Disarmament Agency, *World Military Expenditures, 1970*, p. 28. Albert Axelbank, "Peking Is on the Outside," *Far Eastern Economic Review*, 61, no. 32 (August 8, 1968), 278–79, reports that "the Soviet Union has been placing mobile missile sites in Mongolia."

not view itself as a divided nation where communist power must compete with a noncommunist rival government. "Peaceful coexistence" rather than armed struggle provides the desirable conditions for Outer Mongolia's national development as well as for the eventual attainment of greater independence from Soviet bonds. Although Outer Mongolia, like the Soviet Union, supports the cause of North Vietnam, "U.S. imperialism" seems remote and constitutes no obstacle to Mongolian national aspirations. Under present conditions the alignment of the Mongolian leadership rests therefore not merely on an acute awareness of the balance of power in the area, but also on a certain congruence of Mongolian and Soviet interests. As an editorial in the party organ *Unen* stated, "The main source of our successes in the construction of Socialism comes from tying our destiny to that of the Soviet people." [29] Considering the material progress made by the MPR (thanks to Soviet aid) and the protection the Soviet military shield provides against danger to its survival as an ethnically Mongolian state, there is no good reason why the Mongolian communists need to reexamine such a conclusion at this time.

Together with ready acceptance of the "multi-faceted political, economic, cultural, military, diplomatic, and other assistance rendered by the first socialist country," as Tsedenbal in his previously mentioned *Pravda* article put it, the MPR leadership has adopted the Soviet model in all spheres. For that matter, it is really the only model it has ever known. Whatever differences exist between the two systems today are primarily due to the backward conditions of Outer Mongolia where global concerns are overshadowed by more immediate considerations of economic development.

For some time now, the MPR has played the role of a Soviet forward position against China. Domestic policies tend therefore to be dominated by military considerations. At the same time, the party leadership seeks to transform rapidly a people only emerging from a nomadic existence into a modern industrialized state, with a minimum of detours and loss of time. Obviously, this is not a favorable setting for internal democratization, although modest progress toward the humanization of the communist regime has been made since the days of Marshal Choibalsan – Mongolia's Stalin, who died about the same time as his Soviet counterpart. But on the whole the country, where intellectuals in the Western sense are few, has been little affected by the pressures for political and cultural liberalization which have destabilized communist countries in Europe.

29. *Unen*, March 1, 1970.

However, Outer Mongolia has not remained altogether unaffected by the worldwide trend toward nationalism, which is particularly manifest in Asia. It would be strange if the leaders of a people which once played an important historical role would not dream of charting their own course without Soviet tutelage. In fact, the series of party purges which decimated the upper ranks of the Mongolian communist organization during the fifties and sixties was related to the growth of Mongolian nationalist sentiments reacting against the all-pervasive Soviet influence. That nationalism is growing again in Mongolia, at least under the surface, is evident from the vigor with which such tendencies are being assailed by the party leadership. For example, in expounding the significance of Lenin's teaching, Tsedenbal, in April 1970, had this to say on the subject of nationalism: "The Party will conduct a struggle against the national egoism and the propagation of national exclusiveness and will always exert vigilance concerning the reactionary ideas of nationalism. . . . Communists and working people of the MPR resolutely oppose the anti-Marxist course of the Chinese leaders who, infected by reactionary ideas of militant nationalism and chauvinism, are conducting a violent anti-Soviet policy. . . . They are trying to drive a wedge between the Soviet and Mongolian peoples and harm their fraternal friendship." [30]

The Soviets can ill afford to alienate the Mongolians at a time when they are faced with problems on their western flank and with the Chinese threat in the East, and when they are badly in need of a communist ally who can legitimately claim to be "Asian." But the Soviet Union can even less afford the rise of Mongolian nationalism, which inevitably would direct itself against the dominant role of the USSR and seek support from Peking. The prospects, therefore, for an independent, Mongolian national communism must under present circumstances be deemed very slim. For the moment, the Mongolian communists will have to be satisfied, it seems, with insisting (as did, for example, the director of the Institute for Party History on April 14, 1970) that "the MPRP is creatively applying Marxist-Leninist teachings." Sino-Soviet tensions and the resulting need for tight Soviet control over Outer Mongolia will severely limit any departure from Soviet patterns and policies.

Nevertheless, both Soviet and Mongolian interests favor a certain broadening of the MPR's international contacts, and this in turn may gradually open the gate to new ideas and influences from abroad. The MPR now maintains diplomatic relations with more than fifty states and trades

30. Ulan Bator broadcast, April 23, 1970, of Tsedenbal's *Unen* article of the previous day.

with nearly thirty of them. At present, the MPR hopes for recognition by Japan and the United States, Britain and France having already accorded it. Meanwhile, the Mongolians with Soviet approval are developing closer relations with other Asian communist regimes and parties – especially those of North Vietnam and North Korea – as well as with the independent communists of Cuba. It would be surprising if these contacts did not strengthen Mongolian hopes of attaining more independence from the Kremlin.

It is quite conceivable, therefore, that the as yet mild internal pressures for greater independence from the Soviet Union will call for new purges of the Mongolian party organization in the coming years. For the MPR to break away from its Soviet tutor, however, would require a set of conditions that may not arise for some time to come: as long as the Sino-Soviet conflict continues at the present high level of tension, strategic Outer Mongolia is too valuable a prize for the Soviet Union to let slip from its grasp.

13

North Korea and North Vietnam

BY PAUL F. LANGER

NORTH KOREA

After the Second World War, American forces moved into the southern portion of the Korean peninsula while Soviet troops occupied its northern part. In 1948, the political division of the country was formalized with the establishment of the anticommunist Republic of Korea (ROK) in the south and the communist Democratic People's Republic of Korea (DPRK), bordering on China and the USSR, in the north.[1] From its inception, the communist regime, controlled by the Korean Workers' party (KWP), has sought to bring about a reunification of the divided country under communist rule.

Beyond the 38th Parallel dividing the country, the Korean communists, with their capital in Pyongyang, confront a rival regime in Seoul buttressed by American military, economic, and political power. A communist attempt to unite the country by force, the Korean War (1950–53), brought back American troops under United Nations auspices and proved a failure. Substantial (though recently reduced) U.S. forces have remained in South Korea ever since, and the government in Seoul has gained further protection against communist pressure through a mutual defense pact with the United States.

American and, quite recently, Japanese aid, as well as the effect of the Vietnam War, has stimulated vigorous economic growth in South Korea. Under the authoritarian regime of General Park Chung-hi the ROK also has gained in political stability during the past several years. His govern-

1. The DPRK shares a border of about eight hundred miles with communist China, but borders only for eleven miles on the USSR.

ment not only has been able to ride out without much difficulty North Korean attempts to launch a guerrilla movement in the south, but it has been bold enough to send two divisions to help the South Vietnamese in their war against the north. Obviously, the breakup of the ROK's alliance with the United States and the elimination of the latter's position from South Korea are prerequisites for a successful communist take-over in the south. Hence, the necessity of organizing an effective anti-American struggle in Korea and Japan – and elsewhere in Asia – is the paramount consideration in North Korea's foreign and domestic policies. In his famous speech to the Fourth Supreme People's Assembly on December 16, 1967, Kim Il-song emphasized this point: "What attitude the Socialist countries take toward U.S. imperialism is a criterion that shows whether they fight in real earnest for the advancement of the international revolutionary movement or not." More recently, the growing influence and importance of Japan, which tend to reinforce the position of the ROK, have caused Pyongyang almost as much concern as the presence of American forces in the south.

Another significant factor affecting North Korea's policy is the personality and role of its leader, Kim Il-song. Born in 1912, Kim was active during his youth in the anti-Japanese guerrilla movement in Manchuria, and after the war he returned with the Red armies to his native Korea. He rose in power during the immediate postwar period when Soviet occupation forces controlled the northern half of the country. Subsequently, Kim effectively eliminated his rivals for power, one by one – not unlike Stalin, whom he also resembles in other respects. First he removed the members of the "Soviet faction" (men who had fled to the Soviet Union from Korea); then the "Yenan faction" (revolutionaries who had followed Mao Tse-tung to Yenan); then the "domestic faction" (communists who had survived Japanese repression in Korea or Japan and were now seeking to come into their own). Surrounded by men who shared his Manchurian background and are presumably very loyal to him,[2] Kim emerged in the

2. Joungwon Alexander Kim, "Soviet Policy in North Korea," *World Politics*, 22, no. 2 (January 1970), 237–54, provides an interesting series of tables which show changes in the membership of the Secretariat of the Korean Workers' party between 1946 and 1969. Whereas the early leading group had reflected a diversity of origins and factions, by 1969 the Secretariat was exclusively composed of men who had been associated with Kim in prewar days in Manchuria. Similarly, Chong-sik Lee, "Stalinism in the East," in Robert A. Scalapino (ed.), *The Communist Revolution in Asia* (New York, 1969), provides a list which combines the members of the Secretariat with those of the Politburo of the KWP. Of the fifteen individuals (excluding Kim Il-song), nine had served in Manchuria under Kim, one had been active against the Japanese elsewhere in Manchuria, three belong to the postwar generation, including Kim's younger brother, Kim Yong-ju. The Fifth Congress of the KWP (No-

1960s as the absolute ruler of North Korea. He now heads the party as well as the government and acts as North Korea's commander in chief. Kim's power seems almost as great as Stalin's was and greater than that of Mao Tse-tung, for unlike Mao he is actively involved in the management of day-to-day affairs. Moreover, there is no one in North Korea with the prestige of a Chou En-lai.

To understand Kim's reactions first to Soviet and later to Chinese attempts to bring him to heel, it is necessary to consider the significance of the cult of personality in communist Korea. One is reminded of the glorification of Stalin when one reads such descriptions as the following Pyongyang KCNA account of Kim's appearance at the polls: "Comrade Kim Il-song, smiling all over his face, slowly stepped forward waving to the warm cheers of the crowds. Comrade Kim Il-song, the respected and beloved leader, received ballots from the chairman of the subconstituency election committee and cast them. Then, . . . Comrade Kim Il-song . . . left the polling station amid the warm cheers of the crowds. They loudly sang 'Song of General Kim Il-song' for a long while with infinite adoration for, trust in and overflowing feelings of loyalty to Comrade Kim Il-song, the fatherly leader." Kim, the "iron-willed, ever-victorious, brilliant commander and strategist," [3] like Stalin, must always be quoted whether the subject of discussion is poultry raising, steel production, educational reform, or ideological matters. He is the "sun of the nation" and its "outstanding Marxist-Leninist," and the author of numerous "immortal writings." A pilgrimage to his birthplace ("the cradle of the revolution where the hero of Korea was born") is a must for the foreign visitor, and his rather modest prewar exploits as a guerrilla have been built up to impressive dimensions. Kim is not merely the nominal, but apparently also the real source of all initiatives in ideological, political, military, economic, social, and cultural matters, and – in contrast to Stalin – he is constantly on

vember 1970) further consolidated Kim's power and raised his brother several notches in the communist hierarchy. He is apparently being groomed to succeed his older brother.

3. Kim Il-song is said to have "founded numerous original revolutionary theories," to have "enriched the treasure house of Marxism-Leninism," to have "fully and completely explained all basic problems posed newly in national economic planning," and to have given "perfect answers to all the complex problems awaiting an urgent solution in the question of the proletarian dictatorship." It is standard procedure in Korean communist writings to insert frequent quotations from the leader or to introduce a new paragraph or idea with "Kim Il-song exhorted us (or taught us) as follows: . . ." American and British readers may also recall a full-page advertisement in the *New York Times* and *The Times* of an English version of Kim's official biography which was issued to enhance his prestige abroad.

the move, checking and investigating conditions and the implementation of his plans. Some Korean communist sources state that "Comrade Kim looks after every detail of our work and life with fatherlike affection." Such statements seem to have a basis in fact, as Kim is known for having paid a personal visit to practically every community, industrial plant, or major farm in North Korea. It is understandable, therefore, that when Khrushchev removed Stalin from his pedestal and sought to enforce attacks against the cult of personality throughout the communist world, Kim reacted coldly to such attempts, which merely prompted him to round up and remove his critics. The experience left him with a deep resentment against Khrushchev and against Soviet intervention into Korean affairs.

Kim Il-song, who is always referred to as the "leader of the forty million Korean people" (meaning all Koreans, north and south), is inspired by a fierce nationalism and a powerful desire to unify and shape his nation's destiny without foreign obstruction. Like the Chinese, the Korean communists have a special, colorful vocabulary to describe their basic policies and principles. No term is more important for an understanding of Kim's policies than *chuchi* (also spelled *juchi* or *chuche*), often translated as "self-identity," a word which hardly conveys the significance of that concept and its important policy implications. It is useful therefore to quote in full the definition which official Korean communist sources provide: "Comrade Kim Il-song taught us: 'By the establishment of *chuchi* we mean holding to the principle of solving for oneself all the problems of revolution and construction in conformity with the actual conditions at home, and mainly by one's own efforts.'"[4] This desire to shape policies free from outside interference – Soviet or Chinese – is at the core of Kim's thinking. Thus, in addressing the Fifth Congress of the KWP in November 1970, he asserted that "establishing *chuchi*" is particularly important in Korea because of its peculiar historical and geographic conditions.[5] Kim never fails to stress this theme even when addressing himself to foreign audiences, as can be seen in this following passage from an article in *Pravda* (April 16, 1970): "Our Party has firmly adhered to the *chuchi* line which consists of ensuring that the general principles of Marxism-Leninism and the experience of other countries are creatively applied in accordance with our historical conditions and national features and that the Party always answers its own questions itself and resolves them independently by displaying the revolutionary spirit of reliance on one's own forces; the Party

4. From an important theoretical article published in the KWP organ *Nodong Sinmun* (Labor News) and broadcast (in English), August 27, 1969.

5. See Kim's speech, as monitored by *FBIS* (Supplement), November 16, 1970.

thereby achieved great victories and successes in the Socialist revolution and Socialist construction. Our country has now become a Socialist state with the full right to political self-determination and a stable independent national economy, flourishing national culture, and powerful defense forces."

In assessing North Korea's reaction to the contending pressures of Moscow and Peking, one must keep in mind the Korean leaders' origins and background before the communist seizure of power. Kim and his cadre are not intellectuals or technocrats, but men who, having spent their youth as guerrillas, are quite naturally oriented toward the military. The DPRK is today a garrison state with all the restrictions and austerity that this term implies. The regime keeps the tension at home at a high level by subjecting the entire population to an indoctrination program which aims at making a cadre and a soldier out of every citizen.[6] The party is omnipresent and absolute in its power, and demands complete subordination to its dictates ("unconditionally obey the organization") and total ideological conformity ("Our Party has only one school of thought, only the great revolutionary thought of Comrade Kim Il-song"). At the time of the Fourth Congress (1961), the party had 1.31 million members, about the highest ratio of membership to total population (over 10 per cent) in any communist country. By the mid-sixties membership had exceeded 1.65 million and has probably grown somewhat since. Reminiscent of the Stalinist era, every domestic production drive or political campaign assumes a military character and is conducted in an atmosphere of high pressure. *Chollima*, the winged steed of Korean mythology endowed with supernatural speed, is the symbol of the North Korean regime's intensive effort to raise production levels and to make the economy self-sufficient. But even *chollima* speed has now been declared insufficient: it has been superseded by *kangson* speed ("the new *chollima* speed") and "Pyongyang speed." Meanwhile, 30 per cent of the country's budget is being devoted to military expenditures and every citizen including women undergoes military training.[7] Life in this atmosphere may not be easy to endure, but the regime has certainly succeeded in establishing tight control over its population.

6. *Kulloja* (Worker), the theoretical journal of the KWP, December 5, 1969, quotes from Kim Il-song's writings on this issue as follows: ". . . a vital duty of the dictatorship of the proletariat is to indoctrinate and remold all the people." *Selections from Writings of Kim Il-song*, vol. 4, p. 547.

7. Another measure of the militaristic orientation of the North Korean regime is the high percentage of the GNP it devotes to military expenditures. It is estimated that in 1968 (the last year for which such figures are available) this sector of the economy

North Korea's response to the Sino-Soviet conflict has reflected these characteristic features, although it has been tempered by a realistic acknowledgment of the continued need for Sino-Soviet support against the threat from the south. As the DPRK's strength and self-confidence have grown and Sino-Soviet competition for Kim's allegiance has intensified, one detects an increasingly determined and successful effort on the part of North Korea to assert its political and ideological autonomy from the two communist powers.

Korean relations with Moscow and Peking have passed through a number of phases.[8] Until the outbreak of the Korean War, North Korea remained very much under Soviet control, Kim was only then emerging as the leader. The war demonstrated to the Korean communists the need for modern Soviet weapons. At the same time and more importantly, it was realized in Pyongyang that the intervention of Chinese "volunteers" rather than Soviet aid had rescued the North Korean regime from defeat. China's prestige rose and Soviet influence declined.

From the very beginning of the Sino-Soviet schism, Pyongyang sympathized with Peking's hard-line ideological orientation and strategy because the Chinese rejected "peaceful coexistence" and focused on "United States imperialism" as the enemy. During the late fifties and early sixties this sympathy turned into qualified support, which was reflected in the North Korean position on such issues as Albania's conflict with the Soviets, Yugoslavia's revisionism, and China's attack against India. But, on the whole, Kim continued to see his advantage in staying out of the Sino-Soviet struggle. Meanwhile he used the leverage arising from this new situation to strengthen his own position.

In 1961 Park Chung-hi came to power in South Korea through a military coup, and Kim apparently feared an attack from the south. Turning to Moscow and Peking, he succeeded in persuading both to sign identical defense treaties which gave him protection while implying an acceptance of the DPRK's independence and territorial integrity and a promise of noninterference in its affairs. But, as the Sino-Soviet conflict sharpened, North Korea was compelled to make its choice. Kim could not hope to benefit greatly from Khrushchev's policy of peaceful coexistence, a policy which

took up 18 per cent of the GNP. See United States Arms Control and Disarmament Agency, *World Military Expenditures, 1970* (Washington, D.C., 1970), p. 20.

8. For a discussion of the early years of North Korean policy toward the Sino-Soviet conflict, see Paul F. Langer, "Outer Mongolia, North Korea, North Viet-Nam," in Adam Bromke (ed.), *The Communist States at the Crossroads: Between Moscow and Peking* (New York, 1965).

must have been alien and distasteful to him. Soviet "appeasement" of the United States in the Cuban missile crisis seemed to Kim an abnegation of Soviet strength. Nor was he eager to return to the Soviet fold through adherence to the Soviet-directed Comecon. North Korea thus moved gradually, but more and more openly, toward support of Peking and eventually found itself cut off from Soviet aid.

The significance of this evolution may have been misunderstood or at least not fully appreciated in Peking. Kim Il-song was well aware of the desirability of obtaining Chinese support for his aims. Certainly he felt very much in tune with Mao Tse-tung's assertion of autonomy and his efforts to build independent strength (thus, North Korea congratulated Peking on its successful nuclear tests). This did not mean, however, that Kim was ready to step down from his pedestal and allow Mao to be put in his place or that he was willing to acknowledge Mao's ideological leadership. When the Great Proletarian Cultural Revolution in China got underway and China sought to lord it over all communist movements in Asia, North Korea insisted on its independence. As a result Red Guards in Peking called Kim "a fat revisionist." Relations between the two regimes deteriorated rapidly, as Kim made it clear that he was rejecting "great power chauvinism" whether it originated in Moscow or in Peking. Like the Japanese Communist party with which the KWP maintained particularly close relations,[9] the Korean party resented Peking's rigidity and deplored its anti-Soviet excesses, which could only tend to undermine Pyongyang's own attempts to mobilize all communist forces on a global scale in opposition to "American imperialism." Moreover Peking's cautious attitude in avoiding a direct confrontation with the United States stood so much in contrast with its fiery, anti-imperialist rhetoric that Kim Il-song could hardly place much hope in effective Chinese support for any North Korean action carrying the risk of a clash with "U.S. imperialism."

Moscow appreciated much better the mood in Pyongyang, and Khrushchev's successors were willing to make concessions. The Soviet-Korean détente (which followed the eclipse of Khrushchev in the fall of 1964 and

9. The CPJ's reaction to the Sino-Soviet conflict has generally paralleled very closely that of the KWP. The parties have frequently expressed their concern over the negative effect of communist disunity and have cooperated in attempting to restore a common front. The two parties have long-standing relations and the Japanese party's representative in Pyongyang often provides insights into life in North Korea in his dispatches to the CPJ organ *Akahata* (Red Flag). For a discussion of the special relationship of the two parties and the Japanese party's role in the Sino-Soviet conflict, see Paul F. Langer, *Communism in Japan* (in press), and "The New Posture of the CPJ," *Problems of Communism*, 20, no. 1–2 (January–April 1971), 14–24.

Premier Kosygin's visit to the North Korean capital in February 1965) was facilitated by Kim Il-song's heightened concern about the growing strength of the rival regime in the south and his realization of North Korea's weakened economic and military position, which in part was caused by the cessation of Soviet aid. The Korean Seven-Year Plan was in trouble, and its completion had to be delayed three years (thus ending in 1970) to allow for the simultaneous building up of North Korea's economy and defenses. In both respects, Soviet help could be invaluable. A high-level Korean mission went to Moscow early in 1967 and brought back assurances of Soviet support. Even though this Soviet-Korean rapprochement resulted in toning down Korean objections to Soviet "revisionist" tendencies, it was not accomplished at the price of Kim's surrender to Moscow.

During the past several years Kim, while maintaining reasonably good relations with the Soviet Union, had been patiently waiting for the atmosphere in China to cool off. The KWP sent a high-ranking delegate to the Twenty-fourth Congress of the CPSU which was boycotted by the Chinese party.[10] But this did not prevent Kim from continuing to express views much closer to those of Peking than those of Moscow regarding such issues as "revisionism," the Nuclear Non-Proliferation Treaty, and the need for an international communist conference (the KWP declined to participate). Meanwhile, North Korea has exerted itself to bridge the Moscow-Peking gap and to reestablish a united front of all communist movements capable of providing more effective support to the North Vietnamese struggle – and to the cause of North Korea. Kim Il-song has consistently played down Sino-Soviet differences and has refused to go along with Peking, insofar as it holds that what is at issue between China and the Soviet Union is of fundamental significance. Not long ago, in December 1969, Kim wishfully told an interviewer that the whole controversy was really no more than a "casual family conflict of views." [11]

I

Although Kim Il-song has stated repeatedly that he favors "peaceful reunification," he also has suggested that the peaceful approach to reunifi-

10. The desire on the part of Kim to gain recognition as the equal of the Chinese and Soviet leaders was also reflected in his choice of delegates to the Twenty-fourth Congress in Moscow. Although Outer Mongolia sent its party leader Tsedenbal and so did North Vietnam, Kim did not travel to Moscow, but sent his deputy.

11. Interview with a United Arab Republic press representative, July 1, 1969, and broadcast (in English) by Radio Pyongyang, September 4, 1969.

cation is contingent upon the withdrawal of U.S. troops from South Korea.[12] He visualizes that such an event will occur as the culmination of the successful coordination of three revolutionary forces: those in North Korea; those in South Korea; and the worldwide revolutionary forces backed jointly by the Soviet Union and China which should aim at fighting "U.S. imperialism" in several places to disperse and thereby weaken its power. According to Kim, "Peoples of all countries making revolution should tear limbs off the U.S. beast and behead it all over the world. The U.S. imperialists appear to be strong, but when the peoples of many countries attack them from all sides and join forces in mutilating them, they will become powerless and bite the dust in the end." [13]

In view of the numerical and organizational weakness of procommunist elements in South Korea, Kim has been tempted to supplement their strength with active support from the north. In January 1968 North Korean infiltrators almost succeeded in assassinating the South Korean leader Park Chung-hi, but communist attempts to cause disturbances or to launch through such sporadic action a genuine guerrilla movement in the south proved singularly ineffective — thus confirming Mao Tse-tung's revolutionary theory. The difficulty of creating a revolutionary situation in South Korea has lent added significance to Korean communist efforts to challenge and weaken "U.S. imperialism" in Korea in an indirect way, i.e., by creating difficulties for the United States throughout the world, thereby forcing it to disperse its troops and attention.

In the sixties, North Korea consistently displayed a great deal of belligerence and a disturbing willingness to take risks in confronting the United States. The extreme was reached in 1968 and 1969 with the seizure of the *Pueblo* and the subsequent shooting down of an American reconnaissance plane. Kim Il-song's statement in September 1969 regarding the struggle against "U.S. imperialism" could not be reassuring to the United States — or to the Soviet Union: "Some overestimate the struggle of imperialism, U.S. imperialism in particular, and do not wage an active anti-imperialist, anti-U.S. struggle, thinking that once the imperialists explode an atom

12. The most recent proposal for a reunification of the country was presented in April 1971 by the DPRK Foreign Minister Ho Tam in his address to the Supreme People's Assembly. This proposal involved the withdrawal of American forces; a reduction of North and South Korean forces to 100,000 or less; the abolition of the United States-South Korean defense pact; the confederation of North and South Korea; and the establishment of a unified central government on the basis of free elections in both parts of the country.

13. Quoted by Politburo member and First Deputy Premier Kim Il in a lengthy speech on the occasion of the Lenin Centenary and broadcast on April 21, 1970.

bomb the whole world would perish. We cannot agree to that . . . If the U.S. imperialists are not doomed, why are they getting it in the neck in South Vietnam? . . ." [14]

North Korea's aggressive stimulation of anti-American revolutionary movements in the developing countries, especially in Asia, constitutes a key element in Kim's basic anti–United States strategy. Hence, Kim's report to the Fifth Congress of the KWP urges all revolutionary Asian peoples "suffering directly from U.S. imperialist aggression" (he specifically mentions Korea, China, and the three Indochinese nations) to consolidate their anti-American united front. The DPRK promptly recognized the Sihanouk exile regime (as did China, but not the USSR), and at gatherings of Indochinese revolutionary leaders, Korean representatives often act as if the conflict in Indochina involved them directly.

One might wonder why the Kim regime has not backed up its convictions by sending volunteers to Vietnam, as has its rival, the Park regime. The explanation lies not entirely in the reluctance of the DRV to accept foreign volunteers (which would almost certainly have to include Chinese forces) or in logistic difficulties. The DPRK feels not in a position militarily to risk the dispatch of forces abroad since its army is numerically inferior to that of the ROK. An equally important constraint is probably that the Soviet Union and even China do not favor a North Korean involvement in Vietnam.

An analysis of Soviet pronouncements and behavior makes it clear that the Soviet Union at least sees no advantage in encouraging North Korean aggressive actions. This can be seen in the CPSU message to the Fifth Congress of the KWP (November 1970) which places much stress on the peaceful reunification of Korea and plays down the role of offensive anti-imperialist action. It was also noted that the Soviets promptly participated in search and rescue operations after the Korean communists had shot down an American reconnaissance plane in 1969 and that their eventual support for the Korean version of the incident was much delayed and lukewarm. Kim's often reckless offensive strategy does not fit in with Soviet policy, and the Soviet Union is not likely to assign high priority to the cause of Korean reunification. Peking's attitude may seem more ambivalent. Yet, despite China's voluble support for North Korea's revolutionary pronouncements, Peking's behavior shows no indication of actual support for their implementation. As on other issues, the Chinese leaders' strategy is essentially defensive and cautious. They are not inclined to encourage

14. Kim Il-song interview, July 1, 1969 (cited above).

Kim's adventurist streak, even though there can be little doubt that he can count on Chinese aid should the DPRK be attacked from the south.

A new phase in North Korea's relations with the two communist powers appears to have begun in late 1969. At the time of the Ninth Congress of the Chinese Communist party earlier in the year, Peking's hostility toward Kim Il-song remained evident, as reflected in the absence of any Korean delegates at the Congress. The substantial and rapidly proceeding improvement of relations between Peking and Pyongyang seems to date from September 1969 when many of the leading figures in the communist world gathered at Ho Chi Minh's funeral in Hanoi and conducted important discussions. By that time, the Cultural Revolution in China had run its course, China was reestablishing diplomatic ties abroad and becoming less insistent on ideological purity, and, last but not least, Sino-Soviet relations had approached the brink of war, forcing Peking to reexamine its strategy.

It could well be that Chinese and Korean alarm at the growing Japanese role in Asia – Japanese "imperialism" cooperating with the United States – also played a part in bringing the feuding countries together. In both capitals a reading of the Sato-Nixon communiqué (November 21, 1969), in which the Japanese prime minister stressed the importance of Korea and Taiwan to his country's security, could not but have disturbed the leadership. This interpretation is also corroborated by the joint communiqué – issued in Pyongyang in the spring of 1970 when Premier Chou En-lai, for the first time in twelve years, visited the North Korean capital – which condemned the United States for mobilizing in Japan forces seeking to revive "Japanese imperialism." [15] Accommodation may also have been facilitated or caused by an apparent North Korean decision to abandon the risky, militant strategy in the south in favor of one aiming at long-range efforts to build up an indigenous source of strength – along the lines advocated by Mao Tse-tung.

At any rate, there could be no doubt after Chou En-lai's visit that relations between Peking and Pyongyang, after a hiatus of five years, were once more close and amicable. Kim Il-song enthusiastically welcomed the launching of China's artificial satellite; ambassadors were exchanged between the two capitals; in July 1970 a North Korean military mission, headed by the chief of staff of the Korean People's Army, visited Peking and was granted an interview with Mao Tse-tung with whom they reportedly had "a very cordial and friendly conversation." [16] In the late

15. English text in *Peking Review*, no. 15 (April 10, 1970), 3–5.

16. See *Peking Review*, no. 32 (August 7, 1970), 3.

summer of 1971, the North Korean chief of staff revisited China for three weeks to hold talks with his Chinese counterpart, following close on the heels of bilateral political discussions in the Chinese capital officially described as having been conducted in an "extremely cordial and friendly atmosphere." [17] During this same period a Sino-Korean economic cooperation agreement was signed in Peking in the presence of Chou En-lai. In China, Korean representatives are now welcomed as "comrades in arms" and occupy a seat of honor alongside the delegates from the three Indochinese countries.[18] Kim Il-song's major speech to the Fifth Congress of the KWP was reprinted in its entirety in the People's Daily, and in tribute to his pride and sensitivity, Chinese speakers in May 1971 greeted a Korean delegation with shouts of "Learn from the Korean working class!" and treated Kim like an equal of Mao by calling him "the great leader of the Korean people" and Mao "the great leader of the Chinese people." [19] Meanwhile, Chinese delegations follow each other in Pyongyang with regularity, and Mao exchanges messages of congratulations with Kim.

Since Pyongyang's basic ideological orientation, on the use of revolutionary violence and other important doctrinal issues, had remained similar to that of Peking, and since Pyongyang merely objected to Mao's attempts to dictate to North Korea, there existed at all times solid ground for an understanding between these two communist regimes.[20] This is all the more true because both have important unfulfilled territorial aspirations and in both cases "U.S. imperialism" is the principal obstacle to their satisfaction.

But it seems unlikely that Kim will allow the Sino-Korean rapprochement to go so far as to alienate the Soviet Union, which is now willing to tolerate Pyongyang's autonomous stand and which as supplier of economic aid and of modern armament will continue to be indispensable to the North Koreans. Only by maintaining qualitative superiority over the ROK in military weaponry can North Korea hope to balance the numerical

17. Peking NCNA International Service, in English, July 12, 1971, as monitored by *FBIS*.

18. See *Peking Review*, no. 14 (April 2, 1971), 4–7, on Chou En-lai's banquet and speech.

19. Peking NCNA International Service, May 16, 1971, as monitored by *FBIS*.

20. An editorial in *Nodong Sinmun*, March 18, 1971 (broadcast by Pyongyang Radio on the preceding day, monitored by *FBIS*), states that a revolutionary movement's viewpoint on the use of violence is a major criterion for distinguishing a revolutionary from an opportunist stand.

force advantage of its South Korean rival.[21] To dispel any possible misunderstanding in Moscow, Kim Il-song also was actively moving in 1970 to strengthen ties with the Soviet leaders. This became evident with the visit in April of the chief of staff of the Soviet Armed Forces, Marshal M. V. Zakharov, who, on his departure from Pyongyang, was awarded one of the highest Korean decorations. Obviously, his mission had been a success from the Korean point of view. Kim probably had obtained a promise of more modern weapons and perhaps also new Soviet guarantees. That the Soviet Union is prepared to continue to take an active and helpful interest in North Korea, even if relations between Peking and Pyongyang have improved, is also clear from other developments. In February 1971 the Soviets signed a long-term trade agreement (for 1971–75) with the DPRK which envisaged an expansion of 55 per cent in Soviet-Korean trade. (In 1969 this trade had accounted for almost half of North Korea's foreign transactions.)[22] Brezhnev himself, in speaking about the Soviet party's relations with foreign communist movements at the Twenty-fourth Congress in March 1971, indicated that relations with North Korea and its Workers' party were satisfactory and were taking on new dimensions. A few months later, the Soviet government's newspaper termed the friendship between the two countries "firm and inviolable" and described it as "not of an ostentatious but of an effective nature" and as having "survived the test of time."[23] It seems that by 1971 both Moscow and Peking had tacitly come to accept the fact that Kim Il-song's Korea is now an autonomous unit in the communist world even though it will continue to remain heavily dependent on outside support so long as it has to contend with a strong South Korean anticommunist regime.

II

The Sino-Soviet conflict has allowed the North Korean government to free itself sooner than it might have been able to do otherwise from its powerful communist neighbors' control and to assume an independent stance. This situation also has allowed the Korean communists to find their natu-

21. South Korea represents about two-thirds of the total population of the Korean peninsula, which is now about 43–45 million. As a result, the South Korean forces outnumber their North Korean opponents, the former having about 600,000 men under arms as against 400,000 for the latter. The militia forces on both sides are more nearly equal, numbering somewhere between one and two million each. North Korean superiority in weaponry is particularly pronounced in the air.

22. Moscow broadcast, March 17, 1971, as monitored by *FBIS*.

23. *Izvestiia*, July 6, 1971.

ral place in the communist world – with the growing number of communist states and parties that are beholden neither to the Soviet Union nor to communist China and whose orientation is essentially determined not by the USSR or the PRC but by their own national interests, their own historical experience, and their particular stage of development. This position was clearly enunciated in June 1971 when Kim Il-song signed a joint communiqué with the Rumanian leader Nicolae Ceausescu then visiting Pyongyang. In this document the two parties acknowledged that "an international [communist] center is not necessary." [24]

North Korea under Kim Il-song has thus developed a system that in single-minded fashion aims at rapidly building the foundations for economic, military, and political autonomy under the slogan "self-reliance and self-identity." Kim's regime is a tightly controlled monolithic structure in which only his views count. The North Koreans are objects of unrelenting ideological campaigns, organized by ubiquitous cadres whose task it is to assure compliance with the "dictatorship of the proletariat." The population, as the Korean communists put it, "brims with excitement" and rides a wave of ultranationalism. This supercharged atmosphere offers little prospect for moderating influences which could erode the foundations of the Stalinist garrison state that is North Korea today. Only a general easing of tension throughout the Far East, which would affect the policies of China, the Soviet Union, and the United States and could lead to a gradual dismantling of the barriers that now separate the two halves of the divided country, might start a slow process of evolution toward liberalization in the DPRK.

The projected visit of President Nixon to Peking may eventually produce such a relaxation of tensions in the region of Korea and result in far-reaching changes in the Far Eastern situation. For the Pyongyang regime, however, the immediate issue posed by a possible Sino-American understanding is the need to ensure continued Chinese support for its goal of national reunification and to prevent any bargain Peking might be tempted to strike with the United States at the expense of its Korean ally. The Chinese leadership has in recent months gone out of its way to allay such fears. In addition to the commitments China may recently have entered into in negotiations with previously mentioned North Korean military and economic missions to Peking, Mao has reaffirmed in his messages to Kim China's unswerving opposition to "American imperialism," and the Chinese have repeatedly endorsed Pyongyang's formula for Korean reunifica-

24. Pyongyang Radio, June 15, 1971, as monitored by *FBIS*.

tion. To give further credence to their united front with North Korea, they also have reappointed for the first time in years a Chinese representative to the Korean Military Armistice Commission. Apparently reassured by these statements and actions, the official *Nodong Sinmun* on August 8, 1971, gave implicit approval to Peking's high-level contacts with the United States, describing Nixon's planned visit to China as "the journey of a defeated man" and as a victory of the world's anti-imperialist revolutionary forces.

While South Korea reacts to the new situation by cautiously opening up channels of communication to the communist nations of Europe, the North Korean communists hope to turn the impending changes in the Far East to their benefit by seeking to include the Korean peninsula in the zone from which U.S. forces will be withdrawn when the United States ends its direct involvement in the Vietnam War. Pyongyang reckons that the removal of U.S. troops from the peninsula may weaken the rival South Korean regime which to the dismay of Kim Il-song has steadily grown in strength and self-confidence in recent years.

Encouraged by the fluid conditions which now prevail on the periphery of China, the North Korean communists have by no means abandoned their goal of national reunification, but they appear to be experimenting with a new strategy which places greater emphasis on political negotiations than on hostile confrontation and outright pressure. A new era may thus have opened for the Korean peninsula, when in August 1971 South Korean and North Korean Red Cross representatives, for the first time since the Korean War, cordially talked to each other in Panmunjom about facilitating contacts between members of Korean families separated from each other for the past two decades as a result of the fighting.

NORTH VIETNAM

Like its counterpart in Korea, the (Communist) Worker's party of Vietnam (VWP) sees its primary objective in "liberating the south, defending the north, and reunifying the country." As in Korea, efforts to unite the divided nation have led to military conflict. The struggle in Vietnam has assumed special significance with the massive participation since 1965 of U.S. and other non-Vietnamese forces seeking to shore up the anticommunist regime in Saigon. In the late sixties, fighting also intensified in neighboring Laos, where elements of the North Vietnamese Army (NVA) had long been controlling the eastern portion of the country in alliance with the indigenous (communist) insurgents, the Pathet Lao. More recently, the Vietnam War has spilled over into Cambodia were NVA forces had been availing themselves of sanctuaries for operations in South Vietnam. Thus, what started more than ten years ago as a local insurgency in South Vietnam has evolved into a full-fledged Indochina War with distinct international dimensions. Throughout this extended conflict, both the Soviet Union and communist China have consistently provided the Democratic Republic of Vietnam (DRV) with necessary material and political support.

The United States is currently seeking to disengage its forces while promoting the re-Vietnamization of the war. Meanwhile, the revolutionary movements of the three Indochinese countries have been drawing together under Peking-Hanoi sponsorship. Moscow has indicated from time to time that it would like to see an international conference or some other form of negotiation with the United States defuse the explosive Vietnam issue. Mao Tse-tung, on the other hand, persists in urging Hanoi to persevere in its war against the south. In May 1970 Mao declared that by "strengthening their unity, supporting each other and persevering in a protracted people's war, the three Indochinese peoples will certainly overcome all difficulties and win complete victory." [25] About a year later, Mao (jointly with Lin Piao and Chou En-lai) sent a rather patronizing message to the three Indochinese peoples' revolutionary leadership in which he congratulated them and again expressed his conviction that persevering in a people's war will win complete victory for them.[26] Since the death of Ho Chi Minh in September 1969, the members of a collective communist leadership in Hanoi have been jockeying for position while debating the war strategy in South Vietnam. At the same time, delegates of the United States and of the Republic of Vietnam are continuing to face representatives of North Vietnam and of the Provisional Revolutionary Government across the conference table in Paris. The fate of Indochina thus remains very uncertain.

In analyzing North Vietnam's position in the Sino-Soviet conflict, we will not consider the details of this complex and constantly changing situation, or give an account of the well-known vicissitudes of the war and of U.S. policy. Rather, we will examine the basic factors determining Moscow-Peking-Hanoi relations under the conditions of war. The present situation is much too precarious to permit more than speculation regarding the future international role of North Vietnam. However, it is at least pos-

25. Hsinhua News Agency, *Daily Bulletin*, May 21, 1970.

26. *Peking Review*, no. 14 (April 2, 1972), 3.

sible to clarify Chinese and Soviet interests and policies in Vietnam and Hanoi's response – factors which will play a vital part in shaping the future of Indochina, whatever the nature of the eventual settlement in Vietnam.

I

Since both the North Vietnamese and the North Korean communist regimes face the harsh reality of a divided nation seeking reunification, one is tempted to draw parallels between North Vietnamese and North Korean behavior in the Sino-Soviet conflict. But certain features inherent in the Vietnamese situation create conditions quite different from those in North Korea.

Both countries, located on the periphery of China, were once in the Chinese zone of influence. In contrast to Korea, however, North Vietnam shares no common border with the Soviet Union, and thousands of miles separate it from Moscow. Thus, in balancing Chinese and Soviet influences, the leaders of North Vietnam dare not risk displeasing Peking as North Korea has been prepared to do whenever its interests seemed to conflict with China's recommended policies.

In North Korea and in Outer Mongolia, communist regimes were installed at the point of Soviet bayonets, but no Red Army "liberated" Vietnam. Nor, for that matter, has any Chinese army (although admittedly Mao Tse-tung's victory in China placed, after 1949, vast communist resources at the disposal of the Viet Minh revolutionaries). The Vietnamese communist movement has a long history of revolutionary action. The communists came to power largely through their own efforts and through the political acumen and determination of their leader, Ho Chi Minh. This allows him to assert that "our country will have the signal honor of being a small nation which, through a heroic struggle, has defeated two great imperialisms – the French and the American – and made a worthy contribution to the national liberation movement." [27]

The Vietnamese communist movement from its inception also enjoyed a certain prestige in the communist world owing to the stature of Ho Chi Minh. A contemporary of Mao, but with much greater international experience, Ho had a long and distinguished revolutionary career in France, the USSR, China, and other Asian countries. He was, in fact, the single most outstanding figure in the communist movements of Southeast Asia. Although known as a successful practitioner of revolution, Ho recognized early the importance of nationalism as the most potent force in Asia to-

27. *Nhan Dan*, February 15, 1970, and broadcast that same day by Hanoi.

day. "Land to the tillers" and "national independence," i.e., socialism and nationalism, were the twin slogans which carried him to power. As the official daily *Nhan Dan* put it, "The invincible strength of the Vietnamese revolution is a skillful combination of our people's heroic traditions and revolutionary ideas developed in our era." [28] Ho Chi Minh probably had a better claim to representing the nationalist sentiments of his people than any other revolutionary leader in Asia. It did not require a rewriting of history for Ho to appear in the eyes of his followers as a genuine Vietnamese nationalist. He was recognized as such even by noncommunists. All this created a strong position for the North Vietnamese regime, both in its domestic political contests and in its dealings with Moscow and Peking.

But now Ho is gone. North Vietnam is no longer ruled by a single individual but by a directorate of leadership. Two characteristics of the Vietnamese communist movement deserve mention in this respect because they have a bearing on North Vietnamese behavior in the Sino-Soviet conflict. Vietnamese communism is, of course, remarkable because its founder, Ho Chi Minh, remained its leader for four decades. However, the movement also has displayed exceptional stability in the upper ranks of its hierarchy even though infighting and factionalism have traditionally distinguished Vietnamese politics, and strong differences of opinion are not unknown to exist among party leaders. Further, the leadership of the VWP represents an unusually diverse group of men – ideologists and pragmatists, strategists and planners, theorists and administrators. This diversity, coupled with the fact that no single individual has clearly prevailed since the physical decline of Ho, makes for an organization which favors a division of responsibility among its leaders and tends to resolve its inner conflicts through negotiation and compromise rather than through power struggles and purges. This tendency is reinforced by the need to maintain cohesion in the face of conflicting pulls from Moscow and Peking so as not to impede through disunity a victory in the south which was for Ho and remains for his successors the supreme policy goal.

An analysis of Vietnam's relations with the two communist powers also must take into account the wider context of Indochina. In the case of Korea, the claims of both the communists and noncommunists are satisfied with control over what has traditionally been Korean territory, i.e., the Korean peninsula. The situation is more ambiguous in the case of Vietnam. It can be argued that Hanoi has no objectives beyond Vietnam proper and that its military forces are stationed only temporarily in neigh-

28. *Ibid.*, February 6, 1970. English translation, *JPRS*, no. 50001, March 6, 1970.

boring Laos and Cambodia to assist the war effort in South Vietnam and to give occasional support to fraternal but independent revolutionary movements.[29] It must be noted, however, that communism in Indochina was long a single organization, directed by Ho Chi Minh, and that historically, the Vietnamese have viewed themselves as preeminent in Indochina. There is some reason to suspect that Vietnamese ambitions reach beyond the borders of Vietnam properly speaking. To discourage these widespread suspicions such Vietnamese communist leaders as Prime Minister Pham Van Dong and First Secretary of the VWP Le Duan have stressed repeatedly their regime's disinterested role in supporting the Laotian and Cambodian revolutionary movements.[30]

At any rate, the expanding Vietnamese military involvement in these two Indochinese countries is a fact and is causing difficulties for the Soviet Union (and perhaps even for China), whose priorities and interests in the fate of Laos and Cambodia do not necessarily coincide with those of the DRV. Thus, while giving massive aid to the Hanoi regime, the Soviets have not considered it to their advantage to recognize Prince Sihanouk's Cambodian government in exile which is allied to Peking and Hanoi. This creates a delicate situation for Moscow – only slightly more delicate than the situation in Laos where the Soviet Union recognizes the legitimate Souvanna Phouma government but the Soviet-assisted Vietnamese actively fight for the insurgent Pathet Lao. Moscow, under these circumstances, must ask itself whether or not its aid to Hanoi is being used for purposes which may run counter to its own interests and whether or not support for the DRV is leading the Soviet Union into an ambiguous or even open-ended commitment to what may be Vietnamese expansionist ventures.

29. For a detailed examination of the role of North Vietnam in Laos, see Paul F. Langer and Joseph J. Zasloff, *North Vietnam and the Pathet Lao – Partners in the Struggle for Laos* (Cambridge, Mass., 1970).

30. For example, Premier Pham Van Dong in his address to the Indochinese Summit Conference of April 1970 stated: "The Democratic Republic of Vietnam will always respect the independence, sovereignty, all the national rights and the political regimes of their two neighbor countries . . ." (Hanoi broadcast in English, April 20, 1970). In his massive article of February 14, 1970 (published in *Nhan Dan* of that date and broadcast two days later), First Secretary Le Duan said, "We endeavor to tighten fraternal solidarity between the peoples of Indochina . . . the Kingdom of Cambodia . . . the Kingdom of Laos, on the basis of respect for each other's independence, sovereignty, unity, and territorial integrity." Similarly, the joint statement signed in Hanoi on May 30, 1971, by Ton Duc Thang, president of the DRV, and Prince Souphanouvong, chairman of the Neo Lao Hak Sat, stresses that "the Vietnamese people and the Government of the Democratic Republic of Vietnam once again affirm their desire to see on their Western borders a really independent, peaceful and neutral Kingdom of Laos. . . ."

The most obvious difference between the Korean and the Vietnamese communist parties' present circumstances, however, is caused by the demands placed upon North Vietnam by the fighting in the south. Although in the earlier period of the war much of the burden was being carried by South Vietnamese revolutionaries, the Vietcong, U.S. military pressure has increasingly led the NVA to take a direct hand in the struggle. This in turn has resulted in massively destructive U.S. air attacks against North Vietnam, which have put an enormous strain on this small country's undeveloped and meager resources. Escalation of the war has accentuated the DRV's need for external support. Therefore, as long as the war continues, the North Vietnamese communists will be heavily dependent on assistance from Moscow and Peking if they are not to be compelled to abandon their military struggle. This is fully recognized in virtually every major policy statement by DRV leaders.[31] Any consideration of how to sustain the war effort in the south without creating serious difficulties on the homefront, as well as of the choice of strategy to be pursued in the war, involves the central issue of the assistance the Vietnamese leaders can expect from the Soviet Union and from China. And there is always the question of how they should go about obtaining the maximum from both allies without compromising their own independence. The North Vietnamese thus have seen an advantage in keeping out of the Sino-Soviet conflict whenever their own vital interests were not directly involved, but this balancing act has become more difficult to sustain as Moscow-Peking relations have worsened and as the requirements of an escalating conventional war have made an uninterrupted flow of diverse military and economic aid ever more urgent.

31. See, for example: "Our people have been receiving increasingly great aid from the Soviet Union, China and other fraternal Socialist countries and enjoying active support from the progressive people of the entire world, including the American people. This is a very important factor in the success of the revolutionary struggle in our country." (General Vo Nguyen Giap, *Hoc Tap*, no. 12, 1969, English translation, *JPRS*, no. 49878, February 18, 1970.) "The Vietnamese people's tremendous victory is directly linked to the international Communist movement's powerful support, the invaluable aid of the Soviet Union, the People's Republic of China, the fraternal socialist countries, and the sympathy and solidarity of all progressive mankind." (From Le Duan's speech in the Kremlin, April 21, 1970.) When General Giap gave an interview to Yasir Arafat, the chief of the anti-Israel Al Fatah guerrilla organization, the Arab leader asked him for advice. The Vietnamese strategist gave five major reasons for the Viet Minh's success. The fifth point begins thus: "It is essential that you have international support and backing. International support is essential. Chairman Ho Chi Minh has said: We must depend first on our power and then on the support and the backing of the progressive forces in the world. . . ." (*Ad-Dustur*, April 14, 1970.)

The Vietnamese communists, however, have been aided in their balancing act by the rivalry of Moscow and Peking. Vietnam and its fate are important to both powers, though for different reasons. For China, much is at stake in the outcome in Vietnam. The political alignment of the region along its southern periphery has a direct bearing on its security and on its expectations of being able to shape the Asian continent in a way favorable to Chinese interests. But if Peking cannot permit the DRV to be defeated without suffering the consequences, neither can it allow the Vietnamese communists to win their struggle exclusively with Soviet aid and in a manner contrary to Chinese prescriptions. To keep a hostile Soviet influence from installing itself on its southern frontier, Peking must have at least some leverage – and, preferably, control – in North Vietnam, especially since the orientation of Hanoi is likely to have a direct bearing on the future of northern Laos, which is contiguous to the southern Chinese borderlands. This may explain why Peking did not dare cease its support of North Vietnam, even when the Hanoi regime decided, against Chinese advice, to go to the Paris conference table.

Not as vital, but important nevertheless, is the stake the Soviets have in the DRV. If their global ambitions extend to Southeast Asia – or even if merely the acquisition of pressure points against China is deemed necessary – North Vietnam's friendship could prove a substantial asset. Within the context of its competition with China, the Soviet Union can hardly afford to abdicate its role in North Vietnam. To do so would be to surrender Southeast Asia entirely to Chinese influence, to damage Soviet standing with the national liberation movements, and to confirm Peking's claim that the Soviets today are "fat imperialists" and no longer suitable partners in "socialist cooperation." Neither side is therefore willing to face North Vietnam with an "either-or" proposition, but each seeks to pull the Vietnamese communists in its own direction.

This leads to the question of Chinese and Soviet leverage to control or shape Hanoi's policies. It is often assumed that because of the almost total dependence of the Vietnamese communists on outside military aid and their great need for economic assistance, Moscow and Peking have at least a veto over Hanoi's decisions. But the validity of such a view raises some serious doubts. Both the Chinese and the Soviets would encounter certain obstacles if they sought to translate their massive aid into political leverage, for the competition between them makes coordination of their Vietnam policies difficult and the cohesion of the Hanoi leadership does not permit them to play on factional rivalries. Should either Peking or Moscow show its displeasure by curtailing or cutting off aid, it seems probable that the other party would make a strong effort to replace such assistance – not to mention that the political cost of disowning Hanoi could be high.

Although Hanoi's dependence on Soviet and Chinese aid certainly enhances their influence, this does not necessarily mean that it is in their power to impose their views on Hanoi. In fact, it can be argued that the escalating war not only has increased Hanoi's war burden, but has also raised the stake for the communist powers to such an extent that they can no longer exert effective pressure on North Vietnam. Through the escalation of the war, Hanoi may have actually gained in maneuverability. This is borne out by Hanoi's decision to go to Paris despite Chinese objections, by its strategy in South Vietnam which often violated Mao Tse-tung's prescriptions, and by its decision not to attend the 1969 Moscow conference of communist parties but to give full support to Prince Sihanouk even though Moscow withheld its concurrence. Obviously, coordinated Sino-Soviet pressure on Hanoi would confront the Vietnamese communists with a dilemma. But the Sino-Soviet conflict militates against such an eventuality. Meanwhile, Peking and Moscow appear to be vying for the allegiance of Hanoi.

In this contest, the Chinese communists have enjoyed a distinct advantage. Geographic proximity – the exigencies of the war in the south and the threat to the north – places Peking in a favorable position. China can quickly move its forces, military specialists, and labor battalions across the border into North Vietnam to bolster Hanoi's strength – and it can withdraw them just as easily. Most Vietnamese communist leaders (including Ho Chi Minh) have in the past sought refuge in China, and the Chinese constantly remind the North Vietnamese that there vast land will always be available to serve as a "reliable rear." It is not without significance that Premier Chou En-lai in his congratulatory address on April 25, 1970, to the participants in the Indochinese Summit Conference recalled Mao Tse-tung's oft-quoted dictum: "The 700 million Chinese people provide a powerful backing for the Vietnamese people; the vast expanse of China's territory is their reliable rear area." [32]

Quite apart from these purely military reasons, Hanoi feels a stronger attraction to Peking's revolutionary strategy and world outlook. Unsatisfied in its territorial and political ambitions, disinclined to accept the status quo, poor and underdeveloped, inspired by a spirit of austerity and a desire to transform rapidly the country's social and economic system, North Vietnam can hardly be as close to the Soviet Union as it is to revo-

32. Peking NCNA International Service, May 2, 1970.

lutionary China. The standard Chinese phrase about the two countries being close "like lips and teeth" may not be entirely inappropriate, although it may remind the North Vietnamese uncomfortably at times how much they live in the shadow of China – and how far from Moscow and from Soviet help. Even today, the Vietnamese have not forgotten the long history of Chinese (and Chinese-Mongol) threats to their independence, as is evidenced in the frequent references of Vietnamese communist leaders to past foreign, i.e., Chinese, invasions. General Vo Nguyen Giap, for example, reminded his Vietnamese audience: ". . . in nearly 1,000 years of independence, our people always had to conduct many wars of national defense against foreign aggression in order to safeguard our national sovereignty."[33] A certain natural affinity for Chinese views and policies is tempered – to varying degrees, it is true – by a recognition of the danger which may result from leaning too far to the Chinese side.

No historical memories exist with regard to Russia. The USSR does not threaten the DRV's interests, but it is also in all respects – physically, psychologically, and politically – more remote and less capable in the long run of affecting the North Vietnamese's fate, for better or for worse. In the present circumstances, with Peking and Moscow at odds and with Hanoi in turn engaged in a difficult war against its opponents in the south, the Soviet Union plays, however, a vital role in the calculations of the Hanoi leaders. Only the Soviets can supply the sophisticated weaponry now needed for the war and, more importantly, Soviet assistance can most effectively deter the United States from taking full advantage, if necessary, of its technological superiority. At the same time, so long as the Soviet Union perceives a stake in North Vietnam, it can serve as a counterweight to Chinese pressures and excessive influence.

North Vietnam, therefore, presently has but one real option: it must seek to maintain a cordial relationship with both communist world powers, balancing their influence not only to retain leverage in both communist capitals, but also to proceed along an independent path. This is in fact the course the DRV has long been following, rather successfully. To cite but one example, North Vietnamese leaders almost invariably visit and confer with leaders in both Moscow and Peking when traveling abroad. When VWP First Secretary Le Duan went to the Soviet Union in the spring of 1971 to attend the Twenty-fourth Congress (where he was careful not to participate in his hosts' anti-Chinese attacks, but to give thanks to both countries for their help) and remained there for an unus-

33. *Hoc Tap*, no. 12, 1969. English translation, *JPRS*, no. 49878, February 18, 1970.

ually long six weeks' stay, he balanced what might have been considered a pro-Soviet act by making it a point to pay a reverential visit to Mao's birthplace.[34] Similarly, Soviet and Chinese aid agreements with Hanoi are concluded annually and almost simultaneously. Hanoi's expression of gratitude for such aid is effusive, but distributed in an equitable fashion as is praise for Chinese or Soviet accomplishments. And whenever feasible, Hanoi refrains from commenting in public on issues of controversy between Moscow and Peking.

In reviewing the zigzags of North Vietnam's course with regard to China and the Soviet Union [35] as well as its domestic policy, one is tempted to identify "pro-Chinese" and "pro-Soviet" periods as well as "pro-Peking" and "pro-Moscow" orientations of the DRV leaders. Although these labels are justified only insofar as they describe policy proclivities, they also must be seen in a broader context: what appears to be a leaning to one side may reflect an ideological and political affinity, but it may also merely indicate that a conscious effort is being made to redress the balance of influence of the two communist powers so as to preserve North Vietnam's ability to make its own independent decisions in the light of its perceived national interest. This will explain why the same Vietnamese communist leaders at various times have been described as "pro-Peking" or as "pro-Moscow" and why they often do not seem to act or speak in accordance with the label assigned to them.[36]

II

Soviet efforts to impose "peaceful coexistence" on the communist world met opposition not only in Peking but also in Hanoi. In the late fifties, the North Vietnamese decided to step up their revolutionary drive in the southern part of the country. In 1960 they formed the National Front for

34. According to a Hanoi International Service broadcast in English, April 1, 1971, Le Duan expressed his thanks at the Moscow Congress in these words: "Our victories in the fight against U.S. aggression, for national salvation, are closely linked to the vigorous support and great assistance from the Soviet Union, China and the other fraternal socialist countries, the international Communist and workers' movements, the national liberation movement, and the progressive and peace forces all over the world, the American people included."

35. For a perceptive documented study of Sino-Soviet relations with Hanoi during the mid-sixties, see Donald S. Zagoria, *Vietnam Triangle – Moscow, Peking, Hanoi* (New York, 1967).

36. Thus, General Vo Nguyen Giap, though generally considered to be the foremost member of a "Soviet faction," is nevertheless quite capable of referring to "Mao Tse-tung thought" – which is usually taken as a sign of extreme pro-Peking attitudes. See Hanoi broadcast, April 27, 1970, relating Giap's congratulatory message to the Chinese on the occasion of the launching of China's first satellite.

the Liberation of South Vietnam (NFLSV) and began to invest more heavily in guerrilla activity. "Peaceful coexistence" could not have had much appeal in Hanoi at such a time. Hence, during the early sixties Hanoi took a stance on foreign issues which generally paralleled that of communist China: the Vietnamese communists supported Peking in its conflict with India, attacked Tito's brand of revisionism, and opposed the nuclear test ban. On the Cuban issue they refrained from an endorsement of the Soviet stand. Hanoi's policies during this period reflected its basic quasi-Chinese ideological orientation as well as its optimistic estimate that largely unassisted, small-scale, guerrilla-type revolutionary warfare would succeed in South Vietnam. Since North Vietnam stood to gain little from completely alienating the Soviet Union (even during those years when Hanoi disagreed with Moscow on a number of important issues), it was careful not to let the strains in relations reach the breaking point.

As in the case of North Korea, Moscow at first reacted to Hanoi's closer ties with Peking by applying direct pressure: Soviet aid, a vital factor in North Vietnam's plans for economic development, was cut off. This action alone might not have brought the North Vietnamese back to a more neutral position on the Peking-Moscow spectrum. What eventually caused a reorientation of Hanoi's policy were events connected with the war in South Vietnam. On the one hand, as U.S. forces entered the fighting on the side of Saigon and as U.S. air attacks, early in 1965, began to directly threaten the Hanoi regime, Soviet aid and support became indispensable and the need for such assistance came to dictate policy. On the other hand, the Soviet Union too could ill afford to allow communism to fail in Vietnam. Also, the new situation presented an opportunity for Moscow to balance Chinese influence, to gain a foothold in Southeast Asia, and to weaken and tie down the United States.

The result was a Soviet aid program to the Hanoi regime ranging from advanced military equipment (especially air defense weapons) to machinery and foodstuffs (mostly wheat). This assistance program has since developed into a large and complex enterprise involving convoys of Soviet freighters and the dispatch of Soviet technicians to North Vietnam and the training of North Vietnamese experts, locally and in the USSR. Ivan Shchedrov, a Soviet newspaperman and specialist on Southeast Asia, indicated in early 1970 that in the period from 1955 to 1964 Soviet aid amounted to 320 million rubles out of a total communist aid program to the DRV of 800 million.[37] According to another Soviet source, about one-

37. *Za rubezhom*, January 30–February 5, 1970.

third of this aid was provided as a gift.[38] Other sources confirm that subsequently the Soviet assistance program grew qualitatively and quantitatively to more impressive dimensions.[39] Between January and April 1970, sixty Soviet ships reportedly called at North Vietnamese ports to unload machinery, equipment, and food, and more than two hundred industrial and agricultural projects were underway with Soviet assistance.[40] Radio Vladivostok on January 17, 1970, reported that one ship a day was leaving the Siberian port city for Haiphong and that in addition more than 50,000 tons a month had been shipped to North Vietnam from Black Sea ports during 1969. A Soviet domestic broadcast, monitored by *FBIS*, reported on August 11, 1971, that Soviet ships leaving Black Sea ports had delivered since the first of the year over 300,000 tons of cargo to the DRV. A *New York Times* article, in the fall of 1969, placed the total of Soviet aid to the DRV at 1 billion dollars a year.[41] It was also stated that since 1955 (the year of the first USSR-DRV aid agreement) four thousand Soviet specialists (including engineers, geologists, agronomists, physicians, and teachers) have worked in the DRV, an equal number of Vietnamese have studied in the USSR, and three thousand North Vietnamese have received practical production training there.[42] Some ten thousand Vietnamese are currently being schooled or trained in civilian and military establishments in the USSR.[43]

In sheer magnitude, the Chinese military and economic aid program (estimated at about 200 million dollars per year) cannot rival that of the USSR. Yet its value should not be measured in dollars alone, for it not only provides North Vietnam with a useful bargaining asset in negotiations with the Soviets, but it offers evidence of the Chinese commitment to the DRV. Further, China can supplement North Vietnam's manpower shortage, which the Soviet Union cannot easily do. At the height of the Chinese aid

38. *Krasnaia Zvezda*, May 20, 1971. English translation, *Current Digest of the Soviet Press*, 23, no. 20 (June 15, 1971), 35.

39. See, for example, Eberhard Einbeck, "Moskaus Militaerhilfe an die Dritte Welt," *Aussenpolitik*, 22, no. 5 (May 1971), 300–13.

40. *New York Times*, April 12, 1970, reporting a Moscow Radio broadcast.

41. *Ibid.*, September 29, 1969. Other estimates arrive at a lower figure. Philip Dion, for example, in discussing Soviet policy in Indochina, states that Soviet aid for the last five years has fluctuated between 250 million and 1 billion dollars. See "Fatal Ambivalence," *Far Eastern Economic Review*, 71, no. 12 (March 20, 1971), 24–26.

42. *Pravda*, September 2, 1971.

43. *Izvestiia*, September 17, 1971. See also Colonel A. Leontiev's article in the Soviet Army paper *Krasnaia Zvezda*, September 30, 1971, broadcast by TASS on the same date.

effort, several tens of thousands of Chinese were busily engaged in construction work in North Vietnam, mainly repairing damaged supply lines. In North Vietnamese literature, one frequently encounters mention of Chinese specialists.[44] Their number is thought to be substantially larger than that of the Soviet experts working in the DRV. Similarly, many North Vietnamese are currently being trained in China.

This parallel and competing aid effort has intensified the Moscow-Peking rivalry over the allegiance of the DRV. Competition has been further heightened by Hanoi's return to an essentially neutral position. Hanoi has, of course, continued to seek friendly relations with Peking and even with Albania, but it has also gone out of its way to indicate that Soviet aid is appreciated and that Moscow deserves credit for its show of "proletarian internationalism" – an ever-popular term in Hanoi, which has become especially popular since attacks against "modern revisionism" have to be toned down to avoid alienating the Soviets. This carefully neutral stance has paid off for Hanoi. After the U.S.-Vietnamese incursions into Cambodia and again, in 1971, after the South Vietnamese operation in Laos, both Peking and Moscow signed, within weeks of each other, supplementary aid agreements to compensate the DRV for its losses, and both issued warnings to the United States. In the fall of 1971, Li Hsien-nien, deputy premier of the CPR, visited Hanoi to sign a military and economic aid agreement with the DRV for 1972. Shortly thereafter, Soviet President Podgorny called on the Hanoi leaders to offer assurances of continued Soviet political, military, and economic support – and to balance Chinese influence.

North Vietnamese efforts to reestablish in its own interest some degree of Sino-Soviet cooperation have not been successful despite frequent appeals by the Hanoi leaders. As a result, North Vietnam's position between the two contending powers remains extremely difficult, since support from both parties continues to be indispensable. Certainly it would be desirable from Hanoi's point of view to coordinate the two aid programs and to assure smooth delivery of Soviet aid. It must have been painful, therefore,

44. On June 3, 1971, for instance, Hanoi's international broadcast reported that several Chinese experts working in the DRV had been decorated for their work on "the building of the Dien Bien Phu wood processing factory." How careful the Vietnamese are to balance praise for Soviet and Chinese aid is illustrated by this same news item. It states that Soviet specialists were also decorated for their "help in the designing of various tea mills." Significantly, both groups of foreign experts were given the Order of Labor, Third Class. Similarly, when the Soviet Union and the CPR rushed flood relief to the DRV in the fall of 1971, the arrival of the first Soviet and Chinese aid shipments was announced by Radio Hanoi on the same day and in identical language.

for the North Vietnamese communists to hear the Soviets accuse the Chinese of hampering the Soviet aid effort and of undermining the "struggle against U.S. imperialism." Peking in turn has retaliated with equally strong recriminations, attacking the Soviet Union for sabotaging the Vietnamese people's war and for "engaging in a futile attempt to stamp out the raging revolutionary flames of the Vietnamese people and ruin the fruits of victory." [45] Hanoi has wisely refrained from comment.

The conflict between Moscow and Peking also has been reflected in their differing views on what strategy should be used against South Vietnam. Mao Tse-tung has repeatedly stressed that Hanoi should eschew compromise or negotiations with the "imperialists" and pursue the Chinese formula of a protracted people's war until final military victory. He has made it clear too that such an extended struggle must be won primarily through a self-reliant effort. This, Mao insists, is how "a weak nation can defeat a strong, a small nation can defeat a big nation." [46] This Maoist dictum has its attraction for the Hanoi leaders, but they are aware of the dangers of a protracted war, of the price such a war exacts from an already weary people, and of the difficulty of staying the course so long as the other side enjoys the abundant material support of the United States. Also, it is probably not lost on the Vietnamese that the Chinese formula would minimize the role of Soviet military assistance (consisting largely of the more sophisticated weaponry China cannot supply) and that a reduction of Soviet aid would be politically unwise.

The Soviets, on the other hand, have strenuously sought to create — or reinforce existing — doubts in the Hanoi leaders' minds about the practicability of the Chinese strategic formula and about Peking's intention. They are generally more anxious to achieve a negotiated settlement in Vietnam. They also argue that a sure way to hasten victory is to form a united front of all communist forces in the world, relying especially on the support of the Soviet Union and on the influence it wields in world affairs. If such a front has not materialized and if Soviet efforts on behalf of Hanoi have not been successful so far, this is due in large measure, Moscow insists, to China's unwillingness to cooperate with the Soviet Union. Moscow goes even a step further in placing the blame for the continued costly war on Peking. It asserts that U.S. military action against North Vietnam is the direct result of the Chinese refusal to cooperate with the Soviet Union and of Peking's sermons on "self-reliance." This, the Soviet leaders suggest, signals

45. Editorial in *Jen-min Jih-pao*, February 3, 1970, distributed in English by NCNA.

46. Hsinhua News Agency, *Daily Bulletin*, May 21, 1970.

to the American enemy that China will not intervene on behalf of Hanoi unless directly attacked. How far these Soviet accusations have been carried at times can be seen in the following passage from a Chinese language broadcast emanating from Moscow on March 16, 1970: "Facts convincingly show that the Chinese leaders are more unwilling than those in control of the U.S. imperialist administration to end the war in Vietnam as soon as possible. With their anti-people political and military viewpoints, the Peking leaders have ignored the Vietnamese people's interests, hoping that the bloody war will go on forever."

With the announcement of President Nixon's plan to visit the CPR, the Soviet Union has stepped up its campaign of insinuations, hoping to sow doubts in the minds of the Hanoi leaders about Peking's reliability and intentions. Chou En-lai has visited the DRV to dispel such doubts and Mao Tse-tung has sent a message to Hanoi reiterating that "the Chinese people will, as always, resolutely fulfil their internationalist obligations and give all-out support and assistance to the Vietnamese and other Indochinese peoples in their war against U.S. aggression and for national salvation until complete victory." [47] Despite these reassuring protestations, Hanoi apparently feels uneasy about these developments, to judge by its insistence that the Nixon doctrine aims at dividing the socialist countries and by its studied silence about the possibility of a Sino-American accommodation.

No wonder that the Hanoi leaders, caught between such contending forces and faced with a growing strain on the limited resources of their small country, have at times been at odds with regard to the most effective way of gaining victory in the south. Though little is known about the details of these intraparty debates in Hanoi, public speeches and statements by the Vietnamese leaders give some indication of the focal points of the discussions. In the first place, there is the ever present problem of the degree to which Hanoi should allow itself in its struggle for reunification to become dependent on foreign support. Related to this question is that of how the war should be fought. Hanoi must ask itself if it is willing to mobilize all its resources – whatever the cost – in order to concentrate on a quick thrust to victory (somewhat along the lines of the Tet offensive). This approach, involving great risks, would require extensive outside sup-

47. *Peking Review*, no. 37 (September 10, 1971), 3. Deputy Premier Li Hsien-nien, visiting Hanoi in September 1971, made the pledge of continued Chinese support to the DRV even more explicit when he stated: "The Chinese people will not flinch from the greatest national sacrifices to give support and assistance to the Vietnamese people in their war against U.S. aggression and for national salvation." Peking NCNA International Service, in English, September 26, 1971 (as reported by *FBIS* on the following day).

port and firm backup guarantees from Moscow and Peking. Some leaders apparently have long opposed such reliance on conventional military means and, much in line with Mao's recommendations, have urged the return to guerrilla warfare necessitating relatively little external aid, but presupposing a high degree of stamina on the part of the people and a postponement of the goal of reunification for which the North Vietnamese have been making heavy sacrifices for the past decade.

Decisions regarding the war strategy are in turn intertwined with the problem of domestic growth and of the speed with which the Hanoi regime can advance toward the establishment of a fully developed socialist order. Whatever resources are diverted to the war must be taken out of the domestic development program if the gap is not filled by foreign contributions. This problem of allocation is particularly acute with regard to the shortage of manpower that has long been plaguing North Vietnam and has been further accentuated by the catastrophic floods which ravaged the northern part of the country in the late summer of 1971.

Indications are that out of these debates on war strategy has come a compromise formula which satisfies both sides. Hanoi now is avoiding larger frontal attacks and is preparing itself for a protracted low-cost war should this become necessary because of continuing superior enemy resources and strength. At the same time, it can be assumed that Hanoi is convinced that as U.S. forces are gradually withdrawn from Vietnam it can outlast the United States' will to shore up the Saigon government. Thereafter, it reckons, the war can be brought to a quick end. Husbanding its resources, Hanoi is preparing for such an eventuality.

IV

As is obvious from an abundance of materials coming out of North Vietnam, particularly the lengthy policy statements of First Secretary Le Duan and of chief ideologue and Politburo member Truong Chinh, differences of opinion among the Hanoi leadership also extend to domestic policies. This is not surprising in view of the harsh realities of life in wartime North Vietnam, the serious manpower shortage, the insufficient availability of agricultural land, and the extremely underdeveloped character of the country which must attempt to sustain a never-ending war effort and at the same time provide its people with a sense of progress. From certain superficial similarities with Chinese patterns of economic organization, it has been argued that North Vietnam is in many ways copying the Chinese model in its domestic policies. This impression may have been reinforced by the distinctly Stalinist tendencies of much of the Hanoi leadership. Stalin's writings are still being issued in Hanoi, and the theoretical journal of the 1.1 million-member VWP urges party members to "make intensive efforts to learn from Stalin's revolutionary spirit and persistent struggle and valiant attack." [48] A Chinese orientation also might be reflected in the party's stand on violent revolution. Truong Chinh once stated that his party is "most profoundly imbued with the Marxist-Leninist concept of violent revolution." [49]

Ideologically speaking, Hanoi is not a neutral in the Moscow-Peking conflict, for its orientation puts it closer, much closer, to Peking than to Moscow. This position reflects the nature of the regime and its origins, the problems it faces – particularly the need it feels to change the status quo – and the logical choice of the instruments available to it in pursuing its objectives. Nevertheless the past record of Hanoi's domestic and foreign policy strongly suggests that at no time has the North Vietnamese leadership been content to accept uncritically Chinese advice or the Chinese model. The Vietnamese communists never favored the Maoist doctrine that peasants could lead the revolutionary struggle. They resisted Chinese pressures to introduce the commune system. They rejected the Cultural Revolution as not applicable to Vietnam and made no attempt to emulate the related activities going on in neighboring China. On the contrary, the North Vietnamese repeatedly pointed to their successes in "adapting Marxism-Leninism [not Maoism] to the conditions of Vietnam." So far at least Vietnamese communism has followed an autonomous course despite its strong affinity for Chinese policies. Vietnamese policies and institutions are not carbon copies of communist practices in China or elsewhere.

Precisely what brand of communism will emerge in Vietnam in the coming years cannot be predicted today when the war in the south is still in progress and its resolution can only be dimly perceived. Short of an unlikely complete defeat, it seems most improbable, however, that the Hanoi leadership will abandon the independent course which it has been able to maintain for more than a decade despite the most difficult circumstances. Whatever the final outcome in South Vietnam, Hanoi will have to continue to operate with austerity and discipline if the lagging economy of North Vietnam and the rudimentary state of the desired socialist transformation are to show any signs of progress. The country has suffered immensely, directly and indirectly, from the protracted war. It is in no condition

48. See "The Great Works of the Brilliant Stalin," *Hoc Tap*, no. 12, 1969. English translation, *JPRS*, no. 49878, February 18, 1970.

49. Report on the occasion of a Hanoi cadre conference commemorating the one-hundred-fiftieth birthday of Karl Marx and broadcast by Hanoi, September 16, 1968.

to allow its meager resources to be channeled into nonproductive purposes. Its leadership is bent on creating a strong nation through a further strengthening of the "proletarian dictatorship." [50] Perhaps – some would say probably – the Hanoi leaders have ambitions extending to Laos and to Cambodia. If so, this would require additional effort and resources. Nor can one detect within North Vietnam the presence of influential elements which, as in Eastern Europe, might promote a democratic softening of the political system. As far as one can see into the future, Vietnamese communism is not likely to follow the pattern of the European communist movements. The "revisionist" currents characteristic of Western communism do not fit the circumstances of Vietnam.

50. The Hanoi publication *Tuyen Huan*, March–April 1971, pp. 16–22 (English translation, *FBIS*, May 18, 1971), for example, stated that in the period of transition to socialism the DRV must not loosen, but, on the contrary, must strengthen the proletarian dictatorship.

14

Cuba

BY C. IAN LUMSDEN

Since the overthrow of Batista in 1959, Cuba has continued to lie at the edge of the communist camp as the lone socialist outpost in the Western Hemisphere. In fact, the character and progress of Cuba as a communist state can best be understood in terms of its physical and ideological separation from other communist countries. In 1961 Fidel Castro declared his regime to be Marxist-Leninist, but a decade later Castroism or revolutionary socialism, rather than the communism which is associated with the Soviet Union's stale, bureaucratic regime, still best describes the general tenor of Cuban politics. With the exception of a brief period in the early sixties it has never seemed likely that Cuba's leaders would accept Moscow's current neo-Stalinist model as their own. In short, since the revolutionary process in Cuba has been an autochthonous phenomenon throughout, analogies to other communist states are as likely to mislead as to illuminate.

Cuba's insulation within the Western Hemisphere, as well as within the communist camp, is primarily a result of its revolutionary character. It has directly confronted the respective hegemonies of both the United States and the Soviet Union. Because of its small population, economic underdevelopment, and scarce natural sources of power, however, Cuba's determination to make its own national revolution has always been checked by its dependence upon external factors. It is clear, for example, that without the Soviet Union's military protection and enormous economic aid the revolution would never have survived in its present form.[1] The future char-

1. Castro himself has publicly acknowledged the "decisive" character of Soviet economic aid, and has admitted receiving 1.5 million pesos of military aid from the USSR. *Granma Weekly Review*, January 5, 1969, May 3, 1970. (*Granma Weekly Review* will hereafter be cited as *G.W.R.*)

acter of the Castro regime will depend upon its ability to continue resisting the ideological influence of the very power that ensured its survival in the first decade of its existence.

The leaders of the revolution from the outset recognized Cuba's need to break out of its siege-like state of isolation if it was to preserve its distinctive character. They were undoubtedly aware that their commitment to the transformation of the Andes into the Sierra Maestra of Latin America would entail a direct confrontation with American dominion in the region. But they surely did not expect that the pursuit of this objective would lead to a direct clash with the Latin American communist parties and even to a serious deterioration in Cuba's relations with the Soviet Union itself, which has been seeking in recent years to establish closer diplomatic and economic relations with the region's United States-dominated regimes. The conviction that its revolutionary socialism must expand its present national boundaries has thus led Cuba to engage in a somewhat unequal struggle against the policies and influence of both the United States and the Soviet Union.

Because Cuba lies at a great distance from Moscow, and because its conversion to socialism was voluntarily made by national (and nationalist) leaders whose previous political background was noncommunist, it has enjoyed a much greater degree of national sovereignty than any East European state, with the exception of Yugoslavia and possibly Albania. Fortunately for Cuba the revolution coincided with the emergence of widespread polycentric forces within the communist camp. In addition, the Sino-Soviet dispute prompted the Soviet Union to extend virtually unconditional assistance to Cuba in the early sixties as a means of demonstrating that its economic aid could accelerate the transition of the third world to socialism without having to resort to means that might imperil the peaceful coexistence which has become imperative between the industrialized countries in the nuclear age. Cuba's autonomy within the communist camp has been subsequently bolstered by the Soviet Union's recognition that the United States will not permit it to intervene in Cuba in a manner that is clearly opposed by both its leaders and people, as was the case in Czechoslovakia.

Cuba has taken advantage of these fortuitous circumstances by asserting its national sovereignty to the full. In particular, it has refused to compromise its independence by becoming publicly embroiled in the Sino-Soviet dispute. Cuba's revolutionary socialism, coupled with its forceful brand of nationalism, has involved it in complex and not always consistent relationships with other communist countries. A definition of these relationships is therefore made only at the risk of oversimplification. The difficulty of attempting one is accentuated, furthermore, by the fact that Cuba's political character is still in its formative state.

I

Cuba's mass-mobilization regime differentiates it from the more developed communist countries in Eastern Europe. The European communist regimes are conservative insofar as they reflect values that are increasingly similar to those of the industrialized capitalist countries. A concern for economic growth, increasingly measured by the output of consumer goods, has almost entirely displaced what was once a major goal of communism – to free man from his social alienation. This has not yet happened in Cuba. On the contrary "the transformation of Cuban man into revolutionary man is at the heart of Cuban radicalism." [2]

Although the Castro regime undoubtedly uses mass mobilization to further Cuba's economic development and as a means of political control, its main purpose is to affect the cognitive and behavioral patterns of individuals.[3] Unlike the present leaders of the European communist countries, Castro is very much a utopian thinker who still believes in the ultimate perfectability of man.[4] He assumes that the achievement of the revolution's goals depends upon the complete eradication of Cuba's prerevolutionary values and their substitution by an entirely new world view centered on the individual. The new belief system propagated by the Castro regime revolves around the concept of *conciencia* which "conveys an amalgam of consciousness, conscience, conscientiousness and commitment." [5] It calls for altruism and the rejection of individual material rewards, but it does not seek to submerge the individual in the mass. On the contrary, Cuba's official ideology stresses the importance of self-awareness

2. For a definition and application of the concept of mass mobilization to Cuban politics, see Richard R. Fagen, "Mass Mobilization in Cuba: The Symbolism of Struggle," *Journal of International Affairs*, 20, no. 2 (1966), 254–71. Richard R. Fagen, *The Transformation of Political Culture in Cuba* (Stanford, Calif., 1969), p. 2.

3. See Fagen, *The Transformation of Political Culture*, particularly chaps. 1, 2, and 6, for an illuminating analysis of political socialization in Cuba.

4. Castro's optimism about human nature prompts K. S. Karol "to wonder whether Fidel's pedagogic conception of socialism is not closer to spiritualism than it is to Marxism, causing him to exalt an ideal of man rather than man in the flesh." *Guerrillas in Power: The Course of the Cuban Revolution* (New York, 1970), p. 488.

5. Joseph Kahl, "The Moral Economy of a Revolutionary Society," *Transaction*, 6, no. 6 (1969), 30.

and self-education. Cuba is distinctive, moreover, in the stress that is placed upon the significance of the individual participating in revolutionary programs as a means of creating the "new man." [6]

Such mass organizations as the Committees for the Defense of the Revolution represent the main institutional innovation of the Castro regime. The Cubans have been much less creative with respect to the role of the communist party, a vanguard Leninist organization which is still in the process of formation. Nevertheless, the Cuban Communist party is distinctive for its criteria for membership which emphasize above all else how the individual behaves at work and how he relates to his fellow workers. Candidates are chosen by their peers at work, and mastery of Marxism-Leninism is not necessarily relevant to their subsequent selection and admission to the party. In fact, Castro's populist-style speeches with their infrequent references to Marxism, and not Marxist-Leninist manuals, are the basis of the revolution's ideology. As Castro himself is said to have admitted on one occasion, "the Cubans don't talk very much of Marxism any more." [7] The real ideology of the revolution – Castroism – is highly adaptive, frequently inconsistent, and stresses revolutionary activism. Faith and commitment tend to substitute for revolutionary theory and analysis.

The Cuban Revolution, more than a decade after coming to power, is not yet fully institutionalized. The personality and charisma of Castro still dominate every aspect of Cuba's political system. Cuba's socialist regime would not be overthrown if he were to die or were to be replaced as leader, but there is every reason to suppose that it would experience great changes. Such a complete domination of a country's political structure would not have been possible had Cuba been a more industrialized society or a larger country. What is unique about Cuba is that it is an underdeveloped country with mass communications media that allow its Maximum Leader to communicate simultaneously with virtually the entire population which is small and relatively homogeneous.

The current ideological goals of the Cuban Revolution are greatly similar to the ideas that were persistently advocated by Che Guevara in the early sixties. However, it was not until after Guevara had actually left

6. See Che Guevara, "Socialism and Man in Cuba," in *Che: Selected Works of Ernesto Guevara*, edited with an introduction by Rolando E. Bonachea and Nelson P. Valdes (Cambridge, Mass., 1969), pp. 155–96. Fagen notes "that a primary aim of political socialization in Cuba is to produce a participating citizen, not just one who can recite the revolutionary catechism perfectly." *The Transformation of Political Culture*, p. 7.

7. As quoted by John Gerassi, "The Spectre of 'Che' Guevara," *Ramparts*, 6, no. 3 (1967), 30.

Cuba in April 1965 that the policies with which he had been identified became officially incorporated into the ideology of the revolution. Whatever may have been the real reasons for his leaving, it is clear that they did not revolve around a fundamental ideological cleavage with Castro. The latter may have been disturbed by Guevara's frankness with respect to Cuba's relations with the Soviet Union,[8] and he may have questioned his administrative abilities with respect to the management of Cuban economy, but it is evident that their differences involved timing and practicality rather than principle.[9] Nevertheless, until 1966 Castro refrained from explicitly endorsing his comrade's more outspoken views.

Within a few months of Guevara's disappearance, the first indications emerged that Castro had been fully won over by his arguments and that Cuba would henceforth develop its own quite distinctive road to communism. He admitted on September 30, 1965, that in the past Cuba had made the error of mechanically copying the institutions and practices of the more developed communist countries, and emphasized that Cubans should carefully evaluate their experience, particularly their recent economic policies, to ensure that they did not initiate policies that might deviate from the ultimate goals of communism.[10] A few days after this speech, in which he first introduced the new concept of the parallel development of socialism and communism, he warned other communist countries not to interfere in Cuba's management of its internal affairs and added, for good measure, that it was impossible to conceive of Marxism "as a religious doctrine, with its Rome, its Pope and its ecumenical council." [11] The wide publicity that was given within Cuba at this time to Guevara's virtual ideological testament *Socialism and Man in Cuba* [12] offers further evidence that far from having rejected his views, the revolutionary government was about to make them its own.

Guevara stressed the concept of *conciencia* above all else, a fact which was acknowledged by Castro in his public eulogy to him at the time of his

8. See Guevara's speech on February 24, 1965, to the Second Economic Seminar of the Organization of Afro-Asian Solidarity meeting in Algiers, in which he accused the communist countries of being "accomplices of imperialist exploitation" as a result of their acceptance of the prevailing world market prices in their trade with underdeveloped countries. Bonachea and Valdes, *Che*, pp. 350–59.

9. See Bonachea and Valdes, *Che*, pp. 3–38, for a sensitive analysis of Guevara's relationship to Castro.

10. *Revista del Granma*, October 10, 1965.

11. *Granma*, October 4, 1965.

12. Bonachea and Valdes, *Che*, pp. 155–69.

death in Bolivia. Guevara, he declared, had "boundless faith in the conscience of men" and "saw with absolute clarity, moral resources as the fundamental lever in the construction of communism." Guevara's concern was not merely to revolutionize society, but also to overcome man's alienation from his fellowmen by forging a new revolutionary consciousness within him. Therefore, he contended that "to build communism simultaneously with the material base of our society, we must create a new man." To attain this goal he argued that moral stimuli and collective incentives must have primacy over individual material incentives in Cuba's economy. "Economic socialism without communist morality" was of no particular interest to him. His internationalism was based upon similar considerations. For Guevara, there could be "socialism only if there is a change in man's consciousness that will provoke a new fraternal attitude . . . in relation to all the peoples who suffer from imperialist oppression." But he also saw that the solidarity of the communist camp was essential to the security of its weaker members such as Cuba, and he insisted that it should be prepared to risk a global war, if necessary, in defense of North Vietnam. Guevara's ultrarevolutionary convictions were, of course, diametrically opposed to those of Moscow and of the majority of the Latin American communist leaders who adhered to the concept of the peaceful transition to socialism. His stress upon armed revolution and guerrilla warfare, in particular, represented a direct challenge to the ideological hegemony of the Soviet Union over the communist movement in Latin America. Nevertheless, although many of Guevara's ideas clearly coincided with those of the Chinese leaders, there is no reason to believe that he advocated siding with China in the Sino-Soviet dispute. In fact he criticized China (as well as the Soviet Union) in his final public statement for having placed the Sino-Soviet dispute above the interests of North Vietnam.[13]

In 1966 it became increasingly evident that Cuba's attempt to establish its own independent ideological position along the lines advocated by Che Guevara would be resisted at home and abroad. Castro's frequent and vitriolic attacks on the "servile mentalities" who lent their support to those who did not respect Cuba's "right to build our socialism, and our communism as we consider best" [14] revealed that his new policies had provoked the opposition of the Kremlin and of the old-line communists in

13. *G.W.R.*, October 29, 1967. Bonachea and Valdes, *Che*, p. 159. As quoted by Andres Suarez, *Cuba: Castroism and Socialism, 1959–1966* (Cambridge, Mass., 1967), p. 199. Bonachea and Valdes, *Che*, p. 351. "Message to the Tricontinental," *ibid.*, pp. 172–73.

14. *G.W.R.*, September 4, 1966.

Cuba who still looked to it for guidance. In spite of their opposition, Castro reiterated in the following years Cuba's determination to create its own ideology and to implement its own policies within Cuba.

II

By late 1966, then, it had become clear that Castro would not tolerate any internal opposition to the implementation of the policies for which Guevara had fought. He labeled his internal critics "pseudo-revolutionaries" who sought to compensate for their own lack of revolutionary commitment by denying that of the masses, and warned that unless they changed their views they would share the fate of counterrevolutionaries. Castro explained that if Cuba's leaders had followed the policies set forth by the "pure" economists who emphasize private material incentives, the revolution would never have advanced as much as it had; and he added that it would only continue to advance toward its goal of communism if the Cubans made a conscious struggle to attain it. He declared that the development of the Cuban people's *conciencia* would continue to be stressed, first, because it was essential to Cuba's prospects of eventually creating a truly communist society, and second, because it was "a *sine qua non* requisite for winning the battle against economic underdevelopment." [15] Cuba could not afford to devote resources to the production of consumer goods; in any case, it could never produce enough of these to counteract the counterrevolutionary propaganda emanating from the wealthiest country in the world. The regime had no choice but to strengthen its people's revolutionary convictions and their will to continue the struggle, regardless of the immediate material sacrifices that they might be called upon to make.

On July 26, 1968, Castro gave the definitive account of how the revolutionary government proposed to inculcate a communist consciousness in the Cuban people consistent with the concept of the parallel development of socialism and communism which had first been introduced in late 1965. The revolution's immediate aim, explained Castro, was to ensure that "the essential things are no longer obtained with money." He noted, in this respect, that the revolution had already introduced communism to the children who were attending nurseries and boarding schools where all their needs were provided free, and he promised that the range of services available without charge to the rest of the population, such as medical care, education, and housing, would be systematically extended until it eventually embraced food, clothing, transportation, and recreation. Fur-

15. *Ibid.*, January 21, 1968.

thermore, since Cuba could not entirely eliminate the "vile intermediary of money" [16] until productivity had been considerably raised, the revolutionary government would do everything in its power to lessen the appeal and significance of money. For example, the elimination of all private businesses with the exception of small farmers would ensure that nobody could profit financially from its possession. In addition, the disparity in wages would be gradually eliminated by raising the income of those at the bottom of the scale, and freezing those at the top. Eventually, he claimed, truck drivers would earn as much as engineers. Furthermore, no individual, material incentives would henceforth be offered, either as recompense for overtime work or as recognition of "voluntary" labor in their spare time, to persuade Cubans to increase their output.[17] Castro concluded by repeating his conviction that through education and through personal experience of services provided along communist principles, Cubans would deepen their commitment to the further development of communism in Cuba. These ideas are, in fact, already being put to the test in a few experimental communities, the most famous of which is San Andres de Caiguanabo. In this isolated valley in the province of Pinar del Rio, money is progressively being removed from circulation. With the exception of a few peasant farmsteads, all property is socialized; and all social services and most of the individual needs of its population are provided completely free. The same is true of the Isle of Pines which is almost entirely populated and worked by volunteer youth.

The radicalization of Cuba's domestic policies culminated in March 1968 with the proclamation of a revolutionary offensive that included the nationalization of all the remaining private businesses in Cuba. Most of these businesses had been involved in the sale of food, consumer goods, and services and a minority of them in the production of manufactured products. Castro's measure ensured that the whole of the economy would be state-owned with the exception of farms under 165 acres, which would remain privately owned. Private farming now represents less than 30 per cent of the agricultural sector (the remainder being operated by state farms), but in practice its output is increasingly controlled by the state. It is almost impossible for the peasant farmer to sell his produce directly to the consumer since no markets exist for such transactions. Because farm production is already closely supervised by state agencies, many private

16. *Ibid.*, July 28, 1968, May 28, 1967.

17. Material incentives have not entirely been eliminated yet. See Maurice Zeitlin, *Revolutionary Politics and the Cuban Working Class* (New York, 1970), pp. xxxiv–xxxvi.

farmers have opted to join "micro-plans" by which private land is cultivated in conjunction with state-owned land. The state is responsible for all investments and in return purchases all produce. The peasants retain formal ownership of the land and reap the profits, which can sometimes be quite large (but there is little on which they can be spent). "Micro-plans" are seen as a means of raising productivity while phasing out private farming in a way that will not unnecessarily alienate the peasant.

There is some truth to Cuba's claim that it has become "the socialist country with the highest percentage of state-owned property." It is also possible that "no other socialist country relies as little on market mechanisms as Cuba." [18] Between 1966 and 1968 the Cuban economy became increasingly centralized. A central planning board, *Juceplan*, now purports (all too frequently unsuccessfully) to supervise and coordinate the production of all enterprises. There is admittedly greater devolution of actual administration than there was when Guevara headed the formerly all-powerful Ministry of Industry (which has since been split up and replaced by various new organizations), but the managers of individual enterprises, who enjoy very little local autonomy, are prevented from attempting to raise productivity by offering financial incentive to workers. All profits, and even sales receipts in the case of state farms, are channeled into the national budget and are under the direct control of the National Bank.

At the same time as Cuba's domestic policies were being radicalized, the role of consciousness and will was increasingly emphasized in Castro's foreign analyses. He extolled Vietnam as an example of the extent to which a revolutionary people could overcome almost insuperable odds when they were led by real revolutionaries. He contrasted their behavior to that of the pro-Moscow communists in Latin America who had, he alleged, become even greater impediments to revolution than the local oligarchies. In fact, Castro denied that the former were either communists or revolutionaries for "what defines a communist . . . on this continent [is] his attitude towards the armed revolutionary movement." Castro added that Cuba's support would only be given to those who actually behaved as revolutionaries: "There is a much wider movement on this continent than that of just the Communist parties of Latin America; we are committed to that wider movement, and we shall judge the conduct of or-

18. Carmelo Mesa-Lago, "The Revolutionary Offensive," *Transaction*, 6, no. 6 (1969), 22. Leo Huberman and Paul M. Sweezy, *Socialism in Cuba* (New York, 1969), p. 166. This work contains an excellent analysis of Cuba's recent economic strategies.

ganizations not by what they say they are, but by what they prove they are, by what they do, by their conduct."[19]

Castro's criticisms of the orthodox communist parties – the "Mafia," as he labeled them – and of the role of the Soviet Union in Latin America were so outspoken in 1967 that they led some observers to conclude that the first conference of the Organization of Latin American Solidarity (OLAS), which took place in Havana in August, signaled an attempt on the part of Cuba to form a new international revolutionary movement. These expectations were unrealistic since the Castro regime was still very much dependent upon military and economic aid from the Soviet Union. Nevertheless, it was clear that by 1967 Cuba had carved out a distinctive ideology for itself which was distinguished by a commitment to revolutionary voluntarism that was in sharp contrast to the staid communism which characterized much of Eastern Europe and the Soviet Union. Significantly, the only other communist states with which Cuba enjoyed warm relations – North Korea and North Vietnam – were also small underdeveloped countries that had recently been engaged in a direct confrontation with the United States. Like Cuba, they felt threatened by the Sino-Soviet dispute, and assumed that their national interests would not be served by explicitly aligning themselves with either communist power.

Although Castro has promised Cuba much, it is evident that the revolution has recently achieved less in practice, particularly with respect to economic growth, than his bold predictions would suggest. Accurate statistics on the performance of Cuba's economy are not available.[20] Nevertheless, it is known that sugar production, which is crucial to Cuba's current economic strategy, has fallen far short of official targets in recent years. The new economic program that was adopted about 1964–65, following the disastrous sugar harvests of 1963–64 and the balance of payments crisis which was precipitated by Cuba's early attempts at industrialization and economic diversification, has yet to prove itself. This new strategy assumed that agriculture would be the base upon which the rest of the Cuban economy would be developed. The foreign exchange acquired mainly from the export of sugar was expected to finance not only the modernization of the agricultural sector (and thus to promote the eventual export of beef,

19. *G.W.R.*, March 19, 1967. "To us, the international Communist movement is in the first place just that: a movement of Communists, of revolutionary fighters, and those who are not revolutionary fighters cannot be called Communists." *Ibid.*, August 20, 1967.

20. See Carmelo Mesa-Lago, "Availability and Reliability of Statistics in Socialist Cuba," *Latin American Research Review*, 4, no. 1–2 (1969), 53–91, 47–81.

dairy products, and citrus fruits in addition to Cuba's traditional exports of sugar, tobacco, and nickel), but also the eventual industrialization of the country. For the foreseeable future, the latter is expected to revolve around the supply of Cuba's agricultural products. Cuba has evidently been unable to achieve all its ambitious goals so far, but the vast increase in its gross investment, which rose from 30 per cent of the GNP in 1965 to approximately 31 per cent in 1968,[21] indicates that its growth rate could yet accelerate considerably in the near future. At present, however, the impact of the high rate of capital investment has been negated by the persistent production problems that accrue from a high rate of labor absenteeism and from inept planning which, according to one former economic adviser to the Cuban government, amounts to no more than an alternation of "authoritarian centralization" and "anarchic decentralization." [22]

It would be unreasonable to expect the Cuban people to be over enthusiastic about the current austerity or satisfied to see so many of their efforts squandered by their leaders' mismanagement of the economy. In fact, Castro himself has referred on various occasions to the discontent and flagging revolutionary zeal that have been manifest particularly in Havana and to labor absenteeism which had reached critical levels by mid-1970. Although Castro responded to "the endless number of problems" that confronted Cuba in 1970 by promising to democratize its institutions, particularly the Central Organization of Cuban Trade Unions, there is little concrete evidence to suggest that the government will reverse its increasing tendency to repress dissent and to seek coercive solutions to its labor problems that are epitomized by the new anti-Loafing Law which makes absence from work a criminal offense subject to imprisonment for up to twenty-four months.[23] Significantly, no further advances have been made in the institutionalization of the revolution since 1965 when the Central Committee of the Communist party was established. This organization seems to be quite hollow, judging by the scant information on its meetings, membership, and policy decisions. The first Party Congress has yet to meet even though it was expected to be held by 1967, and Cuba seems to be as far away as ever from drafting its new constitution. Furthermore, newspapers and periodicals which earlier provided forums for diverse views

21. Mesa-Lago, "The Revolution Offensive," p. 24.

22. I. Joshua, as quoted by Huberman and Sweezy, *Socialism in Cuba*, p. 178.

23. See, for example, *G.W.R.*, March 24, 1968, August 30, 1970, September 20, 1970, and December 20, 1970. *Ibid.*, September 20, 1970. See Maxine and Nelson P. Valdes, "Cuban Workers and the Revolution," *New Politics*, 8, no. 4 (1970), 36–48.

within the revolution have disappeared one by one. In short, while economic problems have multiplied, the Cuban people have been given less and less opportunity to exert any influence on the formulation of government policy.

Yet it would be misleading to unduly emphasize the Cuban people's increasing estrangement from the revolutionary leadership without also underlining the persistence of a basic reservoir of goodwill toward the revolution and of loyalty to its Maximum Leader. Cuba may be experiencing great austerity at the moment but the vast majority of workers, particularly rural ones, recognize that they are incomparably better off than they were before the revolution. Consequently, although morale may not be as high as it was in the early sixties, there are few Cubans who are as yet prepared to conceive of a regime without Fidel at the helm, regardless of his admitted personal responsibility for the current state of affairs.

III

In recent years, Cuba's external policies have been as ineffective as its domestic economic policies. Since the much publicized OLAS conference in 1967, Cuba's impact upon the rest of Latin America and its revolutionary movement has become less and less evident. In October of that year Che Guevara was captured and then assassinated in Bolivia. Although the guerrillas have not been completely exterminated in any of the Andean or Central American countries in which they have attempted to establish isolated revolutionary *focos* in an effort to politicize the peasantry (which in most countries are much more numerous than the industrial working class), they have not increased along the lines that had once been projected by the Cuban guerrilla warfare strategists, and there are, as yet, few signs that they ever will. In fact, recent revolutionary activity in Latin America, epitomized by the Uruguayan *Tupamaros*, has been focused on the cities – contrary to the Cubans' onetime insistence that "the basic situation that can produce the vanguard in the revolutionary struggle is not the city but the country." [24] It is still too soon to know whether these newer tactics will prove any more viable than those advocated by Guevara. In the meantime, much of the limelight has been taken away from the guerrillas by the new regimes in Chile and Peru.

Cuba's inability to influence the course of radical events in Latin America is reflected in Castro's assessment of the Velasco Alvarado military re-

24. Cuban delegation to the OLAS conference cited by Sergio de Santis, "The O.L.A.S. Conference," *International Socialist Journal*, 4, no. 23 (1967), 714–15.

gime in Peru as a potentially revolutionary phenomenon demanding Cuba's solidarity. Such an assessment is unrealistic since the junta expressly rejects any association with Castroism or even socialism. Its members had been damned in 1967 by Che Guevara (only a couple of years before Castro's endorsement of the Alvarado regime) as officers of the "puppet army" that had eliminated Peru's guerrilla movement under American direction.[25] The victory in 1970 of the Popular Unity candidate, Salvador Allende, in the Chilean presidential elections also opens up a new perspective in South America which had once been discounted by the Cuban strategists. Further evidence of Cuba's inability to influence revolutionary developments in Latin America was provided by Castro's silence when Mexican students, who had, in part, been aroused by the cause of solidarity with the Cuban Revolution, were massacred in 1968.

Cuba's relations with the Soviet Union have borne a curious resemblance to its relations with the rest of Latin America. In 1967, Castro denounced the Soviet leaders for having extended economic and technical assistance to such governments as Venezuela and Colombia which were simultaneously suppressing guerrilla movements. However, Cuba's attempts to influence the policies of the Soviet Union have proven to be as unsuccessful as its efforts to win the Latin American communist parties over to its strategy of armed revolution. Castro's speech on August 23, 1968, concerning the overthrow of the Dubcek regime, was his swan song with respect to Cuba's endeavor to exert any influence on the Soviet Union's Latin American policies. Castro's endorsement of the Soviet intervention in Czechoslovakia was unexpected, for it was quite inconsistent with the oft-proclaimed principle of nonintervention that Cuba had always insisted should govern relations between communist countries. Moreover, the speech occurred within months of earlier statements by the Cuban prime minister which had implicitly raised and forthrightly rejected the possibility of the Soviet Union using its economic power to intervene in Cuban affairs.[26] In fact, Castro admitted that the invasion of Czechoslovakia could not be justified on purely legal grounds.

25. See Castro's speeches of July 14, 1969, in *G.W.R.*, July 20, 1969, and April 22, 1970, in *ibid.*, May 3, 1970. For a contrasting analysis of the events in Peru see Anibal Quijano, *Nationalism and Capitalism in Peru: A Study in Neo-Imperialism* (New York, 1971). Bonachea and Valdes, *Che*, p. 178.

26. See Castro's speeches of March 13, 1967, and August 10, 1967, in *G.W.R.*, March 19, 1967, and August 20, 1967. *Ibid.*, August 25, 1968. Although Castro gave his support to the Soviet intervention in Czechoslovakia, most of the speech was devoted to lambasting the Warsaw Pact countries for having become increasingly self-

Regardless of what may have motivated Castro to give his approbation to the intervention – perhaps it was his recognition of Cuba's ultimate military and economic dependence upon the Soviet Union – the speech was a humiliation for Cuba. It not only betrayed one of the cardinal planks in Cuba's foreign policy, but it also unintentionally revealed its impotence to have any impact within the communist camp. Castro's approval of the Soviet invasion made clear that whatever may have been his ambitions in the past, his foreign policy was now reduced to mere supplication. He could only demand to know whether the Warsaw Pact countries, consistent with their decision to intervene in Czechoslovakia, would "(1) [cease to draw] closer economically, culturally, and politically to the oligarchic governments of Latin America, which are not merely reactionary governments – and exploiters of their peoples – but also shameless accomplices in the imperialist aggressions against Cuba and shameless accomplices in the economic blockade of Cuba; (2) cease to support those rightist, reformist, sold-out, submissive leaderships in Latin America that are enemies of the armed revolutionary struggle, that oppose the people's liberation struggle; (3) send the divisions of the Warsaw Pact to Cuba if the Yankee imperialists attack our country, or even in the case of the threat of a Yankee imperialist attack on our country, if our country requests it." [27]

Subsequent events within Cuba and official pronouncements by its leaders confirm that Castro had been forced to come to terms with "the political realities" that underlay Cuba's dependence upon the Soviet bloc. Since 1968, Cuba has made no further criticisms of the policies of the Soviet Union or those of the pro-Soviet Latin American communists, and there has been an about-face in the way the Soviet Union has been portrayed in the Havana press. On the centennial anniversary of Lenin's birth Castro removed any doubts about Cuba's future alignment with the Soviet Union. Admitting that the revolution could never have survived without Soviet aid, he added that Cuba's "political and military ties with the Soviet Union [would] never be broken." [28]

The abrupt shift in Havana's relations with Moscow was, to say the least, unexpected, for it had been immediately preceded by the trial in January 1968 of a pro-Soviet "micro-faction" led by Anibal Escalante.[29]

interested in their relations with the underdeveloped communist countries. *Ibid.*, January 7, 1968, March 24, 1968.

27. *Ibid.*, August 25, 1968.

28. *Ibid.*, May 3, 1970.

29. The conviction of Escalante and other former leaders of the pre-1959 Commu-

During the trial it was alleged that the "micro-faction," composed of old-line communists, had sought to rally opposition to Castro's ultrarevolutionary policies. The Cuban government clearly sought to implicate the Soviet Union by its expulsion of a Soviet diplomat at the time of the trial and by its simultaneous announcement that Cuba would not attend the forthcoming meeting of communist parties in Budapest. Furthermore, Carlos Rafael Rodriguez, a leading member of the Secretariat, declared during Escalante's trial that "it was impossible to neglect this situation any longer, one in which a whole series of functionaries and members of Socialist organizations [and] Socialist countries work against the Cuban revolution here and in their own countries." [30]

Since late 1968 Cuba's relations with other communist states have seemingly reverted to the pattern which existed before 1966. In other words, Cuba remains committed to its distinctive domestic policies, and although it may disagree with the course of action of other communist countries or parties, it will refrain from interfering in or commenting on their policies. Furthermore, Cuba will desist from acting as some sort of spokesman for revolutionary movements within the underdeveloped world vis-à-vis the developed communist countries. This does not mean that Cuba has ceased to identify closely with North Vietnam and North Korea and revolutionary movements elsewhere. It merely indicates that the Cuban regime will respect the right of other communist parties to pursue different policies. This new phase of Cuba's external relations contrasts sharply with the activist period between 1965 and 1968. During this time, Cuba was engaged in heated disputes with China, which it accused of carrying out a "criminal act of economic aggression" and of emulating American imperialism in its behavior toward it;[31] it damned the East European states for profiteering in their sale of "junk" to Cuba; it branded

nist party (PSP) confirmed, once again, what had been evident for many years. Fidelistas are firmly in control of all political institutions in Cuba. The only old communist of any significance who plays a prominent role in Cuba today is Carlos Rafael Rodriguez, and there is no reason to doubt his complete personal identification with the leadership and policies of Castro.

30. Cuba actually attended the conference of communist parties that was held in Moscow in 1969, but only as an observer. The speech of Cuba's representative, Carlos Rafael Rodriguez, reiterated – in more diplomatic language than Castro is wont to employ – all the main points that the Cuban leader had made on August 23, 1968, with respect to the policies of the developed communist countries. See *G.W.R.*, June 15, 1969. *Ibid.*, February 4, 1968.

31. Statement by Fidel Castro on February 6, 1966. *Politica Internacional*, no. 13 (1966), 213–26. Cuba's brief but very heated dispute with China in 1966 purportedly revolved around the latter's attempt to pressure Cuba into aligning itself with

the League of Yugoslav communists an "agent of imperialism"; and it charged the Venezuelan Communist party with "treason" for betraying the guerrilla movement in its country.[32]

Cuba has thus reverted to being a marginal member of the communist camp, particularly in its ties with Eastern Europe. Cuba and Eastern Europe and the Soviet Union have different national interests which they pursue at different levels. For example, Latin America is of vital importance to Cuba, whereas it is only of secondary interest to the European communist countries. The latter countries are committed to a policy of peaceful coexistence with the United States and, indeed, to increasing their economic and cultural ties with the West as a whole. In Latin America, the Eastern European leaders pay respect to U.S. hegemony in return, presumably, for noninterference in the Soviet Union's sphere of influence in Eastern Europe.[33] Except for a brief period from late 1964 to mid-1966 the Soviet Union has not even bothered to pay lip service to the possibility of violent revolution in Latin America.[34]

On the other hand, although Castro has not articulated his position with respect to peaceful coexistence since his speech on Czechoslovakia, there is little reason to believe he has revised his conclusion that "relations with the imperialist U.S. government could improve . . . only at the cost of withholding consistent support for the worldwide revolutionary movement." [35] Unquestionably, Cuba links its internal security to the extent to which American power is held at bay in other parts of the world. It has a vital interest in the fate of North Vietnam for, as Castro pointed out in his

China in the Sino-Soviet dispute. Castro contended that the Chinese had sought to use Cuba's dependence on Chinese rice for political ends.

32. *G.W.R.*, August 25, 1968. Castro's speech of August 10, 1967, in *ibid.*, August 20, 1967. See D. Bruce Jackson, *Castroism, the Kremlin and Communism in Latin America* (Baltimore, 1969), for an account of Cuba's relations with the Venezuelan communists.

33. Significantly, the Soviet Union advised the United States that it was going to intervene in Czechoslovakia before notifying Cuba and other members of the communist camp of its intentions. Karol, *Guerrillas in Power*, p. 509. The Soviet Union's acceptance of U.S. hegemony in Latin America (Cuba excepted) is analyzed by James Petras, "The United States and the New Equilibrium in Latin America," in *Politics and Social Structure in Latin America* (New York, 1970), pp. 193–228.

34. For example, the Soviet Union informed the Latin American governments that it disowned the revolutionary resolutions of the Tricontinental Conference held in Havana in January 1966, when the ink had hardly dried on them. See Jackson, *Castroism, the Kremlin and Communism*, pp. 92–94.

35. *G.W.R.*, August 25, 1968.

speech on Czechoslovakia, neither country can be certain of protection from U.S. aggression by the developed communist countries. In the circumstances, the Cubans are cynical of the Soviet interest in peaceful coexistence and they regard such interest as a betrayal of the obligations of socialist internationalism.

Cuba's policy toward the United States continues to be determined by its belief that its own future, as well as that of the other underdeveloped countries, is tied to the overthrow of the United States–dominated global capitalist system. In this respect, Cuba's national interests are clearly different from those of the European communist countries whose concern for improved relations with the developed Western countries reflects their belief that they would benefit by closer economic bonds with the prosperous capitalist countries. In short, from the Cuban point of view, the developed communist countries accept the present world order, they benefit from it, and thus they have ceased to be revolutionary. The situation is quite different for underdeveloped communist countries like Cuba and North Vietnam – that is why they continue to be revolutionary socialist countries. This explains why Cuba is so opposed to Yugoslavia. Far from accepting the possibility that Cuba's revolutionary socialism could eventually evolve into some form of "tropical Titoism" acceptable to the United States, Castro has called for Yugoslavia's expulsion from international communist organizations on the grounds that its internal economic reforms and conciliatory attitude toward the United States make it the principal revisionist force within the communist camp.[36]

Despite Cuba's intransigent opposition to the possibility of improving relations with the United States, its relations with other Western countries, such as France, England, Spain, and Japan have steadily improved in recent years. There is something inconsistent in Castro criticizing the European communist countries for drawing closer to the United States while Cuba does the very same thing with other capitalist countries (as was pointed out by the Venezuelan Communist party in 1967).[37] The truth is, however, that Cuba needs Western trade to lessen its dependence upon the Soviet Union and to secure the technology and capital goods upon which the industrialization of its economy depends. Cuba's external policies are thus much more pragmatic than Castro would care to admit, a fact which should be borne in mind with respect to the future direction of the revolution.

36. See *ibid.*

37. See *ibid.*, August 20, 1967.

IV

Indeed, pragmatism is characteristic of the revolution as a whole, in spite of Castro's thunderous pronouncements from time to time. To be sure, Castro has pursued certain ill-conceived projects, such as the ten million-ton *zafra* (sugarcane harvest), with blatant disregard for the advice of friends and foes alike, and Cuba's commitment to moral incentives has currently acquired the status of official dogma; yet the record of the regime over the last dozen years suggests that it is prepared to discard projects that have forced Cuba to reappraise its policies regarding sugar production, mobilization of labor, and the structure and function of mass organizations, particularly trade unions.[38] The revolution continues to be a revolution without blueprints.

In the circumstances, it is still too early to determine whether or not Cuba will succeed in developing a socialist society that is qualitatively different (insofar as it would combine humanist with revolutionary values), from those of the Soviet Union and other East European countries. Much will depend upon the state of its economy. Its current condition does not, in all truth, augur well for the future. The 8.5 million-ton *zafra* in 1970 represented a record crop, one that almost doubled the figure for 1969, but the large-scale mobilization of resources that made it possible had an adverse effect on many other sectors of the economy. The public postmortem on Cuba's failure "to fulfill the honor of the Revolution" revealed major problems relating to inefficient management, transportation bottlenecks, and labor shortages.[39] The extent of Cuba's economic difficulties was subsequently underlined by its failure to achieve by one million tons the sharply reduced *zafra* target for 1971 of seven million tons.[40] On the other hand, the recent advances that have been made in certain sectors of the economy, as in fish, rice, and nickel production, indicate the progress of which Cuba is capable provided that it formulates and implements its economic policies in a more rational and cautious manner than it has heretofore. If absenteeism is to be overcome, far more attention will have to be paid to the immediate material needs of the masses. In short, the price of

38. See Castro's speeches of July 26, 1970, in *ibid.*, August 2, 1970; August 23, 1970, in *ibid.*, August 30, 1970; September 2, 1970, in *ibid.*, September 20, 1970; and December 7, 1970, in *ibid.*, December 20, 1970.

39. Castro declared on March 13, 1968, *ibid.*, March 24, 1968, that Cuba could not afford to fail to achieve the 1970 target of ten million tons since it involved the "honor of Revolution." Similar statements were made by him on many subsequent occasions.

40. *Latin America*, July 23, 1971.

steady economic progress in Cuba must be the renunciation of Castro's grandiose plans to solve Cuba's economic problems overnight. Such plans have precipitated rash and counterproductive experiments which have led to increasing disillusionment among the masses.

The second major factor affecting the direction of Cuba's future development involves Castro's response to the growing apathy and even disaffection of many Cubans as they have been confronted by setbacks. If Cuba is to avoid following in the footsteps of the bureaucratic, depoliticized societies of Eastern Europe and the Soviet Union, the Castro regime has no choice but to fulfill the early promise of the revolution, that is, to democratize its institutions and allow the Cuban people to participate fully in the making of all decisions that directly affect them. Some grounds for hope, slender though they may be as yet, were offered in mid-1970 when Castro called for a searching reexamination of the role of the communist party and its relation to the mass organizations. But even though he has recognized the need for greater political participation of the masses and for the democratization of such organizations as the trade unions, there is still insufficient evidence to believe that he is prepared to countenance "control of the workers over the Party, of the Party over the Central Committee and of the latter over himself," [41] a sine qua non for a socialist democracy. Moreover any serious step to democratize Cuba's political institutions would run counter to the growing military involvement in an increasing number of civilian affairs. Military officers are now at the head of several key ministries including education and conscripted servicemen, and paramilitary labor brigades have begun to play an ever larger role in agriculture, particularly in the *zafra*.

The immediate prospects for Cuba do not seem too bright but there are some rays of hope. Since nearly half the population is under twenty-one years of age, an increasing number of people will have received their entire education during the revolution. Cuba's youth have been socialized in an environment that has been, for the most part, much more open and egalitarian than that of Eastern Europe and the Soviet Union. Few observers would dispute Richard Fagen's contention that the "first ten years have seen (in addition to hardship, dislocation and bewildering change) considerable material progress, increased distributive justice and a veritable explosion of opportunities for education, social mobility and occupational responsibility; and these positive and palpable achievements go far toward

41. *G.W.R.*, August 2, August 20, 1970. Dumont, *Cuba: Est-il Socialiste?* p. 213. See Zeitlin, *Revolutionary Politics*, pp. xl–xli, for an accurate account of the party's present relationship to the masses.

explaining the continuing popularity and viability of the revolution."[42] How the Cuban people, particularly its younger elements, respond to the regime's increasing tendency to solve Cuba's problems by coercion rather than the open means of persuasion that once typified it, may well be decisive in determining the character of Cuba's future political system.

Since Cuba's geographical isolation is also likely to have a bearing upon its political character, long-term projections about the future of Castroism cannot be abstracted from events in the rest of the Western Hemisphere. For the time being, at least, it seems that the United States has the upper hand in Latin America. There are no organized forces capable of challenging its influence – notwithstanding the emergence of the new regimes in Chile and Peru – and furthermore it is quite evident that the Soviet Union is not prepared to give material assistance to revolutionary movements that attempt to do so. Nevertheless, Latin America's structural problems increase by the day. There has been a constant deterioration in the living standards of the masses relative to that of the middle and upper classes, and an absolute deterioration for the poorest groups, even in countries such as Mexico whose gross national product is rising at a fairly rapid rate.[43] The response of the region's elites to Latin America's structural crisis has almost universally been military and dictatorial in character. How long they can contain the demands for change from students, land-hungry peasants, and the marginal unemployed urban masses is a key question with respect to Cuba's future.

If a serious revolutionary movement were to emerge in Latin America, its impact upon Cuba would depend far more upon the U.S. reaction to it than upon any other factor. Even in the unlikely event that the United States would permit such a movement to come to power, especially since its intervention in the Dominican Republic, it is doubtful that the United States will permit any other country in the Western Hemisphere to under-

42. Fagen, *The Transformation of Political Culture*, p. 160. In a study for the prestigious Twentieth Century Fund, Jerome Levinson and Juan de Onis also arrive at the conclusion that "Cuba has come closer to some of the Alliance [for Progress] objectives than most Alliance members. In education and public health, no country in Latin America has carried out such ambitious and nationally comprehensive programs. Cuba's centrally planned economy has done more to integrate the rural and urban sectors [through a national income distribution policy] than the market economies of the other Latin American countries." *The Alliance That Lost Its Way* (Chicago, 1970), p. 309. See Huberman and Sweezy, *Socialism in Cuba*, pp. 22–64, for an account of the progress that has been made in education and health reforms.

43. See Andre Gunder Frank, "The Underdevelopment Policy of the United Nations in Latin America," *NACLA Newsletter*, 3, no. 8 (1969), 1–9. See also Levinson and Onis, *The Alliance That Lost Its Way*.

go fundamental revolutionary changes, let alone a socialist revolution; [44] and the United States still has an enormous economic and political capacity to prevent such things from happening. Consequently the future of Castroism will be contingent as much upon events in the United States, as upon what happens in Cuba or in the rest of Latin America.

The immediate prospects for Cuba being able to break out of its regional isolation while persisting with its revolutionary policies toward Latin America are not bright.[45] However, Fidel Castro is a complex person: he is a revolutionary socialist, but he is also a pragmatist and a Cuban nationalist.[46] There have been many shifts in policy and surprising turns of events in the short history of the revolution. If it became evident that the economic and political costs of Cuba's continued isolation were too great for Cuba to bear, Castro might yet agree to improving Cuba's relations with other countries in Latin America. This would, of course, entail ending Cuba's active support for revolutionary movements in the region and adopting a more flexible policy toward its individual regimes. Castro has, in fact, already been accused of doing just that by Douglas Bravo, leader of the Venezuelan Armed Forces of National Liberation and the most prominent advocate of Guevara's *foco* tactics.[47] Castro's admission in July 1969 that it was "correct for every country to make its own revolution, in its own way, to fit the conditions of that specific country," and his unsolicited support for the Peruvian military regime lend substance to Bravo's allegations.[48] Moreover, several Latin American governments, including that of Venezuela with which Cuba had once been engaged in the most heated exchanges, have made tentative diplomatic soundings to Cuba, presumably on the assumption that Cuba has either changed its policy toward Latin America or is considering doing so. Fur-

44. See President Lyndon Johnson's statement at the time of the uprising in the Dominican Republic. "The American nations cannot, must not, and will not permit the establishment of another Communist government in the Western Hemisphere." *Department of State Bulletin*, May 17, 1965. See also *The Rockefeller Report on the Americas* (Chicago, 1969), pp. 37–39, 59–65.

45. Admittedly, the Allende Popular Unity government in Chile established diplomatic relations with Cuba in late 1970, but it is most improbable that left-wing movements will be able to gain power in any other Latin American country within the foreseeable future. Significantly, the Velasco Alvarado military junta in Peru has failed to establish relations with Cuba.

46. See the informative biography by Herbert L. Matthews, *Fidel Castro* (New York, 1969).

47. *The Times* (London), January 17, 1970.

48. *G.W.R.*, July 20, 1969.

thermore, there can be no doubt that in comparison to the mid-sixties Cuba's energies are now mainly concentrated upon its domestic affairs. Whether Cuba will persist in the struggle to create the new man, and whether it can succeed in developing a humanistic yet revolutionary society when it has ceased to be actively involved in revolutionary movements in Latin America and elsewhere in the underdeveloped world, remains to be seen.

15

Patterns of Economic Relations

BY PHILIP E. UREN

By 1965, the dream of a communist commonwealth moving forward under a unified plan, which briefly seemed to the communist leaders to be within their reach in late 1962, had become once again just a dream. Indeed, within one year of its embodiment in Khrushchev's famous document "The Basic Principles of the International Socialist Division of Labor," its main tenets had been abandoned and the most authoritative communist publications were openly acknowledging the impracticability of unified planning. "The official communique issued after the July 1963 meeting of Communist Party leaders of COMECON countries did not mention the need for establishing a joint planning agency and indicated that the problem was not as simple as it originally might have appeared." [1] Thus, the years between 1962 and 1965 were in a sense tragic. No matter what one's political predilections may have been, or what imperial motives may have been assigned to the Soviet government, the vision of Eastern Europe and the Soviet Union moving forward in response to a unified plan was impressive from the point of view of scale, if nothing else. The purpose of this chapter is to suggest some of the reasons for the failure of this ideal, to categorize the problems which the East European alliance faces in the field of economic cooperation, and to try to evaluate the present economic situation in Eastern Europe.

NOTE: Professor C. H. McMillan of the Carleton University Department of Economics kindly read the manuscript of this paper and made a number of helpful suggestions.

1. A. Korbonski, *Comecon* (New York, 1965), p. 32.

Patterns of Economic Relations

I

By 1965, the Soviet split with China was virtually total; the Rumanians had made their so-called "declaration of independence"; the Hungarians were already beginning to experiment with what was to become known in 1968 as the New Economic Mechanism; and the currents of change were accelerating in Czechoslovakia. In the meanwhile, party intellectuals and government officials continued their efforts to reconcile those difficult bedfellows – central planning and realistic pricing. There were at that time, as indeed there had been since the notion of "socialism in one state" gave way to that of a "communist commonwealth," two major categories of politico-economic problems facing the leaders of Eastern Europe.

The first included those problems which were primarily political in nature. By far the most important of these was the question of nationalism and national independence; the Sino-Soviet dispute was the most spectacular example, but the desire for an independent national policy existed, in greater or lesser degree, in each of the communist allies. Secondly, the drive toward economic reform was general throughout the alliance and gave rise to both political and technical problems, the political element deriving from the varying nature and speed of the reforms in each member country. Thirdly, there remained the issue of communist economic relations with Western countries, particularly with the Common Market.

The second category of problems was more clearly economic, although it had important political implications. There was first the old bugbear of rational pricing, particularly for foreign trade, in a centrally planned economy. In the late sixties, this perennial issue became more controversial as Soviet economists worried publicly about the Soviet Union's terms of trade with Eastern Europe. Secondly, there was the problem – also not new – of how to develop a multilateral trading system among the planned economies. Without currency convertibility progress was unavoidably slow. Finally, there were the technical perplexities related to specific projects, such as the development of nuclear energy or cooperation on the Danube.

This necessarily simplified categorization of the international economic difficulties facing communist statesmen nevertheless gives some idea of the Herculean task with which they were faced. It is perhaps not surprising that their success has been less than total and that they face the seventies with their fundamental problems still unsolved.

The force of nationalism in Eastern Europe, and for that matter in the communist Far East as well, derives from ancient cultural and historical sources. The difficulties of economic cooperation within the communist commonwealth are in part an expression of this nationalism, and in part, a stimulus to it. There are several fundamental dichotomies within the communist system. The most important, of course, is the genuine division of economic interest between the economy of the Soviet Union and those of its smaller neighbors. This division is widened by the "reverse colonialism" which makes the Soviet Union a major exporter of raw materials and a net importer of manufactured goods. A second division stems from differences in the role foreign trade plays in the economies of the various members of the alliance. The Soviet Union and Bulgaria tend to be less impressed by the need for fundamental changes and for rapid progress toward multilateral trade. This reflects in part the structure of their economies, as well as their political interests and philosophical conservatism. Hungary, Czechoslovakia, and Poland, on the other hand, depend heavily on international trade. They are inclined to be more suspicious of rigid Comecon structures which divert their trade from more profitable markets, impose commitments on them, and impede their economic growth. There is further a close relationship between dependence on foreign trade and propensity for internal economic reform. The concepts of production efficiency, realistic costing, profit, and so on come much more naturally to nations which are, perforce or by tradition, traders. As has been noted, the professional economists, as well as the politicians, in these countries are preoccupied with the notion of "a fundamental reorganisation of the price system, a greater dependence on market forces, supply and demand; a system is envisaged 'which will allow them to choose what they export, to whom and above all for how much, on a much more rational basis than in the past.' "[2]

In contrast, Soviet Russian national interests naturally incline its leaders toward a preoccupation with cohesion, order, and the solidarity of the alliance. In the view of at least some East European officials, a common fallacy in the West is the belief that the Soviet Union is the leading force in seeking the liberalization of trade within Comecon. In their opinion, Soviet officials have relatively little to gain from this in economic terms and thus their concern is largely strategic, while the smaller countries have the most to gain from an effective system of unimpeded multilateral trade.[3]

Thirdly, there is the dichotomy between the developed and less-devel-

2. Andrew Shonfield, "Changing Commercial Policies in the Soviet Block," *International Affairs*, 44 (1968), 1.

3. Although this view has not been published, it is the author's experience that it is widely held by East European officials.

oped nations of the alliance. This is essentially the division between the northern and southern tiers of East European states. Like most less-developed countries, those in the communist world are deeply conscious of their vulnerability to exploitation and of their need for special protection. They are apprehensive that large-scale, "rational" schemes for the development of the whole region will necessarily follow the biblical injunction "to him that hath shall be given, and from him that hath not shall be taken away even that which he hath." This was at least one of the bases of the Rumanian economic "defection" in 1964, and it presents a formidable problem for communist statesmen because it cuts to some extent across the other divisions within the alliance. In the dispute between the "liberal" trading nations and the "conservative" autarkic states, it is possible at least to imagine the victory of one or the other in terms of those categories. Whether this victory went to the multilateralists or to the planners, the "developed-underdeveloped dilemma" would remain. In a decentralized, more market-oriented system, the less-developed countries would remain more protectionist, though eager to maintain planned high prices for their primary exports. In a planned system, the planners anxious to optimize economic growth for the region as a whole would be constantly tempted to neglect the south. In either case the cycle of dissension would begin again.

The general facts concerning the religious, ethnic, and cultural diversity of Eastern Europe are well known, as is the enormous gulf of "custom and fancy" between the oriental and occidental parts of the communist world. It is not our purpose here to elaborate on these basic conditions, but simply to note that they are indeed basic and that they make the task of compromising economic differences infinitely more difficult. The story of Rumania is best known, and it may well be that Rumanian nationalism would in any case have been troublesome to the Soviet Union. The inevitable trouble, however, arose from the correctness and force of the Rumanian assessment that the national economic interest is dependent upon a large measure of isolation and protection, rather than upon cooperation. Less widely discussed is the case of Czechoslovakia, a country with a strong sense of national identity but traditionally well disposed toward the Soviet Union. The logic of its economic situation obliged it to develop national economic policies which, in the event, brought it into conflict with the Soviet Union and doubtless deepened national feelings to the point where a renewed and genuine cooperation with its larger partner must be relegated to the remote future. As Professor Sik stressed in 1967, "To surmount the problems in foreign trade – and, if it does not expand, the Czechoslovak economy cannot grow – it is essential to change the structure of the national economy and make its development more flexible, especially to change the proportions between the share of domestic and imported input in the value of exports and to increase the effectiveness of foreign trade. Of course, this requires a better relation between domestic production costs and prices on world markets. And this, in turn, requires that gains or losses from a specific development of foreign trade have a direct effect on income, both of the production enterprises and the foreign-trade enterprises – instead of going directly to the state budget." [4] This issue of economic rationality inevitably becomes one of national independence.

It was this interaction of economic needs and national aspirations which dominated economic relations among the communist states in the late sixties. That its expression was most dramatic in Rumania and Czechoslovakia should not obscure the general nature of the phenomenon. In all the countries of the alliance there was an increasing awareness of the need for national economic initiatives. This was at least one of the reasons why the executive and plenary sessions of Comecon in 1968 and 1969 could do no more than agree upon the need for reform.

II

Leaving aside the difficulties presented by varying national interests, the second major political problem facing communist leaders in the late sixties had to do with the paradox of central planning versus economic reform. "The root of the problem," according to one scholar, "is that Comecon has entered the era of economic reform with its command economy-oriented superstructure and its arbitrary *modus operandi* essentially unchanged since its early Stalinist beginnings." [5] Perhaps the depth of this dilemma can be better grasped if we imagine the Western nations maintaining their elaborate system of tariff regulation, monetary exchange, and sales distribution while at the same time instituting a government-directed bilateral quota system to govern commodity movements. The one would tend to make the other redundant, but this is only part of the difficulty. If it were simply a question of modifying the superstructure to accommodate

4. Ota Sik, *Plan and Market under Socialism* (White Plains, N.Y., 1967), p. 82.

5. Michael Gamarnikow, "Economic Reforms and Comecon," paper prepared for the VI Internationale Konferonz Studiengesellschaft fur Fragen Mittel – under Osteuropaischer Partnerschaft (Deidesheim, 1970). For an excellent discussion of the current problems of Comecon see Michael Gamarnikow, "Is Comecon Obsolete?" *East Europe*, 17, no. 4 (1968), 12–19.

accomplished economic reforms common to all members, the task would be manageable. But, on the contrary, there is a very large variation in the degree to which individual countries have accepted the need for change.

The primary need in the late sixties has therefore been "to harmonise the internal models of planning and management . . . and the divergent economic policies of the member nations." [6] So far no such harmonization has proved possible because the differences involved are fundamental. The New Economic Mechanism in Hungary, for example, is not simply a matter of tinkering with the arbitrary mechanisms of a command economy. It aims at much more, including the decentralization of important decisions to the enterprises. This is particularly important in the case of the foreign trade corporations which are now judged, like other enterprises, by their productivity and profits. Previously, they had simply implemented their individual sections of an overall import-export plan, but now they operate only within broad guidelines. More significantly, they are allowed to retain a portion of their profits and to dispose of them as they see fit. One managing director told the author that he hoped part of this "profit" would be used to reward the most effective members of the executive staff, particularly the sales staff, while the remainder would be invested in productive enterprises for which good foreign markets had been developed. Furthermore, some enterprises, including at least eight collective and state farms, have been granted the privilege of dealing directly with foreign concerns. The government has, in short, decided to mobilize the energies and expertise of enterprise management in order to push the economy forward within a generally agreed framework.

The difficulties of combining such an approach, which is more or less common to Hungary, East Germany, and Poland, with authoritarian, centrally directed economies of countries such as Rumania, Bulgaria, and the Soviet Union are enormous. Increasingly these difficulties resemble those of East-West trade in the fifties. The "reformist" managers demand access to enterprises in the "traditionalist" countries, while the "traditionalists" call for the coordination of plans and the declaration of firm quotas. If it is true, as most observers agree, that the tide is running in favor of economic reform and more freedom for the enterprises, the bureaucratic superstructure of Comecon must inevitably be modified. In particular, its guidelines and directives must gradually become more general and vague, as the enterprises are allowed more direct contact with one another and more latitude to make their own decisions. But herein lies the third and perhaps the

6. Gamarnikow, "Is Comecon Obsolete?"

most difficult of the political problems facing the organization – the question of economic relations with the West.

More freedom and a greater emphasis on the yardstick of profit in the enterprises may well mean a move toward Western markets. It has been observed that the rate of increase in intra-Comecon trade has decreased sharply during the sixties (see Table 1). At the same time, trade with noncommunist countries has been increasing (see Table 2). There are a number of reasons for this, including the technological gap between the Eastern and Western countries, and the impact of the economic reforms themselves.

Once given the opportunity to make the most profitable decisions, en-

Table 1. Annual Intra-East European Trade Growth, 1956–67[a]

Year	Value (in millions of U.S. dollars)	Percentage of Annual Growth[b]
1956	4,830	
1957	5,940	23.0
1958	6,060	2.0
1959	7,390	21.9
1960	8,080	9.3
1961	8,970	11.0
1962	10,170	13.4
1963	11,030	8.5
1964	11,960	8.4
1965	12,460	4.2
1966	12,540	0.6
1967	13,740	9.6

SOURCE: United Nations, *Yearbook of International Trade Statistics 1967* (New York, 1969), p. 27.

[a] East Europe: Albania, Bulgaria, Czechoslovakia, East Germany, Hungary, Rumania, and the Soviet Union.

[b] The annual average growth rate for 1956–67 was 10.2 per cent; for 1960–67 it was 8.1 per cent.

Table 2. Eastern Europe and the USSR: Distribution of Foreign Trade by Area in Selected Years

Area	1958	1961	1963	1965	1966	1967
Eastern Europe and USSR	62.1%	66.0%	68.7%	66.0%	63.0%	64.1%
Noncommunist countries	29.1	28.6	26.7	29.3	31.6	31.2
Other communist countries	8.8	5.5	4.6	4.7	5.4	4.7
Total	100.0	100.0	100.0	100.0	100.0	100.0

SOURCE: Subcommittee on Foreign Economic Policy of the Joint Economic Committee, Congress of the United States, *Economic Developments in Countries of Eastern Europe, a Compendium of Papers* (Washington, D.C., 1970), p. 544.

terprise managers have not confined themselves to the limited possibilities of the East European region. They have naturally examined the advantages of broader cooperation with industrial concerns in the West where it has seemed that the necessary investment capital and convertible currencies could be obtained. The vertical integration of certain aspects of the Hungarian agricultural industry with West German suppliers is only one example. East German trade with the West increased substantially in 1969, and the Polish authorities continue to cherish their Western commercial connections. Having been at least partly released from planning directives, East Europeans seek the most flexible arrangements possible and these can seldom be found in the more conservative East European countries or under the aegis of Comecon.

The difficulties with pricing are dealt with in somewhat more detail below. It is sufficient at this point to note that the relatively rigid Comecon system, tied to world prices, tends to encourage the more independent managers to seek the higher quality goods available in the West. There is little incentive to import lower quality Comecon manufactured goods so long as convertible exchange is available to finance purchases in the West. Similarly, the rational course is to export the relatively few first-class goods, not to Comecon, but to buyers who will pay in freely convertible currency. Thus Comecon is inclined to become a market in which to dispose of goods that will not sell elsewhere and in which to buy only when convertible currency is not available. This is an overstatement of the case but there is little doubt that economic reform at the enterprise level, combined with the outmoded Comecon bureaucratic structure, has greatly increased the pull of Western Europe or, perhaps more correctly, has led managers to think increasingly in all-European terms.

The question of technology is, of course, closely related to economic reform and pricing. There is perhaps an analogy between the past progress of events within individual countries and the current developments within the communist commonwealth. In the early stages of Soviet national development, the demand for consumer goods was so high that practically anything could be sold. In these circumstances central production plans were feasible, but as productive capacity increased and the market became more sophisticated, a surplus of poor quality goods piled up in the warehouses. Similarly, in communist international trade, marketing was not a difficult problem when all the national economies were recovering from war and decades of neglect. Having reached their current levels of development, "the time when shoddy and technologically backward products could be freely unloaded in the friendly socialist markets is definitely over."[7]

This difficulty is further compounded by the dichotomy between the northern and southern tiers of the communist bloc. The poorer countries are eager to catch up as soon as possible and for this they need the best and most up-to-date capital equipment which, in the most optimistic view, may enable them to "leapfrog" their neighbors, at least in some industries. Such equipment is available in the West and therefore the more developed communist countries of the north have some difficulties in negotiating cooperative agreements with the south. In certain respects, the advantage for both groups lies elsewhere.

Finally, in this question of an "all-European" concept some countries, most notably Rumania, are wary of cooperative arrangements on purely political grounds. Deals with Western firms leave the national sovereignty unscathed, but there is always the suspicion that coordinated production within the framework of Comecon may involve, either immediately or in the long run, some loss of independence.

III

The three major political problems within Comecon interact with one another and are manifested differently in different countries, but they remain at the base of the East European dilemma. They are further complicated by a series of economic difficulties, all of which have political implications.

First, and by far the most important, is the question of pricing. No doubt some progress has been made, but by and large the unkind phrase first used by Frederic Pryor in 1961 remains valid. Pricing in Eastern Europe is a "boiling stew of propaganda, ideology, economic forces and self-delusion." It is, furthermore, at the root of many of the current disagreements within Comecon.

Lacking any other means of relating the domestic prices of the various countries for the purpose of foreign trade, Comecon has fallen back on the yardstick of world prices. Until January 1, 1966, world price averages for 1957–58 were used in Comecon trade. At that time, the base was shifted to the averages for 1960–64. Since this resulted in a downward revision of the prices for raw materials and fuels, it led to serious disparities between the more industrialized countries and those which export mainly raw materials. Furthermore, it has occasioned a good deal of dissatisfaction in the

7. *Rynki Zagraniczne* (Warsaw), April 4, 1967. Quoted in Gamarnikow, "Is Comecon Obsolete?" p. 13.

Soviet Union which is the main supplier of raw materials to the smaller countries. The terms of trade have changed sharply to the disadvantage of the Soviet Union and in spite of a higher volume, the value of Soviet exports has actually gone down. A controversy has ensued between the USSR, with some support from other Comecon suppliers of raw materials, and the other members of Comecon, particularly those from the industrialized north. Soviet writers argue that prices of raw materials should be raised to bring them more into line with production and transport costs, even though this might entail a departure from the world-price-base principle. Others contend that Comecon cannot create its own prices because "comparing real costs in the alliance is still absolutely impossible." [8]

The dilemma is serious and inescapable. If the world price relatives are maintained, enterprise managers, with their increasing freedom of action, will be attracted toward Western markets, particularly for imports of manufactured goods. If, on the other hand, the Soviet Union is successful in raising the prices of raw materials, its Comecon purchasers will in turn be encouraged to negotiate offsetting increases in the prices of their manufactured exports or to seek sources for raw materials increasingly outside the area. In either event, some adverse consequences for intrabloc trade seem to be unavoidable.

A further unhappy result for the Comecon countries is that, with a fixed 1960–64 base and declining world prices for raw materials and agricultural products, they will tend to sell at higher prices within the alliance than outside. For example, as can be seen in the following tabulation, Soviet wheat was sold to Western markets (in this instance, c.i.f. Amsterdam on December 17, 1968) at a price comparable to those of Western wheats.[9]

	Cost Per Bushel (in U.S. dollars)	*Cost Per Metric Ton (in U.S. dollars)*
Canadian no. 2 Manitoba	2.02	74.82
USSR no. 121	1.91	71.48
U.S. no. 2 dark wheat northern spring 14%	1.92	71.11
Argentina wheat	1.77	65.56

On the other hand, the next tabulation indicates the cost of Soviet wheat at the average Comecon price for 1966 (probably unchanged for 1966–70) f.o.b. Soviet border sold to three representative communist countries.[10]

8. Gamarnikow, "Is Comecon Obsolete?" p. 14.

9. *Foreign Agriculture*, USDA, Washington, D.C., 6 (1968), 53.

10. *Vneshriaia Torgovlia, SSSR, 1966* (Moscow, 1967), quoted in Research Report of Research Department of *Free Europe*, April 9, 1968.

	Cost Per Metric Ton (in U.S. dollars)
Czechoslovakia	69.34
East Germany	66.61
Poland	60.34

To better understand this situation, it is worth quoting Lewis Fischer's comments on the meaning of these tabulations: "To meet competition, the Soviet Union is prepared to adjust the price of USSR No. 121 to the price of qualitatively equivalent U.S. No. 2 Dark Northern Spring, regardless of how much higher domestic price and production costs. The [tabulations] also [show] that Soviet wheat sells for higher prices to Comecon members than to buyers on World Markets. Discounting transport cost of $7.00 from the Amsterdam price, the price f.o.b. Soviet border amounts to $64.48 per ton, vs. $69.34 and $66.61 charged to Czechoslovakia and East Germany respectively. During the current Five Year Plan, 1966–70, the Soviet Union has been able to maintain the disproportion in its 'offering.' " [11]

It is naive to regard this situation, as some Western economists have in the past, as simply a question of Soviet exploitation of its weaker partners. There is always a price to pay for regional economic union and, as Michael Gamarnikow has pointed out, there are strong arguments on the Soviet side: "First, there is, indeed, an over-all raw-material, fuel and grain deficit within the Comecon area and only the Soviet Union has the economic potential to reduce these deficiencies. Second, there is some truth to the Soviet claim that under the present terms of Comecon trade the primary and extractive products tend to be undervalued. Moreover, regardless of the supply and demand situation on the world market, the specific conditions prevailing in the Comecon area tend to favor raw-material producers." [12]

What is of interest here is not so much the relative merits of the arguments on both sides of the controversy as the discussion of the issues in open debate. The Soviet Union has very large resources, through the revaluation of the ruble and other more direct pressures, to bring its recalcitrant partners to heel. But this is hardly the way to build a cooperative enterprise in the region. An economic organization from which most of the members are seeking relief or escape is bound to be unstable.

The second technical problem relates to the development of multilateral trade which was a major concern of Khrushchev's document "The Basic

11. Lewis A. Fischer, *Comecon, Agricultural Product Markets,* Agricultural Economics Research Council of Canada, 1970, p. 2.

12. Gamarnikow, "Is Comecon Obsolete?" p. 15.

Principles of the International Socialist Division of Labor." The number of countries involved and, more important, the number of commodities, makes the planning of multilateral exchanges a formidable and perhaps an impossible task. Yet it is generally agreed that only through multilateral balancing can the maximum trading potential of the region be realized. In an attempt to alleviate this problem the International Bank of Economic Cooperation was created in 1964. Table 3 suggests that its achievements have so far been quite limited.

Table 3. Clearing-Ruble, Convertible-Currency, and Credit Operations of the International Bank for Economic Corporation

Item	1964	1965	1966	1967
Total transactions on clearing-ruble accounts (billions of rbls.)	22.9	24.1	23.9	26.6
Total credit transactions (billions of rbls.)	1.5	1.8	1.6	1.9
End-year amount of credits outstanding (billions of rbls.)	0.126	0.204	0.249	0.314
Credit transactions as a percentage of clearing-ruble transactions (2:1)	6.6	7.5	6.7	7.1
Average length of credits (months)	1.0	1.4	1.9	2.0
Transactions on convertible-currency accounts (billions of rbls.)	1.1	2.6	3.8	9.0
Convertible-currency transactions as a percentage of clearing-ruble transactions (6:1)	4.8	10.8	15.9	33.8

SOURCE: *U.N. Economic Bulletin for Europe*, 20, no. 1, p. 51.

The reasons for this limited progress are manifold. They include in particular the fundamentally material nature of Soviet-style planning and management and the consequent difficulities in rendering the Soviet and Eastern European currencies truly convertible.[13] The influence of the more conservative regimes has been of major significance. The continuing preference of the bureaucrats for bilateral arrangements has been an important obstacle to multilateral trade. Frederic Pryor in his 1963 study demonstrated how far the Comecon countries are from reaching their theoretical trade potential.[14] Table 4 indicates the discrepancy between the population and resources of the Comecon countries and their participation in world trade.

13. For an interesting discussion of these issues in light of the recent economic reforms, see M. R. Wyczalkowski, "Communist Economics and Currency Convertibility," *IMF Staff Papers*, July 1966.

14. Frederic L. Pryor, *The Communist Foreign Trade System* (Cambridge, Mass., 1963), p. 41.

Table 4. Percentage Share of Three Groups of Countries in World Trade, 1960–66

Group	1960	1962	1963	1964	1965	1966
Share of World Exports[a]						
Comecon countries	13.1	13.5	13.3	13.0	13.0	12.7
Capitalist countries	65.9	66.2	66.5	67.2	67.7	68.4
Developing countries	21.0	20.3	20.2	19.8	19.3	18.9
Share of World Imports[a]						
Comecon countries	12.7	13.2	13.1	12.6	12.2	11.9
Capitalist countries	65.1	66.1	67.0	67.9	68.7	69.5
Developing countries	22.2	20.7	19.9	19.5	19.1	18.6

SOURCE: *Vnechniaia Torgovlia*, no. 8 (Moscow, 1967).
[a] Percentage of share in total world exports and imports.

The evidence suggests that even within the region there has been little or no progress toward the multilateralization of trade since 1963. A recent quantitative study shows that intrabloc trade remained highly bilateral through the mid-sixties.[15]

There is very little in this record to give comfort to the Comecon authorities. It is difficult to foresee very rapid improvement but, insofar as this remains a possibility, it lies with the "reformers" and the degree of success which they encounter in getting their ideas accepted at the international as well as the national level.

In turning from the complex mechanisms of pricing and multilateral trade to the more straightforward questions of joint projects, the record of Comecon has on the whole been much more encouraging. By the mid-sixties, the Friendship Pipeline, the Rolling Stock Pool, and the Electricity Grid were all well developed. However, in the second half of the decade, as more sophisticated and far-reaching proposals came under discussion, the promise of earlier successes began to fade. Two examples will suffice.

First, in the development of nuclear energy, Comecon's Permanent Committee for the Peaceful Uses of Atomic Energy, under a Soviet chairman, "has repeatedly postponed consideration of meaningful action at the Comecon level." [16] Jaroslav Polach in an excellent review of the advances made in this area noted that "by the mid-sixties so little progress had been made that one by one the eastern European states were compelled to scrap their original plans and draw up a second generation of more modest —

15. J. Wilczynski, "Multilateralization of East-West Trade," *Economia Internazionale*, May 1968, p. 302.

16. Jaroslav G. Polach, "Nuclear Power in East Europe," *East Europe*, 17, no. 5 (1968), 11.

and more realistic – programs of nuclear development. By the beginning of 1968 only two nuclear power stations were in existence in eastern Europe. One, in East Germany, became operational in May 1966 and has been generating power on and off ever since. The other, in Czechoslovakia, is expected to be ready for operation in 1969." [17]

Table 5 indicates how far achievements have fallen short of original plans.

Table 5. Eastern Europe's Nuclear Power Plans Announced before 1960

Year in Which Nuclear Capacity to be Critical	Megawatts of Gross Electrical Power
1960	220
1965	2,100–2,700
1970	6,700–7,400
1975	12,900–21,500
State of capacity, January 1, 1968	
In operation	70
Under construction	150

SOURCE: Jaroslav Polach, "Nuclear Power in East Europe," *East Europe*, 17, no. 5 (1968), 6.

The second example concerns economic cooperation on the Danube which would seem to be a sine qua non for the optimum development of the region. In 1964, the Hungarian government proposed far-reaching plans for cooperation among the Danubian countries. Janos Kadar stated at that time: "The peoples in the Danubian basin live in a community of fate: we must get on together or perish together. There is no other way for the peoples in the Danubian area. If we live under different social systems, we should adhere to the principle of peaceful coexistence. If on the other hand we live under a socialist social system, we should join forces in foreign policy and economic cooperation, in accordance with socialist principles, and should accelerate the development of all of us to the good and happiness of all the peoples living in these parts. This is our policy." [18]

The response to the Hungarian proposal was, to say the least, far from encouraging. The most friendly reply came from the Austrian chancellor who remarked, "It may possibly be here where the Danube connects Western and Eastern Europe that the greatest chance exists to begin to strength-

17. *Ibid.*, p. 3.

18. *Nepszabadsag*, February 12, 1965. Quoted in Charles Andras, "The Slow Drift to Danubian Cooperation," *East Europe*, 17, no. 2 (1968), 21.

en understanding between East and West."[19] The reaction from the communist countries was less positive, and the Soviet Union ignored Kadar's initiative. All of this suggests that the strategic interests of the "socialist community" are deemed to override any broader schemes for regional cooperation.

IV

Thus, Eastern Europe in the second half of the sixties presented a confused mosaic of old purposes and new hopes. Logic and the force of circumstance moved all members of the alliance toward economic reform, but old fears, rigid bureaucratic structures, and ideological concerns prevented the development of a coherent "new model." Old and new divisions criss-crossed one another so that general agreement on economic cooperation proved impossible. It was in most respects a gloomy picture, disappointing both to the more imaginative leaders in Eastern Europe and to those outside the communist bloc who desired some progress toward real cooperation between the two Europes.

But the picture can easily be painted in too dark colors. Many of the shortcomings and difficulities in the Comecon system have their counterparts in Western economic groupings, including the Common Market. A narrow and irresponsible nationalism is not a monoply of the East European countries, nor are the problems of large and small, developed and underdeveloped members in an alliance exclusive to Comecon. The balance between planning and the market mechanism is a dilemma which all statesmen face, communist and noncommunist alike. There have also been times when Western countries have been alarmed by the pull of Eastern markets, particularly in the depressed areas of the West. Pricing for raw materials and agricultural products is not a question which has been neatly answered by the noncommunist world but rather a perennial problem which is contained rather than solved. The mechanisms for multilateral trade are considerably more flexible in the West but still protectionism and economic nationalism raise difficulties.

What then is the essential difference, if any, between the "disarray" of Comecon states in economic affairs and that of the Atlantic community? Essentially, there seem to be two considerations. The first is that the trend toward economic reform in Eastern Europe threatens or can be judged to threaten the security of the Eastern alliance. The Eastern communist regimes, and particularly the Soviet elite, depend largely upon their separateness, their insulation from the rest of the world, and their identity as a

19. *Ibid.*, p. 23.

different kind of society for their survival. Reform in many respects implies joining the rest of the world and, to put it perhaps rather crudely, "admitting" the rest of the world. Secondly, the problems for Comecon states, although in many respects not different in kind from those faced in the West, are much more acute. This is the result of the relatively short history of the communist experiment and the concomitant need for rapid change.

It is always possible, of course, that there will be a reversion to former rigid practices in the economic affairs of Eastern Europe. It is certain that the evolution of new models will be slow and that the associated disputes will be acrimonious. It is unlikely that Western statesmen can influence the process very much and it is perhaps unwise for them to try. In conclusion, however, the author may be forgiven for recalling some words which he wrote in 1966 and which still seem relevant. "It seems appropriate to note the curious paradox in Western thought which presents every Communist transaction in the Western world as 'economic penetration' and every Western transaction in the East as a weakening of our position. This kind of analysis indicates a lack of confidence which ill befits our economic strength and our political conviction. It is unlikely that we shall wean Communist statesmen from their convictions by selling them goods however needed and valuable. But it is no more plausible that they will remain unaffected by increasing contact with the efficiency of our system and the abundance which it furnishes. While it is an unrealistic, and perhaps an undesirable dream that we should expect the abandonment of socialism in Eastern Europe, it seems at the very least a reasonable hope that increased commerce will produce some identity of interest and some impetus toward change. To deny this is to overestimate the efficiency of Communist control systems and to undervalue our own success. But in the end, we must return to the choice between precarious security and uncertain hope." [20]

20. Philip E. Uren, comment on H. Gordon Skilling, "Canada and Eastern Europe," *Canadian Slavonic Papers*, 8 (1966), 29.

16

Patterns of Political Change

BY TERESA RAKOWSKA-HARMSTONE

There is nothing novel about the forces of nationalism either in Eastern Europe or in Asia; the preoccupation with economic reform and development has always been characteristic of communist states, as have been the pressures from their people for greater individual and cultural freedoms and for a better life. All these forces seem to have converged, however, in the 1960s and appear to be accelerating into the seventies, introducing new dynamics of change into the societies which, until recently, had been assailed for their "stagnation" by critics and apologists alike. Although numerous factors may be singled out as contributing to the new dynamics, two landmarks stand out as catalytic agents: the Twentieth Congress of the Communist party of the Soviet Union which opened up new avenues in domestic political process through de-Stalinization; and the Sino-Soviet dispute, which rent apart the world communist movement and signaled the emergence of new trends in the relations of communist states with "fraternal" states and with the noncommunist world.

De-Stalinization, initiated by Khrushchev at the 1956 Congress, has shaken the philosophical foundations of the communist system. By destroying the myth of Stalin as the infallible and indeed divine leader, Khrushchev also destroyed, however unintentionally, the myth of infallibility of the party that Stalin had built and led, and thus undermined the very legitimacy of the Soviet system and its claim to universality. The impact, tentative but spreading in Khrushchev's era, has resulted in a general malaise of communist elites which have begun to question ideological and institutional orthodoxy, and to search for a new legitimacy and for novel ways of building a socialist society. Inevitably, in their search for sources of strength, they have turned toward their people, a new alliance in most cases but one which promises benefits to both sides. National communist leaders have strengthened their base of support, and the people have discovered that government is more receptive to their demands. A newfound solidarity and a sense of purpose are to be seen in each country's pursuit of common national goals and in its resentment of outside interference.

The Chinese challenge to Soviet supremacy has irretrievably destroyed the CPSU's position as the leader of the world communist movement. Though Tito's 1948 defiance of Stalin might have been secretly, if doubtfully, admired, the Sino-Soviet dispute made it legitimate, so to speak, to pursue one's "own road to socialism" and to try policies and solutions different from those developed by the Soviet comrades, providing that, given geographic proximity to the Soviet Union, one did not question certain basic doctrinal assumptions too loudly and did not violate certain basic constraints.

The crisis of legitimacy and the Chinese challenge combined have released forces of change which inexorably press toward ever greater differentiation in the domestic and foreign policies of communist states, undermine the unity of the international communist movement, and render questionable the Soviet interpretation of the Marxist dogma, the Soviet model of communist society, and the very principle of Soviet leadership. There is no going back to status quo ante.

I

The crisis of legitimacy affected the Soviet communist elite as much as it did the elites of the ruling and nonruling communist parties throughout the world. For the first time in more than thirty years it became possible to question the fundamental principles of doctrine and the basic assumptions governing communist parties and communist states. The way was opened also for weighing the record, domestic and international, of the CPSU, the assessment to be made not by outsiders but by members of the communist elite. The shattering impact that the denigration of Stalin had on communist intellectuals may best be compared to the shock a believer experiences when the certainties of his faith are suddenly declared invalid. An underground poem, written in the period following the Twentieth Congress by, allegedly, one of Russia's well-known poets, illustrates the point:

> I am building on sand, and that sand
> Only recently seemed to me to be a rock.

It was a rock, and has remained a rock for everybody,
But for me it fell apart and began to flow away.

But I am faithful to the construction program;
Backed up against a wall, hanging by a hair,
I am building on sand which is flowing under my feet,
Slipping out from under my feet.[1]

This disillusionment was not confined to the Soviet Union alone, but was felt even more strongly throughout Eastern Europe. The views expressed in the mid-sixties by Robert Havemann, an East German scientist and life-long party member (since expelled), are typical of the Eastern European communist intellectuals' agonizing reappraisal of their beliefs and their relationship to the party and to society: "Before the Twentieth Party Congress I was a Stalinist. My complete turning away from this mental attitude resulted from the revelations of the Twentieth Party Congress in 1956. . . . The foundations of my belief crumbled under the impact of this earthquake. That, which I think today, that, which I write today, is reconstruction from the rubble. . . . I am in doubt, I am troubled. I make an effort to reflect upon everything myself. . . . Before the Twentieth Party Congress everything the Party said was sacred for me. The Party had the right to censor and to suppress all these ideas which it did not share. Today I know that the Party leadership does not have the right of censorship. I know that everyone of us, inside and outside the Party, has the right and the duty to form an independent judgment, to have an independent view." [2]

Generations of communist leaders struggled unsuccessfully for years under Big Brother's watchful eyes to adapt the Soviet model (developed by Lenin and Stalin from their own understanding of Marx to fit the heritage of Imperial Russia) to societies with differing demands and requirements and a wide variety of political cultures. The model's credibility at last open to question, they turned to national traditions in their need to validate their rule. The lucky few who had gained power by their own strength

1. One of the "Poems from the Underground," in Abraham Brumberg (ed.), *Russia under Khrushchev: An Anthology from "Problems of Communism"* (New York, 1962), p. 415.

2."Warum ich Stalinist war und Antistalinist wurde," a letter to the Free German Youth periodical *Forum*, reprinted in *Die Zeit* (Hamburg), May 7, 1965. Havemann was expelled from the SED for his revisionist views. The questioning of the Stalinist doctrine spread rapidly in Western European parties; the Italian party, for example, has adopted many of the revisionist views. The French party remained orthodox, but went through a crisis which resulted in the expulsion of Roger Garaudy in February 1970.

rather than by the might of the Red Army have from the beginning based their authority in their national heritage – a constant source of friction between them and the Soviet Union. Now the turn is coming for others, if they are to survive in the face of mounting domestic pressures and the bankruptcy of old formulae.

The conscious, if cautious, effort to evolve one's own "national model" of a communist society, which, though comprehensible and acceptable to the people, would retain basic socialist principles, was characteristic of the ruling communist parties in the late sixties. Among communist elites *apparatchiks* still survive (even they have to make concessions to the new demands, however), but the group now in ascendancy is the pragmatists, who represent a strong nationalist commitment. Younger, and frequently better educated than the old style leaders, they are impatient with Byzantine murkiness and the appalling inefficiency of the system, and they attempt to run their countries in a more efficient way giving first priority to national needs and demands. For them, ideology and interests of the "socialist commonwealth" are distinctly of secondary importance. Among ideologues, some tried to reconcile orthodoxy with the need for new philosophical justifications, but many were swept aside because they could not adapt or, like Havemann, because they went too far in their bitter appraisal of the system. The keynote in the reformers' search for a new legitimacy has been the emphasis on broadening the popular base of support. The preoccupation with legitimizing the role of the masses has dominated the policies not only of the pragmatists but also of those ideologues who are anxious to escape the repetition of the crippling and ideologically indefensible phenomenon of the "new class."

As seen from the review in this volume specific policies vary in response to local heritage, ideological commitments, and power constraints. In all cases, however, there is the new emphasis on national determinants leading to the "nationalization," as it were, of communist regimes, although the degree of emphasis ranges from cautious use of national symbolism to outright identification of the ultimate perfection of socialism with a national state. Economic reforms have been a part of the new model in all the communist states. Called forth by the orthodox need to advance on the path of economic development, these reforms have come increasingly to serve the purposes of new legitimation, reflecting the leaders' preoccupation with improving the standards of living and thus satisfying the material demands of the hitherto deprived and increasingly restive populations. Economic reforms have resulted in varying degrees of "goulash communism," have brought a degree of back-door liberalization, and have facilitated ever broader contacts with the noncommunist world.

Liberalization has also been an element of the new model, especially in countries where liberal-democratic traditions are a part of the national heritage. While greater individual freedom and protection of civil rights are among the strongest popular demands, concessions in this sphere are the most dangerous for the survival of the reformers, on the one hand, or for the system itself on the other. True to Western European tradition liberalization opens the door to political pluralism, which in turn undercuts the very raison d'etre of the party – its monopoly of political power. Few of the party reformers are willing to contemplate this alternative as is apparent even in cases like Yugoslavia and Czechoslovakia. The Czech example of 1968 also points to the second danger, that of a Soviet intervention to stop reforms which, in its judgment, have gone too far on the road to liberalization.[3] Liberalizing tendencies have been so strong in Eastern Europe that in almost all cases of economic reform partial retreat has been necessary to avoid the danger of concurrent liberalization. One cannot escape an impression that all the ruling parties are trying to gain the popular goodwill by either economic concessions (as in Hungary), or nationalist emphasis (as in Rumania), to bribe their people away from their dreams to be able to choose freely from among competing political alternatives.

The collectivist aspects of the traditional cultures in the Asian communist states and their relatively undeveloped economies have minimized the pressures for liberalization. But their different political heritage and their mass peasant base made the search for new political and economic models even more imperative than that in Eastern Europe. The emphasis on nationalism is especially crucial there for mobilization of popular support, in view of the peasant's traditional identification with his locality and his memory of colonial interference.

The search for a new and better model of a communist society, as well as the need to justify ideologically the rejection of the Stalinist model, has led communist intellectuals to the sources of Marxism. Disenchanted Eu-

3. The Czechoslovak reformers' sin, that of building their own model of socialism, was made explicit by Vasil Bilak, member of the Presidium of the Communist party of Czechoslovakia (postinvasion), in a Radio Prague broadcast, November 5, 1970: "They wanted to write off, in what was called a 'creative way,' everything that has been created by the Soviet people in the past 50 years under the leadership of the CPSU . . . [and they] reached as far as the need to draw up a new, specifically Czechoslovak model of socialism." Quoted in Ota Sik, "Prague's Spring: Roots and Reasons," *Problems of Communism*, 20, no. 3 (May–June 1971), 2.

ropean communists seeking an escape from the sterility and inhumanity of the official doctrine and a return to the humanist values of the Western heritage attempt to find support in the "original" Marx, especially "young" Marx, and other socialist thinkers. On the other hand, official Soviet and Eastern European ideologues, committed to the justification of the present system, attempt to revalidate its basic ideological and operational assumptions through a revival of Leninism. Asian communist leaders, while paying homage to Marx as their source of inspiration, have largely endowed their ruling ideologies with their own charisma, in a manner reminiscent of the establishment of Leninism-Stalinism. It is Chairman Mao in China who is the fountainhead of ideological formulae and of the simple set of basic "truths," the value of which is sacerdotal rather than intellectual, and which serves to legitimize the total social, economic, and political transformation of the Chinese society. A similar role was played by the late Ho Chi Minh in North Vietnam and is now being played by Kim Il-song in North Korea.

The "Marxism with a human face" discovered by East European revisionists embodies many traditional humanist values. The questioning of the doctrine led to total apostasy for many, while others hover uneasily on the borderline between partial rejection and selective adaptation. Strapped in a straitjacket of Soviet-generated and Soviet-imposed orthodoxy, the revisionists are primarily preoccupied with trying to escape somehow the central dilemma of what Leszek Kolakowski, a Polish philosopher and himself a leading revisionist, calls the "blackmail of a single alternative": "The problem of a single alternative is one of the most important of our time. It most adequately expresses the experience of the Stalinist era and the main tendency of the political Left resulting from that experience. The whole complex of recent political and intellectual attempts at the ideological renaissance of the revolutionary Left — attempts whose effects and effectiveness cannot be foreseen at present — may be characterized generally as an attempt to break through the traditional Stalinist *blackmail of a single alternative* in political life. The permanent Stalinist line was, in fact, to try to create situations where every criticism of Stalinism would amount, objectively, to an automatic adherence to the reactionary camp, to an automatic declaration of solidarity with capitalist imperialism. Stalinism forestalled all social criticism by labeling it counterrevolutionary." Remarking further that persecution under the Stalinist system, as in any system that has become "an end in itself," has always been a "hundred times more violent" for heretics and dissidents than for recognized enemies, Kolakowski concludes that the phenomenon cannot be regarded "as a natural self-defense of a political organism against an invasion of foreign bodies," but as "an attempt to develop an epidermis invulnerable to stimuli likely to produce evolutionary changes — a symptom of regression in the social process." [4]

The sterility and lack of social relevance of the official doctrine have also been stressed by other revisionists. Seconding Kolakowski here is an unlikely companion, Andras Hegedus, the ex-prime minister to Rakosi, Hungary's "Little Stalin." Commenting on the lack of social relevance of historical materialism (which he calls "Stalinist sociology"), Hegedus, now turned revisionist, forecasts greater differentiation for socialist countries under the impact of the rediscovered Marxist sociological tradition: "Although claiming to be scientific, this sociology hardly lived up to this claim, since it avoided confrontation with social reality and refused to admit the possibility of further development. In recent years, we have witnessed a return to reality and discovered that there is a sociological tradition in Marxism which permits of further development. . . . there is a trend toward extending Marxism by confronting its theoretical concepts with actuality. In socialist countries it is likely that Marxist sociology will mean further differentiation." [5]

It is the concept of the leadership role of the communist party and its monopoly of political power which is at the heart of the "single alternative" dilemma. The denial of this monopoly, as well as the recognition of the right of other political forces to exist and the right to pursue political alternatives other than those offered by the party, is the essence of revisionism. The reassessment of the role of the party leads also to reassessment of related concepts such as the relationship between the party and the working class and between the party and the society, the working class' access to power and its participation in the political process through dialogue and gradualist concessions, and eventually through an electoral process with more than one party available. All these lead ultimately to a reappraisal of the relationship between socialism and democracy and to the recognition, however reluctant, of the value of pluralism.

Yet it is precisely the concept of party leadership which is at the base of the survival instinct of the ruling parties, the one issue on which there can-

4. Leszek Kolakowski, "Responsibility and History," in *Toward a Marxist Humanism: Essays on the Left Today* (New York, 1968), pp. 96–98. Kolakowski was expelled from the party and is now in the West.

5. *Kortars*, December 1968, quoted in *East Europe*, 18, no. 2 (1969), 29. Hegedus was reprimanded for his views by the Hungarian party, but retained his party membership.

not be a compromise. All the Eastern European parties, even the most revisionist among them, the Yugoslav League of Communists, still adhere to the principle of the party's leading role. The Czechoslovak Communist party under Dubcek, which, on the eve of the Warsaw Pact intervention was facing the danger of being submerged in political pluralism, has paradoxically embarked on the path of reform in order to strengthen and to legitimize the system and the party's role within it. The revisionists in and out of power are compelled to operate on the fringes of their theoretical discoveries, attempting with varying degrees of success to "square the circle," i.e., to maintain the party's political monopoly while at the same time allowing a limited degree of recognition to social and economic forces, with major effort directed at absorbing their political impact within the existing party-government structures. Revisionists such as Kolakowski and Djilas, who developed their philosophy to its logical conclusion, have placed themselves beyond the "political pale" in their respective countries.

Within permissible limits, however, all East European parties have experimented with economic and social reform and some revisionist ideas.[6] Apart from constraints imposed by the need of the ruling parties to remain in power, the Soviet definition of permissible limits was made clear by its invasion of Czechoslovakia.[7] Revisionism minus Soviet restraints, but with internal ones still operating, can be observed in Yugoslavia. There, the leading role of the party is carefully preserved, but appears tenuous, for its ability to command is severely curtailed by political and economic decentralization, internal democratization, and the formation of pressure groups, reported by observers to be vigorous and aggressive in pursuit of their "selfish" interests. The leadership is nevertheless preoccupied with the need to maximize direct popular participation to avoid the twin evils of Stalinism: bureaucracy and privilege. Although openly discussed, political pluralism is not officially regarded as the logical outcome of reform. Instead, it is hoped that group interests can and will be accommodated within the Yugoslav League and under the umbrella of its auxiliary organizations. At least one member of the top leadership is known to have said that "a gradual overcoming of one party monopoly is possible without the creation of political groupings outside the self-managing socialist structure of society." [8]

6. See chaps. 3–10 above.

7. See chap. 3 above.

8. Mitja Ribicic, Yugoslav premier, in "Draft Documents for the Ninth Congress of the League of Communists of Yugoslavia," *Komunist* (Belgrade), 1968, quoted in *East Europe*, 18, no. 3 (1969), 38.

The Soviet regime's stand on the issue of the leading role of the party is unequivocal. The orthodox formulation of the concept of the dictatorship of the proletariat was restated in the wake of the Czechoslovak invasion during the commemoration of Lenin's centenary.[9] While not adverse to partial reforms, the CPSU has become increasingly uneasy over Eastern European revisionism and its domestic impact, and, despite mounting internal pressures for liberalization, recognition of minority rights, and economic rationality and benefits, its policies are increasingly reverting to the Stalinist mold. In the eyes of a lone open dissenter the party's policies carry the seeds of its own destruction: "In order to remain in power the regime must change and evolve, but in order to preserve itself, everything must remain unchanged." [10] Though simplistic, the opinion carries a grain of truth and in this context is applicable also to Eastern Europe.

Intellectuals are the bearers of revisionism and, not surprisingly, cultural freedom is suppressed throughout the communist world, although restraints are relatively mild in Yugoslavia and increasingly muted in Hungary. In most other countries, following brief, limited, and varying periods of thaw, repressions and a new emphasis on ideological reeducation were characteristic of the late sixties. The seventies promise little change. The Soviet Union has had its writers' trials, the expulsion of Aleksandr Solzhenitsyn from the Writers' Union, the resignation of Tvardovskii from the editorial staff of the one liberal journal, *Novyi Mir*, and the arrest of Andrei Amalrik. Repression of Soviet dissidents continues, but, unlike in Stalinist times, it seems to breed more rather than less disaffection. A "Scientific Opposition" has joined a "Literary Opposition," and Soviet youth appear pessimistic and dissatisfied.[11]

The exuberance of the Prague spring is no more; intellectuals, the first victims of purges following the invasion, are faced by new restrictions resulting from the May 1971 Fourteenth Party Congress, the keynote of which was "Long live the Soviet Union." In Poland repressions proceeded the events of March 1968, and the economic thaw introduced by the new Polish leadership in the spring of 1971 aroused only cautious hopes among intellectuals who, this time, look toward the Hungarian model of cultural self-restraint rather than to Czechoslovakia's intellectual ferment, which

9. See for example V. Platkovskii, "V. I. Lenin o diktature proletariata," *Kommunist* (Moscow), no. 17, November 1969, and other Soviet theoretical journals.

10. Andrei Amalrik, *Will the Soviet Union Survive until 1984?* (New York and Evanston, 1970), p. 22. Amalrik was arrested in June 1970.

11. See Lewis S. Feuer, "Intellectual Opposition," *Problems of Communism*, 19, no. 6 (November–December 1970), 1–16.

was at its height under Dubcek. Rumania, a pioneer in independent foreign policy, remains circumspect in granting internal freedoms; restrictions also remain in other bloc countries. Even in Yugoslavia the spring of 1971 brought new efforts to impose censorship on the much too free public discussion of the country's political and economic ills.

The views of dissident intellectuals on freedom and humane values are typified by a courageous (and suppressed) letter by Solzhenitsyn written in response to his expulsion: "It is high time to remember that we belong first and foremost to humanity. And that man has distinguished himself from the animal world by THOUGHT and SPEECH. And these, naturally, should be FREE. If they are put in chains, we shall return to the state of animals."[12] Nevertheless, the official response to pressures for greater cultural freedom emphasizes the existence "of a single alternative," as can be seen in this warning issued by a Central Committee secretary of the Polish United Workers' party to the Polish Writers' Congress in February 1969: "The Party will consistently oppose and eliminate from cultural life all that is politically hostile and ideologically alien to socialism and combat signs of anti-socialist activities waged under a cloak of freedom."[13]

As if to underscore the long-range futility of the party's efforts, the following statement of the Polish Episcopate read in Polish churches on January 1, 1971, expressed the broad spectrum of individual, social, economic, and national freedoms. It condemned the government's forcible suppression of the December 1970 riots in the Baltic cities, and appealed for: "The right to freedom of conscience and freedom of religious life together with full normalization of relations between the Church and State; the right of freely shaping the culture of one's own nation, according to the spirit of the Christian principles of coexistence of people; the right to social justice, expressed in fulfilling just demands; the right to truth in social life, to information according with the truth, and to free expression of one's views and demands; the right to material conditions which insure decent existence of the family, and of each individual citizen; and the right to such an attitude towards the citizens that they are not insulted, harmed or persecuted in anything."[14]

12. Aleksandr Solzhenitsyn, "An Open Letter to the Secretariat of the Russian Republic Writers' Union," November 12, 1969, quoted in "Chronicle of Current Events," *Novoe Russkoe Slovo*, no. 11 (6), December 31, 1969.

13. Stefan Olszowski, secretary of the Central Committee of the PUWP at the Seventeenth Writers' Congress, *Trybuna Ludu*, February 8, 1969, quoted in *East Europe*, 18, no. 3 (1969), 48.

14. Quoted in *East Europe*, 20, no. 2 (1971), 45.

The rejection of Stalinism in China has its roots in forces different from those in Eastern Europe, the most important of which are its political culture, its stages of revolutionary and economic development, and the party's road to power. The "single alternative" still rules in Peking but in its Maoist rather than its Stalinist guise, and the party's principle of leadership has been blurred by the role played by the People's Liberation Army, and overshadowed by the direct ascendancy of the Leader. Revisionism has been replaced in China by permanent revolution, and the individual's rights and freedoms by the collectivist mass participation in the building of a new society on Maoist foundations. The masses, in direct communication with the Leader, serve to combat the same twin evils of Stalinism, bureaucracy and privilege, that the revisionists abhor, for these have also been the scourge of the traditional China. Chairman Mao's insistence on the perpetuation of the revolutionary pitch is in opposition to the desire of party and state bureaucrats to consolidate and institutionalize their power, and the struggle between them has resulted in a specific rhythm in Chinese developments, with revolutionary leaps (the Civil War, the Great Leap Forward, and the Great Proletarian Cultural Revolution), alternating with periods of consolidation. In personal terms this dialectic has been reflected in the Mao Tse-tung–Liu Shao-ch'i dichotomy and, after the Cultural Revolution, presumably in the dichotomy of Mao and Chou En-lai. It is interesting to note that Mao and Tito, the two extremes on the communist spectrum, are both preoccupied ideologically with the "new class" dilemma, and, in the building of a "socialist" society, both attempt to find ways to escape the need for a Soviet-type privileged bureaucracy which oppresses the masses and sacrifices revolutionary goals to self-perpetuation. Mao's path has led through collectivism and revolutionary rejuvenation; Tito's through emphasis on the value of popular participation in politics and the reassertion of individual and group rights.

II

The primacy of politics, enforced under the Stalinist model of command economy through centralized planning and the party's control over supply, distribution, wages, prices, and currency, has been the cardinal rule in the economic decision-making of communist states. In the sixties, however, mounting economic problems became an important cause of the dissatisfaction with Stalinism, and generated a need for economic reform in all but a few communist states. In the Soviet Union and Eastern Europe the command model had served the exigencies of development at the mobilization stage, but its efficacy at the postmobilization stage [15] has come to be questioned because of the slowdown in the overall rate of economic growth (dangerous in the face of capitalist competition), as well as the general stagnation and waste, the decline in productivity, and the shortages and poor quality of consumers goods. Economic reform in Eastern Europe became a matter not of choice but of necessity.

The need for improvements in the rate of economic growth, in labor productivity, and in the equalization of supply and demand made it essential to replace direct economic control mechanisms with indirect ones at least in part, in order to elicit response to market demands and to utilize better the profit motive and entrepreneurial elements in the economic process. Communist leaders tend to agree on the need for reform and the general direction it should take, i.e., a degree of decentralization in the existing systems of planning and management. Specific measures, however, and their implementation have been hampered by a recognition of the political implications of decentralization, and by the erosion of the party's leading role inherent in the introduction into the political process of forces outside its direct control. "The crux of all the reform blueprints . . . ," says a specialist in the field, "is a gradual transfer of the decision-making powers (at least in the field of micro-economics), from the party establishment and the central administrative apparatus to the new managerial class – and in time, theoretically, through the mechanism of the market to the mass of consumers." [16]

The nature of the reforms and their effectiveness depend largely on the approach each individual country has taken toward the key variables of socialist economy: the relationship between the plan and the market; the amount of freedom allowed to enterprise managers; and the degree of control over prices. Since planning is the hallmark of socialist economy, none of the reform movements envisaged the scrapping of a general plan, but the degree of decentralization and thus the effectiveness and scope of the reforms have hinged on the proportion of the planning process reserved for decisions by the central authorities (the planning "from above") and those allowed to individual enterprises or groups of enterprises (the planning "from below"). The greater the share of planning "from below," the greater the degree of decentralization and managerial (and market) inputs in the economy. Only the major reformers (Yugoslavia, Hungary, and

15. As defined by Richard Burks in *Technological Innovation and Political Change in Communist Eastern Europe*, Rand Corporation (RM-6051-PR.), August 1969.

16. Michael Gamarnikow, "Political Patterns and Economic Reforms," *Problems of Communism*, 18, no. 2 (March–April 1969), 13.

Dubcek's Czechoslovakia) have reduced the share of planning "from above" to the level of general guidelines and indicators, and only the first two (as of the date of this writing) have abandoned the prevalent practice that once the plan is adopted, it is legally binding. Arbitrary price determination is also generally maintained, and partial attempts are made – by major reformers only – to free some prices to respond to the market.[17]

In most cases the reforms have consisted of half-measures, the leaders in each country being caught in an unhappy dilemma between the demands of economic rationality on the one hand, and the imperative of the party's monopoly of power on the other. Amalrik's caustic description of the Soviet reform points to the problem common to all: "The so-called economic reform . . . is in essence a half-measure and is in practice being sabotaged by the party machine, because if such a reform were carried to its logical end, it would threaten the power of the machine." [18]

Still, even in the case of partial reforms, substantial benefits resulted from improved economic performance, particularly in increases of productivity, equalization of supply and demand, improvements in living standards, and, most important, improvements in the economic growth rate. Inevitably some drawbacks also appeared, such as a trend toward inflation and unemployment, a growth in wage expenditures, and an adverse balance of trade.

There is no question that the specific problem is political rather than economic. Measures which make good economic sense are not acceptable politically because they are an obvious impetus to free market pluralism and liberalization. In Yugoslavia, as noted above, the role of party leadership was seriously undermined by the reform movement, and a strong thrust toward liberalization accompanied reforms in Hungary and Czechoslovakia. The Czechs openly acknowledged and even promoted the political consequences of their reform, but were not allowed to continue. Hungarians, fearful of a similar fate, have attempted to minimize the political aspects of their reforms and to maintain and to emphasize the party's leading role. In the aftermath of August 1968 only Hungary remained of the major reformers within the Soviet bloc, and signs of retrenchment became visible in other countries where partial reforms had proved successful, as in the GDR, and even in the Soviet Union where new managerial freedoms are more apparent than real. At the same time it should also be

17. See Harry G. Shaffer, "East Europe: Varieties of Economic Management, I and II," *East Europe*, 19, no. 2 (1970), 20–30, and 20, no. 1 (1971), 35–40.

18. Amalrik, *Will the Soviet Union Survive Until 1984?* p. 30.

noted that countries like Bulgaria and Albania, where little or no reform had been initiated during the sixties, began cautiously to experiment in 1970.

A new impetus to reform in Eastern Europe may have been signaled by the December 1970 riots in Poland, where the pent-up economic grievances of the workers' elite swept Wladyslaw Gomulka out of power. The new pragmatic leadership of Edward Gierek seems more attuned to the desperate urgency of the country's economic needs, and is again moving toward reform, twice planned and twice delayed earlier. It also appears that the lesson of Gomulka has not been lost on other communist leaders. For the first time since the establishment of the system of Stalinist command economy, its *economic* shortcomings have become transformed into *political* action by the very workers whose wishes the party can no longer ignore – not because of ideological reasons but because of the workers' basic importance in the postmobilization economic stage, a point to which I shall return later.

None of the developed communist countries can escape the necessity of reform if they want to avoid economic stagnation and decline and the resulting political consequences; yet the conflict between the free market forces and the party's monopoly of power remains. Given the comparable Czech and Hungarian experiences, it appears that as long as economic experimentation does not challenge the primacy of the party directly, it will be acceptable to the Soviet Union, even if in the process some of the party's decision-making powers are eroded. At the same time a search goes on for other ways out of the dilemma. One solution, adopted most widely, has been to open up the party ranks to the new managerial class and thus to contain new forces within the orthodox power structure. It is a moot point whether this practice results in the politicization of managers or whether it leads to the "embourgeoisement" of the party. Both opinions have been expressed in assessing the situation. Another possible solution, enthusiastically embraced by Soviet leaders, is the application of new computer technology to economic planning, which, it is hoped, will combine centralized political control with economic rationality, and will accommodate market demands without conceding any substantial decision-making powers to local interests.

The role of the workers in the political and economic affairs of the communist states assumed an increasing importance in the sixties, coming into focus in Poland's Baltic riots. The revisionists have long been worried by the leaders' practical disregard of the basic Marxist assumption that in a socialist society producers participate directly in the management of productive forces, and by the hypocritical assertion that the state acts on behalf of the producers and that workers' interests, by definition, are identical with those of the state. Therefore, an important part of the reform in Yugoslavia and Czechoslovakia (and a similar abortive effort in Poland in the fifties) has been the introduction of workers' councils, their power ranging from actual self-management (Yugoslavia) to a "partnership" with the state (Poland). The Czech attempt, like their whole reform, has been scrapped, but their effort to defend the gains of their "spring" provides us with a classic formulation of the producers' role as seen by the reformers: "The only possible way the bureaucratic administrative model of our socialist society can be transformed into a democratic model is by decentralizing the state's control over ownership rights and transferring it to those in whose interest the socialist enterprises operate – namely the workers' councils in the enterprise." [19]

The idea of a "partnership," as typified by Poland, was contemptuously dismissed because it retained the dominant role of the state. In promoting producers' rights in the partnership, however, Czech reformers understood "producers" to mean a workers' collective rather than individual managers, an important distinction in their view between a "socialist" and a "capitalist" market.

The 1970 Polish events forced the communist leadership within the Soviet orbit to reexamine the workers' rights and responsibilities in their producer-consumer capacity, and led to a new emphasis on the role of the trade unions. In the light of current announcements, the unions are to transmit real workers' needs and grievances to the leadership and to have a say in economic decision-making, but they still will be denied the right to equal partnership. At the plenum of the Polish Central Council of Trade Unions (February 1971), its chairman, Kruczek, asserted that "workers' criticism has shown that trade unions have not rightly fulfilled their basic function as representatives of interests and defenders of the working class," and that, in production matters, they should act "from the crew point of view" rather than from that of the administration. He also criticized Polish unions for their "excessive submissiveness" in not opposing unrealistic economic concepts and decisions.[20] Echoing these statements, President Ceausescu of Rumania declared that the old con-

19. Rudolf Slansky, Jr., *Prace*, February 18, 1969, quoted in *East Europe*, 18, no. 4 (1969), 31. Workers' councils in Czechoslovakia were formally abolished in July 1970; shortly thereafter control over trade unions was consolidated and their number substantially reduced. *Ibid.*, 19, no. 2 (1970), 50.

20. Quoted in *ibid.*, 20, no. 4 (1971), 42.

veyor belt role trade unions played for the party was no longer "adequate to the present state of Rumania's social development" and called for a bigger role for workers' representatives in factory management.[21] It is too early to tell whether under this program the influence of the workers in the economic decision-making process will be other than nominal, but at least the leaders realize that their interests and demands can no longer be ignored.

Another aspect of the impact of even a partial reform on East European societies is their developing economic cooperation with the West and particularly with Western Europe. This has flourished in relations not only between states but also between individual socialist enterprises and capitalist firms. Numerous agreements and protocols provide for cooperation in production, marketing and sales service, technology and research, and even investment projects, ranging from small pilot ventures to huge undertakings. Here again Yugoslavia and Hungary lead the way, but East Germany, Poland, as well as Bulgaria are also involved. Rumania, which cautiously began economic connections with the West in the sixties, has significantly forged ahead in this area in 1970–71. A characteristic feature of East-West economic agreements is the transfer of capital and technology from the capitalist to the communist countries. The capital needs of the communist states can no longer be satisfied by squeezing agriculture and consumers, which had been so effective at the mobilization stage; the technological needs of their advancing economies can be met only by the West.[22] Although all such exchanges are carried out under the aegis of the communist governments involved, they clearly favor entrepreneurial habits and elements within communist societies, and foster closer and increasingly more intimate contacts with the capitalist world.

The demand for the type of economic reform present in the developed communist societies is absent in Asia where the key problem, as in Russia in the 1920s, is the need to develop and to industrialize. Nevertheless, in Asia as in Eastern Europe, the Stalinist model has been found wanting, because of its obvious pro-urban, pro-bureaucratic bias, and the depressing long-range effects it has had on agricultural productivity and the welfare of the peasant masses. Stalin's deliberate squeeze of agriculture to gain capital for industrialization is contemptuously dismissed by Mao Tse-

21. Jonathan Steele, "Polish Revolt Starts a Thaw," *Manchester Guardian Weekly* (London), April 3, 1971, p. 6.

22. See Michael Gamarnikow, "Industrial Cooperation: East Europe Looks West," *Problems of Communism*, 20, no. 3 (May–June 1971), 41–48.

tung as counterproductive: "The agricultural policy of the Soviet Union has always been wrong in that *it drains the pond to catch the fish.*" [23]

Instead, the Chinese decision (which, despite internal political upheavals, has increasingly shown its validity in the economically undeveloped peasant society) has been to concentrate on a labor-intensive rather than a capital-intensive type of development, and to give priority to agriculture rather than to industry in the development timetable. This priority has been reaffirmed in the aftermath of the Cultural Revolution.[24] Emphasis has been placed on stimulating agricultural productivity through educational as well as participatory methods, with state procurement kept at a level which allows for reinvestment and for the development of auxiliary industries essential for the production of consumer goods, a further incentive to productivity. The countryside is the focus of economic development, with industry reduced to a subordinate role, and the huge Chinese manpower utilized to the utmost in the absence or shortage of advanced technology. Specialized services are provided by a tremendous shift of the population from the cities into the villages, and by the fanning out, through the countryside, of "barefoot" doctors and "barefoot" technicians. While the primacy of politics is maintained for mass educational and mobilization purposes, Maoism places major emphasis on such economic values as increases in productivity, the need for material incentives (in the sense of economic and social success guaranteeing better standards of living), and entrepreneurship, which is reflected in the glorification of innovation and ingenuity that make for a collective success.[25] The key production unit in agriculture, as elsewhere, is a collective, and collective rather than individual endeavors are markedly stressed. Bureaucracy (inherent in the Soviet extension of the state's managerial powers) is regarded as inimical to grass-root mass efforts, as is individual entrepreneurship (prized in Eastern Europe) because it deprives the collective of its most enterprising elements, and thus decreases its chances of success. The Chinese way of economic development is very much the collective way, while East Europeans have increasingly turned toward the individual as the basic variable in economic progress. The differences in their stage of development notwith-

23. Mao's comment on the 1966 Hupeh proposals as quoted by Jack Gray, "The Economics of Maoism," in *China after the Cultural Revolution* (New York, 1970), pp. 126–27.

24. The Red Flag, as quoted by Norman Webster in *Globe and Mail* (Toronto), February 19, 1970.

25. Gray, *China after the Cultural Revolution, passim.*

standing, both have diverged from the Soviet model in direct response to specific national needs.

III

Much has been said in this volume about nationalism, for it is the major unifying theme in any discussion of the sixties and in every projection into the seventies. In all the communist states, without exception, nationalism has reasserted itself as the most significant force, inclusive of the revival of that familiar phenomenon, Greater Russian chauvinism. For communist leaders nationalism has increasingly become the source of new legitimacy and the strongest link uniting them to the people they govern.

Nationalism was one of the dynamic influences which shaped the destiny of Eastern Europe and the Balkans in the past, and its relation to communism has not always been complementary. Initially it had been highly dysfunctional to the establishment of communist systems in countries with long-standing enmity toward Russia, such as Poland, Hungary, or Rumania, where communism was identified with traditional Russian imperialism. The new communist governments clearly owed their ascendancy to the invading Red Army, and had few popular roots in national, political, or class loyalty. This was not true in Bulgaria and Czechoslovakia, however, which had traditional ties of friendship with Russia (Czechoslovakia also had a sizable communist party), and in Yugoslavia, where communism provided a unifying force in an environment of multinational hostilities and in the struggle with another enemy, the Germans.

The relationship between communism and nationalism changed in the later stages of development of East European politics, following 1956. Through the ascendancy of "national" factions within the communist leadership (the persecution of which under Stalinism gained them substantial popular sympathies), communist governments began to identify *with* national interests and *against* Russian hegemony; this transformation gave them a stronger base of mass support and a new sense of legitimacy. Emphasis on national determinants and the pursuit of national interests have become the functions of that popularity. Ironically, the Soviet Union has emerged as the great catalyst of the new nationalist alliance between communist governments and the people of Eastern Europe. Almost every East European communist government has tried, at one time or another, to defy the "Big Brother," a praiseworthy move in the eyes of their people. In 1956 as in 1968 the upsurge of popular support swelled behind leaders who resisted Russian encroachments on national sovereignty.

In Asia the nationalist-communist alliance has characterized developments since the Second World War (and even before) because from the very beginning communist movements there identified themselves with the anticolonialist struggle and hence with the growth of new nationalisms. This alliance has been at the roots of the popularity of Asian communist governments. At the same time it has also made them reluctant to obey Soviet dictates, adopt Soviet models, and accept Soviet leadership. It is sometimes difficult to determine whether a Mao or a Ho should be regarded as a communist first and a nationalist second, or vice versa. In the Asian context, and unlike their European counterparts, they have enjoyed a veritable monopoly of nationalist leadership, with little competition from noncommunists.

The CPSU's insistence, ever since 1919, that the national interests of the Soviet state are identical with the interests of the world communist movement posed the major problem in relations between communist parties and, after 1945, in relations between communist states. Early defiance by national parties was suppressed, and all such rebellious acts were forbidden under Stalin, even though the first successful challenge was made by Yugoslavia in 1948. No concessions were granted to the national requirements of states within the Soviet bloc until the fifties. The establishment of Red China, the death of Stalin, the rapprochement with Tito, and the events of 1956 all compelled the CPSU to recognize, however reluctantly, that each communist country has a right to pursue its "own road to socialism," providing it does so within the framework of "proletarian solidarity," the limits of which were none too clearly defined. The Sino-Soviet conflict, characterized by fierce competition as well as a struggle to determine which one, the CPSU or the CPC, has the true "philosopher's stone," has offered smaller states their first opportunity to take advantage of this right to pursue their own brand of socialism. The disarray in world communism and the resulting polycentrism are now permanent, despite Moscow's attempts to reunify the communist countries and to reassert Soviet supremacy – efforts which are only successful when backed by armed Soviet might.

The famous Brezhnev doctrine – the doctrine of limited sovereignty – formulated to legalize the intervention in Czechoslovakia and to prevent further intensification of the revisionist-nationalist trends in Eastern Europe, supplies the justification for the use of force. The limits which the doctrine imposes on the "own road to socialism" make it difficult to distinguish it from the Soviet conception of "our way": "There is no doubt that the peoples of the socialist countries and the communist parties have and must have freedom to determine their country's path of development.

However, no decision of theirs may be allowed to damage either socialism in their own country, or fundamental interests of other socialist countries, or the worldwide workers movement, which is waging a struggle for socialism. Whoever forgets this, places sole emphasis on the autonomy and independence of communist parties, lapses into one-sidedness, and shirks his internationalist obligations." [26]

In other words, "proletarian internationalism," as defined by the Soviet comrades, takes precedence over the concept of a nation's "own road to socialism." Not a new formulation, the doctrine is a direct extension of an early Bolshevik policy applied to the rebellious borderlands, which stated that the right of proletarian unity is historically the higher right than that of national self-determination, and therefore must prevail in case of a conflict.[27] In the 1960s, it was the contiguous communist states that had assumed the characteristics of the borderlands. The use of force is an extreme measure, and its threat is supplemented by a major effort by the Soviet Union to integrate the bloc militarily, through the Warsaw Pact, and economically, through the Comecon – an effort that is proving increasingly frustrating because of the reluctance of the member states to cooperate, as became apparent in Rumania's open defiance of Soviet restraints.[28] There is little need here to stress the obvious, but let it be said that the foreign policies of communist states which are outside the perimeter of Soviet power are fully based in their leaderships' perception of their countries' national interests. But even the most "loyal" among the Soviet client states, such as East Germany, Poland, or even Bulgaria, justify their loyalty in terms of national interest and popular support, and tend more and more to pursue national goals regardless of the needs of "fraternal" states and their common, Soviet-inspired policies. The search for national advantage has made them seek relations with the noncommunist world, in the hope of

26. Leonid Brezhnev at the Fifth Congress of the PUWP in November 1968, *Pravda*, November 13, 1968. Secretary Brezhnev strongly reiterated the tenets of the doctrine at the Fourteenth Congress of the Communist party of Czechoslovakia in May 1971. A major portion of his speech was devoted "to stressing continuing need for interdependence among Warsaw Pact states against class enemies at home and abroad." *New York Times*, May 27, 1971.

27. See T. Rakowska-Harmstone, *Russia and Nationalism in Central Asia: The Case of Tadzhikistan* (Baltimore and London, 1970), chap. 3.

28. See chap. 8 above. An International Investment Bank was established by Comecon in 1970, the major purpose of which, according to *Trybuna Ludu* (Warsaw), June 2, 1970, is to exert economic influence on the development of relations between the Comecon countries, and especially to orient "investment processes in directions compatible with the principles of international specialization and the international division of labor." Quoted in *East Europe*, 19, no. 2 (1970), 42.

acquiring economic and technological benefits and under the impact of traditional cultural and diplomatic contacts. Within the bloc itself the old specter of a Balkan entente has reappeared with the new and vigorous Yugoslav-Rumanian partnership, which threatens to include Hungary (as it did Dubcek's Czechoslovakia) and to isolate Bulgaria, Russia's lone friend in the area.

At the beginning of the seventies Rumania was the only communist state in the Soviet orbit openly pursuing a national foreign policy and international contacts with the Western world (including the United States) and with China.[29] Although Rumania is the only country which is overtly defiant of the Soviet Union, even the most loyal states, such as the German Democratic Republic, have felt the urge to establish a more independent position; and others, while officially following the Kremlin line, are oriented basically by nationalistic goals in foreign policy. Nevertheless, the Soviet influence is still predominant. For example, there are some indications that the May 1971 change in the leadership of the GDR may have been occasioned by Ulbricht's lack of flexibility in subordinating East Germany's national interests to the Soviet need for a rapprochement with the German Federal Republic.[30] East Europeans' attitude toward China, as voiced at the Twenty-fourth Congress of the CPSU in April 1971, was the official measure of their allegiance to Soviet leadership in the international arena,[31] but apart from this and other crucial issues where conformity was

29. Ceausescu (who also exchanged state visits with President Nixon in 1969–70) was greeted with exceptional enthusiasm in Peking in June 1971. Not only was he personally escorted by Chou En-lai on a trip to Nanking and Shanghai, but he also talked at length with Chairman Mao in the presence of all members of the CPC's Politbureau Standing Committee (with the exception of one, reportedly in disgrace). From Peking Ceausescu went to Pyongyang and Hanoi. *Washington Post*, June 7, 1971.

30. According to Wolfgang Leonhard (conversation in Ottawa, May 1971), the sequence of events immediately preceding Ulbricht's "retirement" clearly indicated that he tried to assert his independence in defiance of the official CPSU line, and, as a result, was replaced by Erich Honecker, a lesser but more compliant personality. Leonhard's analysis is based on the comparison of Ulbricht's behavior at the Twenty-fourth Congress of the CPSU and the reporting (or lack thereof) of his and his delegation's activities by *Pravda*. In his speech at the Congress Ulbricht did *not* condemn China, and he emphasized his personal friendship with Lenin, both cardinal sins from the point of view of the present CPSU leadership. The listing of the GDR delegation in *Pravda* was especially significant. After the speech, Ulbricht's name, which headed the initial listing, was dropped, and Honecker's name substituted. There was only one other mention of Ulbricht subsequently: a small item reporting that he went to see the head of the State Planning Committee who discussed with him correct methods of socialist planning.

31. Ceausescu and Ulbricht were the only two Eastern European leaders who did

required, they continue to pursue nationally inspired policies. Typical aspirations of national communist leaders were voiced in Czechoslovakia in its all too brief period of freedom: "The citizens of Czechoslovakia must have a certainty that if, together with the Soviet Union, we support such foreign policy we do so on the basis of our own judgment, our own evaluation of the situation, and that we can defend the policy to the public. In the same way they must have the certainty that, should the leadership . . . have any doubt about . . . a proposed common policy, it may present its own views and discuss them . . . without fear of pressure and recrimination." [32]

Clearly, nationalism is in the ascendant among the communist states and will inevitably lead to ever stronger assertion of their national interests and to more frequent defiance of Soviet hegemony and policies whenever they trespass and violate these interests. The use of force to stop the trend, while temporarily effective, is in the long run self-defeating and counterproductive, for the dynamics of nationalism gain new strength with each intervention and serve to weld more closely together the people and their governments in an anti-Russian alliance.

The disruptive force of nationalism does not stop at national boundaries, and the new vigor of national self-assertion has also affected the domestic politics of multinational communist states. Soviet minorities have obviously become more restive, and there is evidence that national groups are pressing strongly for a larger share in decision-making and for greater national and cultural autonomy; there even is some indication of separatist trends in the western borderlands.[33] Pressures by national minorities are apparent also in other European and Asian communist states, such as Czechoslovakia, Hungary, and Rumania, China and North Vietnam. National pressures by the Yugoslav nationalities have resulted in all but formal erosion of federal powers. The constitutional proposals introduced late in 1970 for enactment by mid-1971 provide for a collective presidency

not condemn the CPC. Given the Polish debt to China in 1956, Gierek's tirade against China was particularly significant; undoubtedly a quid pro quo for the Soviet support of his leadership at home and for Soviet financial help in meeting Polish workers' economic demands.

32. *Rude Pravo*, June 13, 1968, quoted in *East Europe*, 18, no. 1 (1969), 17. A joke circulating in Prague after the invasion illustrates the dilemma: "Czechoslovakia is the most neutral state in the world. It does not even interfere in its own affairs." Quoted in *ibid.*, 18, no. 4 (1969), 28.

33. See T. Rakowska-Harmstone, "The Dilemma of Nationalism in the Soviet Union," in John W. Strong (ed.), *The Soviet Union under Brezhnev and Kosygin: The Transition Years* (New York, 1971).

and hand over economic decision-making powers to the constituent republics. In fact, to quote the Yugoslav premier, "republics have become states." [34] Paradoxically, the ethnic nationalisms of Yugoslavia, which had been eclipsed by communist-inspired unity in the war years, now appear to have revived to the point where they threaten the very solidarity of the federal state — affording yet another example of nationalism's ascendancy over communism.

IV

The title of this volume, *The Communist States in Disarray*, may be considered to imply more than is warranted by casual observation. After all, the only visible "disarray" is between Russia and China, the old maverick Yugoslavia, tiny Albania, and the cautious new maverick Rumania. Czechoslovakia, like Hungary in 1956, has been brought back into line, and there are signs of a revived effort on the part of the Soviet Union to enforce obedience among those who are within easy reach of the Warsaw Pact troops. Still, the dynamics of political forces pressing from below all point to greater differentiation rather than renewed conformity, to the assertion of particularistic rather than "proletarian internationalist" interests, to the development of new political, economic, social, and cultural forms best suited to an individual state's own national and political heritage.

Although the trends and pressures are similar, the response differs in each case depending on a whole range of variables, such as geopolitical position, traditional political culture, and degree of economic development. In some communist states the major demand is for democratization; in others, economic decentralization; in still others, national self-assertion. In domestic politics (including those of the Soviet Union) the extent and the depth of change varies from far-reaching to minimal. In the international movement the monolithic character of communism is a thing of the past, even though strong common ties remain.

Add to this "disarray" the entry into the political arena of the new generation. The young communist cadres appear to be more pragmatic than ideological and relate more to their national than to their communist heritage. The ordinary youth, the future "masses" of communist countries, seem to be apathetic ideologically and in pursuit of immediate personal advantage, as well as clearly susceptible to "decadent" Western ways. The new generation as a whole (with the possible exception of China) indi-

34. Mitja Ribicic, quoted in *New York Times*, April 12, 1971.

cates an abysmal failure of "communist upbringing," and symbolizes the basic sterility of the Soviet version of Marxism-Leninism and its general bankruptcy.

The resurgent nationalism and the pressures demanding the freedom to pursue one's "own thing," including political liberalization and economic rationality, all point to particularist solutions. Moreover, and despite appearances, these tendencies operate in an increasingly favorable environment, characterized by an overall decline in Soviet influence, effectiveness, and credibility, and by the corresponding need of local communist elites to establish their credibility and legitimacy in local, national terms. This in the general framework of competing universalist claims of the two communist superpowers, which negate the old claim to one ultimate truth and open new alternatives for the smaller states.

Turning now to cohesive factors, it can be said that Marxist-Leninist ideology has always been of doubtful value in uniting the communist world (especially when confronted with nationalist demands), since its effectiveness is largely the function of the effectiveness of the power of the Soviet state. Whatever its past value it has now been destroyed except in the most general and thus meaningless terms, and has been replaced by local versions, such as Titoism or Maoism, which reinforce the particularist trends. There remains the consideration of the power of the Soviet state, still as formidable as ever and enhanced by its nuclear capacity to "overkill." The freedom to use this power seems to have been eroded, however, and while armed intervention to attain political objectives still can (and does) occur, it cannot be used in cases of minor infractions and annoyances generally indulged in by the smaller states. Moreover, its use in major crises has now become increasingly awkward. This is the result of the growth of the new "objective" factors, such as the rise of China, a powerful rival both demographically and geopolitically and itself nonamenable to invasions like that of Hungary or of Czechoslovakia; the stronger local roots of the communist regimes and their progressively complex pattern of foreign relations; and the changing international scene. In addition there are cogent "subjective" factors, the key to which is the change in the style of Soviet leadership, its frequent lack of resolution and consensus, and the consequent absence of the "will to act." In any case, while the growth of centrifugal forces may be checked and temporarily turned back by the use of military intervention, it cannot be stopped permanently.

The outward calm and relative stability of the "socialist commonwealth" thus do not negate the underlying disarray of the conflicting and ever more differentiated interests of national communist elites, which reflect powerful forces working from below in patterns as dysfunctional to Soviet and bloc interests as they are functional to the revival of traditional national entities and cultural models. Relieved of their ideological strait-jacket, preoccupied with economic needs, and increasingly responsive to national demands and popular approval, each national party has embarked on its own adventure. Their timetable, like their emphasis, vary with needs and constraints; their progress is frequently stopped and sometimes reversed. In the long run, however, they are not to be diverted from their new separate course.

Notes on the Contributors

Notes on the Contributors

ADAM BROMKE is chairman of the Department of Political Science at Carleton University. He has authored and edited several books, including *The Communist States at the Crossroads.*

JOHN C. CAMPBELL is senior research fellow with the Council on Foreign Relations. He has written a number of books, including *Tito's Separate Road: America and Yugoslavia in World Politics.*

VINCENT C. CHRYPINSKI is a professor of political science at the University of Windsor and the author of several articles on Polish politics.

MICHAEL COSTELLO is with the Research Department, Radio Free Europe, where he specializes in Bulgarian affairs.

MELVIN CROAN is associate chairman of the Department of Political Science at the University of Wisconsin. He has written many studies on East Germany, including the chapter in *The Communist States at the Crossroads.*

GABRIEL FISCHER is an associate professor of political science at Acadia University. Formerly with the Institute of International Relations in Bucharest, he has written extensively on Rumanian affairs.

ANDREW GYORGY, a professor of international affairs at the Institute for Sino-Soviet Studies, The George Washington University, is the author and editor of numerous books, including *Eastern European Governments and Politics.*

PAUL F. LANGER, of the Social Science Department of the Rand Corporation, is the author of several books on communism in Asia, including *The Red Flag in Japan.*

C. IAN LUMSDEN is a member of the Political Science Department at Atkinson College, York University. He has written extensively on Cuba, including the chapter in *The Communist States at the Crossroads.*

Notes on the Contributors

PETER R. PRIFTI is with the Center for International Studies, Massachusetts Institute of Technology. He has written several articles on Albanian politics.

TERESA RAKOWSKA-HARMSTONE is an associate professor in the Department of Political Science, Carleton University. Her specialty is communist politics and she recently authored *Russia and Nationalism in Central Asia: The Case of Tadzhikistan.*

H. GORDON SKILLING is the director of the Centre for Russian and European Studies, University of Toronto. He has written numerous books and articles on Eastern Europe, and especially Czechoslovakia, including *The Governments of Communist East Europe.*

PHILIP E. UREN is co-director of the School of International Affairs at Carleton University. He has authored and edited several studies on communist economic relations, including *East-West Trade.*

JOHN W. STRONG, an associate professor of history and former chairman of the Soviet and East European Studies Program at Carleton University, has written extensively on Sino-Soviet affairs and recently edited *The Soviet Union under Brezhnev and Kosygin.*

FERENC A. VALI, a professor of political science at the University of Massachusetts, is the author of several books, including *Rift and Revolt in Hungary.*

Index

Index

Index

Index

Index

Index